DOG OBEDIENCE TRAINING

Revised Edition

DOG OBEDIENCE TRAINING

Revised Edition

BY

Milo Pearsall

AND

Charles Leedham

CHARLES SCRIBNER'S SONS · NEW YORK

Copyright © 1958, 1979 Milo Pearsall and Charles Leedham

Library of Congress Cataloging in Publication Data

Pearsall, Milo.
   Dog obedience training.
   Includes index.
   1. Dogs—Training.   2. Dogs—Obedience trials.
I. Leedham, Charles G., joint author.   II. Title.
SF431.P38   1979   636.7'08'3   79-65993
ISBN 0-684-16158-3

1 3 5 7 9 11 13 15 17 19   V/C   20 18 16 14 12 10 8 6 4 2

Printed in the United States of America.

*For Margaret and Mary Lee
and, aptly enough, two dogs named
Black Charger and Black Douglas,
who started it all*

Acknowledgments

The pictures in this book were taken by Wally and Warren Bushman, Bill Coursen, and Ken Downs, and many of the charts and diagrams were prepared by Mr. Downs. We are also indebted to the owners and dogs who consented to act as models, and to Mr. Scott Piersol of the Casa Linda, Daytona Beach, for his cooperation.

We are grateful to the American Kennel Club and to Mr. Jim Dearinger for invaluable help with facts and figures on dogs, registration, obedience trials and titles. We gratefully acknowledge the permission of the AKC to reprint the "Obedience Regulations" and to quote from other AKC publications, all of which are copyrighted. We gratefully acknowledge, also, the permission of the Gaines Dog Research Center to quote portions of their publication "Touring with Towser."

Contents

Preface to the Revised Edition

In the years since *Dog Obedience Training* was first published, the authors have worked with, taught, and watched closely the training progress of thousands of dogs and their owners. Tens of thousands more owners and dogs have learned the pleasures and rewards of obedience training with the book alone, from simplest companionship training to the highest obedience titles awarded by the American Kennel Club, as the book has come to be recognized as the standard guide and manual on the subject of training. These years of further experience with direct teaching and training, the comments and reactions from the book's users, and continual experimentation and reexamination of every point and technique have together led to the changes, refinements, and improvements in this revised edition.

You will find here both a gentle method of training, using an absolute minimum of force or none at all, and obedience achieved through working *with* a wonderfully cooperative animal who wants to and will do almost anything to please you if you show him what you want—clearly, carefully, and with praise. In obedience competition at dog shows, nothing is more pleasing than watching a dog go through the competition exercises with a bounce in his step, with a clear eagerness to do just what his owner and handler asks of him, because they trust and love each other and are working *together*. The same is true in basic home companionship training: a well-trained dog who has learned elementary manners and responds happily to his owner is a joy to behold. Both show and home obedience are the result of a gentle approach, demonstration, consistency, and understanding, and in the new *Dog Obedience Training* we take you step by step toward these goals.

We wrote this book originally to make dog training better, easier, and more fun for owners and their dogs, and we have been pleased with the results we have seen. We have revised it for the same reason, and we wish you and your dog a long and happy life of working together, trusting each other, and enjoying the close companionship that obedience training can bring.

Introduction

Every minute you are with your dog, you are training him. By your every action and attitude, by what you say to him and how you say it, by your tone of voice, you are teaching him to be affectionate or reserved, courageous or timid, responsive or withdrawn, obedient or disobedient. It is something you cannot escape, even if you should want to, for once a puppy leaves his mother and litter mates and moves in with you, his attitude toward the world will be learned largely from you.

If he learns from his first contacts with you, and from all his future contacts, that he is loved and respected, that he has a definite place in the family and that certain things are expected of him, he can be what you have always wanted in a dog, and perhaps even more. It is to this ideal that we have dedicated this book. You cannot spend all your time on obedience training of your dog, but in your training sessions can be established an owner-to-dog rapport that is very nearly impossible otherwise. If training is done with kindness and love and respect, your dog will learn to respond to you in a marvelous degree. At the same time, you will learn how to treat him outside of training. He will in addition become obedient, and his obedience to your commands will again color your attitude, making for a relationship that is more than owner and pet—it becomes truly owner and companion.

You will not find in this book a collection of pretty maxims about dog training—neat capsules of methodology that say, in effect, "If you do this, he will do that." We ask you to think about training, about your dog and his reactions, and then apply the means of approaching each item of training that we have found to be most effective. There is no substitute for thought and understanding in training, any more than there is in any other facet of life. This is what we ask of you again and again in every section of this book, and this is what we hope you will do.

If there could be any one capsule statement of our ways of training, it would center around the words "praise" and "gentleness." Praise is the keystone, the foundation of training and a good relationship with your dog.

He learns through praise, and he forgets the sting of the necessary corrections because you praise him immediately after. Gentleness, too, is an essential. You must, in training, use scientifically applied force at times to demonstrate to your dog what you want done, but the force must be carefully calculated and applied without anger or rancor, and only to the degree necessary. You are working with one of the most responsive and intelligent and loyal animals alive, and only through gentle and understanding treatment will you realize his full potentialities.

Do not misunderstand us. This is not a brief for a hesitant and over-protective approach to either your dog or his training. Pampering can have equally as bad results as harshness; too little insistence on the proper performance of any obedience exercise is quite as bad as too much. But there is a middle way: insistence with understanding and knowledge of your dog and how his mind and emotions work. This middle way, the understanding and knowledge that make it up, are what we propound, along with various items of information that we think are helpful both in and out of training.

The full potentialities of a dog, any dog, are generally nowhere nearly realized by the average person, or the average owner of a dog. A dog is too often thought of as "nice to have around," "fun to romp with," and as that only—to be locked in or out as the occasion requires, locked in the cellar when company comes, struggled with, and worried about. It is difficult for someone not familiar with obedience to comprehend the ease and pleasure of living with a dog who will respond promptly and willingly to a quiet word, a click of the tongue, a snap of the fingers, or almost to a thought.

Another thing you will not find in this book is magic, or the "easy" way of training. There is no really "easy" way of training, or at least not in the sense of lack of application. To train a dog, you must put forth effort. It is our conviction, however—and it has been borne out through work with thousands of dogs of every variety and temperament—that directing your effort along the lines we suggest will show far more satisfactory results than any other method. There are tricks to every trade, and dog training is no exception. Such "tricks," as we explain, will sometimes have almost magical results when applied to a dog who has been unable to learn by another method, but there is still no substitute for the thought and understanding behind each such "trick"—those you must have before you can apply the "trick" effectively.

There are extremely few exceptions to the statement that every dog can be trained, and certainly no exceptions to the fact that every dog should be trained. Age, after a certain minimum, is no limiter. Whatever type of training you may be interested in—home training, ring training, tricks, tracking—all these we have treated. All these you can do. It is our hope that you will do them, for a well-trained dog, even at the most basic level, is a joy to own and a pleasure to be with.

DOG OBEDIENCE TRAINING

Revised Edition

CHAPTER 1

Choosing the Pup

To paraphrase the old French recipe: First you get a dog. Then you train him. The kind of dog you get depends on you, of course, and on any number of factors of convenience, temperament (both of owner and dog), what you want a dog for, and conscious or unconscious tendencies toward one breed or another.

If you already have a strong leaning toward one breed, the best we can suggest is that you examine your choice in light of the considerations discussed later. Breed likings can be strong and irrational things, though, not easily subject to examination in the cold light of reason. One owner of a Doberman known to the authors would have none other because of a movie he had once seen in which a lean and beautiful Doberman played a supporting role as the minor villain. The owner of a majestic Great Dane admits his affair with the beast began in a showing of *The Hound of the Baskervilles*. This Holmesian epic was equipped with a monstrous Dane leaping over the misty moors in the title role, inexplicably fitted out with a prop set of saber-tooth fangs.

How many collies found happy homes on the basis of the appeal of Lassie will never be known, but their number is legion, even as the number of German Shepherds inspired by Rin-Tin-Tin and Strongheart. The breed going best-in-show at Madison Square Garden each year inspires its own small flurry of popularity.

There are major cycles of breed popularity for which there is no particularly good explanation. For many years the Cocker Spaniel held undisputed place in American homes as the most numerous pet, then the Beagle, and for decades now the Poodle has been the top dog, according to American Kennel Club registrations. Within the major cycles are smaller cycles, many of them regional. On the Eastern Seaboard some years ago the fancy was Scotties, preferably with unpronounceable and obscurantist Gaelic names. Then the Poodle held sway, and then a rash of Boxers, in turn giving way to Chihuahuas. In the late 1970s the Doberman moved from earlier distant placing to number-two spot, perhaps simply because of the appeal of the breed, or perhaps because in uncertain times a large dog with a fierce appearance and reputation fills a need for both companionship and protection.

Whether you already have a breed in mind or have just decided that it is time you got a dog, the best possible thing you can do is go to an all-breed show. Once there, you can take a good close look at some of the best specimens of your favorite breed, or simply wander around and window-shop. With an interest in obedience, it is best to pick a show with attached obedience competition where you will have a chance to watch different breeds in action in the ring. Each of the two basic types of show—match and point—has its advantages for the window-shopper. Many point shows are benched, which means that when the dogs are not actually in the show ring they are in small stalls arranged by breed groups. Thus the dogs are in one place in some quantity, affording you a better opportunity to look them over. On the other hand, at a match show the atmosphere tends to be more informal. The exhibitors sit, stand, or walk around with their dogs on leash when not in the ring, and the opportunities for striking up conversation are greater.

When you have more or less decided on a breed, or on several possibilities, talk to the owners at the benches or at ringside. Most owners will be glad to tell you anything you want to know about their breed. Remember, though, that when you talk to an owner at a dog show you are talking to an avid partisan of that particular breed. You will learn a great many of the facts of life about dog owning and about that breed, but you will also find that his breed is brave, loyal, obedient, resourceful, trustworthy, and so on all through the catalog of the major virtues. And you will in all likelihood also find that any other breed is mean, vicious, dull-witted, coarse, and tinged with dubious ancestry. It takes a little skepticism and judiciousness to separate the woof from the warp; nonetheless, you will find out more about the different breeds of dogs by assiduous conversation and careful observation at a dog show than anywhere else.

To find out when and where a dog show will be held near you, look in any of the dog magazines at your local magazine or news dealer, or pet shop, or write to the American Kennel Club (51 Madison Ave., New York, N.Y. 10010) for help.

PUREBRED OR MONGREL?

Probably the most basic of all considerations is that of whether you want a purebred dog or a mongrel. If the circumstances (of which price is not an inconsiderable one) incline you to a mongrel, all the above advice on dog shows is of course superfluous, as is much of the following material on competition obedience and temperament. For when you acquire a mongrel pup, you are taking pot luck of the chanciest sort.

If you get a mongrel pup from a friend, you at least have the advantage of knowing something about its mother and some clue as to the ultimate size, coat, coloring, intelligence, and disposition of the "cuddly child" you take into your household. But if the pup arrives via pet shop or animal shelter you are deprived of even this. Knowing nothing of the ancestry or age of your acquisition, you may not know until much too late that the lovable bundle of fur has turned into a lumbering giant with hair like a llama. This outcome is unlikely, as constantly mixed breeding tends toward the average, but it emphasizes the uncertainties you acquire with the aptly named "Heinz."

The controversy over the intelligence of purebred versus mongrel has raged for centuries, but it is neither true that street-roaming mongrels have naturally sharper wits than "pampered" purebreds, nor that constant mixing has somehow scrambled the brains of mongrels. Dog for dog, the mongrel is probably fully as intelligent as the average purebred. The major advantage of the purebred is that the mixed mutt does not offer known instinctual traits. It is these known traits in the purebred that offer such a variety of choice, and such possibilities of temperament matching to the prospective owner.

Additionally, if you are interested seriously in obedience work, there is the serious handicap that only obviously purebred dogs are allowed to compete in the dog show obedience ring.

PUREBRED DOGS

There are three terms that apply to such dogs: purebred, registered, and pedigreed ("thoroughbred" is incorrect when applied to dogs). In general, a dog will be all three, but not necessarily. A purebred is a dog whose ancestry is 100 percent of a single breed; a registered dog is one registered with the AKC as certifiedly purebred; and a pedigreed dog is simply a purebred whose ancestry for several generations is officially attested by a written and signed pedigree.

The American Kennel Club, the ruling authority of purebred dogdom, officially recognizes and accepts for registration 122 breeds. These range from the giant Danes and Irish Wolfhounds to the Chihuahuas and the Mexican Hairless, and encompass anything in size, coat, temperament, intelligence, and aptitude that anyone could want. These breeds are divided into six major groups:

> Sporting—dogs used for the hunting of game birds.
> Hounds—racing dogs and game hunters.
> Working—shepherds, guard, and rescue dogs.
> Terriers—rodent hunters.
> Toys—very small pet dogs.
> Nonsporting—catchall group.

In addition, seven more breeds are officially recognized as purebred by the AKC and accepted in obedience rings, though not for breed judging beyond a "Miscellaneous" class at some shows. It is extremely unlikely that any of these breeds will come under your consideration in the choice of a pup, as the majority are almost totally unknown even to veteran "dog people." Miscellaneous breeds at this writing include such exotics as Spinoni Italiani, Australian Cattle Dogs, and Tibetan Spaniels.

Any attempt at describing each of the AKC dogs would take a book in itself, and providentially the AKC has done just that. We can recommend highly the AKC's *Complete Dog Book*, which has pictures of each breed, a short history of each, and the accepted standard of the breed. This latter can be especially helpful to you when you have gotten down to shopping around within one breed, as the standard sets out in clear terms just what is most desirable in physical conformation and temperament for every breed. If you read it closely and keep the major points in mind while inspecting dogs, you may well avoid serious mistakes in choosing.

SOME BASIC CONSIDERATIONS

Temperament is probably the major factor that will guide you in your choice of a dog. The pup you buy now will be your companion for many years, and it is his disposition and personality that you will be living with rather than his looks. Within the AKC's 122 breeds is every range of temperament from the lethargic to the hyperactive, from extra friendly to highly reserved, from comic and playful to serious.

It is of course impossible to make any broad generalizations on temperament, particularly as temperament can vary widely within the same breed. Here again the best possible guide is personal observation and whatever advice you can get from friends and people at shows. You should, as much as possible, try to get a fairly close match between your general outlook on life and the known characteristics of a breed. A generally jovial and outgoing owner is not likely to be happy with a moody and reserved dog, and the constant running and whirling of a vivacious terrier could very easily drive a sedentary or nervous master to distraction.

In the young puppy, certain general outlines of character will show. If, for example, you want a very friendly dog, by all means choose from the litter the pup that first runs to you and greets you with glad tail wagging and licks. If you prefer the reserved type, then choose the one who hangs back and minds his own business despite your opening blandishments. But be careful in this case that his reserved air is not the result of some fundamental defect like illness or deafness, or the result of timidity in general.

There can be no guarantee from the actions of the pup as to his final disposition. The basics are there already, but so much depends on his environment while growing up, on your treatment of him, that you can really only establish the basics, and then work from there. Some traits should be strictly avoided, such as timidity. A pup who already shows a basic fear of his environment at the age of three or four months will probably never become courageous. But the average happy, active puppy can be molded into whatever you want—and that is what obedience training is for.

If you are firmly set on some particular temperament, the best course is to start looking at older puppies or even at mature dogs. By the time a dog is, say, a year old, his personality is largely formed, and in buying a dog of this age you can be pretty sure of what you are getting. But buying an older dog has its drawbacks too, as will be discussed later.

One friend of the authors' took this "older dog" way in choosing his dog, however, with no ill results visible to date. For reasons best known to himself he wanted a highly aggressive Doberman. Touring the kennels, he looked at pups in the six-to-nine-month age group, and to each dog he liked the looks of he applied his personal test, which consisted of running suddenly at the dog with a stick as if to hit him. When he found the one pup who nearly tore his chain out of the wall in a snarling return lunge, he had found his dog. It took a good many repeat visits to the kennel—steak in hand—before that pup consented to have anything to do with him, but once a truce was effected they lived happily ever after.

Completely at the other extreme was the young couple who took home a soft and cuddly German Shepherd pup and lavished much affection on him. They were completely inexperienced with dogs, and somehow seemed not to have realized that pups do grow up. The inevitable, in their case, happened when one day they found themselves with a year-old, 70-pound reasonable facsimile of a wolf in the household. The day he tried an experimental snarl when they punished him for some misdemeanor, they were frightened silly at the sight of all those big sharp teeth on their erstwhile bundle of joy. The dog, of course, realized very quickly that he had the controlling hand in things, and until the day the couple managed to return him to the kennel (and an unusually accommodating kennel it was), he ruled the household with an iron paw. It happens that in this case one of the authors spent several hours with the dog a few days after his return, and a gentler, friendlier dog could hardly be found. It was simply a case of the owners' having no idea of what they were getting or what they really wanted when they got their pup.

Size is another factor that should figure heavily in your selection. Both for your own comfort and for the happiness of the dog, you should judge as carefully as possible the maximum size of dog you should have. Keeping a large dog in a small apartment can be literal cruelty. Even in a house in the city or in a development or suburban area, where you may have to keep the dog inside most of the time, too large a dog can be inconvenient. Particularly if he is an active large dog, your nerves might be completely undone, along with your precious bric-a-brac, by ponderous lungings and crashings about. As a fairly good rule, the difficulty of traveling with a dog increases in direct proportion to his size—and the amount of traveling you do is another factor in choosing a size. A Chihuahua can be carried almost anywhere quite conveniently in a small traveling case, but public transportation officials tend to get quite stuffy about Great Danes, and a Dane even in your private car takes up enough room for several humans.

If you are undecided whether to get a long-haired or a short-haired dog, your decision can be very quickly made on the basis of the time you are willing and able to put into grooming and picking up shed hairs. The long-haired varieties require constant grooming, plucking, combing, cutting, and brushing if their coats are to be kept in even tolerably good condition, and when they shed, the evidence is everywhere in abundance. The short-haired breeds seldom require more than a regular brushing with a good stiff-bristle brush, and when they shed it is considerably less evident and annoying.

MALE OR FEMALE?

Almost every dog owner you talk to will give you a different reason for choosing either a male or a female as your dog. In actuality, the difference is small indeed. The male dog of almost any breed tends to be slightly larger, if that is a consideration. In serious obedience work the male has the advantage of being eligible for the ring all throughout the year, while the female is barred when she is in season. On the other hand, the female is less likely to be thrown off in the ring by other dogs' smells, as is the case sometimes with the male. Neither sex is conspicuously the better performer.

Around the house, the female suffers only in that her twice-yearly "season" (ten to twenty-one days each time) entails close watching against the possibility of unwanted pups. She may also go into a false pregnancy after a season, and consider herself very delicate and motherly for a few weeks, which can be wearing. And during those seasons, you may have the neighborhood males baying about the house until you're ready to call the law. Commercial preparations diminish this overpowering attraction—ask your pharmacist or pet-supply dealer about them—and cut down the problem, but none of them, obviously, eliminates the impregnation problem if your bitch is loose and a male comes upon her. On balance, the male dog may spend more of his time than you think proper baying about someone else's in-season female, is far and away more likely to try to pick a fight on the street, and occasionally will try to drag you off bodily, while walking, on the sweet-scented trail of some in-season female, lo these three days gone.

Another minor consideration, if your dog-walking time is at a premium, is that, once housebroken, the average female relieves herself as soon as she hits the street, and then will be glad to take as much of a walk as you care to give her. The male is the more ruminative of the two; if he feels like holding it for a while, no power on earth can persuade him to accommodate your wishes. Male dogs are very territorial, as are many male wild animals; one of the major ways of marking a territory is to lift a leg on an outpost, for each dog's urine has an individual identifying scent easily detected and recognized, at least as "stranger in town," by another male. In the territorial confusion of city and town streets, this marking has lost almost all its original instinctual purpose, but males nonetheless continue their ancestral habits of leaving warning notices at selected points around their turf. Investigation of all areas is also necessary, to find out who's been around lately—with a challenging overspray required at some points where particularly interesting calling cards have been found. Your male will happily stroll around until he has found exactly the half-dozen spots he wants to anoint on that particular walk, and time has no meaning until he has found them.

ONE DOG OR TWO?

Two dogs in one household can be twice as much fun as one, but the problems of keeping more than one dog can increase all out of proportion to the number of dogs, or at least seem to. The major argument advanced in the cause of two dogs is that they will keep each other company, and that playing together they will do less damage to property during the chewing stage as puppies. Both of these claims need close scrutiny, because they are both true and false.

Two dogs may indeed keep each other company, whether the owner is at home or away; on the other hand, they may merely tolerate each other and be just as lonely when the owner is gone as if they were alone. They may, in fact, decide one day that even toleration is too much to ask, have a serious disagreement while the owner is off shopping, and leave him with one or more badly damaged dogs when he returns. Even the most deceptively friendly pair of dogs can have a falling out over a seeming trifle, much like their human owners. But when two healthy dogs decide to disagree, the result is generally more than hurt feelings if there is nobody around to restrain them. It isn't inevitable, but it does happen, particularly with two males. A male and a female together offer less risk, and two females together seem fairly safe but the risk is always there.

The argument that their playing together while you're away prevents damage to the furniture is open to serious doubt. Two rambunctious puppies are just as likely as one to decide that your possessions make wonderful toys. Many a two-dog owner has been greeted at his door by the sight of a room seemingly knee-deep in sofa-cushion stuffing and his beloved pups happily playing tug-of-war with the remains of the covering. Even the perfectly innocent play of two dogs, especially dogs in the medium-to-large size, can be nerve-racking and damaging. One New York City couple with two Doberman pups has trouble because of overfriendliness. The two, a year old at this writing, are happiest when careening around the apartment in seemingly savage mock battles involving much snarling and clashing of fangs. Imagine, if you will, two 70-pound dogs crashing full tilt through your legs, caroming happily off furniture, clawing into fast turns on your best rug, and all accompanied by blood-curdling sound effects. True, they will outgrow their rambunctiousness with maturity, but in the meantime the apartment is about as peaceful as Bunker Hill.

Here are some other practical considerations: (1) Two dogs eat twice as much as one. (2) All your inoculations and preventive medicines will cost you twice as much; and as dogs seldom have the consideration to take sick or be injured at the same time, your trips to the vet will double. (3) Housebreaking will be more than twice as hard, as very young puppies without fail operate on distinctly different schedules, necessitating twice as many rush trips out of the house or to the papers and leaving open the possibility of accident by one while the other is being attended to. In the middle or near the end of housebreaking, one pup may make a mistake when you're not watching—which is the way it always seems to happen—and you run the not inconsiderable risk of correcting one for what the other did, or not being able to make a correction at all for fear of making this mistake. Two pups, believe us, are more than twice as hard to keep the requisite sharp eye on as one. (4) Training problems will increase manifold, what with the necessity of training each dog separately and the almost inevitable difference in learning rates.

Do not, however, take the above as an indictment of the idea of more than one dog. If you're willing to devote the extra time and effort to the cause, you will be amply rewarded, because two dogs can be much more than twice the fun.

AGE OF THE PUP

How old should the pup be when you get him? Three to four months is the ideal age, for many reasons. By that time, the pup is well weaned from his mother and fairly well embarked on life. At four months he is just about ready for housebreaking. The first signs of his personality will have begun to show. He will have learned a great deal about relationships with other dogs through his contact with his litter mates. Before three months, the pup is little more than a mass of instincts; and what happens then is best left to what he learns from contacts with litter mates and the breeder's family.

Some fascinating research studies have shown that in the period just after one month of age a puppy is actually the most open of all to learning. This openness, however, is more of a problem than a benefit to any but the most expert trainers. Unless training and handling are done with exquisite care, a month-old puppy can be mentally scarred for life simply because he *is* so completely open to learning what life is all about, and careless mistakes or mistakes resulting from inexperience can be extremely damaging to him. The number of things that can go wrong physically with a very young puppy are overwhelming, too; thus we recommend strongly that you stick to the three-to-four-month age range in choosing your dog.

As the pup gets older than four months, his desirability as a pet acquisition falls rapidly. By five or six months he may have developed strong emotional ties with his kennel man, difficult to transfer to yourself. The central idea in getting a young puppy rather than an older one or a grown dog is that his first affection, after the instinctual stages, can become firmly fastened on you and you alone, without divided loyalties. Aside from that, the earlier you begin molding the pup's outlook on life to suit your own, the better your personalities are going to mesh through your life together. A pup older than ten months begins to come into the "grown dog" category in the problems he may present you with. If he has lived in a kennel for ten months he will be completely unhousebroken, and his free-and-easy ways of taking care of his needs will be much harder to correct than a four-month-old's. Whatever bad habits he may have acquired will have a much greater chance of being well set and much harder to erase and replace with good ones. And, again, he may have developed attachments to his surroundings and current owners that will be hard to transfer to you and your home.

This is not, mind you, as stern a warning against older puppies and grown dogs as it may sound. Many, many older pups and fully grown dogs have found happy homes and have become beloved, faithful companions and marvelous pets. Dogs are remarkably resilient creatures and can adapt to almost anything life brings them. It's just that if you have a choice—and you usually will—you should stick to the three-to-four-month age range in a puppy. It's better.

WHICH DOG FOR OBEDIENCE?

Much has been written, and much more said, about the obedience capacities of the various breeds. If you are interested in serious competition obedience work, you may be looking for the "right" dog, the one who learns and performs best. Every trainer, including the professional, has his own personal choice in dogs for training, and is usually quite vocal about it, but the basic fact is that any breed can be trained in obedience and can achieve the highest degree, the UD (Utility Dog).

In forty AKC obedience trials across the country during one month, the winners of first place in the Utility Classes (the most advanced classes) were Shetland Sheepdog (7), German Shepherd (5), Golden Retriever (4), Standard Poodle (3), Doberman, Boxer, Dalmatian, Pomeranian, Collie, Papillon, Border Collie, and Great Dane (2 each), and German Short-haired Pointer, Miniature Poodle, Weimaraner, Cocker Spaniel, and English Springer Spaniel (1 each).

Among the winners of other classes in these same forty shows were Norwegian Elkhound, Miniature Pinscher, Schipperke, Labrador Retriever, Pembroke Welsh Corgi, Miniature Schnauzer, Welsh Terrier, Samoyed, Chesapeake Bay Retriever, Rough Collie, Pointer, Smooth Fox Terrier, Brittany Spaniel, Irish Setter, Boston Terrier, Dachshund, and Wire Fox Terrier.

There could hardly be a greater diversification of breeds than those represented above, with dogs of every size and from each of the six AKC groups, yet each dog outscored all competition in a class open to all breeds.

While any dog can be trained, as shown above, certain breeds are generally somewhat easier to train than others. The most likely candidates for the "easiest to train" accolade are those of the Working Group. These dogs—German Shepherds, Dobermans, Boxers, Collies, and the like—have a long heritage of working at command, and this aptitude for obedience is an inherited characteristic. Yet the Poodle, a member of the catchall Nonsporting Group, is generally acknowledged to be one of the most intelligent of dogs, and perhaps the quickest to learn. The Poodle, however, has as a drawback his capricious and playful nature. He may work perfectly one day, and the next day seem never to have heard of obedience.

In the Sporting Group, another group with a history of working on command, Golden Retrievers have interestingly established themselves as among the very best in high-scoring precision work in obedience rings, outclassing any of the Working Group dogs. In 1977, the AKC for the first time established a championship title for obedience dogs (see Chapter 6, "Utility and Beyond") that requires winning first place at a number of obedience trials. The first dog to win the title of Obedience Trial Champion was a Golden, who managed to take his final points just twenty-three days after the title was established. The second, almost immediately thereafter, was also a Golden Retriever, and Goldens in that same year won the "Highest Scoring Dog in Trial" prize at 200 of the 773 trials where this award was given.

Still, any dog of any breed can be trained, and trained to do well, in obedience competition. Every breed, without exception, is represented among the winners of the AKC's obedience titles. So, in fact, can any mixed-breed be trained to do anything a purebred dog can do. Who knows, perhaps better. But as mixed-breeds are not permitted to enter into obedience competition, no one will ever know.

The size of the dog is something to be considered, from the viewpoint of trainer and handler. Chihuahuas and Danes are as easily trainable as the next dog, but their physiques are something to think about before you start on one. Especially if you are not a particularly large human, you may not feel equal to the pushing and hauling that are in store for you when you tackle the training of a Great Dane, a St. Bernard, or an Irish Wolfhound. These dogs are all in the over-100-pound class, and there is no small amount of effort involved in pushing a really recalcitrant giant canine into the sitting position if he happens not to feel like sitting. At the other end of the scale, the really tiny toy breeds require considerable delicacy in handling, because too hasty or forceful a correction could seriously injure a toy.

BUYING THE PUP

By this time you've decided on the kind of pup you want, and the big question faces you: Where do I get it?

The answer is: By all means, from an established, reputable breeder and/or kennel. There are three good ways to find out about breeders in your area: the AKC, breed clubs, and shows in the area. The AKC maintains a Breeder Information service purely as a courtesy service to those interested in buying a dog. They will send you a selection of ads for puppies of the breed you are interested in, from their *Pure Bred Dogs* magazine. The breeders listed may be in your general area, but if it's a numerically unpopular breed you're interested in, don't be surprised if the nearest breeder is several hundred miles or more distant.

It's worth picking up a copy of *Pure Bred Dogs* at your news dealer, if he carries it, as it has extensive advertising by breeders of almost all breeds. The AKC, however, cannot recommend any one kennel—and their listing carries no guarantee of the quality of the puppies sold. The listing only means that the kennel or breeder is in good standing with the AKC; that it has not been involved in any deal or transaction that would cause the AKC to withdraw registration or showing privileges from it.

The national breed clubs (see the AKC's *Pure Bred Dogs* for a listing of breed clubs) are generally glad to be of assistance to anyone interested in buying a dog of their breed, and a letter to the secretary will bring you the names of affiliated kennels in your area. At shows, too, you can generally contact breeders, either through just walking around and striking up conversations at the benches, or watching for the kennel signs on the benches.

Pet shops are another matter entirely. While there are many clean, honest, and reputable pet shops throughout the country, the ethics and standards of a large percentage are open to serious question. The bouncing, wistful pups in the window have an appeal unequaled in window displays, but they are definitely not for the buyer seriously interested in a good, lifelong pet. While it is undoubtedly true that pet-shop dogs have become excellent, healthy, and loyal pets, and that champion show dogs have in rare cases come from such a shop, the odds are distinctly against you. You have no way in the world of knowing the quality of the shop's stock, extremely little chance of finding any former customers to talk to, and a not inconsiderable chance of getting a complete dud. Pet shops are the places where many breeders will get rid of their "culls," poor-quality dogs from good litters . . . and you can bet that the cull's parentage is untraceable and he himself unregisterable. This is not, however, meant as a blanket indictment of pet shops. Some are excellent, clean, and aboveboard. Their dogs are healthy and the owners anxious to build and maintain a good reputation. But unless you have some source of excellent advice, don't gamble on the chance of accidentally finding one of the good ones.

Buying a puppy is not very different from buying anything else, except perhaps that a first-time buyer of a dog is generally far more ignorant of the "product" than the buyer of a car or a refrigerator. The major principles to be observed are as follows: (1) Find out as much as possible about the breed before beginning to shop. (2) Take a good long look around before buying, and don't let yourself be stampeded into buying anything until you're completely satisfied that it's what you want. Always remember that, barring accident, you're going to spend a good many years with your dog, and a dog is not the kind of thing that can be traded in on a new and different model with any great ease.

With your list of breeders in hand, and your desires firmly fixed in mind, you can now start shopping. Be sure to call ahead of your kennel visits, to find out if there is any puppy stock available and to let the breeder know you're coming. Breeders are not open fixed hours daily like a store, and most puppy showing is by appointment. The breeder will be glad to give you as much information as possible over the phone, including directions on how to get there. And when you do get there, remember that the breeder is not a clerk bent only on making a sale; he is an independent businessman who loves dogs, and he is just as eager to make sure his puppies get placed with the right people as you are to get the right pup.

The first step is to look the kennel or breeding quarters over carefully. Satisfy yourself that the "plant" is clean and well cared for. But don't be offended or feel immediately that something is wrong if the breeder asks you not to come right into the kennels proper. He's rightly concerned with the health of his pups, and if you've come straight to him from another kennel on your shopping tour he simply can't take the chance that you might be innocently carrying a vagrant dog-disease germ from the last place. A virulent strain of disease brought in from outside can literally wipe out a kennel—it has happened—and so the breeder is well within his rights in exercising a certain caution. You can tell quickly enough without walking right into the kennels whether everything is clean and in order and if the place "feels" right. If not, make your excuses and walk out quickly.

Up to this point, we'll say, everything has gone well, and the puppies have been brought out for your approval. Right then and there, watch out! The appeal of a clutch of tumbling puppies can be overpowering, and the time to hitch up your sales resistance is right then. Look them over carefully with a skeptical eye and feel perfectly free to ask as many questions as you can think of about their parentage, their health, their prospects, and anything else that comes to mind. Talk it over thoroughly with the breeder. He wants to make a sale, true, but he also wants to make sure he has a satisfied customer. A breeder's reputation can be very quickly scuttled by a few vocally unhappy owners of his pups, and this he wants of course to avoid.

Watch the pups carefully. Look for good strong bones. Look for clear eyes and a playful disposition. Watch for a good coat in healthy condition. Snap your fingers behind the pups' backs to check their hearing and alertness. And if you've found one you think is the one for you, don't hesitate to ask the breeder to take his temperature and show you the reading. The temperature of a healthy pup will be up to 102°. Above that watch out, for temperature is the surest known indication of the state of a dog's health.

If you've conscientiously shopped around among the available breeders, and now think you've found *the* pup, start all over again. Look very, very closely at this little animal who may share your life for the next ten years. Watch all his reactions carefully, particularly how he reacts to the people around him. If he recoils from people, he may have been mistreated, or he may be naturally timid. Avoid him like the plague, but don't rule out a dignified pup who is simply reserved about people. You can tell the difference if you've looked at a few litters. Then, start asking questions about his ancestry, if you haven't already satisfied yourself on that score. Most breeders will be eager to show you a pedigree already drawn up for the youngster. Make sure that he is already registered as one of a litter, and that he is fully eligible for registration with the AKC.

Get all the medical details straight on your pup. Get a written statement from the breeder detailing which preventive shots the pup has had and whether he has been wormed and if so when and how. Get the details of the pup's diet so you can continue to offer him familiar food when he is abruptly thrown into the strange surroundings of your home.

Most important, get him checked by a reliable veterinarian. If at all possible, have the vet come with you to the kennel to give your choice a thorough examination. But if you *do* take him away with you to the vet, and leave a deposit or the full price, have the understanding clearly in writing that the pup is returnable for a full refund if the vet turns thumbs down on him. Whatever you do, take the vet's good advice, even if it means returning the most lovable little bundle of fur you have ever encountered. He won't advise against a dog without good reason, and if you take a sick or weak puppy, you are in for nothing but large doses of trouble. By all means, if there is any reluctance on the part of *any* seller of a pup to have a medical examination done by a vet of *your* choice before the sale is completed, pick up your hat and politely but firmly do not touch the deal with the traditional pole.

WHAT WILL IT COST?

Very generally speaking, a purebred puppy costs between $150 and $250, with the majority of the prices in the high half of that scale. You will rarely, if ever, find a good pup selling for less than $100, and in some cases the prices are well above $250, depending on the breed, ancestry, and the prospects of the pup. While there is no sure way of telling which pup of a litter is a future show champion, many pups show apparent good prospects early, and the breeder will set a higher price on these specials, hoping to sell them to someone interested in breed showing and future breeding of his own. If you are looking for a pet and an obedience dog alone, the best thing is to leave these show prospects out of your considerations.

When the question of payment comes up, most breeders of course prefer cash in hand when they part with the pup, but many will be glad to make arrangements for split payment if you can satisfy them that you are a good credit risk. Dog buying very rarely gets into the true installment range, though. Most breeders simply won't be bothered with small monthly payments and won't want to get into anything beyond a three-payment deal. So if you're not paying cash, plan to pay at least one-third of the pup's price at the time, and the rest in two equal payments, probably at monthly intervals.

Prices vary within a breed, but you will find that the variation from one breeder to another is relatively slight for an average pup. If you find a pup whose price is unusually low, tread with caution. Dog buying is one field in which it is never wise for the novice to go bargainhunting. If the price is exceptionally low, there is a good likelihood that something is wrong somewhere. One extra veterinarian's bill can eat up the difference in price if you get hold of a lemon, or you may well pay many times the difference in price in your disappointment with a poor specimen.

There's very little haggling over price in dog selling. The price is the price, and that's about that. Of course, there are breeders who do haggle, but most of them won't take it very well if you try to knock their price down. Occasionally a breeder will shave his price if he takes a liking to you and if he feels that his pup will find an exceptionally good home with you. Don't count on it, though.

CONDITIONS OF SALE

In most cases, there are no conditions attaching to the sale of a puppy. Once you have paid for him, he is yours to have and to hold. The breeder may ask if you intend to show the dog in breed—to him a highly pertinent point. A breeder's reputation rests solely on the quality of his dogs, and the major way that quality is proven is through breed ring awards and championships. Therefore, if he has what he thinks of as a particularly good litter, or pup, he will want it to be shown in order to add to the glory of his line. The breeder may, in fact, refuse to sell a pup unless he has some sort of guarantee that you will show, or that you will allow him to show it. Our advice is that you stay clear of this sort of arrangement, especially the latter sort. A "guarantee" of this sort can result in having your dog away from you several times during the year if the breeder takes him for conditioning prior to a show, or takes him on one of the "circuits" of the dog show world. Steer clear of any showing guarantee if you just want a pet and obedience dog.

It is a good idea, too, to avoid any entangling alliances in regard to the future breeding of your pup. The breeder may ask you to allow future use of a male at stud if he turns out well, or ask you to guarantee future mating of a female, or an option on future pups or litters. These stipulations are rare, but they do occur: good breeders devote a great deal of study to genetics and blood lines and matched breedings to improve the breed, and they like to keep things as much under control as possible. In all likelihood you, as a pet buyer, will never run into any of these things, but if you do, think over the consequences before you agree.

REGISTRATION AND PEDIGREES

As explained earlier, registration simply means that a dog is registered with the AKC. This in turn means that he is certified as a purebred member of one of the AKC's 122 breeds, usually attested to by the fact that his parents were registered, and so on. When a litter is born, the breeder registers the litter as a whole. He may already have an individual registration certificate on each, which he will give to you at the time of sale.

In either case, a first individual registration listing you as the owner or a Supplemental Transfer Statement must be sent to the AKC, which will send you a registration certificate naming you as owner. Both these forms, with instructions, are reproduced on the following pages. If you are buying

APPLICATION FORM FOR REGISTERING DOG WITH AKC (blue). To be filled out by litter owner, and signed by litter owner AND new owner of dog. Fee ($4.) must accompany application. Use this form for recording ORIGINAL transfer only - for subsequent transfers, use Supplemental Transfer Statement.

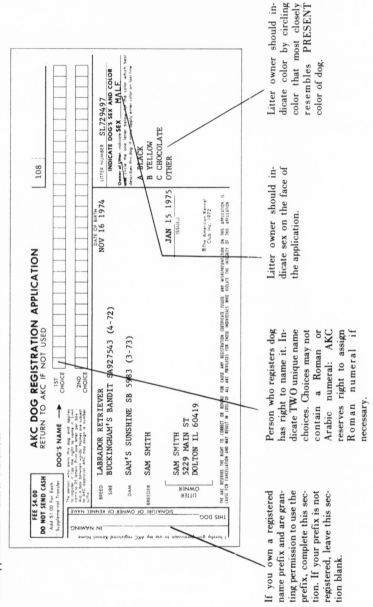

If you own a registered name prefix and are granting permission to use the prefix, complete this section. If your prefix is not registered, leave this section blank.

Person who registers dog has right to name it. Indicate TWO unique name choices. Choices may not contain a Roman or Arabic numeral: AKC reserves right to assign Roman numeral if necessary.

Litter owner should indicate sex on the face of the application.

Litter owner should indicate color by circling color that most closely resembles PRESENT color of dog.

FEE $4.00
DO NOT SEND CASH
Add $1.00 For Each
Supplemental Transfer

AKC DOG REGISTRATION APPLICATION
RETURN TO AKC IF NOT USED

108

DOG'S NAME →

1ST CHOICE

2ND CHOICE

The person who owns this dog and applies to register it has the right to name it. Limit name to 25 letters. Print one letter per box plus a box between words. Names are subject to AKC approval; AKC may assign a number suffix.

BREED   LABRADOR RETRIEVER
SIRE   BUCKINGHAM'S BANDIT SA927543 (4-72)
DAM   SAM'S SUNSHINE SB 5983 (3-73)
BREEDER SAM SMITH

SAM SMITH
5229 MAIN ST
DOLTON IL 60419

LITTER OWNER

THE AKC RESERVES THE RIGHT TO CORRECT OR REVOKE FOR CAUSE ANY REGISTRATION CERTIFICATE ISSUED. ANY MISREPRESENTATION ON THIS APPLICATION IS CAUSE FOR CANCELLATION AND MAY RESULT IN LOSS OF ALL AKC PRIVILEGES FOR THOSE INDIVIDUALS WHO VIOLATE THE INTEGRITY OF THIS APPLICATION.

DATE OF BIRTH
NOV 16 1974

LITTER NUMBER SL729497

INDICATE DOG'S SEX AND COLOR   MALE
Owner of litter, indicate SEX
Circle the one letter beside the color which best describes this dog if owner slightly enter color on last line

A BLACK
B YELLOW
C CHOCOLATE
OTHER

JAN 15 1975
ISSUED

©The American Kennel Club Inc. 1972

SIGNATURE OF OWNER OF KENNEL NAME

THIS DOG.

IN NAMING

I hereby give permission to use my AKC registered Kennel Name

Reverse side of blue application form. In buying a dog, do not accept an application that has not been properly completed in Section "A" by the litter owner.

INSTRUCTIONS: PLEASE TYPE - OR USE **PEN, NO PENCIL.** Erasures or Corrections may cause return of application for an explanation.

SEC. A MUST BE COMPLETED IN FULL AND SIGNED BY OWNER OF LITTER (AND CO-OWNER IF ANY) SHOWN ON REVERSE SIDE

ONE box MUST be checked

☐ I (we) still own this dog, and I (we) apply to The American Kennel Club to register it and have ownership recorded in my (our) name(s).

☐ I (we) certify that this dog was transferred DIRECTLY TO THE FOLLOWING PERSON(S) ON FEB 4 75
mo day year

MUST be filled in by owner(s) of Litter
PRINT NAME(S) OF PERSON(S) TO WHOM DOG WAS DIRECTLY TRANSFERRED MR. & MRS. JAMES JOHNSON

ADDRESS 631 HARRIS ST. LOUIS, MO. 63120

Signature *Sam Smith*
OWNER OF LITTER AT BIRTH

Signature
CO-OWNER IF ANY) OF LITTER AT BIRTH

SEC. B TO BE COMPLETED AND SIGNED BY THE PERSON(S) NAMED IN SEC. A ABOVE PROVIDED the person(s) owns the dog at the time this application is submitted to the A.K.C. If the person(s) named in SEC. A has transferred the dog to some other person(s), DO NOT COMPLETE SEC. B Instead - obtain a Supplemental Transfer Statement form from the A.K.C. Instructions for its completion and use are on the form.

I apply to The American Kennel Club to have Registration Certificate for this dog issued in my (our) name(s) and certify that I (we) acquired it DIRECTLY from the person(s) who Signed Sec. A above and that I (we) still own this dog. I (we) agree to abide by American Kennel Club rules and regulations.

New Owner's Signature *James Johnson*
New Co-Owner's Signature *Joan Johnson*

Name PRINT JAMES JOHNSON   JOHN JOHNSON
Address 631 HARRIS   631 HARRIS
City ST. LOUIS State MO Zip 63120   ST LOUIS State MO Zip 63120

REGISTRATION FEE MUST ACCOMPANY APPLICATION. MAKE CHECKS, MONEY ORDERS PAYABLE TO THE AMERICAN KENNEL CLUB. DO NOT SEND STAMPS OR CASH

FEE: $4.00 plus $1.00 for each additional transfer of dog represented by Supplemental Transfer Statement.
FEES SUBJECT TO CHANGE WITHOUT NOTICE

When completed and submitted, this Application becomes the property of the American Kennel Club
Mail to: THE AMERICAN KENNEL CLUB, 51 Madison Avenue, New York, N.Y. 10010

Litter owner must complete Section "A" by indicating date of transfer and printing name and address of person(s) to whom he is directly transferring the dog.

Litter owner must sign Section "A" verifying details of transfer. Separate and individual signatures of ALL co-owners are required. Husband and wife must sign separately.

If new owner named in Section "A" intends to keep dog and register it in his ownership, he should sign and complete Section "B". (Separate and individual signatures of all co-owners are required.) If the dog is to be transferred again do not complete Section "B".

SUPPLEMENTAL TRANSFER STATEMENT (gray). Only the first transfer by the litter owner is to be recorded on the blue application form shown above. If further transfer of the dog is to be made before the application is submitted for registration, the former AND new owner(s) must complete this Supplemental Transfer Statement, and attach it to the completed blue form. A fee of $1. (in addition to $4. fee required with blue form) must accompany each transfer application.

SUPPLEMENTAL TRANSFER STATEMENT
NOT VALID unless attached to the AKC Dog Registration Application

SEC. A MUST BE **COMPLETED** AND **SIGNED** PERSONALLY BY PERSON OR PERSONS WHO TRANSFERRED THE DOG. *

I certify that on (month) FEB (day) 28 (year) 75 I delivered or shipped the (breed) LABRADOR RETRIEVER _____ DIRECTLY TO:

(sex) M (color and markings) YELLOW from litter No. SL729497

PRINT NAME(S) JOHN JONES

ADDRESS 123 BROADWAY, AKRON OH 44322

SIGNED _James Johnson_   SIGNED _Joan Johnson_
FORMER OWNER — PERSON TRANSFERRING DOG   FORMER CO-OWNER (if any)

INVALID IF SIGNED IN BLANK

SEC. B MUST BE **COMPLETED** AND **SIGNED** PERSONALLY BY NEW OWNER (AND NEW CO-OWNER, IF ANY) NAMED IN SEC. A ABOVE, provided he still owns the dog and wants registration certificate issued in his name. If the dog has again been transferred, do not use this Sec. B, but make out Sec. A on another of these forms.
I apply to The American Kennel Club to have registration Certificate for this dog issued in my/our name(s), and certify that I/we acquired it DIRECTLY from the person(s) who signed Sec. A above, and that I/we still own this dog. I agree to abide by American Kennel Club Rules and Regulations.

New owner's personal signature _John Jones_

Print:
Name JOHN JONES
Address 123 BROADWAY
City/State AKRON, OH 44322

Co-Owner's Signature If Jointly Owned _____

Print:
Name _____
Address _____
City, State _____

*READ INSTRUCTIONS ON REVERSE SIDE

R 48-9 (4-74)

Former owner(s) must complete Section "A", indicating date of transfer, breed, color, sex, and litter number of dog, and must print name and address of *person(s) to whom* *dog is being directly transferred*. Former owner(s) must sign Section "A" verifying details of transfer. (Separate and individual signatures of all co-owners are required.)

New Owner(s) of dog who applies to register it, should complete Section "B". (Separate and individual signatures of all co-owners are required.)

a puppy represented as purebred *and* registrable with the AKC, take heed of the AKC's own cautionary statement on the matter of "papers":

> Failure to get AKC registration "papers" causes more grief for buyers of purportedly purebred, registrable dogs than any other problem except sickness. It has long been common practice to explain inability to provide the proper registration application, at the time the puppy is sold, by saying, "AKC hasn't sent the papers yet," or some other similar excuse, the essence of which, it is the American Kennel Club's fault the papers are not available.

The tone of that statement is slightly defensive, but for quite good reason: the AKC has attained and maintained such an excellent reputation and solid authority as the guardian of purebred dogdom that the organization's name is often enough used to ill effect as a loosely given verbal "guarantee" that the puppy in question is a good one. Again, on that subject, the AKC's own quote:

> There is a widely held belief that "AKC" or "AKC papers" and quality are one and the same. This is not the case. AKC is a registry body. A registration certificate indicates the dog as the offspring of a known sire and dam, born on a known date. It in no way indicates the quality or state of health of the dog.

Caveat emptor, in other words. But most of this is unnecessarily cautionary if you are dealing with a reputable breeder. You'll get your litter registration transfer or ownership transfer, and that will be that. Whatever the case, be prepared to wait patiently for your certificate, as the AKC registers over a million dogs a year, and the formalities take time. Three weeks is about minimum, and sometimes it takes a little longer. Be sure to have an understanding with the breeder as to who will pay for the registration and/or change of ownership, as the AKC makes a nominal charge for this. For your own peace of mind, send in the signed application yourself, for then you know it has been done (although, again, with any reputable breeder there is no question of its being taken care of once the breeder says it will be done).

When your certificate arrives from the AKC it will have on it the name of the dog, the names of his sire and dam, his registered number, the name of the breeder, and your name and address as owner. The registered number is especially vital, as it is by this number that your dog is kept track of in AKC files for the rest of his life. The code letter preceding it denotes group (W for Working, H for Hound, etc.) and the figures currently run to six digits. If you ever have cause to look into your acquisition's ancestry, you will find that originally the AKC simply gave a number, such as 345,678—but when they got to 999,999 they decided things would get unwieldy in the seven-digit range and began to issue numbers with the prefix "A." Those ran along for a while and then someone saw the handwriting on the wall as registrations poured in, and the present group prefix system was adopted. The millions of registrations that have poured in since even that change was made have forced the addition of more letters; so your dog's number, if he is, say, a Sporting Group dog, will begin with "S" plus A, B, C, D, or a succeeding letter before the actual registration number begins.

The pedigree of your dog is simply a listing of his ancestors for as many generations back as interest you. Many breeders will supply you with a pedigree already drawn up (usually three or four generations) at the time of sale, as they are intensely proud of the breeding of their pups. These pedigrees are usually on a nicely designed pedigree blank supplied by one of the dog-food companies, and will be signed by the breeder as being true to the best of his knowledge. If you want to go further and have a signed and sealed affirmation of ancestry, the AKC will look up and make out an official pedigree for you if you supply them with the name and number of your dog. The organization charges a nominal fee for either a three- or four-generation pedigree.

An official pedigree is a nice thing to have around the house, and a moderate sprinkling of Champions, Obedience Trial Champions, and/or UD's in your pup's family tree can be a matter of considerable pride to you.

NAMING THE PUP

The AKC says, "It is the person who owns the dog and applies to register it, who has the right to name it." If your pup has already been individually registered (aside from being part of a litter registration), he will come to you already tagged with a long and impressive name, usually including the "kennel name" of the breeder, as in "Fotheringale Farms Fancy." Breeders like to have their kennel names used in the registered names of their pups, as a matter of pride. Even if the pup is as yet unnamed, the breeder may ask you to include his kennel name in its official name, but you are under no obligation to do so. If you make the original registration, you can tag it with any name you choose, so long as the name is no longer than twenty-five letters (by AKC regulation), and that is his official name forever. Unfortunately, if the breeder has registered your dog individually and named him, *that* name is his forever, for the AKC refuses (for quite good reasons, incidentally) to alter the registered name of a dog.

The tendency in choosing the official name of a dog is to the multisyllabic, to identify him among the thousands of other dogs of his breed. Names also run to strong similarity in each breed, being generally of a ponderous or massive nature for the giants, Germanic and fierce-sounding for many of the working breeds, sometimes cute and precious for the toys, and along nationality lines: French for Poodles, Gaelic for Scotties, Chinese for Pekingese, and so forth. Depending on your breed, you might find yourself owning something grand like "Destructor the Invincible von Hapsburg" or something so coy and ludicrous you want to hide when you see it applied to your very own. But there it is—you're stuck with that name if the breeder registered your pup individually.

But there is hope in the dog's "call" name, which is what you choose to call him under nonofficial conditions. If you should happen to acquire Destructor the Invincible, nothing in the world keeps you from calling him plain "Gus" if it strikes your fancy. Frequently, the dog's call name is part of his official name. For example, friend Destructor could be called "Des" or "Vince" or "Hap," as a shortening of part of his registered name. It's entirely up to you.

A word of caution, though: Try to make his name a little distinctive—away from the Spot, Rover, Queenie line. Also, if possible, make it of one or two syllables (for ease in calling) and preferably something with a hard consonant at the beginning. This makes for a stronger-sounding word when you want his attention, which will be often enough. Particularly if you are interested in serious obedience competition, make the call name short and snappy, *individual* (it could easily confuse him to hear his name called from an adjoining ring while he's in the process of performing in his own ring), and definitely try to avoid having it sound too much like any of the standard obedience commands, for much the same reason. If you want to call your dog "Peel," "Deal," or even "Heel," fine and dandy, but he can become mighty mixed-up if he's trying to do good work in the ring while his name, or something very similar, keeps ringing out from the area next door.

When *you* file the registered name, his call name of course can be part of it, and there's nothing to prevent you from including your own name, too. "John Smith's Mike" is a perfectly acceptable name, if you want it that way. In any case, he's your dog now, so call him what you will—he won't mind much what the name is, as long as you call him.

CHAPTER 2

Pretraining

The moment you bring the young puppy home, training begins. As an adult dog, he will represent the total of his experiences with you. What you permit him to do, what you forbid him, what you encourage him in, and what you persuade him to do by active training—these are going to pattern the behavior of the mature dog.

More important than any of these, though, is *how* you permit, forbid, encourage, and persuade him. How you treat him will depend entirely on your attitude toward him and on your conceptions of what a dog is and how he works. The dog's mind does work in certain ways, and it does not work in others. If these ways are clearly understood, three-quarters of the problems of civilizing and training will be solved from the outset.

A dog can and does do certain things. He learns certain patterns of behavior, and he learns to avoid other patterns. He learns to respond to words of command, positive and negative. He learns to love and hate. He can learn to do an astonishing variety of things that can easily lead to the conclusion that he has thought the situation through, but it just isn't so. He cannot follow any extended line of reasoning, equate cause and effect over any period of time, reach rational conclusions about series of events, or do most of the many mental acrobatics some people hold the dog capable of. No matter about the wonder dog you heard of from Aunt Matilda—who bought the groceries, priced the chops, and translated from the Hebrew— old Shep may be the nearest thing to a human being on the block, but it isn't because he ponders the state of the world, but rather that he has a certain combination of instincts and training and an expressive face.

Along these lines is the experience of one of the authors with a "talking dog" in England. She was a German Shepherd, billed as "Rita the Talking Alsatian," and her specialty was mathematics. She would bark out the answer to the most abstruse problem you could think of as long as it was a whole number, and preferably a low one. There is no sillier feeling in the world than that of facing a dog and saying to her, "Rita, what is the square root of eighty-one" and expecting to get an answer. But she was put to the test and came through admirably. Although she *could* count up to ten, as demonstrated by her barking the right number of times for a number of fingers held up, she couldn't answer any problem her handler didn't himself know the answer to, which pretty well gives the game away after a while. Rita had simply been trained with almost unbelievable patience to respond to minute signals and cues—you could do it with your own pup if you wanted to devote your life to it. We don't recommend it, though. It might be a bit uncomfortable explaining to your friends why the dog handles the family accounts.

Whatever "thinking" as such can be taken to mean, the dog does not think constructively about training. However intelligent he is, however sensitively he may react to your feelings, whatever instincts guide him, you will be avoiding a great deal of trouble in training if you hold fast to the fact that the dog is an animal—a creature of limited intelligence, however lovable, motivated by desire for pleasant sensations and avoidance of unpleasantness. What you want him to do you must demonstrate to him, again and again, without expecting any sort of thoughtful cooperation. He will cooperate to the extent that performance of what you want is made pleasurable to him, and nonperformance is made uncomfortable. He has not, and never will have, a conscience. He has no concept of right or wrong, should or shouldn't. He may look guilty at times, but he doesn't feel tht way; all that "hangdog" expression on his face means is that he has detected a threatening attitude in you and he's worried about that, not about whatever it was he did or didn't do.

There are many things you should not do when handling and training a dog, and these, along with what you should do, will be taken up with each particular point in training. There is, however, one overriding principle to follow in all your contacts with your dog, and that is the basic one of love and confidence. Your dog must never get the feeling that you have withdrawn your love and affection from him. It is something that he will never understand, and will in fact never connect with either performance or nonperformance. Insofar as you can manage it, he must never associate unpleasantness with you—and that is easier than it sounds. When it is necessary to correct him, the correction is made to be associated in his mind with his misdeed of whatever nature, and he will accept it as such. It's easy to see that no good will come of giving him the idea that *you* will correct him for misbehavior, for if he should manage to get that idea firmly in his head he'd run wild as soon as you were out of sight.

The object of your training your dog is to make him an acceptable companion and to equip him to live in your civilized world without giving offense, and, in the later stages of training, to make him even better to live with and, in fact, actually useful. As to whether training makes a happier dog we have serious doubts. We have never been able to discern any significant difference in inner happiness between a well-trained dog and a messy lout—the difference lies in the reactions of society to him. The ill-trained or untrained dog tends to get booted about and generally disapproved of when he comes into contact with society, while the trained dog gets a pat and a biscuit. And there you have it: the dog is going to be trained for your benefit primarily, and only secondarily for his. You want him around because he's your dog, and it's a lot pleasanter to have him around if he has manners.

When you bring your puppy home, you are faced with a number of simultaneous problems. He has to learn to love you, which isn't too difficult if you're even barely civil to him (and believe us, he doesn't care a hoot about you for a while; he *learns* to). He has to be taught to control himself in the basic sanitary considerations, and he has to learn respect for such things as your possessions and your household routine.

First of all, the pup must have some place in the house that is exclusively his own. In the first days, this is not necessarily the place that will always be his, as the problem of housebreaking will dictate his preliminary quarters. In whichever room you're going to assign as the housebreaking room, make him a comfortable bed out of something old and discarded of yours: a pair of pants, an old dress, a tattered blanket, or whatever. Old clothing serves the dual purpose of giving him something soft to lie on, and of having your smell predominant in his sleeping quarters. You can, whatever his size, make him a low box of sorts, but make it something he can get into and out of by himself. Otherwise, he will be forced to soil his own sleeping quarters when you're not around to lift him out—and even the youngest pup hates that sort of thing.

One good solution to many problems is the "crate," used by most professionals in the dog world, and by a great many other owners. The crate is an affair of heavy aluminum wire "mesh" forming sides and top, and with a solid bottom, almost always constructed to fold for storage. You can find them advertised in dog magazines and sold at any dog show big enough to have supply concessionaires, or at your local pet-supply store. The ideal size is big enough for an adult dog of your breed to stand and sit and turn around in comfortably with headroom to spare, and wide and long enough for the adult dog to lie or sprawl without being cramped.

A crate, not to mince words, is a cage; but as bad and restrictive as that may sound to the inexperienced dog owner, it isn't at all what it sounds like, at least not if it is used intelligently. It is not so much a cage as a home for your pup; with an old blanket or something similar, it can be quite a comfortable home. True, it has a door that can be fastened shut, but confinement is really not the basic point, except at limited and specific times and for limited and specific purposes. A puppy's (and a grown dog's) crate becomes his special place, his home within your home, his refuge and retreat. If it is treated that way from the beginning, your pup will come to consider it as exactly that—*his* place.

If you're going to use a crate, then, heed these words from the beginning and forever into the future: Being in the crate must always be a pleasant experience for your dog. He must *never* ever be spoken to harshly when he is in his crate; he must never be chastised or punished when he is in there. It must *always* be a secure, safe place for him to be. That's the way it becomes his home, his castle, his refuge, rather than a restrictive cage.

Whether it be a crate or low box, he should in any case have a specific place that is his own home from the moment you bring him into your home. The crate or box should be in the corner of the kitchen, which will almost certainly be his housebreaking room. There he can lie or sit, in his own personal reserved area, and watch and listen to everything that's going on in his new domain. As soon as you get him in the house take him to his bed—box or crate—and plop him there. He'll probably be tired out and ready for a good sleep, as the trip from the kennel will have been pretty wearing for him. If he goes right to sleep, all well and good. If he wants to roam around right away, let him—but only in the housebreaking area. And as soon as he steps foot outside his bed, housebreaking begins.

Resolve yourself to practice considerable restraint for the first few days and weeks. Let his housebreaking room be his home and *keep him there*. However much it may delight you to see the cuddly little devil shambling about your living room, weakly nosing and investigating things, you will have lost considerable ground even before you start, when he relieves himself on the Persian carpet. He's going to have a long life to wander about the house, and he'll be just as cute when he makes those first investigations *after* he's housebroken.

HOUSEBREAKING

What you are faced with is a young animal who is only just beginning to have control over the sphincter muscles that control his functions. This control is still weak, though it has been building up largely due to his unwillingness to soil his own quarters. Your job now is to concentrate his attention on further control, and to extend the unwillingness to soil his sleeping area to an unwillingness to make a mess anywhere in the house.

This assumes a pup in the 3–4 months age group. Any pup much younger than that will simply not have enough muscular control to do what you want him to. If, for some reason, you have gotten a younger pup (and we advise strongly against it, for this and other reasons), about the only thing you can do is wait for the right age. Almost any attempt to housetrain a pup before he is physically ready for it will only confuse and bewilder him, and will set back all your training efforts a long way.

The most practical method of housebreaking, all things considered, involves preliminary paper breaking for the puppy. He first learns that newspapers spread on the floor are the place to go, and then his attentions are progressively directed to the outside as the preferred place. Pure housebreaking from the beginning is very difficult, particularly for city dwellers who may live on the seventeenth floor of a large apartment house. The young pup will find it necessary to relieve himself a great many times per day, and if you have very far to go before you hit the street you will become exhausted, discouraged, probably wet, and won't accomplish much.

But despite all the popular lore, housebreaking is neither a hard nor extensive job. Ten days to two weeks will see the worst of it out of the way. True, at the end of that time the pup won't be completely trained, but the bulk of the work will have been done. Keep in mind only that the job requires as constant vigilance as does caring for a newborn child. But if you do it right there's a great feeling of accomplishment, and it's done for his lifetime.

The housebreaking regimen we recommend, while not hard, is one that requires constant attention. We realize full well that household chores, child tending, and other considerations may make it impossible, even for a week or so, to keep a beady eye constantly on the pup. What we have laid out is the "ideal" way to go about it—if the pressure of other affairs keeps you from living up to the letter of what follows, it isn't as serious as all that. Follow the instructions as best you can without shattering your domestic life; omissions and mistakes of a minor sort will, at worst, only prolong the housebreaking period. One caution, however: Never under any circumstances violate the basic rule of keeping the pup in his housebreaking area until housebreaking is done. This requires no extra effort, and is really the key to the whole thing.

The procedure can be helped along from the beginning if you exercise control over the intake as well as the outgo. The young puppy is fed at fairly regular intervals as a matter of course (see Chapter 11, "Feeding and Health," for more on this). He should also be watered only at specific times. Give him his water bowl about an hour after he has finished eating and let him drink as much as he wants then, rather than leaving water always available. About half an hour after the watering, either start watching him carefully or take him out—just about then the hydrostatic pressures in his bladder and bowels add up to "time to go."

It isn't practical to watch the pup *all* the time, and he will have to go at other times, aside from just after eating and drinking. Hence the papers. They are provided only secondarily for sanitation and ease of cleaning— primarily they serve as a focus for the pup's attention. Through them he first learns there is a place to go—and places not to go.

The ideal housebreaking room is the kitchen, combining as it does a tiled or linoleum floor (or at least one without a rug) and in many cases a back door leading outside. Even in an apartment, the kitchen is the usual place, simply because of the floor. Whatever you choose as his room and the housebreaking room, put down several layers of newspaper, being sure that you cover the floor space completely. Then, with papers on floor and pup on papers, wait for him to use the facilities. When he relieves himself, praise him, and pick up the sheets he used right away. Sterilize and deodorize the section of floor underneath with a good strong soap or disinfectant so that the smell doesn't draw him back to the same spot. With one small area of papers used, discarded, and cleaned after, the hope is that next time he'll use another papered area—if he does, repeat the process of praise and cleaning. If he doesn't, and you're lucky enough to catch him at it, try to distract his attention with a firm "No!" and carry him to a papered area to finish, and praise him. If you weren't watching, take him gently over to the wetted spot, push his nose at it, tell him, "No, bad dog," and then take him outside immediately. If the weather is bad or for some other reason you can't take him outside, simply plunk him on a papered area —but outside is clearly preferable. This will begin to give him a connection between the outside and relieving himself, but don't expect him to light up at the idea right away. If possible, take him to a spot that other dogs use. The smells there, combined with encouragement and "Good boy" from you, may even induce him to contribute his own small puddle. Let him know effusively that he's done a wonderful thing by using that spot.

The business of pushing his nose at whatever he did needs a bit of clearing up at this point. The operative word here is "at"—very definitely not "into." The idea is not to shame or humiliate him by pushing his nose into his urine or feces—a fairly disgusting act—but to let him get some idea of what is going on. If his nose is pushed close enough for him to get a good whiff at the time you're saying firmly, "No, bad dog!" he has a chance to make the connection. Otherwise, unless he's caught in the act, a correction only confuses him.

Overall, with the papers, what is hoped for is a steady progression toward the door leading outside. If you have a back door leading outside from the kitchen, aim him there. If you've an apartment, aim him at the kitchen door, which will eventually lead him outside, even if only past a hallway, twenty-seven floors in an elevator, another hallway, and a disapproving doorman. Here again the papers serve as a focus and a guide—through them you can lead him to the door. If you should have the rare good fortune of your pup's using first the papers in the far corner and progressing steadily, one sheet at a time, to the door, luck is with you indeed. Otherwise, if he uses the one nearest the door first, replace that sheet with one from one of the corners, symbolically declaring the bare corner out of bounds. Work away from everywhere else toward the door, shifting papers when necessary, until the last set of papers is right by the door.

He is going to make the mistake of not using the papers a good many times. Each time, scoop him up if you catch him and put him on the papers to finish, and praise him. Even if too late, take him to his proper spot after your correction.

If you are so situated that the kitchen door leads outside, a good trick after the last paper by the door has been used is to put a sheet half under the door to lure him farther. When that is used, place one with about a quarter protruding into the room. Keep at it until he goes to that sheet—correcting him all the while for the inevitable mistakes. You will probably find that he will next go directly to the door, looking for the paper after the last quarter sheet has disappeared, and your battle is won. Keep an especially close watch for his searching after the paper is gone, and take him out immediately. In an apartment, simply watch closely after the last paper is removed. When he begins to look around for it, take him out to the street and wait, no matter how long it takes, for him to relieve himself.

The "no matter how long" can sometimes be very long (we hope the weather is at least reasonably good), for you may run into the problem which has faced a good many housebreakers. The puppy has firmly learned that the only place he is supposed to go is on the papers; therefore, logically enough, if there are no papers outside, no go. One sly way of getting it done is to take a few sheets of newspaper along when you take him outside, however peculiarly your neighbors may look at you. It does work sometimes. Otherwise, you must be prepared for a siege, at least a time or two, for he will determinedly hold himself in, utterly convinced that that's exactly what you want. Be prepared—it is worthwhile to take a book with you and prepare to sit on a park bench or a stoop as the hydraulic pressures build up in the pup. One way to get over the hurdle is to be sure that he has no water at all during the night, then let him drink his fill first thing in the morning, and then shortly thereafter get him outside. And wait. It can take literally hours for the breakthrough to come; when it does, he may think he's done something wrong. This is an occasion for- immediate and overwhelming praise.

During the paper period, you will be able to see very easily whether he has made the connection. To the beginning owner and trainer, few sights are more glorious than the first time his pup deliberately uses a paper rather than the floor; the pup will probably show his pride of accomplishment in every line of his body. Watch his reactions to the whole process, and adjust the speed of taking up the papers to how well he seems to be getting the idea.

The night is another problem again. You can't keep an eye on him then, so he *must* be restricted to his housebreaking quarters. If he's been taken out after his last meal and watering, the pressures on him won't be too great, but he still may have to go during the night. If he has used the papers during the night, praise him. If he has used the floor, take him to the spot, chide him, and take him outside quickly. He'll get the nighttime idea soon enough.

It is here that the crate can be even more useful. When a pup has reached three and a half to four months, assuming you've been giving him elementary housebreaking training, he should be able to control himself during the night, particularly if he is kept in his crate sleeping quarters by a closed and latched door; he will normally perform marvels of retention in order to keep from soiling his sleeping area. If, during the night, you hear him making significant noises, by all means get up and let him out of the crate and onto the papers or outside, but he will probably be able to hold it in till then. If for some reason he simply can't help it, and unavoidably relieves himself on his blankets or pad, there's no correction you can give him. It was something he couldn't help. Just clean and air out the padding and the crate floor thoroughly, let the whole thing go for a few days—leaving his crate door open at night so he can get out and use the papers—and try again.

When the day arrives in which he has kept his room completely clean, he is almost ready to be introduced to the rest of the house. Let one more errorless day go by, just to be sure it wasn't chance, and then that evening or the next day give him his freedom of the house. Let him sniff around and explore as much as he wants. Keep a close watch still, as prevention of a mistake is a hundred times more important and effective than correction after the fact. Keep to his outing schedule after eating and drinking, and be careful not to play too roughly or scare him, as too rough handling or a fright may cause him to lose control involuntarily and wet the floor.

The final, unwatched introduction to the remainder of the house should wait until he has gone several days with no mistakes under your supervision. This applies to nighttime also; he should be kept in his housebreaking room for the night until the three or four mishapless days have passed—to prevent accidents. Then, when his day of complete freedom has arrived, issue him his passport to the house. Have faith in him—if you've done everything patiently and well up to now, you may never have another moment of trouble with him.

If something has gone wrong, and it can happen, there is only one thing to do: Start all over again. Allow him one mistake in the house as benefit of the doubt. After the second mistake, take him right back to the housebreaking room covered with papers and treat him as though it were his first day in the house. Don't swear at him—it's not his fault. He may not have quite enough sphincter control just yet, or you may have pushed things a little too fast for him. For whatever reason, the lesson hasn't been firmly enough imprinted in his mind, and the solution is a complete refresher course. Go through the whole thing again, but don't be vindictive. Make the corrections and give the praise just as before. It's rough luck, but sometimes it does happen, and you've just got to sweat it out. When he's through with the second time around, he'll be the best-behaved dog in the block and he'll go through the tortures of the damned rather than relieve himself in the house.

HOUSEBREAKING THE OLDER DOG

If you have acquired a dog of over six months from a kennel or breeder, the problems will be much the same as with the three-month-old puppy. They will be slightly easier because, being older, he will be able to exercise firmer control over himself if he wants to. And they will be harder because of the unrestricted ways he's been used to in a kennel run.

Papers are of little use with such a dog. He is old enough so that he has the necessary concentration for simple corrections. Confine him in the kitchen or in whatever room is easily cleaned, or use the wire crate as with a younger puppy. Set up a steady vigil, and when you see him becoming uneasy—either searching around in the housebreaking room for a place to go, or getting clearly restless in the crate—take him outside immediately and wait for him to relieve himself. If you're not in time, give him the puppy correction and take him outdoors.

Here too, with the older dog, proceed with caution when you give him the run of the house, and if necessary start all over again with a second course if he makes a second mistake after his liberation.

With the older dog, suppositories are a help in teaching that bowels are moved only outside. Giving a dog suppositories strikes many people as a highly unpleasant way to go about things, and if you really object on aesthetic grounds you can housebreak without them. It's just easier that way. If you do decide to use them, follow the advice of your veterinarian in the method of administration and in choosing the kind to use. And of course use only a gentle suppository, with moderation.

About half an hour to an hour after the older dog has eaten, apply the suppository. Take him out immediately thereafter and lead him to wherever you want him to learn to go. Repeat as necessary and your training problems are highly simplified.

STREET AND YARD BEHAVIOR

When, in housebreaking, you take your dog "outside" it may be your yard, or it may be the city or village street. In any of these cases there should be certain definite spots for him to go. If it's your yard (city or country), you'll want to designate some special corner for his defecation. Whenever you take him out, always take him to that spot and keep him there until he has gone. It requires occasional policing up with a shovel and old papers, but it's preferable to having him litter the yard at random.

In the city or town you'll be faced with the sidewalk-curb situation. In many municipalities, it is flatly against the law for you to let your dog soil the sidewalk. In any case, it is an offense against common decency. When you take him out, take him directly to the street just over the curb and make it understood that that is the place. If on your walks you find him squatting on the sidewalk, pull him firmly but gently over to the street and keep him there. He'll learn quickly enough that the sidewalk is forbidden.

The urination problem is something else again. Females squat, and they can be taught to squat only in the gutter. Males, though, eventually learn to lift their legs against some convenient vertical object. It's pretty useless to try to teach them to do this in the street proper, as there's nothing much there to lift against except a neighbor's car. And that is something of an offense in itself as the acid in dog urine corrodes chrome or paint quicker than almost anything else. Therefore, it is fairly accepted practice to allow him to lift his leg on fireplugs, trees, and telephone posts pretty much anywhere along the sidewalk. There is probably a law against this, too, in some places, but it isn't likely to be enforced if you are only a little judicious about spots, the spots you choose. Don't, for example, allow him to use someone's doorway. Or young trees, if possible. Keep him away from people's precious front-lawn shrubs, too. Aside from these, you and he will have little or no trouble with leg lifting.

INSIDE THE HOUSE

It is of such great importance that any spots inside the house be thoroughly cleaned, deodorized, and disinfected that we will emphasize it again. The smell of urine, so helpful in the gutter, draws the dog to that same spot again and postively encourages him to use it. The male is especially drawn this way to "cover" any such place. If, in later days, when he has learned to lift his leg, he tries an experimental squirt at furniture, attack that spot with fury and clean it to a fare-thee-well. Apply your correction first, of course. There are commercial preparations on the market to remove the stain and odor of urine, and they are mostly effective. But there is no substitute for a thorough scrubbing with soap and water, and disinfecting; a strong disinfectant odor acts very effectively in covering up any residual urine odor.

HANDLING AND PLAYING

During those first weeks, most of which he will spend in the housebreaking room, the puppy is something more than just a housebreaking problem. Like all children he will spend a good deal of his spare time sleeping and quite a lot of it in eating. When he's awake, though, and feeling playful he can still be a lot of fun to have around, restricted though he is.

One of the first things he must learn is the comfort of your touch. When you first bring him home, he has been used only to the feel of his mother and of the other puppies in the litter, and it may take a while for him to get the idea that being fondled and handled by you is something highly pleasant. To get him into it, try to get down to his level, aside from the disciplinary moments involved in housebreaking. Try to be, in your moments of play together, another puppy. He may be a little hesitant at first because of your peculiar body odor—no offense, mind, but to a puppy, smell is almost everything, and you will smell distinctly peculiar to him. However, once he accepts your smell and gets used to it, he will remember it—favorably—for the rest of his life. He *will* be taken in, even though you are rather large and odd-smelling for a pup. You can play with him just about as roughly as he feels like, but remember that when it comes to a delicate pup, you don't know your own strength. Let him set the pace, and don't force him to play if he seems drowsy or disinterested. Rule: Let him come to you.

Don't taunt him by slapping at him, however gently, or grabbing at him. Shove him around all he wants, and tumble him gently, but never tease him. Growling isn't a bit cute in the puppy: it encourages nastiness and aggression. Differentiate, though, between playful grumbling and growling, and true aggressive growling. There is a difference, and a marked one. If, while you're playing, he seems to be getting serious, calm him down with the command "Easy!" Tone of voice is very important here; make it a caution, a gentle but firm warning. If this doesn't get results, put him firmly back into his bed or crate and close the kitchen or crate door. Then let him think it over for a while. This is not a punishment, but a correction to let him know gently but firmly that this sort of thing doesn't go.

He likes little better at this stage than chewing on things. When you play with him, he'll dig at your hands and fingers with his needle-sharp baby teeth. There's no need to reprimand him if the chewing is moderately gentle—it is, after all, just his method of playing with you as another pup. Young pups chew at each other all the time and are none the worse for it. Your pup's mouth and teeth are one of the focal points of his body; having no hands to grab and hold things with, his mouth assumes the functions. It is as senseless to reprimand him for grabbing that way as it would be to punish a human child for grabbing with his hands.

Teeth may hurt, though. So if he begins to lacerate your hands take him back to his bed. As he grows older, he may continue to want to grab your hands, and if he does you can teach him to moderate his grip when you tell him, "Easy." This is done by prying his mouth open gently when the bite becomes too hard, repeating at the same time the command "Easy." Choose any command you want, but "Easy" is a good one that won't con-flict with any of the standard obedience commands he'll learn later. After this has happened a few times, he'll learn that "Easy" means to let up, not necessarily to stop biting entirely. He will come, in fact, to be able to give all the appearance of chewing his way through your arm in three easy bites while not even denting your skin.

Your pup will never have any real intention to hurt you, but if you have mauled him too roughly in play he may instinctively snap a good one at you. It is his nature to protect himself first of all, at least before he has learned to love you as his master. And snap he will, if he feels he's getting the short end of things. But blameless though he may be in this, it is one time where he will have to take the blame for your carelessness. Give him a very firm "No!"—firm but not shouted—to let him know you're distinctly displeased, then be sure to give him a pat of praise. This is one of your first experiences with "praise after a correction," and it's a good time to start getting used to the practice. It is the most natural thing in the world for a novice dog owner to tend to be angry, and continue to be angry, but this is the worst thing he or she can do; the dog must learn that some things are forbidden—and thus the correction—but he must *not* learn that you are angry with him. If you are angry, and stay angry, he will learn nothing except a certain amount of caution in approaching you, because he simply can't understand, a minute or two after the event, what it is you're angry about. All your anger does is confuse him. So . . . correct, then praise, and break off the situation, but in a friendly fashion. And resolve never to let that same situation arise again.

TOYS

Because of his great and enduring interest in chewing on things it's a good idea to let him have one or two toys that he can keep in his play area. Give him a ball of hard natural rubber, or a strip of hard leather. Wooden toys, soft rubber toys, or anything else that may be torn up too easily are on the strictly forbidden list for a young puppy. Anything that comes loose in his mouth will be swallowed, and a piece of soft rubber can end up blocking his small intestine, which can either make a very sick pup or kill him. The danger of wooden toys is obvious, with the possibility of splinters cutting his mouth or lodging in his throat or stomach.

Anything you give him from a pet shop or pet department in the way of a toy must be thoroughly examined both before and after giving it to him. Before buying it, give it a thorough test with a fingernail. If you can pry up a bit of it that way, don't consider it. After you've given him something, watch carefully for a few minutes to see what he does with it. If he is able to chew small pieces off, take it from him and throw it far away. He won't be happy about this, but you can divert his attention to something else and soon he'll have forgotten all about it.

His chewing also serves the purpose of helping along his teething. An excellent toy for this purpose is one of the specially treated natural bones found in almost any pet department. It is a section of bone that has been chemically hardened to the point where he can little more than scratch it after hours of arduous chewing. You can let him have one of these in complete confidence, as it's impossible for him to hurt himself by chewing on it. And don't worry if his chewing on it, or on anything else at this stage, seems highly violent and likely to knock out his teeth. That's what's supposed to happen. He'll lose two sets of baby teeth before he acquires the adult set. The idea of chewing on something hard is to loosen up the old to make way for the new.

Natural bones are excellent if judiciously chosen. Any of the beef long bones or knuckle bones, raw, provide the pup with days of chewing pleasure. Even cooked, if a bone is solid, let him have it. Be careful, though, of the smaller animal bones, and even the soft and/or splintery kind from beef. Rib bones, for example, are bad. The bones of any fowl or fish are about the worst thing you could give a pup.

As a general rule, don't give him anything as a plaything that is an old version of something new that is forbidden to him. Old shoes or gloves may seem the ideal castoff for him, but you are only casting temptation before him. He has no way of distinguishing between the old and the new. One day it will be the old shoe, and the next you will lose your expensive brogans. And you can't reprimand without confusing him utterly and undermining his faith in you. A shoe is a shoe is a shoe as far as he's concerned.

You can give him a clean old rag to chew on and to tug around. It won't hurt him. With this, and with your finger, and with anything else that's long enough for both of you to get hold of, he'll love to play tug-of-war. About this you will hear some contrasting opinions. You may hear that you should never play tug with the pup because (1) you're likely to deform his teeth and jaw, (2) he'll learn the power of his jaws, and (3) he'll learn to defy you.

If you observe common sense in playing, nothing will go amiss. First, there's precious little chance that he's not going to learn the power of his jaws at one time or another. There's no use trying to keep this from him. And in pulling, if you exercise a bit of moderation, you don't stand any chance of deforming his jaws. Hold on only hard enough to be considered a stationary object and you'll do no more harm than if the rag were stuck on something. Pull gently in the opposite direction and he'll enjoy himself hugely. Do not, though, jerk suddenly to try to get it away from him. That's what can do the harm. A sudden, hard jerk can give his head quite a snap, and it will shake him up a bit.

TEACHING "GIVE"

A valid point in objection to tug-of-war is that it might teach your dog to defy you. But this, like some other dog lore, is a maxim designed to keep dog owners from having to think; a little thought and training shows the way out. That way out is to force him to release his grip on the cloth or whatever when you tell him, "Give" or "Out." Besides quelling any defiance at this point, the "Give" lesson lays the groundwork for future obedience work. To teach this, simply insist firmly and gently that whatever he is holding on to at the moment be released on command. When you're tugging together, say "Give" and then pry his jaws apart with your fingers. This is done by taking hold of his muzzle from beneath and pressing with the thumb and fingers about halfway back along the jaw, forcing the lips against the teeth.

You'll find, if you want to experiment, that it's very nearly impossible to pull his jaws apart by brute force, big as you are and little as he is at the time. What you're doing is pitting yourself against one of the strongest muscles in the world, the masseter, which supplies the immense power of jaws both canine and human. But by squeezing the skin of the mouth against the juncture of his upper and lower teeth, you are applying pressure that he will want to relieve rather than fight. He'll quickly enough open his jaws to save himself discomfort. Try it on yourself a couple of times to get the idea—put your thumb on one cheek and your forefinger on the other and then squeeze hard together. Painful, isn't it? You do *not* want to hurt your pup—and you will see from experimentation on yourself that it can hurt. So apply the lips-against-teeth pressure only enough to persuade him to open his jaws and give you the item he's holding in them. If you are calm and patient about it, the situation is not likely to develop into any sort of struggle.

When he has opened his jaws and perforce released whatever he was holding, take the object and praise him highly for what he has just done. Do this occasionally during the tug-of-war, and also when he's playing with other things like his rubber toy or bone. No matter how much he seems to be enjoying it, tell him, "Give," and apply the persuasion unless he releases it at once. A few times of this and he'll let go quickly at the word, and the defiance problem is no problem at all. Don't bedevil him with it, though. Give him the command and the persuasion a few times a day until he has learned it thoroughly, and then infrequently thereafter unless it is used for some practical purpose. Don't jerk or try to jerk anything from his mouth when you say "Give." Nothing will inspire him to hold on harder than a jerk in the opposite direction. Don't be inconsistent about making him release things once the command is given. A command must *always* be obeyed, from the very first time it is being taught. If you are playing and tell him to give, and then go on tugging happily, or josh with him about it, he is rapidly going to get the idea that commands are actionable only every so often, or perhaps only when you say so a second time with your voice raised. Not good.

PICKING UP THE PUP

In housebreaking, in playing, for weighing, and all-round, you'll be picking him off the floor a good many times during his infancy and youth. You can, with astonishing ease, undo him by picking him up the wrong way. Be as careful with him as you would with a human baby—although for once the baby analogy is a bad one. The puppy should neither be picked up by the chest and shoulders nor should he be cuddled or carried on his back. Grabbing him, from front or back, by the shoulders and/or front legs can pull that region seriously out of whack. We won't go into the anatomical considerations, but it is a very bad way to go about lifting him. Nor do we recommend the "natural mother" method of grabbing him by the scruff of the neck, logical though that may seem. By the time you get him he'll be past the neck-scruff stage and such treatment will hurt him.

The right and easy way to do it is to put one hand or forearm under his rump, folding the hind legs forward, and the other hand under his chest and shoulders. Keep the hand as far forward on his chest as you can, either from front or back, and his weight will be distributed so that he's safe and sound. Aside from the possibility of physical damage, the "shoulders only" method of lifting will scare him. Animals hate to dangle in space, no matter how firmly they are held by the front. The same applies to holding him, once lifted, on his back. It's an unnatural position for a dog, and he will panic and try to get himself twisted around. Put yourself in his place and picture yourself being hoisted by your legs and then dangled upside down by a giant.

TEACHING HIS NAME

By constant repetition and by the tone of your voice, you will teach the pup his name means him, and that when he hears it, you want his attention. When you're playing with him, repeat it to him in a coaxing and friendly tone. Later, you'll be using it with most of the commands you give him involving action on his part (rather than "Stay" or "Wait," for example). At the beginning, though, be sure that when he hears his name it is always associated with pleasantness. In correcting him for housebreaking or other mistakes, don't use the name at all. Just "No!" Do use his name when you feed him—to reinforce the association with something good.

FURNITURE

Some dog owners believe that a dog is a dog, and that his place is on the floor exclusively. Some feel that he is a member of the family; that he should be allowed on chairs or sofas if he feels like it. And there are attitudes in between that may dictate permission for him to get up on one "favorite chair." Generally the split is between country and city, with country dogs being relegated to the floor and city dogs having the run of the place. You can do it either way, as long as you decide in the beginning and stick to your policy.

If he is going to be strictly a floor dog, then he must *never* be allowed on any piece of furniture, right from the start. Even when he is first allowed out of his housebreaking room you mustn't pick him up and hold him on your lap on the couch. Being up on the couch with you *or* solo holds little distinction for him, and it will only confuse him later if you deny him the privilege. When he's little, he won't be able to negotiate the height, so there's no problem with his climbing up. As he grows and investigates new horizons, he'll try to climb up just to see what's there. Push him off gently and tell him, "Off," a few times and he'll get the idea. Later, he may perversely decide that the soft couch or chair represents heaven on earth to him and occupy it while you're out of the house. You can't correct him directly, as you'll never catch him up there despite evidence that he was. (There's a wholly apocryphal but still delightful story about a dog whose owners had this problem. They could never catch him up on his favorite chair because he'd hear them coming up the walk and jump off. But they would feel his warmth still in the cushion and chastise him every time. They thought they had him cured until one day, peeking through the front window on returning, they saw him standing in front of the chair blowing on the cushion.)

If you decide that he's going to be a full member of the household with all privileges, the problems are only those of dirt and reactions. If he comes bounding in from a muddy or snowy outside and leaps directly onto your best petit-point upholstery you may wish you could trade him in for a parakeet. This isn't necessary, as he should be trained to wait at the door for a quick cleaning with an old rag after a particularly messy run. By the time he's old enough to bound onto chairs easily, he will be old enough to have learned the "Stand" and "Stay," and there the problem endeth.

As far as reactions go, this is really something between you and your friends. Somewhat fastidious friends who come to visit may find dogs on furniture disagreeable, particularly if the dog has to be shooed off the chair they're about to sit in. Again, a later bit of training is the solution to this, in which he is relegated to his quarters while those particular guests are there. If he's a chair sitter in your house, he may try to be one when he goes visiting with you. And although your friends may be glad to see him, and dog lovers withal, they may be of the dog-on-the-floor variety. So set up a rigid rule for him: Okay at home, forbidden elsewhere. Don't make exceptions with the occasional friend who doesn't mind him on his furniture. Keep the rule hard and fast and he won't be confused, provided you keep him on lead so he's under control. It's always better to avoid the problem rather than make a correction after the problem has occurred.

CODDLING

Far before written history began, man and dog came together on the basis of mutual assistance. The dog helped track down game and defend the cave or hut against marauders both animal and human. The man provided shelter and a supply of food. Out of that relationship grew affection and companionship. Withal, the dog has never given up his right to be an individual, standing on his own feet beside his owner and master.

In our opinion, one of the worst things that can happen in dog rearing is to take away this individuality—to coddle all the "dog" out of a defenseless pup. One of the most painful sights is the dog who doesn't know he *is* a dog—who's been pampered and petted and cooed over until he's good for nothing but more pampering and petting and cooing. True, the working function of the dog has declined sharply and the companionship side of the relationship is in the ascendant, but there is no reason why the dog cannot be a respected individual within the household.

When as a puppy he has problems, give him a chance to work things out for himself. If he gets tangled up in something, let him try to get himself out unless you see he's about to panic or can't manage at all. Let him work out the problems of stairs by himself. If he gets hurt, give him sympathy and fix it up, then leave him alone. Above all, don't be afraid of discipline. Good discipline for the pup means a far happier life for both of you; it doesn't mean continual beatings and/or scoldings. We've seen people who "just couldn't bear to hit the little dear." Without fail, the "little dear" has been a spoiled monster unfit for human society. We've also seen, at the other end, the poor pounded pooches who crawl warily from one restriction to the next, never getting a chance to enjoy life. The middle course between the two extremes is an easy one to find, with a little thought.

The middle course is, in fact, essential for obedience. It is flatly impossible to teach the pampered pup anything wihout a long period of readjustment for both pup and owner. While we recommend obedience training as the solution for behavior problems, it is a far easier thing for everyone concerned if the behavior problems are never allowed to arise in the first place. In the next chapter we spend some time discussing corrections for various situations, all of which comes under the heading of discipline. The most severe correction requires a healthy clip under the muzzle. You probably will have to hit your dog at one time or another, but one or two firm cracks, scientifically and fairly administered at the proper times, can prevent you from ever having to hit him again, and you can save yourself irritation, frustration, and endless disappointment in your dog. Throughout this book we take up one or another aspect of discipline and permissiveness at the appropriate places. You'll find, as you train your own dog, that he can be allowed an astonishing amount of freedom and status without getting in the way, if he is raised in the middle course.

LEAVING THE PUP BY HIMSELF

When the pup has come to have the run of the house by himself, he may get lonely when you go out. It's not surprising—he's come to think quite a lot of you, and he wants you to be around. In his housebreaking room, particularly if he has his bed or crate there, where he can be secure and comfortable, he's never sure whether he's alone in the house or not, and thus is less likely to make lonesome noises. If he does, you can get a start on training him not to make lonely noises when you're out by letting him get the idea that he shouldn't make them when you're there. If he wants your attention when you are in another part of the house or apartment, it is a good idea to come to him occasionally and play, as it builds up the feeling in him that you are a team and that he can communicate with you. But also, when you are busy, or simply as a matter of preliminary training, tell him, "No, that's enough," in a firm tone after he has made his first request for your attention and company. Most important, do something about it if he doesn't stop. Go straight to him, and lay it on him firmly and gently that he is to shut up. Not harshly, but firmly, putting your hand gently around his muzzle if necessary to show him that you want him to be quiet. Then pat him and leave. Repeat as necessary. He will be confused at first, as the idea of noise being unappealing is totally foreign to a dog, and particularly to a puppy, so you must exercise extreme patience. He will learn that a bark or two or some other noise is permitted, but that if it doesn't get a friendly response, he is to cease.

This sort of training may prevent later problems, but still, when you're out of the house or apartment later and he can look everywhere and not find you, he may take to letting all and sundry know that he doesn't like being left alone. His complaining can be a fearsome irritation to neighbors. To correct it, which you should at least try, you have to catch him in the act. Leave him one day with all the appropriate ceremonies, and leave the front door unlocked and even unlatched. Then lurk about in the hall or around the corner of the house; at the first howl—beyond an allowable tentative bark or two—charge back, fling open the door, give him a strong "No, that's enough!" and shut the door again. That will shake him up a little, and make him less likely to do it again. If he tries it again, repeat the correction. Be careful to do a neat job of lurking—he has fearfully acute ears, and of course his sense of smell, and you might not be fooling him at all if he never seems to howl when you're just outside the door.

Chewing on forbidden items and forgetting his housebreaking while you're away are more serious. For some reason, dogs seem to do both of these very shortly after the owner leaves—perhaps out of pique, we don't know—and this gives you the opportunity to use the same sort of correction as with loneliness noises. It may take a little more waiting, say, ten or fifteen minutes, but you're very likely to catch him in the act when you come in unexpectedly.

One word of caution, though: Unless you catch him absolutely red-handed, don't do anything about it right away. Whatever he's been up to, he'll greet you joyously when you come in. Greet him cordially, at least for a moment or two, and then affect to discover what he's done. Take him to it, make sure he knows what the situation is, and give him a very stern "No, bad dog. Shame!" If it's a housebreaking misdemeanor and it happens more than once, you may have to give him the refresher course. But first, examine your conscience and make sure you haven't been asking too much of him. If he's still in the paper-breaking stage and he misses the papers when you're out, then it simply means you haven't trained him well enough. It's not his fault. If he's beyond that stage and into the outdoors-only stage, remember that you can't ask miracles of him. A puppy simply has only so much ability to control himself, and if you've left him for more than six hours, there's not much he can do about it, try though he might to hold it in.

If the problem is chewing, correct him with the object chewed on. Shake it in his face, and give him the same stern "No, bad dog. Shame!" correction. Then put the object away, and come back and praise him to let him know that it isn't just your being mad at him in general. That may be a bit hard to do if he's ruined your best pillow or pair of shoes, but remember that he has to associate the correction with the wrong, and not with general ill temper on your part. The last thing you want to do is teach him to expect unpleasantness from you, except where unavoidable. That is why you must never immediately reprimand him when you come into the house; after a few times, he'll get the idea that your coming back means unpleasantness, and he'll run for cover instead of greeting you happily. More dog owners than we can tell you have told us, "But he *knew* he'd been bad. Why, as soon as I came in he looked guilty and ran away." Figure out for yourself what had been happening to make the dog run away whenever the owner opened the door.

If there is a chewing problem that you can't solve with corrections on returning, then the simple solution is to eliminate the problem, at least temporarily, by eliminating his access to the chewables. Leave him in the kitchen when you go out, with the kitchen doors closed; then there won't be tempting cushions, shoes, and other things for him to chew on. After doing that three or four times, and always greeting him happily when you return, try him out in the house again. If there's chewing, go back to three or four times in the kitchen. It's a very hard idea for him to get, make no mistake about it, but it often gets through. Or at least by the time you've done it a number of times, he's past the bad lonelies and at least partially past the bad time when teething encourages him to chew on things.

One thing you should prevent before it happens is chewing on lampcords or other electrical wires. An inquisitive puppy is quite likely to chew on anything so conveniently sized and available as a wire. He may get away with it, but a vigorous chew can short-circuit the wire through the pup's mouth, which will at best give him a bad burn. Coat all the wires in your house with Musterole, citronella, or any of the commercial "Keeps Dogs Away" items. A light wipe with any of these will make the wire unpleasant to the taste—just be sure that what you use is unpleasant and not poisonous. However, if the cords are not in his normal path to be tripped over and he's been well supervised on being introduced to the different rooms of the house (a gentle "No" followed by "Good boy" if he sniffs and investigates wires), he is much more likely to be content to play with his own toys and ignore wires.

JUMPING UP

Big dog or little, jumping up on people should be discouraged firmly from the beginning. It may seem cute at first, but the big dog in later life can knock people down with a firm planting of the front paws, and even the littlest can leave muddy footprints and rip expensive hose. The habit is easily broken by giving him a good thump in the chest with your knee just as he comes up. Don't even correct him verbally. Catch him in the chest with your knee just hard enough to throw him off balance and over, and then sympathize with him over the accident. Keep doing that and he'll be puzzled by the inexplicable thing that happens to him every time he tries it, but he'll chalk it up as one of the many mysteries of life and seek other outlets for his affection. And with no hard feelings between you. The little dogs require the same treatment, but with the ankle or foot—just a shove, not a kick. Make it seem as casual and accidental as possible. And whatever you do, don't step on his toes to try to cure him. This is sheer senseless cruelty when correction can be done without hurting him at all.

PROTECTION AND RESTRAINT

As the pup grows older and learns that you are his property, he will probably begin to feel protective both about you and about your house. Or *his* house, as he sees it. He may begin to develop a strong dislike for the idea of anyone else's coming in. Many dogs are, if anything, too friendly and welcoming to almost everyone, but many aren't, and aggressiveness should be controlled and directed from the beginning.

To control this, he must learn to go to his bed or crate on command. Decide on one word to use as a command for this. "Place," "Bed," "Kennel," or "Crate" are possibilities, but you can use any other word you like. Whatever it is, get in some practice with it as soon as he has the freedom of the house. Give him the command—in a normal tone of voice, but clearly a command—and put him in his bed or crate. Once there, praise him and pet him and let him know all is well, that you are pleased with what he did, even though you did all the doing.

Clearly, the first few times you do this, he won't have the faintest idea what it is all about, but he'll catch on. He will almost certainly want to pop right out again and come into the living room, but don't let him. Patiently, gently, at every attempt, put him back in firmly, giving him the command each time you make the correction. For the first several times, you will have to stand right by and see to it that he stays put. Then gradually you can go farther and farther away without his leaving. In the beginning, don't be hard-nosed about it. After a few times of putting him there with the command, and his popping right out, and your putting him back, be prepared with a "release" command. The release word can be "Okay" or something like that, but definitely don't say something on the order of "Come on out," as the command "Come" is reserved for a very specific action in later training. With your release command decided on and ready in the beginning training, and after you've put him back several times, quickly give the release, and praise him for that just as he's about to leave again. Or, if he *is* staying where he was put, give him the release and take him out of the bed or crate, again praising him for what *he* did.

This takes a little time, but he must learn to respond to your "Go to your place!" command regardless of where he is in the house, and remain there until he's been released by another command. This procedure makes it incumbent on you to be careful and thoughtful about your part. *Always* release him with your command. Don't, for example, send him to his place when you're going to bed at night, or when you're going out of the house. It is simply too much to expect of a puppy—or even a grown dog—for him to remember several hours later that he is supposed to be under a command. The crate can be very useful in this training, as after the first few times you can close the door after you have given him the command and put him in, leave it closed for a few minutes, then open it when you give the release command. That will help sink the whole idea into his head.

Continue the "Place" training until he goes of his own accord on command. And again, be patient. By this time he loves and adores you and hates to leave you. The leaving is something he doesn't want to do at all, so you must be firm about it, and willing to give the lesson over and over again. Remember why it is that he is at first unwilling to go, and you'll be less likely to lose your temper and rant at him.

When he has learned "Place," you can use it for the doorbell and visitors. When the doorbell rings, send him to his bed. This prevents over-friendly rushes at people he likes, and growls and aggression toward those he doesn't like or distrusts. It won't interfere at all with his protective instincts, because once he has learned the "Place" lesson thoroughly, you can allow a certain discretion—in which he is allowed to stand by, or sit by, when the bell rings, and watch what's going on.

Now you can begin to make a differentiation between friends and strangers and delivery boys at the door. When friends come in, release him from his place and introduce them. Literally that. Let him come out and show him your friendliness and acceptance of your visitors. Go so far as to introduce them formally. Even though the words mean nothing to him, your tone and manner as you do so will convey everything to him. And you can convey the right tone best if you are actually introducing your friends to him. If for some reason he takes a dislike to a visitor, never allow him to show any aggression. At the slightest sign of a growl send him immediately to his bed and keep him there for a while. Then let him out to try again. If he still shows active dislike for your guest, send him away until the friends have gone. He'll learn soon enough that your friends are not to be menaced.

Don't introduce him to delivery boys and salesmen. If someone comes into your house strictly on business, make the pup keep his distance. When a delivery boy comes, send the pup to his place and keep him there. Later, he can learn to stand by the door and keep an eye on things. But for the moment let him learn his distinctions by being kept at a distance. If, from his bed, he makes threatening noises at service people, well and good. Neither encourage nor discourage his attitude, but simply make sure that he stays where he is.

All this is extremely valuable groundwork in obedience and in protection of you and your property. As far as the protection goes, remember that his being kept at first in his bed won't reduce it. You don't want a dog that snaps at anyone, no matter how sinister. The factor of protection in a dog is his presence, the amount of noise he will make if anything goes wrong, and the uncertainty in the mind of anyone with evil intentions that he won't really have a hand taken off. As far as your friends and guests go, there can never be any excuse for the slightest show of hostility toward them, unless of course they have actually mistreated him. If a visitor in your house decides to brain you with a chair, or lifts a trinket or two in a kleptomaniac mood, don't expect your dog to make up for your mistakes in judgment. Keep him in his place, make him be friendly, or at least not actively unfriendly, toward your friends, and let him keep his distance from others.

NOISES, THUNDER, AND BELLS

The young pup, like the young child, has an instinctive dislike of sudden noises. Curing him of fear reactions can be done by exposing him to noises under circumstances ordinarily pleasant to him. For example, you can make a racket with pots and pans when it's feeding time and he's busy gobbling, starting easy and working up until he will eat happily through a full cantata for dishpan, fortissimo. Get him to understand that there's no harm in loud noises and he'll come to take them like a veteran.

Thunder and telephone and doorbell trouble almost always can be traced to the owner of the dog. If you leap into the air and crawl under the bed when it thunders, don't be surprised if the pup starts doing the same. He thinks it's the right thing to do, and he will quickly sense and absorb the fear you have. If you're really terrified of thunder, keep his welfare in mind and sit with gritted teeth through the worst, patting and reassuring him the while. It might even cure you.

Dogs get panic reactions to the doorbell and phone in the same way. Eventually a dog begins to associate the doorbell with company and may get excited at the prospect, but that is another matter. If his owner is galvanized into action by a bell, he'll learn the same patterns by association. Next time the bell rings, see if it's you who's teaching him to jump and run in circles.

THE COLLAR AND LEASH

Within a few days after the pup has arrived at your house he will be ready to be introduced, gradually, to the collar and leash. His first collar can be a cheap affair, because he'll outgrow it before long. Get him one of leather, the width adjusted to his size. If he's short-haired, get him a flat collar wide enough so that it can't possibly cut into his neck. If he's long-haired, get one of the round leather variety. The reason for this is that though the flat is the better collar, a wide-enough flat collar will press down and mat the hair of a long-haired dog, tangling it considerably and making life uncomfortable for him. And make it a perfectly plain collar, with only a strong buckle and a solid, one-piece ring for attaching a leash. If you must have studs or other ornaments, by all means have them, but they will only make the collar heavier and more of a burden to your pup. Ornaments on the collar may make you feel good, but they won't impress him or his friends a bit.

Before you put the collar on him for the first time, play with it around him for a while. Drag it over him a few times and treat it as a plaything. If he wants to chew and tug on it a bit, let him. Convince him that it's an entirely harmless object. Then, one of the times you're passing it over and around his neck, buckle it on loosely. Practice the buckling a few times beforehand so you don't make a butterfingered mess of the process and panic him. If you do it right it'll be on and fastened before he realizes what's happening to him, and the victory is won. He may object, and object strenuously, to having it around his neck, but pet him and reassure him, and let it stay. He'll find it doesn't hurt him, and he'll get used to it before long. The first time on, buckle it loosely. When he's a bit more accustomed to it, adjust it to just the right fastening—tight enough so he can't slip it off, but loose enough so you can put your fingers between it and his neck without squeezing overmuch.

It'll take him a day or two before he's thoroughly resigned to the fact that the collar is there to stay. Then you can begin to introduce him to the idea of the leash. Here is where the greatest caution, patience, and tact are required, for it is not at all uncommon for serious troubles to arise with the first leashing if you don't do it right. A sudden snapping on of a leash and the consequent restraint can give your dog fits and generally send him into a three-layered panic that he won't recover from for some time to come.

The thing has got to be done gently. When he has accepted the idea of the collar, play around him with the leash a bit, then snap it on. Don't hold on to the leash at all—let him drag it around with him and get accustomed to the idea of having it on. Leave it on him for a few minutes, then take it off for a while, then put it on again. This stage can be accomplished in a day. Even the most timid pup will soon get over any fright if the leash is not used to restrain him right away. If, in his moving about, it catches on things, release it for him, and let him drag it about some more. But don't use it to restrain or hold him. You'll see quickly enough when he has become accustomed to the idea. Let him get firmly used to the idea that it will not hurt him, then take the first steps in using the leash as a restraint.

Try holding on to the other end of the leash now. Go about it gradually and gently, and at first do nothing more than hold on to it. When he pulls away, as he will, go along with him wherever he goes. Make as much of a game of it as you can. Then when he is used to the fact that it pulls on him slightly, exert a little gentle pull. Gradually increase your pressure until you are standing or sitting in one spot and he is restricted to a circle with the radius of the leash. Again, he won't like it much, but reassure him when he reaches the end of his tether. The final step is to exert a positive pressure so that he is forced to leave wherever he is and come along where you want to go. Go easy and gradually, and give in to him every now and then if he seems really unhappy, but finally insist that when you pull it means get moving. Don't jerk or yank—just bring up the pressure until he has to move. With little or medium-sized dogs it won't be much of a test of strength, and even with the large variety you should be able to pull it off.

Get in a good bit of practice with the leash before you use it the first time on the street. That way you'll both be more confident about things, and you'll avoid public shrieking on his part and tooth gnashing on yours. You'd be surprised how many nice old ladies can spring out of the ground waving umbrellas and police threats if your in-training pup so much as whimpers on the street. Get the difficult parts over in private, as much as possible. And the more you practice with the leash at home, the better off you personally will be. If this is a first dog, the experience of being on one end of the leash will be just as strange to you as it is to him. If you're unsure of yourself and your handling of the leash (and it is a minor art), all your unsteadiness will transmit itself right down that six-foot length to the pup and make *him* unsure of things. You've got to be the fount of wisdom and steadiness in his world, so live up to it.

THE TRAINING COLLAR

The training collar, a device consisting of a length of nylon cord or light chain (usually chrome-plated) connecting two metal rings, can be introduced any time after the pup has become used to his leather collar. Some dogs do not have a leather collar to start with and are introduced directly to the training collar, which brings up practically no problem. If the training collar is his first one, put it on just as you would the leather one, slipping it over his head with a deft movement at the same time you would have buckled the other. The length of nylon or chain is made into a loop by slipping the nylon or chain through one of the rings until the other ring keeps it from going any farther. Presto, a loop. Or rather a collar.

Whether to use nylon or chain is entirely up to you, but consider these points: Chain collars are sturdy and traditional—tens of thousands of dogs have been trained with them—but they do present some problems. Unfortunately, it is very, *very* difficult for beginning trainers to remember that they must never, *never* hold the dog on a tight leash. You'll be hearing a great deal about the importance of this later. If you do hold your dog on a tight leash—and you will, we're sorry to tell you—a chain collar can cut away the hair on his neck, and with enough abuse actually start scraping away the skin on his neck.

Whichever type of collar you buy for him, be sure that it is of exactly the right length and width or size. The length is easily determined: Measure the distance around his head from his throat to the highest point of his skull (the smallest circle that will just slip over his head) and add an inch. Keep a check on this as he grows, so you can replace the collar later with a larger model when necessary. The width must be adjusted to the size of your dog. Make it as light as possible but not so light that it cuts into his neck when you have to apply pressure with it. If chain is your choice, be sure also to get a chain in which all the links are rounded, not "jewel-cut" or ground flat along one or two sides. They're pretty, but the grinding of jewel-cut chains makes sharp edges that will catch and pull his hair.

There's a very definite right way to put the training collar on, and it should always be put on this way. To do this, hold the collar with one ring between the thumb and forefinger of each hand. Lift your left hand until it is directly above the right at the full length of the chain. Then let the chain slip down through the right-hand ring until both rings meet. With the right hand take hold of the half of the chain nearest the left-hand ring, releasing the right-hand ring, and separate your hands. The ring that was in your right hand should now slide freely along the chain between your hands, and the collar is ready to slip on the dog as he faces you.

This may seem to be a great deal of trouble over nothing, but it has a point. With the collar on this way, you have greater control over the dog when he is walking on your left side, which is where he should be when walking or in training. When you pull with the leash on the "live" ring of the correctly placed collar, the body of the collar slips through the "dead"—inactive—loop and pulls itself up tight immediately. With the collar on wrong, a pull simply exerts pressure on the other side of the dog's neck without tightening. And tightening, *with a quick release*, is the whole point of the training collar if you need to use the live ring.

A simple way of checking whether you have it on correctly is to see whether the chain or nylon comes *over* his neck and through the inactive ring, rather than under and through. Another check is to pull the collar gently tight, then let the free end drop on the dog's right. If the collar is on right, the whole thing should immediately loosen. Otherwise, the loose end will flop over and hang from the inactive ring.

Using the collar with the lead attached to the live or the dead ring is up to you and depends on your dog. Training should be done with the least possible force and discomfort for your dog. When you start every element of training with the leash on the dead ring, you are simply giving a gentle pull to his neck, via the collar, when you use the lead. Sometimes it is necessary to use the live ring, which gives a momentary tightening of the collar, but we recommend you use it that way only when it appears absolutely necessary, and then go back to the dead ring for further training.

Get your dog used to wearing the training collar early, as it will be a great help in teaching him to walk correctly with you on the street. And a final point about training collars: *Never* put on or attempt to use any variety of "spike" or "pinch" collar with your dog. They are only for extremely unmanageable dogs; if now or at any time later in training you honestly come to believe that your dog is unmanageable without a special collar, you have no business trying to work with him yourself. Turn the problem over to a professional trainer, who is the *only* person qualified to use a spike or pinch collar. In all probability he will not have to use such a thing, but leave it to him. Never—and we cannot emphasize this too strongly—*never* try to use a spike or pinch collar on your dog.

COLLAR OR HARNESS?

Although many people with small breeds of dogs feel that the proper thing for walking is a harness affair, we definitely recommend against it for any breed. With one of the larger breeds you'd be letting yourself in for a lot of trouble with a halter, for a full-grown dog of the larger sizes may be stronger than you when it comes to pulling. If he knows that a sudden pull means a contest of strength, he may hesitate little on seeing a particularly appetizing cat or place to smell down the street. If, however, it means near strangulation to pull against you he'll think about it for a while.

The right way to put on the training collar. The chain comes over the head and through the "dead" ring.

Even with the tiny breeds, including the toys, a light collar is far preferable to a harness. Constant pulling against the harness, by however light a dog, can be irritating. It can also pull his shoulders out of shape if he does it enough. The collar, on the other hand, can only make him momentarily uncomfortable.

THE PROPER LEASH

The best possible leash to get is one of flat leather or webbing, preferably half an inch wide or even more. You may have to shop around to get it, for pet stores and departments go in heavily for fancy and useless little

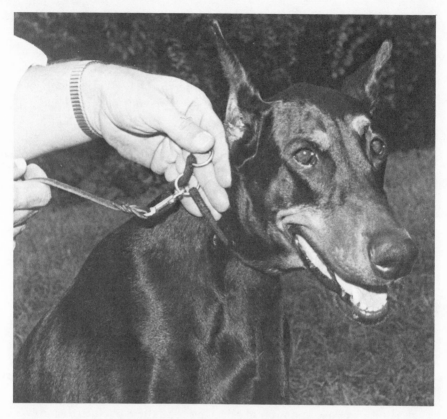

Lead attached to the "dead" ring of a light nylon collar, which is still put on as recommended, in case the "live" ring must be used.

plastic leashes, thin leather ones, and, unfortunately, chains. Avoid all these even if the shop owner recommends them with passion. Any very thin leash of whatever material will cut into your hands if you have to use any force on it (and you will), and a chain is suicidal. It will cut rashers off if you're not very careful. Make sure it is of good leather or solid webbing, with a loop big enough to get your hand through, firmly stitched at the other end from the snap.

The snap itself is of great importance, too. There are many designs on the market today, including two good traditional kinds—one with a sliding rod at one side of the snap held firmly in place by a spring, and one with two flattened curved-metal "hooks" that slide alongside each other to make a secure catch for the ring of the collar. Make sure that whatever snap you choose is strong enough for your dog but light in weight and easy for you to operate, a design that is not likely to catch on anything and come open accidentally. Avoid completely the fancy snaps you will see on some leashes, especially the kind that comes apart at the tip of the snap and is held together by a spring. That one will come apart one day on a hard pull with the leash and you might lose a dog.

The length of the leash is important only in that it should be comfortable in your hands without excess length to get in your way when you're walking or training. Most people can handle one quite efficiently if it's between four and six feet long; six feet is in fact a good maximum length because some municipalities that require leashing at all times in public specify that the leash shall be no longer than six feet. Don't waste money on anything longer with the idea of giving him a little more freedom—you and he will get all tangled up in it. The longer leashes you may see in pet stores are for tracking or other special purposes where considerable length is required.

CATS AND OTHER DOGS

There is no natural antipathy between dogs and cats. Dogs are set on cats in the street by witless clods who seem to think it's funny, and the dog's natural prey instinct makes him chase anything that runs. If there's a cat already resident in your house when you bring the puppy home, they'll learn to accept each other, and even like each other, if they're left to themselves. Make the introductions slow and easy, and keep an eye on things. Don't force either of them on the other and all will go well. If as the pup grows older he develops a desire to chase the cat around, put a stop to it, no matter how friendly all this seems. In the heat of the chase they might accidentally hurt each other, and things would get serious. After a few trial chases are discouraged, the growing pup will get the idea, and the dog and cat will live happily ever after.

On the street, teach him simply to ignore cats and other dogs by keeping him on leash and under control at all times. If you approach a cat on the street while walking, keep the pup in close and tell him to heel (to be learned later) and make him mind his own business. If necessary, use his name with a cautionary and rising tone (remember that his name should not be used as a correction, but in this case simply to get his attention and let him know there's something to be thought about), then follow it with a sharp "No!" command if required, or "Heel!" (once he understands the heel command). Use a snap on the lead to get him back to your side if he lunges. And never, *ever* simply restrain him by holding him tight with the leash! He'll always keep an eye on cats you pass, but he won't bother with them if he is discouraged uniformly from the beginning.

Other dogs on the street constitute more of a problem, because both parties will want to investigate each other. Up until he's at least six months old, strictly discourage any close contact with other dogs in the street. Nobody knows what curious germs a stranger might be carrying, no matter how clean he looks, and a good mutual sniffing is the surest way known to man or dog for transmitting those germs. When he's old enough to meet his fellows, allow the contact cautiously at first. If you let them get together, be cautious about pulling them away from each other, as there is a very strict protocol about dog meetings that you shouldn't violate. Their first stiff-legged contact is a wary one usually, and each is looking sharply to see if the other will flinch. If neither does, and they are of the same political persuasion, they will draw apart in a very dignified manner. But if you suddenly yank one away, the other will take that as abject withdrawal and will want to tear yours apart.

If your pup is aggressive by nature, keep a firm hand on him in dog meetings. A growl or a snap should be discouraged sharply by a strong "No!" and a yank back into position at your side. Remember, though, that aggressive behavior on his part toward another dog is very likely to be one of his ways of protecting you—strange dogs are to him much more dangerous to the realm than most strange humans. If, on the other hand, he's excessively timid about meeting his peers there's very little you can do about it. Pushing him at another dog will terrify him and may warp his relations with other dogs for life. Let him be and wait hopefully for signs of courage. As in all meetings with dogs and dogs and/or cats and/or people, don't ever force the issue.

As far as having other dogs in your house, or taking your pup to another house with a dog, simply exercise caution. Don't visit either way until he's past six months and full to the ears with the proper inoculations. When you go to another house, expect the resident dog to be wary and protective. Let things take a natural course. Follow the same procedure with visiting dogs in your home. It does happen at times that two dogs will take a violent dislike to each other, for no reason apparent to the friendly humans involved. If so, just shrug your shoulders and make the best of it. If they really don't like each other, they shouldn't be brought together. They'll probably never hold hands, even after years of forced proximity.

CARS AND TRAFFIC

In the city, where he will always be on leash outside the house, the problem of chasing cars and bicycles is solved simply by a yank back on the leash and a stern command to stop it. Actually, city dogs on leash hardly ever seem to develop this taste in recreation. Country and town dogs, though, quite often have to be broken of the habit. Here, the best correction is prevention. As soon as the pup shows any tendency to chase moving vehicles, set up a situation where correction can be automatic and convincing.

Tie on to his collar a very light chain or rope and fasten a stick about three-quarters of the way between his neck and the ground. Fasten the stick in the middle so it will swing, and then arrange for a car to be driven by, and for someone to ride a bicycle along the road. You can sit by and not say a word, for the stick will do the correcting for you. When he starts to run, the stick will crack painfully against his front legs and soon drive out any interest he may have had. Repeat this a few times, and then try him without the stick. He should be cured, but if not, put it back on. Repeat until he is through.

Also in the country, you may have the opposite problem: that he hasn't the brains to get out of the way of a moving car. Here, again, the situation itself is the only cure. Get an accomplice to drive a car slowly along the road or a driveway and maneuver the pup into the way. If he still sits or stands there as the front bumper approaches, have the driver toot the horn in the pup's ear. That'll move him off in a hurry unless he's stone deaf.

Traffic in the city may be a problem to the dog who's always on leash outside. He never has a chance to learn the traffic facts of life. You can teach him respect for cars by the method described above, and teach him respect for the street by never allowing him to run out into it, except for his brief excursions to relieve himself. When you're on your walks together, make it a firm practice to stop at the curb before crossing. Make him sit if you want, but at least make him wait at the curb for a word from you before going into the street. Be consistent—never let him bound ahead of you at the end of the leash, for as he grows older he'll get faster and stronger, and one day might leap out into traffic.

RIDING IN CARS

When you brought your pup home from the kennels the first day, you may have had your first experience with the carsick dog. Some dogs take to cars naturally and never have a sick moment. Others are nauseated by the motion of the car and other factors and get sick at the thought of going for a ride. The central problem is one of confidence—he has to be made to feel sure of the situation, and of his surroundings. Consider it from his point of view. Suddenly he is thrust into a strange-smelling monster of steel and padding, closed in a small place that immediately starts moving and bumping about, assaulted in the nose by gasoline smells, in the ears by motor and horn noises, and in the eyes by the frightening sight of the world swaying and rushing by him. Small wonder some dogs get upset.

You can start things out right by not feeding him for an hour or so before taking him for a ride. That takes some of the physical load off his system. And then carry things out gently and in a manner calculated to instill confidence in him. If you're driving alone, by all means let him snuggle up to you on the front seat; pet him and talk to him. Let him sit with you in the car for a few minutes before you start up, until he has gotten used to it. Then start off slowly, reassuring him all the while. Drive only around the block the first time, so you can get him out of the car before he has a chance to get sick. Then increase the length of the rides until he becomes a veteran.

During the introductory rides, keep as close an eye on him as you can and still drive. If he shows any of the preparatory signs of throwing up (usually a sort of slight hiccuping), stop as quickly as you can and get him out. But if he beats you to it, let him go until he is empty. Then go on for a bit and see if he becomes resigned to it. Whatever you do, when he is sick don't chastise him in the slightest. He can't help it, and any attempt at correction or any disapproval will only confuse and bewilder him, and may make him sicker yet. If he throws up on your lap, just sigh and clean it off as best you can. Better, though, to take the precaution of spreading an old blanket or an expendable sheet over the front seat and your lap beforehand.

Once he's gotten over car sickness, or if he never had the problem, you can direct your attention to persuading him to ride where you want him. Your early attentions and permission in letting him ride beside you on the seat won't substantially affect the job of persuading him to take his proper position. Wherever you want him, put him there and make him stay. If he moves, correct him with a firm "No!" and put him back.

Later, as he makes the car his own, you'll run into the problem of windows if he's middle-sized or larger. Most dogs who get to like riding in cars love to stick their heads out of the window like a railroad engineer. You may think this is quite all right, and if so, let him crane for all he's worth. But keep in mind the possibilities that (1) he may get something large and gritty in his eye that way and do it permanent damage, and (2) if he learns that poking his head out is okay, he may carry his protection of the car a bit beyond the bounds of propriety. For some reason, dogs defend cars even more fiercely than they do houses, so be aware that he might just reach out and snap a sirloin off an innocent passerby who happened to brush against the car while you're parking. It's better to let him know that the windows are strict boundaries.

For car riding, it is essential to make one very strict rule and never deviate from it: He cannot leave the car until you give him permission. Later he will learn the commands "Sit" and "Wait," and you will be able to use them in the car situation. When you drive home and stop, he'll dance around in his anxiety to get out and into the house, no matter how much he enjoyed the ride. Make him sit and stay until you give him the "Okay." It can save his life, and it can save you the nasty spill you might take if a large or medium-sized dog came charging out between your legs as you were trying to disentangle yourself from the car.

TABLE MANNERS AND FOOD REFUSAL

Although feeding and its related problems will be taken up in a separate chapter, table manners and food refusal properly belong under pretraining. Table manners are simple. They involve his staying away from the table when you're eating. You can, of course, allow him around and throw him tidbits from your plate if you want to, but quite a few people feel strongly about dogs at table, and you may have them over for dinner some night.

After he's been given the freedom of the house, he'll come up to the table at lunch or dinner and fix you with an appealing, mournful look as though never a morsel of food had passed his lips these three days gone. You know it isn't true, and he knows it isn't true, but there's no harm in trying. Send him to his bed for the remainder of the meal, and then release him. If he persists from meal to meal, keep sending him away and making him stay. After a while he'll catch on. He'll just lie around the house and ignore you completely, and you can eat in peace.

Food refusal is a little more complicated problem. It's something all dogs should learn, for their own good and for yours. There are, sad to say, people in the world who hate dogs enough to poison them just on principle, and many a fine dog and longtime companion has been lost that way. If your dog trustingly takes food from anyone who comes along, he stands a fair chance of getting at least an upset stomach, even if he never runs into a poisoner. Doting strangers will try to feed your dog an unholy variety of stomach-turning items, and he'll probably happily gobble any and all such.

For your own well-being, food refusal is a good idea. Too many homes have been burgled by someone with the foresight to bring along a handful of hamburger to pacify the household dog. To prevent this, lay the ground-work by never allowing anyone outside your own household to feed him anything. Never, that is, unless you specifically tell him that it's all right. Don't tempt him for a month or so, just to let the idea get firmly es-tablished that food flows only from you and yours. Then, if you want, get a friend to offer him some tidbit that he likes specially well. As soon as the friend offers it, tell the pup, "No!" quite firmly. By this time he'll know full well what "No!" means, which is why it's best to wait until you have some measure of control over him. Repeat this treatment until he refuses the morsel offered without your having to tell him "No!" Then, when he is steady, tell him "Okay" and let him take it. Alternate permission and re-fusal until he refuses the food without fail and takes it willingly when you permit it. The reason for this two-way training is that someday you may have to leave him with friends or at a kennel and you don't want him to starve to death just because he has faithfully learned never to take food from anyone but you. Don't allow him to show any aggression toward the offerer, and don't worry yet about his refusing things when you're not around. Just get the basic idea across.

A thief or poisoner can also throw his offering onto the ground, and a dog should learn that he is to eat nothing unless it is in his feeding bowl or he gets it from you or with your permission. It'll also save him from getting sick from tainted food left lying around. For the moment, though, don't take any positive action in this line. Lay the groundwork by never letting him pick up anything from the floor or street to eat. If he approaches some-thing on the ground, steer him off with a "No!" and if he's grabbed it al-ready, put the "Give" training to use and take it from him.

SOME GENERAL CONSIDERATIONS

There are, as you have seen, a great many things the young puppy has to learn in his first weeks and months in your home. All of them he will learn if you learn to be a good teacher and practice patience and kindness in your teaching. Space out the lessons and don't bedevil him with overtraining. Take it slow and easy in all things, for up to now he's having a time on his own sorting out the world around him. On your side you know that he will become quickly attached to you. He will learn to want to please you, not from any innate joy that pleasing you gives him, but from realizing that pleasing you brings him fondling and praise, while displeasing you brings corrections and confinement. There is no natural perverseness in him, no matter how much it may seem so at times. When he sets his will against yours, it is not just for the setting, but rather that his way is dictated by instincts and his otherwise natural way of life. When he opposes you it's for a reason. Try always to look for that reason and take it into account in training.

If you've gotten him safely and well through pretraining, he will be at the barely civilized level, fit to live with but just only so. Basic training as taken up in the next chapter will teach him the elements of behavior above and beyond controlling his natural impulses, and will fit him to be a true companion and member of your household.

CHAPTER 3

Basic Training

Although this chapter is entitled "Basic Training" and the next "Novice," both together comprise the work necessary to pass the Novice Class work in AKC obedience trials. At the same time, the training taken up in both chapters is what we consider as basic grounding for the well-behaved dog above and beyond the elementary manners acquired in pretraining.

We recommend strongly that you train, in following the two chapters, exactly as though you were preparing for the ring, even if at present you haven't the slightest intention of ever going into competition obedience at a dog show. All the exercises included in AKC Novice work are based on practicality (Heel on Leash, Heel off Leash, Recall, Stand for Examination, Long Sit, and Down), as we will point out as each exercise is gone over. One of the reasons for our recommendation is that you may easily acquire an interest in ring work as you progress in training. It has happened to thousands of dog owners, and it is many times harder to retain a haphazardly trained dog to perform all the exercises correctly than it is to begin right. Obedience training to show standards takes very little extra effort and is rewarding in itself.

BEGINNING BASIC TRAINING

The pup should be at least six months old before you begin serious work on obedience training. As with most age specifications, this one is subject to variation depending on the dog. It may be that you have a canine genius in your household, ready for work at the age of four months. Dogs have been started in training earlier, and in fact we know of at least one who qualified for the basic AKC obedience degree, the CD, or Companion Dog, at the age of six months. This is the exception—and in this case the trainer was a man of considerable experience in the field who had the ability to recognize extra talent in the very young puppy, and to adapt standard training procedures to his precocious charge. If this is your first dog (since childhood) and your first attempt at training, we recommend that you hold off until at least six months. We've seen too many dogs who've had their puppyhood shattered by too early attempts at the imposition of the concentration and discipline necessary, and who, though trained after a fashion, never worked happily or well.

Many training classes stay several months above the line by refusing to accept dogs until they are eight months old. Professional trainers who take dogs to train for others prefer that they be one year old before they begin. At one year, the nominal maturity age for a dog, he will be adult enough really to give his attention to the task at hand, and there will be little problem with frolicsomeness and a wandering mind. The various institutes that train dogs as guides for the blind set one year as their minimum age limit. So take counsel from those whose lives are devoted to dog training and wait awhile before beginning on your pup.

Ease of training isn't the only factor in waiting. Your dog is, after all, a puppy—young and playful, full of the joy of life, sniffing and sprawling and tail wagging. As a member of your family he deserves to be allowed to enjoy his puppyhood even as a child enjoys his all-too-brief childhood before being intensively prepared to face the world on his own. Training, properly done, can be fun and basically enjoyable for both you and the pup. Still, it involves disciplines and restraints, concentration and corrections, learning and unlearning. Enough that in his first month or so he has had to learn to control his natural functions, to respect visitors, not to chew on your possessions, to release his treasured playthings on command. Let him enjoy the fruits of his elementary civilization for a while before going on to more serious endeavors.

There are, however, many training classes these days for beginning pups—sorts of kindergartens—geared to the pup as young as two or three months. Under the guidance of skilled professional instructors, these classes can be useful and fun, with dog socialization a major objective, teaching the puppies about the world outside their homes and owners, and introducing them to society early in life. The way it is handled, the dog is allowed to be a puppy, while being gently directed along a course that will be helpful later on. You'll learn a lot from such a class, too.

BASIC TRAINING

At the other end of the scale, you can totally disregard the hac. business about an old dog and new tricks. We have seen dogs entere training up to the age of eleven years and qualifying for degrees at twelve and thirteen. The fact that the older dog will be a bit more set in his ways is counteracted by his increased ability to concentrate. If he's been yours all that time, your relationship will have become so firmly established that your position as giver of commands will be unquestioned; unless, of course, he's been badly spoiled and/or unmanageable all his life. But with the average older dog, training is definitely indicated.

DISCIPLINE AND CORRECTIONS

Training requires discipline. Discipline in the case of the dog means attention to the matter at hand and ultimate performance of the required exercises. Discipline also means, equally as importantly, concentration and self-control in yourself. Before the dog can learn what you want to teach him, you must understand thoroughly what he is to learn, how he is to learn it, and how he feels about it. You must resolve never to lose your temper, never to display anger to the dog, never to correct him for your own mistakes (except in the rare instances we will mention), and *always* to remember that you're working with a dog. That last may seem obvious, but it isn't. People who are having their first contact with training often tend to lose sight of what they are working with. They impute curious and overly human motives to the dog: vindictiveness, obtuseness, spitefulness, and other unpleasant human characteristics. If this major mistake is assiduously avoided, the training processes can be genuinely enjoyable and effective.

As a first rule of obedience training, keep always in mind that the dog is never punished. He is corrected. When possible (and this is nearly always), he is corrected immediately after the commission, or omission, occurs. He does not, and never will, understand punishment. While you can say to a child, "You did thus and so yesterday and I'm going to spank you for it," you can't do it to a dog, for remembrance of isolated mishaps past is beyond his capacity. The dog lives in the moment, with no real understanding of the concept of the past or the future. He will anticipate and expect things that are going to happen soon, but tomorrow, or even later today, is an alien concept to him. And yesterday, or even earlier today, means little more to him except as habit patterns have been laid down, and people or commands or things from the past come to his attention and excite conditioned responses.

We don't mean to say that the dog doesn't remember anything, for he most surely does. He remembers you, and your friends, and his toys, and the things you have taught him, and your house, and his favorite run in the woods. And while we won't get into the argument over whether he consciously thinks about things when they are out of sight, we will say that one-time occurrences mean nothing to him once they are over. Even the veriest novice would reject the idea of punishing a dog for not having sat yesterday. But as the gap between not sitting and punishing grows smaller, the tendency arises to feel that punishment is justified, that "he knows why he's getting it." It simply isn't so—the separation in time of a minute, or even ten seconds, is enough for all connection to be lost in the dog's mind.

Of corrections there are two types: demonstrative and restrictive. We speak throughout this book simply of "correction," and in each case the type will be apparent, but for the moment let's examine these two distinct types.

The demonstrative correction is one which shows the dog, by physical guidance with leash or hand, what is expected of him. When he is learning, say, to heel, the snap on the lead pulling him back to the proper position by your left side is demonstrative. It is in effect a compulsion, in that you compel him, however gently, to do as you wish. It can be applied in many degrees of force, and can, when training has progressed, even be a purely vocal correction to call his attention to what he is supposed to do. In pretraining, you will already have applied a good many demonstrative corrections, beginning with the first time you rushed him to the papers or outside.

In the restrictive correction, you prevent him from doing something undesirable. In many cases the line between the two is hazy, as in the example just given of heeling. When you snap the lead to force him back, are you demonstrating where he should walk, or are you preventing him from walking elsewhere? It's a philosophical point in such a case, depending on how you look at it. Generally, the strong restrictive correction is given literally to correct his behavior. If, for example, he becomes rebellious during training, the strong correction is called for. This may mean firm handling with the leash, or it may mean striking the dog. And this latter requires a discussion of its own.

Striking the dog is something to be done only *in extremis*. When he is struck, he should be hit only in one place, under the chin, and with only one thing, the fingers of your open right hand. He should be struck *only* for positive misbehavior uncontrollable in any other way, and never—repeat, *never*—for failing to do something. You can, in fact, make it a rule that he should be hit *only* if he becomes aggressive—threatens you, growls at you, or snaps or bites.

There are many good reasons for striking him under the chin when necessary. A blow anywhere else on the body, or on the side or top of the head, can injure him internally. A blow under the chin, applied with the proper force, can only snap his teeth together and shake him up a bit. The chances of catching his tongue between his teeth are slight indeed, as he's a good deal faster on his reflexes than you are. Of course, the force has to be calculated with considerable nicety, all of which leads back to the vital issue of never losing your temper while training. A full roundhouse swing, even under the muzzle, could rattle his brain pretty badly. With a toy breed, even a six-inch swing might, at full steam, nearly snap his head off.

This consideration is behind the "fingers only" restriction. With your open fingers you have considerably less chance of miscalculating your own strength, plus the fact that the open-finger blow is the maximum ever required, regardless of the size of the dog. Try it under the edge of the table and you'll see that you can deliver a pretty nasty crack with your fingers, without even moving your wrist. If the time comes, use your good judgment about the force of the blow. Of the hundreds of people who have been taught this correction, never has there been a case where a dog has been injured by it.

Hitting him with the hand, incidentally, won't make him "hand shy" if you do it right. When you give him this sort of correction he is always on lead and unable to duck. So you connect. One of the things that makes a dog hand shy is being swung at. If the dog can get away, or if you rush at him swinging and hollering, he's going to get distinctly unhappy associations with that good right hand of yours. The cardinal rule in all this is a simple one: Don't miss. If he is not in a position where missing is nigh onto impossible, don't swing.

The other thing that will cause him to distrust you and your intentions with that right hook is the lack of immediate praise after you've corrected him. But more on that in a moment. First we want to lay down a rigid rule: Never hit the dog with *anything* but your hand. No leashes, no sticks, no switches, no buggy whips, nothing. The folded newspaper, by the way, is a bit of interesting mythology designed to keep you from having to think through the business of corrections. True, the resounding whack of a paper may scare the wits out of him, and unless you larrup him with the Sunday *Times*, sports section and all, you don't stand much chance of hurting him seriously. But if you follow this method you are letting yourself in for (1) being unable to correct him until you have found and rolled up a newspaper, (2) teaching him to be scared of sudden loud noises, and (3) instilling a fundamental dislike for newspapers that could seriously affect his literacy.

A critical point here is that you *must* praise him immediately afterward if you've had to hit him. To the beginner this seems completely wrong, but you *must* do it. That way it is a correction, but you're demonstrating with the praise that you still love him. If he snaps again as you're attempting to praise him, hit him again, then return to the praise in order to calm and reassure him. It may sound totally wrong, but we guarantee this is the only right way to handle it.

PRAISE AND PLAY

Praise is the motive power in the training of your dog. In training, it is to be applied in liberal doses, at all opportunities. It is administered when the dog does something right, and, paradoxical though it may seem, when he does something wrong. Don't fall into the "easy" solution of giving him tidbits as rewards for the performance of exercises. The food reward will work, but eventually it'll have to stop and then you've got a problem. You'll either have to face him down when you start withholding the goodies, and endure his thoughts of you as a pretty cheap character, or you'll have to substitute effusive praise for food. In which case you'll be right back with us and praise. It's strictly against AKC rules to give an obedience dog any offering of food in the ring, but praise between exercises is unlimited. If your dog is used to bribery, he may decide in the middle of the ring, "No food, no work," and go on strike. For which we wouldn't blame him a bit, if he'd been trained to expect worldly goods for his efforts.

Praise when he does right needs little explanation. When he is first learning, give him praise when he has done something, even if you have had to guide, shove, and haul him into it every step of the way. All the work in the beginning stages may have been yours, but praise him as though he'd done something colossal. When he gets a glimmering of what you want and tries it experimentally, praise him to the skies. And even after he is a veteran, having performed the same exercise a thousand times perfectly, praise him every time as though it were the first. Praise him with your voice, telling him, "Good boy!" and "Good dog!" and even "Well done!" or whatever. This is one case where there is no reason to stick to a single word or phrase—the tone of your voice tells him all he wants to know. The words are for you, because it's easier for you to sound praiseful while saying "Good boy" than while pronouncing "The rains in Spain." You could do it with practice, but why bother? And praise him with your hands, particularly with your left—of which more later. Pat him, stroke him, fondle him, scratch him. But let him have your touch as a reward and assurance that all is well. Sometimes you'll find you get a better response when you use both vocal praise and hand contact; with some dogs and at some times it may be better to use just your voice, or just your hands. Try it several ways when you're working at basic training. See what it takes to cheer him on without allowing him to explode and get out of control because you've made such a fuss over him.

Praise when he has done something wrong may be a bit harder for the neophyte to understand, but it is perhaps even more essential than praise for good work. It assumes a good constructive correction first to straighten out whatever he has or hasn't done. Then praise to take his mind off the fact that it was you who did the correcting. As we have said before and will say again, the correction must always in the dog's mind be a natural outgrowth of the wrong, or of the failure to perform whatever is wanted. If you correct him, then come in immediately with praise; it lets him know that you are still on his side, still love him, and that all is well in the world. Correction, done fairly and firmly, earns you his undying respect, if followed by praise and unaccompanied by any display of displeasure or withdrawal of affection, however momentary. Take this as another firm and basic rule of training: Always praise after a correction.

Play is important in training, too. While the training period itself must be kept businesslike, a period of carefree play and romping should always follow, as something of a reward. As soon as the training period is over, let yourself go and romp with him. Although he'll probably never think of it as an actual reward for having been cooperative, the play will establish completely friendly relations between you. No one but an old hand at this sort of thing can maintain a completely icy calm during training, and things may get a bit strained around the edges before the period is over. If so, the play puts things back on the right footing. He'll forget about the corrections in his joy at wrestling or running with you, but the lessons will still be there.

"HEEL!" AND "SIT!"

The goal in the heel and sit, which are taught simultaneously, is to train the dog to walk at your left side, neither lagging nor forging ahead. When

you halt, he is to sit quietly by your side and wait for further develop-
ments. The practical advantages of this training are evident—walking along
city streets is paramount among them.

In preparation for heeling you will have been out on the street with him
a good many times. Through hours of having his freedom restricted by it,
the leash will have become a nuisance, but a tolerable one, something to
shrug off and live with. This is of course a general rule, to which there are
exceptions. If your particular pup is still at odds with the leash, hold off
until truce is declared. There are as many types of dog, and reactions to the
leash, as there are dogs in total. Through leash walking you should by now
have a fairly good idea of how he will react to his first lessons in heeling—
whether he will take it well, or actively fight it, or get hysterical, or curl up
and die at the thought. Keep these first reactions in mind, as the course of
heeling training will be largely dictated by them.

Choose as a training area someplace where there is enough room to walk
a bit in any direction, and where there will be no interruptions: a field, if
you can get to one conveniently; your yard; a quiet sidewalk; even your living room, as a last resort. Make sure the collar is on correctly and snap the
lead on to whichever ring you're going to use; we recommend starting with
the dead ring and progressing to the live ring only if necessary. Fold the
loop of the lead and any excess length into your right hand so it won't be in
your way. Then take hold of the lead near the collar with your left hand,
close to your dog but not forcing yourself to bend over or strain sideways.

Maneuver yourself around so that he is more or less by your left side
(guide him gently, don't haul him into position), then do three things simultaneously. Call his name and give the heel command together, "Mike,
heel!", step forward with your left foot, and gently slap the fingers of your
left hand against the lead to help get him started. You'll obviously have to
release the grip of your left hand on the lead to do this, but what we want
you to do, from the beginning of heel training, is to abandon the idea that
you're pulling or hauling on the dog to get him to walk alongside you. Keep
your left hand *at* the lead near his collar, not *on* it. And don't haul with
your right hand, either. The lead is used to guide him gently, to demonstrate to him that you want him to walk along at your left side. It isn't a
contest of strength—it's instruction.

There's little reason he shouldn't come right along with you, so keep
your tone of voice pleasant and coaxing, and step right out. When he gets
out of a position generally at your left side, slap or flip your fingers against

the lead near the collar, indicating the direction you want him to move in in order to get back more or less into place, and each time give the command, "Mike, heel!" Don't make it a sequence of command and then correction. Make it absolutely simultaneous. Then, immediately afterward, praise him with a warm "Good boy." In fact, keep a pleasant, coaxing conversation going with him: "There, that's it, right there, good boy, that's the way."

He can deviate from position forward, to the side or the back. Forward or to the side means at least that he is moving in the same general direction you are, and requires only continued gentle corrections to get him back into position, accompanied by command and followed by praise. If you feel, as things go on, that a slightly stiffer correction is needed, particularly if he hangs back badly, change the snap from the dead ring to the live ring. A quick, light snap on the lead, tightening and immediately releasing the collar, will get his attention. Then return as soon as possible to the dead ring. Above all, don't get into the habit of overcorrecting. You're teaching him something entirely new by demonstrating to him that you want him to walk at your left side when he hears the command, "Mike, heel!" Be sure he begins to understand and is not performing through force and fear.

A slightly more serious problem arises when he doesn't move at all, or tries to charge in the other direction once you've started off. Again, a correction is needed, the amount of force behind the snap on the lead depending on the size and temperament of your pup. You may have to do it several times. Don't be timid about it, but don't go overboard, hauling away, muttering, and cursing. It *will* work out. We have yet to see a dog or puppy who couldn't be taught the basic idea of heeling in a session or two, and you should be starting to "read" your dog by now, learning what's going on in his head by his reactions to what you do. If he doesn't understand at all what you're trying to teach him, if he is confused, then *you* are doing something wrong, not he.

When he's gotten up to your side and you are striding along together in an orderly fashion, praise the pull back especially warmly. If he's big enough to reach without bending double, pat him with your left hand, holding the lead in the right to keep up the corrections. Otherwise, make your voice give all the praise. While he's in position, let the lead hang slightly loose and give him continuous praise for being where he is. Don't hold him firmly in position with the lead, but always keep a short enough hold for an immediate correction.

PROBLEM DOGS

A real problem is the pup or dog who resents the idea of training to the point where he takes active steps to put a stop to it. The dog inherits from his wild ancestors the instinct to try to become leader of the pack, and he may choose this time to have a showdown with you. No matter how good your relations have been up to this time, it can happen. Usually it won't, but if it does, the time has come to establish once and for all who is going to be boss in the particular pack consisting of you and him.

First, though, go back to the beginning and try to regain his confidence in you. If you have the snap fastened to the live ring, return it to the dead ring. Walk around a bit, shaking the lead gently to let him know he has nothing to fear. Keep the lead loose, and give him the gentlest of corrections to urge him to move in a specific direction. Coax him along with his name and anything else that comes to mind. If you can avoid a showdown, all well and good. The problem may come up again from time to time, so think it through, and don't just jump in hauling away at the lead, making a contest of it. Run with him a little, and when he gets going, use the lead to bring him up sharply. As soon as he's been jolted to a stop, praise him and apologize for your clumsiness. Tell him what a terrible thing it was that you accidentally held on to the lead too tight. He'll forgive you, not knowing that it's going to keep on happening. Apologize profusely after every time it happens. He'll begin to think you're a pretty clumsy lout, but he'll watch out for the jerks on the collar and he won't get mad at you.

This may cure him. If not, showdown time has come. When you start back into serious heel work, keep a very close eye on him, watching for the first sign of a curled lip or snarl. Work with a very short lead so that your hand is near his collar and ready to hold tight if need be. When the snarl comes, grab his collar with your left hand at the back of his neck, lift him just enough so that his front feet are off the ground, and connect under his chin with a good crack with the right-hand fingers. Just having his feet off the ground will take some of the fight out of him. Immediately, then, loosen the collar and praise him. Keep hold of the collar with your left hand and keep your right hand ready to go again in case it's needed, but praise him effusively with words. Watch him closely. If the resistance seems to be gone, straighten up and start off with a snap and "Mike, heel!" and go right into heeling. It may take several fairly stiff corrections to straighten him out, but this method is infallible. If you're firm and quick you stand little chance of being so much as nipped. And praise here after the correction is of extreme importance, to take his mind off the fact that he's been hit, and to let him know that you love him still and all that, but that you're having none of the snarling business.

The two vital things to remember are: Do not display any temper or fear, and especially do not use this correction when he is just being stubborn; only apply it when he makes it perfectly clear that he intends to lacerate you a little if you insist on trying to train him. Then make it good.

Possibly the worst of problem dogs is the hysteric. When the lead is put on for training he may sit, lie down, roll over, or even stand on his hind feet and try to climb up the lead with his front feet. What he is afraid of is the lead and the increasing restriction that is being placed on him through it. The cure is a simple repeat of the original introduction to the lead as he runs free around the yard or house. He'll trip on it and stumble, and tangle and disentangle himself; but let him work out his own problem of getting more used to it. When you put the lead on, attach it to the inactive ring of the collar, the one that will not make the chain pull up tight when he steps on the lead and yanks himself. By leaving him alone with the lead, you allow him to regain his own confidence in the state of the world without having at the same time to worry about you and commands and what to do next.

Gradually, then, take him out for walks, using more and more restriction as you go, adjusting the progress to his own progress in confidence and lack of resentment and hysteria. Don't force him at all; keep things at the pace he sets, and a week or two should see the problem over. Gentle corrections and especially fulsome praise are indicated for this type of dog once you are back in the training schedule.

MORE HEELING

Up to now, about all you will have been able to do is give your dog the idea that he is to stick close to your left side while you're walking along. The next thing is to teach him to stick with you when you turn either left or right, or around, and to adjust his pace if you slow down or start trotting or running.

When you begin making turns with your dog, work on the left turns first. This way, you'll be guiding him around the turn with your left leg, which obviously gets in his way if he doesn't turn, and using your left hand on the lead as you turn on your left foot. That's the way to do it: Turn on your left foot, and bring your right foot around and step off with it first. Then, after a few left turns have been accomplished, try a few right turns, turning on your right foot and swinging your left around and stepping out with it. Do the turns gradually at first, making more of a small quarter-circle than a sharp turn. Guide him along gently with light snaps on the lead to keep him in place. Praise him and coax him along with you on the turns, remembering to praise after every snap of the lead and to give the heel command with each correction.

The snap and your use of it are extremely important, here and in all training. Doing it properly is one of the hardest things the beginning trainer has to learn. "Snap" to some people sounds a little harder than necessary, but it is a standard term; it means that you use one hand to give a quick indication to your dog that he is to move in a given direction. To snap, pull sharply, but as lightly as possible to get the effect you want, and then *immediately release* by loosening the lead. You are guiding, demonstrating, and teaching, *not* hurting your dog or hauling him around. You must *never* keep the lead tight while training—or at any other time, for that matter.

If you learn nothing else from this book, you will have learned more than a surprising number of dog handlers learn, even in classes. If you simply haul your dog along at heel, or haul him around on the turns with the leash tight, he is learning nothing at all except that you have a leash in your hand while he has a chain or nylon loop around his neck, which gives you a considerable advantage in a hauling contest. You snap, as gently or as firmly as required, then release immediately. And praise. Remember this maxim, engrave it on your mind: If you *ever* have the lead tight except for a quarter-second during a snap, you are *wrong!* If the lead is snapped on to the live ring of the collar, you will be choking him, and continuing to choke him, which accomplishes nothing positive. If it is on the dead ring, the collar will be cutting or sawing into his neck, which does no good either.

The about-turn is simply an extension of the right turn. While walking, slow down just slightly at first to give your dog a small warning that you are going to do something. Then turn around and go in the opposite direction, always making the turn to the right. Don't spin in position or do a military about-turn. This would leave your left foot out behind you to block your dog's progress as he's circling to try to stay with you. As you start the turn, call your dog's name to warn him that something's about to happen, give him a heel command, turn on your right foot, and step out with your left.

Throughout all your heeling and turns, walk always at an even pace—just

fast enough so that he can step along smartly. Don't adapt your pace to his
once you've gotten into it. Use the lead to make him keep up with you, or
down with you, at the pace you've chosen.

When he has mastered the turns—a matter of several days of training—
you can begin the "slow" and "fast." While walking with him at heel in a
straight line, slow down gradually until you are moving quite slowly. Keep
him with you, using commands and the lead. Then gradually increase your
pace until you are again walking normally. To teach him the fast, reverse
the procedure. From a normal walk slowly increase your pace until you are
trotting along at a fairly good clip, again using snaps on the lead and the
heel command to keep him right at your side. Don't break into a full run,
because at this point the temptation will be almost irresistible for him to
break into a real lurching gallop. Even with a mild trot you will encounter
the problem of his trying to romp with you once you begin going fast. As
soon as he breaks his pace, slow down, giving him a strong correction with
the lead. Then start up again, increasing your pace more gradually this
time. Keep a close lead and keep him well under control as you speed up.
You'll have to break him of romping while you're increasing your speed, as
it's quite difficult to keep a good snapping lead control and puff out firm
commands and praise once you've gotten up to a respectable pace.

Although you may seldom want to run with him at heel, especially off
lead, there may come times when you do want to. Teaching him to stay at
heel can prevent some pretty nasty work trying to slow down a really
charging dog who's gotten worked up to a full run. In the show ring you'll
be required only to work up to quite a mild trot, really not much more
than a jog; but you must be able to demonstrate that he'll stay at your side
whatever your pace.

When going into or coming out of either the slow or the fast, "float" into
or out of them. Don't suddenly start running, or creeping along, and don't
return to normal pace with a jerk. With his shoulder directly by your left
leg he has to have some small warning of your intentions to change pace. If
you don't help him out, he'll develop the habit of lagging or forging ahead.

THE SIT AT HEEL

Teaching the dog to sit requires a little more work than heeling. You
have to learn to use both hands in smooth coordination and to bring him to
the point where he will sit automatically when you come to a halt.

Don't bring in the sit too early. Let him get well accustomed to walking at heel before you begin it. Then, once you have started, make it a firm rule that when you come to a stop while heeling, he sits, unless you have given him a different command; but this will come later.

A little preliminary work on the sit is in order, using what we call the "tuck under," as demonstrated in the photos. Gently holding the pup's collar with your right hand at a point behind his head, place your left hand across his rear just above his hocks. Exert pressure forward with your left hand as you draw back gently with your right, "tucking under" his hind quarters into the sit position with the command "Sit!" He'll learn very quickly that the word "sit" means to get into that position. When he begins to understand what it means, you can transfer to guiding his rear down with your left hand, with very little pressure needed.

While walking in a straight line with your dog in heel position, slow to a halt, taking several steps to do it. As you're taking those steps, prepare yourself for the sit-at-heel lesson by releasing the lead with your left hand, and taking up the slack with your right hand moving over to the left. Come to a halt on your right foot, bringing your left foot up even with it, just as you say, "Mike, sit!" This way, your "guide foot" is the last one in motion. Just as you stop and give the command, place your left hand flat on his shoulders and move it rapidly but smoothly down his back until it is directly over the end of his rib cage. Command him, "Mike, sit!" and at the same time pull *straight up* on the lead with your right hand and press down firmly with your left. Release the pressure of both hands immediately and reassure him with hands and voice. But keep a close watch and keep your hands close to position. If he tries to get up or shies from position, pull the lead up again and push down on his rear gently but firmly and repeat the commands. Follow this command immediately with "Stay!" If he tries again, correct him into position and again, "Sit, stay." Keep him there for a few moments, then start up forward again, always taking the first step with the left foot, telling him to heel and snapping the lead if necessary.

Do not, at this point, attempt to teach him to sit under any other circumstances than in stopping at heel. Getting him to sit while in front of you or at a distance follows later in a natural sequence of training. Concentrate on the sit now as part of heeling and get it down firmly before progressing to anything else.

The simple sit method applies to any breed and size. With large or medium-sized dogs there should be no trouble in applying the simultaneous moves of the hands. With the very small breeds you will have to

The gentle "tuck under" with a very young pup. One hand steadies him at the chest, the other is at the hocks. The table is used here only for demonstration visibility.

The hand on the hocks moves forward, tucking pup's legs under and gently lowering him to the "sit" position.

bend over considerably to get the left-hand move done, but do just that: Bend over. Don't, with any size, squat or kneel down to teach the sit. Stay on your feet so that he doesn't get the idea that you have to be down with him to get him to sit.

The pull directly upward is important. It serves to stop his forward motion, keeps his head up when sitting, and gives a pressure in the general direction of what you want him to do. Be especially careful not to pull the lead across your body with the right hand, as this will pull his head in that

Very little force will be necessary with the left hand in teaching the "sit." Use only enough to guide his rear down.

direction and encourage crooked sits. If you are working with a very large breed, say, a Scottish Deerhound, you can pull the lead slightly back as you pull up, to aid you in exerting the proper pressures. Or if the dog really needs a push, still hold on to the leash but move your right hand around to give him a rearward push on the chest as you exert downward pressure on the rear with the left hand.

The position of the left hand is important, too. If you push on him too far forward, in the middle of his back, he will brace his hind legs and resist the whole idea. If you push too far back on his rear it will make him tend to hunch his rear forward when sitting. Keep the hand, after sliding it down from his shoulders, directly over the rear of his rib cage. The purpose of the slide from the shoulders is to reassure him by not bringing a sudden and unexpected pressure to bear on his posterior.

As in all training, adjust your pressure carefully to the dog, using only enough to force the action you want and to demonstrate to him what it is you're looking for. Use as much force as necessary with the big ones and go carefully with the toys and miniatures. They have delicate leg bones, and rough handling can either scare them badly or actually injure them. You may want to keep up the kindergarten "tuck under" a little longer for some individuals of both the small and the very large breeds, since many times the bigger dogs resent pressure on their hindquarters. Not only that, a really large dog like a Dane who resists a push downward on his rear can be quite a challenge—but the "tuck under" will do away with resistance.

When you have him firmly at the sit, don't start up immediately into the heel again. Let him sit there for a few moments. It is far easier to teach a dog the wrong thing than the right, and if you start up again right away he'll get the idea that what he's supposed to do on a halt is to bump his rear on the ground and then pick it up right away and start off. By making him wait patiently you're also teaching him to work at command rather than by a learned routine. As he's sitting there, reassure him continually with praise and a repeated "Stay!" The constant repetition of "Stay" will keep his mind on his business and lay the groundwork for more intensive stay work in future training.

Once he seems to have learned that he is supposed to sit when you stop walking, stop using the left hand. When you halt, give a snap upward with the lead, commanding "Sit!" The free left hand can now be employed to advantage in making him sit straight. Walking along with you at heel, his hindquarters will be in line with his head and the direction of travel, and it is just as easy for him to sit perfectly straight as it is for him to swing his rear around in any direction. From the first time, at the beginning adjusting the direction of your downward pressure with the left hand, and later using it purely as a lateral corrective measure, insist that the sit be straight. Try not, though, to shove his rear around once it has hit the ground. Keep a close eye on proceedings as you are about to halt, and use the hand to guide his posterior as it moves to the ground.

When he will sit with only the lead correction, use it gradually less and less but still retaining the verbal command. Work with him several days, always commanding, "Sit!" when you halt, before you try to leave commands and corrections out altogether. Then, one day, come to a halt while heeling and see what happens. Ninety-nine chances out of a hundred he will surprise the life out of you by coming smartly to a sit and looking extremely proud of himself. Praise and praise him again, and after a few moments start up the heeling again. If he doesn't immediately sit, use the leash to snap him into position without a command, continue this for a while, and later try him solo again. It won't take long.

Put him through complete routines now. Forward, left turn, right turn, fast, normal, about-turn, slow, halt, forward, halt, right turn, halt, and so on. Mix it up thoroughly so that he doesn't get to expect any definite pattern of events, but will follow your lead wherever you go. And always, when you start up again from a halt and sit, use the "Mike, heel!" command, and always start on your left foot.

TURNS AND FIGURE EIGHTS

By now your dog should be fairly proficient at heeling and halting, and you can begin to sharpen things up. Start going into your turns more sharply while still giving him all the help you can. On the left turns, swing on your left foot so that your right leg comes around in front of his face to let him know what is up. Try giving him a light snap backward on the leash just as you are about to turn left, to hold him back slightly and draw his attention. On right turns, turn on your right foot and swing the left leg around to guide him. Snap lightly a bit forward and to the right as you are about to go into the turn. Work on these until you can turn sharply to the left or right with him staying perfectly at your side.

The next step is circling completely to prepare him for the figure eight. As you are walking along, start out by making a very wide full circle to your left, coaxing and correcting him along as you go. Then make a full wide circle to your right. Work with him on these circles, making them increasingly smaller in radius as you go along and he gets the idea. On the right turns, work until you can turn almost in place and have him swing around you at heel. On the left, continue decreasing the radius until he himself is almost swinging around in place as you circle around him back to the original line of travel. Don't let him crowd you or swing wide.

Mix the circles up, going from a full left directly into a full right, and then again into the left, making the circles ever smaller. Then you can progress to the formal figure eight. For this, place two chairs, or any other similar objects, about eight feet apart on the ground or floor and proceed to walk a figure eight around them with him at heel. When you've both mastered this, do the same exercise around two members of your family, or friends, standing in place of the chairs. Keep the dog firmly at heel with his mind on his business. If he tries to sniff either chairs or people, snap his head into place. If he shies away on an inside turn, make the turn wider and then slowly decrease it with constant reassurance until he thinks only of being where he's supposed to be and pays no attention to the objects you're going around. But give him plenty of leeway on the inside turns so that he doesn't have to brush against anything.

With the figure eight mastered (which is, among other things, preparation for walking along crowded streets and all the consequent turning around people), the training in the heel proper, on leash, is completed. You should be able to walk anywhere with the dog without having to think about his being there, or about his entangling people or signposts with the lead. Such problems as do arise will come up in the first heeling and sitting, and the later practice in turns and circles will simply be a matter of continued application by both of you.

HEELING IN GENERAL

While training and heeling, wear whatever you will for the training periods. A swirling skirt flapping right beside his head may put him off a bit and make him heel a little wide, but if that's what you're going to wear while walking with him, let him get used to it. Small use it would be always to wear slacks while in training, and then expect him miraculously to get used to the idea of a skirt.

All the work is done on lead. Don't give in to the temptation to take him off lead "just once" to see how he will do, no matter how well he seems to have it down. It will give him the opportunity to make a mistake at precisely the wrong time in the schedule, and will set you back considerably.

For every exercise in this chapter, and until you have progressed to the Novice work in Chapter 4, *keep him on lead at all times!*

Make your training periods fairly short—about fifteen minutes at a time. Get in two of these periods a day and he will have just about as much learning as he can absorb without getting thoroughly bored with the whole thing. Give him plenty of praise during the training, and play with him afterward. Keep it fun for both of you, and progress will be faster and better. Try not to train always in the same place, or he'll come to expect that he has only to work when you take him there.

If you always step out with the left foot first when you want him to come along at heel, he will learn to take this as a sort of signal. Later, in the "stay" work, you will step out with your right foot when he is to remain— which helps him keep things separate.

Mix up the work as much as possible. Keep him from thinking that any one move comes naturally after another, except the sit when you halt.

Work as a team. True, you're training *him* to heel with you, but at the same time you're learning how to walk with him and handle him so that it's as easy for him as possible. Don't adjust to his walking pace, but keep in mind that it's the two of you working together, not him working for you.

Use verbal commands at all times during the training. Eventually you will need only to say "Mike, heel" when you start up from a halt. But work very gradually toward that state. Give your commands clearly and firmly, without shouting. Use corrections only when necessary, and then apply them firmly and properly.

The verbal command you use, the "Mike, heel!", is a two-part command, and should be used as such. Calling his name is to draw his attention and prepare him to do something. After that follows the command for one action or another, in this case heeling. Later in training he will become accustomed to the situation and to listening for commands, but in these beginning stages, make just a slight hesitation between his name and the command, to give him time to alert himself to what is coming.

THE STAND

This exercise is a very important one and is taught both on lead and off lead, but you won't get to the off-lead stand until the next chapter, "Novice." It is important that the stand on lead be taken up at this point, before going on to the down and the stays in the sit and down positions. Therefore, let's take a moment to examine what the stand means.

One of the objections that people preparing dogs for the breed ring have against obedience is that it trains the dog to sit promptly when the handler comes to a halt. This could be damaging to the dog's chances of winning in a breed ring, where he is expected to keep up and alert at all times. If the stand is taught now, after the basic work of heeling and sitting, the dog learns firmly that stopping doesn't always mean sitting; it means sitting only when there is no contrary command to stand in place. The ability and training to hold a standing pose can in fact be very positively valuable to breed exhibitors, teaching the dog to stand quietly before and during an examination by a judge.

Another common objection of breed exhibitors to obedience training is that it kills a dog's alertness, his sharpness, the élan that sets a top dog apart from others. This point bears discussion, for it has in the past, unfortunately, been valid. Earlier methods of training involving punishment (striking the dog, scaring him by throwing chains and other objects at him) made for a dog who did indeed, though trained, lose some of his spirit. Even today a trainer who loses his temper in training, is overly harsh, or proceeds illogically in training will have at the end a dog who, if not actually cowering, has lost his alertness and responsiveness.

We guarantee, however, that a dog trained by the methods we outline, and with the attitudes we encourage, will not show these effects. So long as the dog is treated with respect and kindness and is allowed to retain his natural dignity and self-respect in training, he will lose none of his show-ring sparkle. He may even gain some. It is simply unfortunate that earlier means of training gave the results they did, and that the prejudice against such training and its results still remains among breed exhibitors.

The stand also has two very practical out-of-ring applications. If, in heeling in muddy terrain, you want to stop but don't want your dog to sit in the mess, tell him to stand as you come to a halt, and he stays on his feet and remains clean. For grooming it is invaluable. With the large dog on the floor, or the small one on a table, his training to hold a standing pose for minutes greatly facilitates the necessary brushing and combing.

The stand is taught from heel. With a medium-sized or large dog, as you are walking along, suddenly take a long step out in front of him, holding the lead in the left hand, and turn to face him with your right hand thrust in front of his face, palm open in the universal gesture for stop. At the same time give him the command "Stand!" and then "Stay!" If he tries to keep on going, push your right hand at him again and repeat the commands. If he tries to sit, you will have to resort to the small-dog correction.

For small dogs, as you are walking, suddenly step to your right out of the line of travel and turn to face the dog. With your right hand snap back lightly on the lead to stop his progress and use your left hand to block the forward motion of his right hindleg as you command, "Stand!" Don't grab the leg—just use the hand, fingers stiff, to block it. Whatever his size, he will be very unlikely to try to sit, because of the unusualness of the situation. Instead of stopping in place, you have moved out of position; and with hand either in front of his face or against his leg, you indicate something entirely different to him.

Once he has been stopped at a stand, keep repeating to him the commands "Stand!" and "Stay!" to reassure him and steady him. Move back to your position at his side slowly, repeating commands and praise. Then move off in your original line, commanding him to heel. Take three or four steps and stop, telling him to sit. Start up at heel again, and repeat the stand routine, praising and reassuring.

The stand-stay is taught as soon as he will stand motionless at your side. As it is the first time he is expected to stay in one place or position without having you right by him, use great patience in persuading him to hold his pose. One time when you have stopped and he is standing, use the right hand as an additional stay signal again, in front of his muzzle, and move slowly around his head, holding the lead in your left hand so that it passes over his head. It is especially important that during this first move you keep repeating "Stand, stay!" along with praise. Keep moving all the way around him counterclockwise until you are back at heel position.

Despite his steadiness at your side, he may show a desire to move during the circling. After you have drummed into his head that he is always to stay at your side, at heel, you now want him to stand still while you move. He may try to follow you around at heel as though you were doing a tight circle to the left. To avoid movement on his part, slide the collar around so the rings are at the top of his neck and hold the lead so it is straight up in the air, snug but not with enough pressure to indicate to him that you want him to sit—and remember, snug, *not* tight. Repeat the command "Stand, stay!" as you start to make your circle to the left. The goal is for him to stand rock-still while you circle around him, although if he follows your movement with his head there is no cause for correction.

If he tries to follow you around, tell him firmly, "No, stand, stay!" and use your free hand to make a correction. If he should try to sit before you finish the circle, don't correct him with a snap on the lead. Just stop and with the back of your hand under his stomach, in front of the hind leg nearer you, lift him back up on his feet into the stand position, repeat the command, and complete your circle to the heel position. Perform the exercise a few times with the snug lead before progressing to doing it with a loose lead.

When you can circle him and he is steady, try moving—right foot first—out to the front of him. When he is in position, back away from him slowly, repeating the "Stand, stay!" command and using your open right hand as a

In teaching the "stand," use left hand as shown—not holding the leg, or supporting the body, but "blocking" the leg.

stay signal until you are at the end of the lead. If he tries to move to you, check him immediately with your hand and the lead. Get to the end of the lead by slow stages: first just a foot or two in front of him, then three or four feet, and finally the full length. Modify that "full length" in this stay, and in all the others to come, to this extent: Let the lead hang from his collar until it touches the ground, then move as far away as you can with the lead still touching the ground at one point. This keeps the lead from exerting any pressure on him other than the weight of a very short section, and keeps you from making any inadvertent tugs that would confuse him when he's trying to keep still.

Don't keep him standing there without you for more than fifteen seconds or so, only long enough for him to get the idea. Then when you return, circle around to heel position, passing him on your left and holding the lead in the left hand so that it passes over his head. When back at heel, wait a moment, then take three or four steps forward, with command to heel, and come to a halt, whereupon he should sit.

If you've been following all the steps patiently, insuring that he is perfectly steady at each stage before going on to the next, the stays with you at the side and behind him can be accomplished in the same lesson with the "stay in front."

When he is steady with you in front, move gradually off to the right to the end of the lead, with lead still touching the ground, using the same corrections for moves on his part, again repeating "Stand, stay!" constantly to reassure him. Then from heel position move directly back of him to the lead's length. This will be a little harder, as it is hard for him to keep track of where you are, and he will crane around to watch you. Don't try to correct the head turning, but concentrate on complete steadiness in the rest of his body. Again, keep up the talk to him to let him know you're still there, and to keep his mind on the business at hand. From the side and the back, don't go around him to heel, but return directly to position. When you return to position, don't step off immediately in the heel. Wait five seconds or so before you move, rather than let him get the idea that he should start up as soon as you're back at heel.

In all the stand-stays, mix up the work with all the other exercises he has learned up to this point. Do one stand-stay, then heel him around a bit, interposing some stops and sits. Then stand him again, then more heeling. Don't get his mind completely on the stay to the detriment of his other training.

THE SIT AND STAY

The sit and stay is merely a repeat of the methods you have used to keep him in one position while standing. The command and signal to stay are the same in any exercise—stand, sit, or down—where you're teaching your dog to remain in a given position until you have returned to him. Follow the same procedures, first steadying him while you walk around him, then to the front and then to the side and back. You will probably not encounter any problem of moving, as by this time the concept of the stay will be firmly fixed in his mind. He will be sure that you are coming back to him when you step out for wherever you're going, and he will sit patiently until you've come around, or from in back. Again, if any problems are encountered in the first circling, *come back around* to make the correction, rather than completing your circle. Again, let the leash touch the ground when you're standing away from him.

In the sit-stay, as in the stand-stay before and the down-stay to follow, there is a standardized stay signal that is universally used. As you give the stay command, the open hand, either one, is chopped sharply toward the dog's muzzle, stopping an inch or so in front. The motion is toward the muzzle from in front, and need be only very short. In first training, the right hand is easier to use, for you can bring it around your body in quite an impressive sweep, then stopping just short. Time your stay command so that it rings out just as your hand stops. Later in training you can use either hand, in quite an informal gesture of palm-before-nose to indicate stay to him, but for the present make the gesture quite large and definite.

THE DOWN AND STAY

It is with the "down," which should be the simplest of exercises, that some people have had the worst problem in all training. Some trainers advocate pushing the dog down forcibly. Some do it with the leash, either pulling him from below or using the foot to force the leash and dog downward. If you have a dog with hysteric tendencies, or one who has fought the leash and training before, any force at this point is guaranteed to send him straight into a six-ply panic. If you try to force him down, either by pushing with your hand or pulling with the lead, he has something to fight, and fight he will. He'll brace his front legs to a fare-thee-well and you're in for a struggle that you'll have to win. This will make you mad, and him mad, and the training program will be up the spout.

We have taught the down without force and without resentment on hundreds of dogs, with never a serious problem. It shows him what you want him to do, and it reassures him while you're doing it.

With the dog sitting at heel, tell him to stay, and kneel beside him. Reach over his back with your left hand and take one leg in each hand, thumbs down, holding on just below the dog's elbow. Then lift his front legs slightly off the ground and push them somewhat out in front of him. Hold him there a second to reassure him. Simultaneously, give him the command "Down!" and lower his front to the ground. At the same time, with your left elbow (or forearm or even wrist with smaller dogs), tip his hindquarters off balance toward you so that he comes down with his haunches sideways under him rather than straight and braced to rise. There is nothing for him to fight, as the hind legs are slewed sideways under him, nipping in the bud any tendency to try to rise to the sit or stick his

The "down-stay" signal for a small dog. When working from the front, stay close at first to reassure him.

rear up in the air. And the front, with his legs in the air out in front of him, simply lowers to the ground. All the while you are as close to him as you can get, with your arm around him, praising and reassuring him that all is well.

Once he is down, stay with him and move your left hand slowly from his leg up to his shoulders, leaving it there with slight pressure, repeating, "Down, stay!" and "Good boy." Keep a slight pressure on his hindquarters with your elbow (or forearm or whatever) until he shows no sign of trying to scramble his rear feet back under him. Then slowly move the elbow away and maintain only the pressure with the hand.

When he seems steady in the down, slowly get up yourself from your crouch, keeping the light pressure on with your left hand. Here is where the break is likely to occur—seeing you get up he will try, himself. If slightly increased pressure with the left hand on his shoulder doesn't keep him in place, combined with a firm, "No, down, stay!" don't fight it. Let him get up and then repeat the entire process. This time make your move to a standing position more slowly and be extra sure that he is steady before moving. Lighten the left-hand pressure until the hand is no more than resting on the shoulder, and then take it off entirely.

On the original down, you may run into the problem of the dog trying to walk backward on his hind legs once you get the front legs up in the air. You can curb this very easily by putting your left leg and foot or knee squarely behind him as you kneel to take hold of him at the sit. He may back a bit, but he will run into your leg and have no place to go. Once he's stopped, proceed with the down as if nothing had happened.

Throughout the exercise keep a good hold on the lead, close to the neck with your right hand, even as you pick up his right leg. If he shows any tendency to fight the action, you have a good short grip on him and can get in an immediate, firm correction. In this case, fighting you can only mean curling the lip or snarling. Once again, the occasional dog may have let things go this far on sufferance and decide that now is the time for a mastery dispute. No method of downing in the world can make him change his mind if he is so decided. If he does dispute you, follow the firm correction procedures outlined above under heeling, and proceed with the lesson when the issue is decided.

When you are able to stand erect while he is at the down, you can teach him the release, which is the "sit." Let him stay down for a few moments, increasing the time as you go along, and then tell him to sit. Give him a firm snap upward with the lead, to get him to a sitting position. If he tries

First step: Take hold of both legs just below the "elbow."

Second step: Lift both legs out in front.

Third step: Ease dog to the ground.

Fourth step: Straighten up slowly, steadying dog with your left hand.

The left knee behind the dog prevents him from backing while you "lift" him down.

to stand, push his rear down with the left hand in the approved manner. Continue with the down until he goes down on command without any lifting or other touching on your part. Remember to praise him at every point, and to keep praising him as he improves and begins to go down without help.

The down-stay will be even simpler, as he has had previous practice with the other two stay positions. Repeat again the circle, the move to the front, and the moves to the side and back. Go slowly until he is steady, repeating the commands and praise until you can leave him in any direction for about fifteen seconds without saying anything beyond the original "Stay!" when you step away.

Once again, mix up the down and the down-stay with all else he has learned up to this point. Heel him, fast and slow and with turns, give him a down-stay, more heeling, a sit-stay, more heeling, another down-stay, and so forth. Again, you will be teaching him to work strictly at command, with no anticipation of a particular order of things. And between the lessons in the new exercise he will be sharpening up his work in all the others.

When he is quite steady at the down-stay, increase his steadiness by stepping over him as he is at the stay. Give him the stay command, then take a high side step to your left, over his back, and stand at his left. As you raise your foot and go over, keep reassuring him that all is well by repeating "Stay!" and "Good boy." Move only very slowly at first, for a sudden move of a foot over his back will make him break. Then, as you are standing at his left, take a side step in the same manner to your right and back to your original position. Be careful that you do not touch him with your feet as you go over, and do not jerk on the lead. This maneuver teaches him confidence in you, and makes him less likely to break because of distractions.

RECALL

The recall, or "come," is done at first from heeling. To start, be sure the snap of your lead is on the dead ring of his collar. While walking along with the dog at heel, suddenly back up three or four steps, calling to him, "Mike, come!"; then snap back on the lead to get him to come around. He should swing around in surprise at this new development and come straight at you. When he is directly in front of you, facing you squarely, quickly command him, "Sit!" You may have to reinforce the sit with a sharp upward snap on the lead, but don't reach over and use your hand to whack his rump down. Let the lead do the work here. He already knows what the sit is all about, and the lead will be enough to get him used to the idea in the new situation.

If the turning causes him to slue his rear out of line, then you'll have to run backward a few more steps until he straightens himself out. Don't use your hand to straighten him out except as a last resort, and never use your feet. If you push him around with your foot to make him sit squarely in front of you, he'll get wary of feet, and we want him to come in as straight and close as possible, with complete confidence. Keep the lead shortened as he comes in so that you can get in a good correction on the sit, or if he tries to move on past you on either side. A move to either side calls for a sharp snap with the lead to bring him up short and get him sat. Don't try to haul him back to directly in front of you if he is way off course. Get him sitting, and keep a tighter control the next time.

When he has sat approximately in place in front of you, praise him verbally and tell him to stay. Wait a moment or two, and then walk around him to heel position, reinforcing the previous sit-stay training with continued "Stay, stay!" as you go around. Once he has come into the sit, the

As you step back, while heeling, dog comes around to walk in and sit in front of you in first recall.

walking around is a simple repetition of what he has learned on the sit-stay. There should be no problems at all at this point. If there are, return to the sit-stay corrections.

Don't attempt to get him to come in on the recall in any other way at this time. Your control over him won't be good enough yet to accomplish it without a lot of unnecessary tugging and hauling, all of which will strain your relations. And again, mix up the work.

Above all, when he does come at your command, *never* call him to you to punish or reprimand him. *Always* go to him to make a correction. This is a major reason that some dogs never come to their owners happily; they have been called and punished. Just imagine how often you would respond happily at the call of a friend if you often got hit when you went. The dog feels the same way. *Always* make it a pleasure for him to come to you.

GO TO HEEL

At this point, toward the end of basic training, you can take up the "go to heel," or as we will refer to it, the "heel" as opposed to "heeling." In this, the dog learns to move from his position directly in front of you to a position at your left side—ready to walk at heel or to be left in a stay. He will also learn, almost by himself once he has mastered the basic idea, to move to heel from any position near you.

Having learned heeling, the idea has been dinned into him that the command "Mike, heel!" means that he is to keep at your left side. It requires little further work to make him understand that when he is at rest away from your side, he is to get there quickly at the command. For show and for practical purposes, there are two ways he can get from in front of you to heel position: either by moving to your right and around to heel, or by moving to your left and swinging himself around into position. The method you use is entirely a matter of personal choice. Our own preference is split—we recommend the "left" heel for small dogs, and the "around" heel for larger breeds. This is based on the fact that it is easier for a large dog to come around and walk directly into position, while a small one can switch his rear around into place quite handily. One other consideration, and this a purely practical one, is that if you have your dog on leash, and an armful of packages, he will wrap the leash around you, doing an around heel. This is a minor consideration, even as are the ease-of-movement ones previously mentioned. So the choice is simply whichever you happen to prefer, or better, whichever your dog prefers. Try him out with both ways and see which one is the easier for him. If you let *him* make the choice, your training may well be a happier thing for both of you.

First, the around heel. With the dog facing you in front, take hold of the leash quite close to the collar, and give him the command "Mike, heel!" As you do this, take a short step backward with your right foot and pull him along to your right side. As he gets to your rear, move your foot back into position, reach around behind with your left hand for the lead, and guide him around into heel position at your left side. As he gets there, give him the "Sit!" command, and praise him generously. The backward step as you're giving him the first pull is for two reasons: The motion of your foot helps him get the idea of going in that direction, and it gets your weight farther back so that you can snap him more effectively. You can drop the foot movement as soon as he gets the idea.

As he is coming around, guided by the leash, give him encouragement and repeated commands, and praise him. There is little likelihood that you will have trouble getting him to move. But if for some reason he just digs in and sits there, resisting the whole idea, start him off with a good sharp snap on the lead to get him on his feet. Don't try dragging him around all the way on his rear, as this can develop into a struggle. Snap him onto his feet, then keep him going with further snaps. From the very beginning, insist that he sit straight at your side when he gets there. Use your left hand (switch the lead to your right as he comes around) to nudge his rear in the right direction as he's lowering it for the sit. Don't wait until it's down and then try to move it. Correct the sit as he goes down.

When he is doing everything satisfactorily under lead urging, drop the "Sit!" command as he gets into position. With your left hand on his rear and your right on the leash, make him sit, just as you did the sit in heeling—without a command. Then continue your work until he performs the heel with nothing but the original "Mike, heel!" command.

To repeat the exercise, from the very beginning mix up the way you get him in front of you after each heel. One time, when he has come to heel, tell him to stay and step around in front of him, then repeat the heel. Next time, walk forward with him at heel and do a recall from heel to get him into position. You are, at the same time, reinforcing his training on both the recall and the stay.

If he is slow in coming around, get him around faster by stronger snaps with the leash, and later by any urging that increases his speed. Slap your left leg with your hand, use his name, and praise him as he comes around. Soon he will practically leap around to get to heel.

The left heel is taught in much the same way. Here, as you give the command "Mike, heel!" take a step backward with your left leg and pull (or snap) him toward your left and back. Get him back until his rear is just past the original position of your left leg, then guide him around in a half circle *to his left* and into position as you move your leg back into place. Your leg here is even more of a guide to him than in the around heel. If you have a

Right foot is back to guide dog, leash urges him around to heel position in "around" heel.

With the left foot back, dog is guided around from "sit in front" to heel position in the "left" heel.

very large dog, you may have some difficulty following to the letter the instruction to pull him back to your left until his rear is even with you, but moderate the procedure to fit the situation.

    As he gets into position, give him the "Sit!" command just as in the around, and drop the command when ready. Urge him to move faster by verbal persuasion and snaps on the lead, and correct his sit as he goes down.

Whichever way you have him heel, be careful that he works on your command only, once he has learned what to do. Quite often a dog quickly catches on to the fact that from a sitting position in front of you, you are going to want him to go to heel soon, and he will anticipate your command. Insist that he stay seated in front of you until you give him the command, and snap him back sharply with the leash if he tries to move. To keep his mind on his work, once he has learned the heel, mix it up by occasionally not having him heel. When he is sitting in front, you go around him to heel once in a while. Then get him in front again, and do a heel. Also, vary the time you have him sit in front of you before you give him the "Heel!" command. Wait as much as a minute, no matter how uneasy and anxious he gets. And whatever you do, don't try to fool yourself and him by slipping in a quick "Mikeheel!" if he starts to come around before your command.

You will also encounter the problem of the "crooked sit" in front of you when he has learned the heel. Knowing that he will probably have to go to the right, if he goes that way to heel, he will come to a sit in front of you facing toward your right rather than sitting squarely in front. As we suggest in the next chapter, "Novice," for off-lead work, this can be cured by taking a backward step and commanding him again to come when you see his rear going down crooked. Keep taking backward steps and recommanding, "Mike, come!" and guiding him with the lead, until he sits squarely in front of you.

When you have taught him the heel, by either method, add the variation of coming to heel from in back of you. Leave him at the sit-stay and walk straight forward until you come to the end of the leash. Then, commanding him to heel, snap him forward into position with the leash. Later in training, you can if you wish have him move to heel from any position close to you. This can be valuable training for corrections if he later loses his accuracy in sitting. But do not have him do this from any distance, now or later, or he may be confused in the straight recall, and never be exactly sure, even with distinct commands, whether he is supposed to run in and sit directly in front of you, or run from a distance directly to heel. You could, with patience, teach him to distinguish, but there is no practical value in it.

GENERAL BASIC TRAINING

As you begin basic training with your dog following this chapter, be sure to teach each exercise exactly in the order laid out here. We have given them to you in that order for very good reasons, primary among which is that he learns something in each that he can apply to the next lesson. He learns the sit at heel before he needs to use it as a release from the down; he learns the sit-stay and walkaround before it comes up in the recall, and so on. Keep to the order.

During and between the exercises you and he have learned, there are some general considerations to keep in mind. An important one concerns the words of command you use and how you use them. The simple and directly descriptive words used in this chapter and the ones to follow are the words in general use: heel, sit, down, stay, stand, wait, steady, easy, come. Others you will be using are equally standard and descriptive, such as commands used for decades by tens of thousands of trainers and words as commands that your dog cannot confuse with other commands. You can go to a hundred obedience trials without hearing any deviation from them, but if you want to be individualistic there's nothing to stop you. Tell him "Sassafras" instead of "Sit" if you feel like it, or anything else that comes to mind. But once you've started out, stick to the word.

When you've established your command words, don't embellish them. In his early training, it's going to be hard enough for him to connect your mouth sounds to actions without your garbling up the words with a lot of associated verbiage. If you have a problem on the sit, for example, don't chatter at him, "Hey, you, siddown, blast it, sit, sir!" It means nothing to him. Or if you insist on being conversational during training, at least have the decency to supply him with a handy reference dictionary so he can translate all that into "Sit!"

The words you use in praise can be many and varied, of course. There, it's the tone that counts for the most part, although he'll probably learn the meaning of "Good boy" and a few other associated words. Thinking or not, dogs are intelligent creatures, and yours already may know more words than you suspect, just from sitting around the house with his big ears open.

The extent to which a dog can learn his required words is sometimes astonishing. Not long ago, one of the authors traveled to Staten Island, New York, to look at a year-old Doberman he was considering buying. The dog was shown off, and demonstrated that he had had a thorough course in obedience. Later, while coffee was on and general conversation ensued, the dog wandered around sniffing at things. At one point, the lady of the house said to her husband, "Put the cake down on the table there," and midway in the sentence came a resounding crash as King went to the floor. Out of that sentence, uttered in a perfectly normal tone of voice, he had picked out the word "down" and responded like a shot.

When you're giving your commands, sing them out loud and clear. Don't mumble. And don't shout. As far as the use of his name with commands goes, there's a simple rule to follow: When you want him to move somehow, use his name in conjunction *always*. When you want him not to move, don't use his name. His name calls his attention sharply and prepares him to do something.

Praise can be given both by hand and verbally. Generally, when he's at your side you can reach down and give him a few good thumps on the left side while you're going along. Otherwise, use your voice as warmly and sincerely as you can. With the hands, use only the left hand for praise as far as possible, keeping the right for signals and correction. It'll help him keep straight later on as you get into the use of hand signals.

The leash is the wonder weapon of training; without it you would stand slight chance of training anything. But keep in mind that it is a training tool and not a magic device. Just because he has it on he won't necessarily obey. You've got to use it, and correctly.

Keep your training periods short. About fifteen minutes twice a day is right. Don't keep at it until he is bored. And don't bother him throughout the day with a snippet of work here and there. In a later chapter we'll issue a warning about badgering him around the house with commands to no good purpose, but for the present he's off leash in the house, and you shouldn't say so much as "Boo!" to him unless he's on lead at this point. Not letting him make a mistake is just as vital a part of training as is showing him the right thing to do. Wait for the practical applications until considerable control off leash is effected.

CHAPTER 4

Novice

When you begin to work with the dog off lead, in this chapter, you will experience for the first time true control of the dog. Above and beyond the specific arts of heeling and sitting and staying, and all the others the dog will learn in later training, you are working now for control. This is the ultimate goal: to reach the point where your dog unhesitatingly obeys your commands under any circumstances and at whatever distance.

All obedience work is aimed at control, and some of the later exercises we cover in advanced work are taken up as much for the development of it as for any practical application. Control, too, is the reason behind our continued stressing of precision in all your work. The idea is that your dog must do *exactly* what you tell him, and not just a near approximation. The situation is quite similar to that of training troops. The constant drilling, with manual of arms and marching in columns and right face and about-face, are for the purposes of an army directed primarily at establishing control of the men and instilling instant, unhesitating obedience to the commands that make an army work. Drilling is an exercise in conditioning the mind to work in a certain way; obedience exercises for the dog are much the same sort of conditioning. And where army drilling work is useful in moving bodies of men in an orderly fashion, so the basic dog-obedience exercises have their own extremely practical applications.

As one cannot reasonably expect a dog to comprehend "When I say this, you do thus," desired actions and responses to commands must be drilled in until they become almost reflexes. The dog at first learns his lessons by the application of a primary stimulus—forcing him to sit, for example—and at the same time a secondary stimulus, the command, is given to him.

Soon, the secondary means exactly the same to him as the primary did. The best-known example of this primary-secondary transfer is the famous experiment of Pavlov on the salivation of dogs. The Pavlov experiment, briefly, involved giving food to dogs in his laboratory, and at the same time ringing a bell. He continued this, day after day, until the ringing of the bell was firmly associated in the dogs' minds with food. Then he rang the bell without offering food. The dogs immediately began to water at the mouth, proving Pavlov's thesis that even unconscious bodily reactions can be "trained" to react to a secondary stimulus. In this case the food was the primary, the ringing of the bell the secondary. It isn't recorded just how disappointed Pavlov's dogs were when the food didn't show up when the bell rang, but probably even in old age they watered at the mouth when a fire engine went by.

The process of training a dog is a repetition of much the same pattern of primary-secondary substitution. You have been doing it in basic training. The primary stimulus in teaching the sit is the combined pressures of one hand on the rear and the other on the leash. Soon the secondary "Sit!" becomes in his mind associated with the action. Finally, the secondary stimulus alone will produce the desired action. We want to emphasize this because a full understanding can eliminate one of the major possible difficulties in training, that of a wrong attitude toward your dog. Let us suppose that on one of his experimental runs, one of Pavlov's dogs had failed to salivate at the bell. Pavlov would have looked more than somewhat silly, and would have accomplished nothing, if he had sworn at the dog, "Double-blast you, why didn't you salivate?" You will accomplish just about as much if you blame your in-training dog for not responding properly to your commands. And you will confuse and frighten him to boot. What you must do when your "experiment" doesn't produce the desired results is to examine your procedure and find where the fault lies in you and your methods—not in the dog.

As you get further along in training you will have to use the primary stimuli less and less as your dog gets into the habit of making the necessary associations. There are, of course, slow dogs who take as much time to learn an advanced exercise as to learn the basic sit, but in most cases you will find that something really advanced, like directed jumping, which you probably can't imagine your dog ever learning, will come to him in the regular course of things if the proper obedience foundation has been laid.

Through all the basic training of you and your dog, you have been establishing the transfer to the secondary stimulus (the command) with leash in hand, ever ready to reapply the primary stimuli when needed. Now, in Novice work, you will be working without the leash, and you must be sure before you start that the lessons of basic training are so firmly in your dog's mind that a command is all that is needed for good performance.

Here, attitude is doubly important. Once off lead, the dog is under no control but that of your voice and command. If he is ready, you must have faith in him, and show him your faith. You must be ready to think like him, to examine the mistakes he makes in the light of what you know about the way his mind works. You must be generous with praise for a job well done, and you must know positively what went wrong before you apply a correction. As the exercises grow more complex, with several different required actions blending into one performance, you must be very careful not to correct at the wrong time for a part of the performance ill-performed, lest he get the feeling that he is being corrected for another part that he did right. Remember that by now a "No!" is to him a strong correction; be careful how you use it. Be ready to forgive mistakes repeatedly, even as you correct them. And practice patience, patience, patience.

PREPARATION FOR OFF LEAD

The first step is perfection in the dog's work on lead. He must be able to go through all the exercises—heeling, the down, stand and sit with stays, the recall from heeling, and the heel—without your making any lead corrections. To test this, go through the work with the lead on the dog, but out of your hands. Loop the lead through your belt, or stuff it in a pocket, or hang the free end over your shoulder, always allowing enough slack for the dog to make the turns. Start out at heel and go through all his heeling work. Give him all the praise and encouragement and extra commands necessary as you walk along. Try to talk him into staying in place, but keep your hands off the lead. If he strays, it almost certainly means that you have been holding him in place, consciously or unconsciously, during the on-lead heeling, and now you see the results. To correct straying from position, simply take hold of the lead for a quick, gentle snap, then let it go again.

If the heeling goes well, try the stand, sit, and down with stays, leaving the lead again attached to his collar but lying on the ground. Go through the complete routines in all three positions, to the front, the back, and the sides.

If he has worked well in everything, with no need for corrections other than verbal, you are ready to take the leash off for advanced Novice work, most of which is simply an extension of basic training. However, be very sure of yourself and the dog before you try it. Going off lead too soon has been the source of endless frustration for countless dog owners and trainers. The temptation is strong to get away from the lead too soon, and then the mistakes begin to pile up. The dog wanders off course, he gets corrected both improperly and unjustifiedly, he becomes confused and resentful, the owner loses his temper, and sweetness and light go out of the window with the training program.

Be sure you can go through the *entire* routine without using the lead for *any* corrections; if not, keep the lead on for another week and then try again. During the repeat week, concentrate on the mistakes your dog made that kept you both from going off lead. If all goes well, take off the leash and go right through all the exercises again. You'll probably be stunned that he does do it—everything right down the line. Keep the leash in your hand, just to let him know it is there if needed, and for your own peace of mind. In all likelihood you won't have to use it. In fact, many city dogs do their heeling better off lead than on, surprising though that may seem. To them, being put on lead has come to mean freedom through being taken to the street on lead. Sometimes it pops up right away, and sometimes the dog doesn't make the distinction until later in training. If you're interested only in obedience around the home, it won't bother you at all.

If minor problems develop in the first heeling off lead, put him back on for a few minutes and apply strong corrections where the faults have shown up. Then try again without the lead. One short application may solve the problem. If it doesn't, repeat the week-on treatment. It takes patience and determination not to try to muddle through somehow once you've gotten the lead off, but the week or two invested in sureness will pay off many times over in lack of troubles later. Unfortunately, there's just no other way out of it. If you try dragging your dog around by the collar or the scruff of the neck, or have to resort to slapping his rear down on the heeling sits, or anything else, you're beginning a losing battle with trivia. Get it right, on lead.

HEELING OFF LEAD

Once he has heeled successfully off lead there is little more to do but practice with him. Mix up your work together as much as possible, fast and slow, left and right turns, circles to the right and left, about-turns. Try stopping from a fast and from a slow. Do your figure eights around trees, people, rocks, and holes in the ground, around two cars parked in a lot. Get him used to heeling steadily under all circumstances. Don't be afraid to go back on lead momentarily to solve a specific problem. If, for example, he is nervous about cars, or ecstatic about them, put him back on lead while doing your figure eights around cars. When he is steady, take it off again.

Use verbal commands and encouragement as much as you need to, pat your leg to urge him into place, and be generous with praise. As you're doing corners and circles, keep telling him to heel if he has any hesitation. As you go along, you'll be able to cut down the repeated commands gradually until you need to say "Heel!" only when you start up. Remember in your heeling, too, always to start off on the left foot. It's a big help to the dog, and if you are consistent about starting with the left, and leaving him on the right, he'll be surer of what to do, and you'll incidentally be laying the groundwork for later work with signals.

THE STAYS OFF LEAD

From the stay on lead to off lead is a simple step—you have only to go farther away from your dog, which you are now able to do as you no longer need hold on to the leash. As with all training, work up to it gradually. Leave the leash hooked on to his collar a few times. Beginning with the sit, work your way slowly from the leash's length in front of him. Take it by easy stages, and you'll be surprised to find that within one training session you will be able to stand thirty feet or more away from him without a break. Work up to the same distance away to the sides and to the back, and then progress to the down and the stand. As you go farther away in each position, keep repeating "Stay!" and "Good boy" to reassure him until he seems steady, then drop all but the original "Stay!" command as you leave. Be sure not to try to keep him in place with the fierce power of your flinty stare—it will do more harm than good. Never glare or stare at your dog when he's at the stay; you will obviously want to keep an eye on him to be sure he's still staying, but look over him or above his head. Eye contact will create uneasiness in many dogs and is more likely to cause them to break than to keep them steady.

Problems here can only be solved by going back to the beginning and working on lead until steadiness is acquired. Among the problems you may encounter is the dog who tries to come to you as you are walking away, or who waits a few moments and then begins a creep toward you. Go back to the beginning, on leash, stepping only out to the end of the leash. Then, with the leash still on, start upping your distance more gradually this time, coming back sooner from the more distant positions and repeating a firm "Stay!" to keep him where he is. In the sit or down, don't expect him at this point to stay for more than five minutes. Hold your requirements for the stand-stay to about two minutes, as standing motionless is very tiring for the dog. He will slowly learn to hold the pose longer, but don't put too much of a strain on him too soon.

Another problem is the dog who tries to change his position when you have left him—sitting from the down or stand, lying down from the sit or stand. Check to be sure you have left him in a natural, comfortable position. He should simply be standing, or sitting, or lying down, not in some artificial, unnatural position that will cause him discomfort if he attempts to maintain it. Remember not to glare. If there are still problems, go back to your practice on lead, and work them out there.

THE PLAYFUL DOG

When the dog is off lead at some distance from you, he may leave his position and run around playfully. Usually it is because he is still very much a puppy at heart, even at this stage; or it may be that, at whatever age, he finds himself for the first time completely unrestrained and it seems like a long-awaited chance for a good run. This is one of the reasons you must be especially sure that all his preliminary training has sunk in well before you attempt to work off lead. But unexpected playfulness happens even in the best of families, and you may have to face the problem. The first precaution, of course, is to do your beginning off-lead work in a place where a serious runaway can't get hurt. A fenced-in yard or section of a park is best, or a field in the country is good. True, it is difficult for the city dweller to find such places for training, but for the safety of the dog never try your first off-lead work in some place, such as a parking lot, where an unthinking run could take the unsophisticated dog onto a street, where serious injury might result.

Wherever you are training, the cardinal rule of coping with the playful runaway is: *Don't chase him!* To run after him is the worst possible mistake you can make, for no matter how much you may shout orders or entreaties at him, he will take your running to him as a gilt-edged invitation to run farther and make a great game of tag. If you are in an area where he can't come to any harm by running about, stay where you are and try to get him either to come back to you or stop where he is and wait for you to approach cautiously. Using his name with praise and entreaties may get him to come, albeit erratically, to you—provided you stay where you are. Crouch down as if you were ready to play, and he is more likely to come running in. Try also giving him the command to sit or down, just to see if it works. It just might, because by the time the situation occurs, his responses to those commands should be almost automatic.

If he does sit or go down at a distance, walk—do not run—to him. Keep his attention by repeating "Stay!" and "Good boy" to him as you approach, and don't make any sudden moves with the lead you want so desperately to get snapped on to his collar. He can make a very successful break for it when you have your hands almost on him, so keep it casual until you actually have the leash snapped on. However you get together again, don't under any circumstances attempt to punish or correct him for having run away. He won't connect it with the running away at all; but rather with having returned to you or having obeyed your command to sit and stay. Let this happen once or twice and you'll have a serious problem on your hands, for he won't listen to a thing you say, but will start running hell-for-leather once he gets a good lead.

Even if the circumstances are such that he is heading for danger in his run or is making for the tall timber, again don't chase after him. Try to get his attention by shouts and whistles, and then run away from him. Paradoxical though it may seem, that is the best way to get him back. Back-pedal in the opposite direction from the way he is going. If he's running away in play, he'll turn and chase you instead of your chasing him. When he gets close, though, don't make any sudden grabs as he'll only sheer off and keep going. He may keep going anyway, and if he does, just reverse and keep running away from him until he either gets tired of it all and comes to you peacefully or plops down. If possible, with his attention on you, run behind some trees or a building; it'll shake him up a bit that *you* are trying to get away from *him,* and he'll come belting over to look for you. And again, once he has come to you, praise him and let him know all is well once you get him on lead. Don't sulk or yank him about to get even for the near heart failure he gave you, or the next time he won't come back so quickly. Let him know by your attitude that he did a wonderful thing in getting back to you.

Go back again and start the stays on lead, and this time when you would have left him off lead completely, tie to his collar a long length of light clothesline. String it out along the ground before you tie it on, and then when you leave him at a stay, don't keep the line in your hands but walk along it, keeping one foot on the line at all times. If he stays, all well and good. If not, you've got a foot on the line and can bring him up short if he makes another dash for it. Even if he's big enough to yank you off your feet if he goes suddenly, you'll find that a running dog trailing thirty feet of line is a good deal easier to get hold of than one without. Leave a little slack at his end of the line, so that if he decides to get playful you can let him take a bound or two before he is brought up short. Just as you see the line about to jerk him, give him a strong "No!" Try to time it so the "no" reaches him just as the line pulls him off his feet. It'll get across to him that you are in control no matter how far away he happens to be, and as he saw you leave empty-handed he'll wonder how it all happened.

STAND FOR EXAMINATION

In competition obedience, the idea behind this exercise is to teach your dog, on your command, to stand still off lead and allow himself to be touched and examined by the judge without showing shyness, fear, resentment, or hostility—all while you are standing facing him about six feet away. The exercise has practical applications in the breed ring, for advanced training where your dog's height may have to be measured to set the height of jumps, for later work in the Utility Class, for grooming, and especially for the times when a veterinarian must examine him. If your dog is thoroughly trained to allow himself to be handled and looked over by strangers when you tell him to stand and stay, you are a long way toward having solved any problems of overaggressiveness or shyness in the dog. And this training will not lessen any dog's effectiveness as a watchdog. In fact, the dog who will not allow examination when commanded is such a liability that he should never be considered as a pet or watchdog by anyone but a recluse or hermit with gold under the floorboards. Such a dog, if his reactions are aggressive, is an extreme danger to your friends and neighbors, and a danger to you through the lawsuits that will result if anyone is bitten or seriously frightened by him. Ritualistic and formal though the obedience-ring specifications for the "stand for examination" may seem to you, we urge strongly that you train your dog to these specifications in any case.

Proceed with the stand-stay training exactly as you have with the sit-stay and the down-stay until you feel he is steady enough to try it off lead. Remove the lead and put it out of sight somewhere. Stand your dog, give him the stay command, and walk casually away from him. Don't back away as this can encourage him to break and come to you. About six feet away, turn to face him, but don't stare at him. Wait a few seconds to be sure he is steady, then give him another stay command to remind him of what is going on. Walk slowly to him, keeping your head up and neither staring nor glaring. Repeat the stay command, hold out your hand for him to sniff; then, standing slightly to his left by his left shoulder, touch him lightly on the head, body, and hindquarters using the fingers and palm of one hand.

Give him another stay command and walk back to your position six feet in front and facing him. Wait a few more seconds, then walk around him to heel position. Then you can either start heeling with him again for a few paces and finish with a sit, or simply tell him "Okay" to release him. Now shower him with praise. Unfortunately, there's no way you can praise him *while* he's standing, except perhaps for a calm, occasional "Good boy," since praise during an exercise like this often will excite him and actually cause the break you don't want. Better to wait until it's over, unless you've learned that he can receive a reassuring word of praise and still remember he's not supposed to move, except for a permissible wag of the tail. If you do run into any problems, go back to work on lead until you're sure he is steady and ready to try it again off lead.

When you are able to give him the complete examination, call in the help of a member of the family or a friend who knows the dog well. Leave the dog at the stand-stay and walk to the end of the lead just as before, and ask your "judge" to examine the dog. Be sure that he or she knows full well how to go about it, especially the first move of allowing the dog to take a brief sniff of the right hand before any touching is done. A dog generally figures that anyone who comes up to him with a hand extended, *palm downward*, to allow him a smell doesn't mean any harm. It's an important point.

As the "judge" makes the first light examination of the dog, keep a specially close watch for any moves, repeating "Stay!" and "Good boy" to reassure him that all is well and that you want him to stay. The examiner should approach from the right as you have been doing (your right, the dog's left) and when he has finished the examination, step back without going around the dog. Keep this up until your dog will submit to a thorough examination. You can then vary the procedure with the "judge" approaching from any side (but not from the back), and circling around the dog in his examination.

When that stage is past, somehow secure the services of a complete stranger (to the dog) to do the examining. Repeat exactly as before, working up from a very light few touches on the dog's head and back, to a full examination. For the first approaches of the stranger, stand close in front of the dog with the leash held close, and watch for any signs of fear, resentment, or aggression. Cure these by constant corrections with the lead, and reassurances. In the case of a really shy dog, be very generous with praise and reassurance, and make sure that the examiner approaches slowly and gives the dog plenty of time to take the preliminary sniff, and that no sudden moves are made. Next, if possible, get another stranger to come up and give a thorough examination without any preparation. And somewhere along the line, be sure to have both a woman and a man do the examining. Some dogs, for reasons of their own, will submit to a man examining them, but shy at a woman, or vice versa. Try it also with children. The idea is to get him to stand for an examination by anyone, when you tell him to.

A practice examination. "Judge" approaches at dog's left, goes over him gently. Note loose lead.

"Judge" examining a dog at the stand, off lead, the final step in training for the exercise.

With both friends and strangers examining the dog, finish the exercise after every examination by circling back to heel position. Give him plenty of praise as you release him.

RECALL

One of the most useful, if not the most basic, things the dog has to learn is coming quickly when called. Despite its importance, we have put the teaching of the complete off-lead recall this far back in the training schedule because of the several other things that have had to be learned before a successful recall can be taught. We don't mean that you shouldn't have your dog come to you, or call him, before you reach this point. It would be impossible to keep a dog around the house this long unless he responded to your summons in some measure. But the formal, obligatory recall should wait until now. Foremost among the things he must learn is control. Specifically, the dog must first have learned thoroughly to stay when told, and to execute a preliminary sort of recall from heeling. The recall from heeling as an introductory step is an especially important one, as it eliminates the necessity of having to jerk the dog up from a sitting position to get him into motion. While heeling, he is already in motion and has only to learn that "Come!" means to move directly to you and sit in front. Now he can learn that the familiar command means to get up from wherever he is and start moving.

First, work with him until he can do the recall well from heeling off lead. Then, when he appears ready, put him in a sitting position, on lead, and give either the command "Stay!" or "Wait!" For decades, it was standard practice to leave a dog with the command to stay when performing the recall, relying on extra training to make him understand that at times "Stay!" meant that he was to remain until the handler returned to heel, and that at other times it meant to stay there until called. After trying it both ways with thousands of dogs and handlers, we are convinced that using the command "Wait!" when it is to be followed by a command to do something else is far preferable: it makes a clear distinction in the dog's mind, and never raises the question of what he is to do when told to stay. He stays.

First, work with him until he can do the recall from heeling well off lead. Then, when he is ready, put him in a sitting position, on lead, and tell him to wait. Walk out in front of him to the lead's length and, facing him, command, "Mike, come!" Give a gentle snap on the lead to help him understand what you mean, and guide him in until he sits in front of you. As you urge him in to you, keep repeating "Come!" with his name, encouraging him with "Good boy" and praise to suit. When he will do this on lead but without corrections, take him off lead and repeat until he will come the six feet to you in good order.

Each time he comes in to you, finish the exercise by commanding him to heel, and then praise him. Don't give him any physical praise as he sits in front of you; it is just too much of a temptation to him to jump around and play. A quiet "Good boy" is not out of order at this point, but generally save the praise, once he has the exercise fairly well in hand, for when he has gone to heel.

When he will do the six-foot recall off lead, you can start to increase your distance—but slowly and gradually. Whatever you do, don't make the very common error of pride or overconfidence, jumping immediately from a few feet to a long recall of thirty feet or more. First, try it from eight feet, and if that works well, from ten, and so on. If you go at it properly, it will work very well. As you extend your distance, also increase the time you stand facing him before you call him. This helps steady him, and takes away any idea that as soon as you've walked away and turned around, he's going to be called in a second or two. Using the "Wait!" command instead of "Stay!" carries with it that problem: He knows full well he's supposed to stay where he's left only until he gets further word from you, and he may be overeager. It is a very small disadvantage, and well worth the trouble it saves in teaching him otherwise, that "Stay" means one thing one time and another thing the next time.

Wait, also, before sending him to heel when he has come in to sit in front of you. But don't wait too long. He is after all intelligent, and it seems logical enough to him to try to go directly to heel without all the bother of stopping in front to stare at you. Watch for this; it happens with almost every dog som time in the course of training, and you will see it happen with dog after dog in Novice at AKC obedience trials. It requires only thinking through, patience, and insistence on your part that he sit in front and wait for your command to go to heel. But above all, don't try to cheat and make it seem okay by giving him a quick command to heel if he either doesn't wait in front of you or comes to you and starts to go straight to the heel position without sitting. It won't fool him at all, and will just start him in bad habits.

The major problem you may run into here is that of the dragging recall. The dog gets up, yes, and comes to you, but with no will at all, drooping along as if the temperature were 107° in the shade. Almost without exception this results from faulty training—you have punished the dog when he came to you, or committed some other cardinal sin of training that makes him reluctant to come when you call. The one-two solution for this is to examine your training history to find out just what it is that makes him reluctant, and then cure the habit by making him come in faster. The best way we know involves the assistance of a friend who understands what you're working on and who has a good sense of timing and the ability to follow your instructions precisely.

You'll also need a long lead—a length of light clothesline will do nicely—

with a snap on the end of it. You can tie the line to the dog's collar, but it is a cumbersome business, and it's much better and easier just to get a cheap lead somewhere, or use an old one, cutting off the snap and putting it on to the line.

Snap the lead of the long line on to the dead ring of the dog's collar and position the ring and snap under his chin. Give him a "Wait!" command and then lay the line down straight in front of him as you walk away. Your helper should already be in position, about thirty feet in front of the dog. You walk out, hand him the end of the lead, and turn, walking perhaps a step or two forward, to face your dog. After waiting a moment, give your dog a good strong command, "Mike, come!" Here is where the timing comes in. Your assistant must give the line a sharp snap *exactly* when the word "come" issues from your mouth. The correction is made, and you aren't associated with it, for your dog can see perfectly well that you haven't done anything. In fact, it is a good idea to reassure him and get some enthusiasm into the recall by clapping your hands and making a fuss to get him coming at a trot, getting his attention to you rather than to your helper.

Don't repeat this device more than a few times. It should be effective but can be overdone. And don't yank on the long line, or have your assistant yank on it, to speed up a lagging recall; it will only make your dog like the idea of coming to you less and less. Try running a few backward steps away from him, patting your legs and calling to him as you go. Make something of a game of it—run away from him, always going backward. Keep repeating the backward run until he speeds up to a respectable trot or run as he comes toward you. Then slow down gradually so that you come to a stop just as he is a pace or two from you.

Use this same technique if he begins to sit crooked in front of you. Many dogs, having learned what's going on, come in well but sit facing whichever direction they're going to go when they start to heel. It's just a labor-saving idea he's invented that seems only too sensible to him. If, as he comes in, you see him about to sit crooked in anticipation of the "go to heel," take a step or two backward with another "come" command, and this time, when you stop, be ready to reach down and correct his position. But be very careful not to overcorrect on the sit. Coming to you is supposed to be enjoyable. If you nag at him harshly every time about whether he's sitting straight, it will take most, if not all, of the fun out of it for him. It is much more important that he come in to you running, and happily, and is welcomed when he does. With occasional gentle corrections you can straighten out the sit situation as time goes on.

Taking him off lead when he has reached the point of coming in smartly at a thirty-foot distance is a process of tricking him past the stage of conversion from lead control to voice control. It is at this point in training that many dogs, if taken suddenly off lead, decide to make a run for it, or simply sit there and do nothing. If he's really off lead, there's nothing you can do but come back cursing under your breath for some repeat training. But you can fool him for the time it takes to establish the necessary control. First, have him come a few times with the long line lying on the ground between you and him, still attached to the collar, with you holding your end, but letting it drag as he comes in. Then, stretch it out over the thirty feet and take him to the snap end, putting the snap on his collar, and walk down the line until you come to your end, where you stand on it. If he comes at your call, fine. If not, you have the lead there to make your corrections. Then—and here is the deception—with the line stretched out on the ground, take him to the snap end and go through all the motions of snapping it on without actually doing so. Don't drop the snap to the ground with a great thunk or you'll destroy the illusion; rather, leave a few spare feet of line at his end so you can set it down gently behind him. Then walk again to the end of the line exactly as before and call him. And there you have his first free recall from a distance.

Work on this a few times. After the first few times, you won't have to bother with the pantomime snapping on of the lead. Then, when you come to the end of the line, step to the right or left a few paces. Call him in. He won't follow the line as if it were a railroad track, but will come directly to you. Finally, you will be able to dispose of the deception entirely, and he will come in to you over any distance. Use the backing-away trick on the longer recalls to speed him up if necessary.

When he will do a long recall proficiently, you can start working him with distractions. Call him to come away from members of the family, or from friends, from food, or away from other dogs. Always put him back on lead for the first few lessons with each new distraction, and keep him on lead until you are satisfied that he will come immediately. Get him to come to you from any position—sit, stand, or down. And teach him to come immediately, even if he is running around at play, simply by using the long line on him when he is playing, and giving a sharp snap on it to get him coming in if he ignores the command.

You may feel, if your dog comes quite happily to you most of the time around the house and out in the open, that you really don't need this sort of training in the recall. But training must establish a response when you want it, not when he is in a good mood and feels like responding. It may save his life, and it will definitely save you frustration.

DISTANT CONTROL

Teaching the dog to sit or lie down while at a distance from you is, like the recall, an extension of the work you have been doing on leash. Up to now, you will have been sitting or downing him only at your side, on leash. As with the other exercises, the idea of the training is to get obedience to the command so firmly entrenched in his mind that it will make no difference where he is—"Down!" means just that, and the same with "Sit!" When your dog has shown that he will respond instantly to the commands, both on leash and off, at your side, move around directly in front of him (but not at the full length of the lead). Give him the command and be ready to correct with the leash. Progress to off leash at a distance with both commands, slowly as always. You won't be able to give him any corrections from a distance, with or without a lead, so be sure he works very well close up and on lead before you move out. Work out any problems by moving right back to him and giving him a refresher course on lead. One principle to keep always before you in this work is that, once he has learned the exercise and has shown that he can and will do it without fear or resentment, he must always do it on the *first command.* Nothing is so detrimental to discipline and control as letting him get away with just sitting there while you rant at him. At whatever stage, when you tell him "Sit!" he must sit, without any further word from you. Don't make the mistake of waiting a moment to see if he'll do it, or urging him again and again. If he doesn't sit, get in a correction immediately, get back to a position where you can apply a correction simultaneously with the command, and work until he responds at once. This sort of obedience and control on leash must be established before you can hope for control off leash. We repeat this to the point of boredom because it is so vitally important to successful training.

If you've done some training before, you may have found that you have serious problems getting your dog to do something on the first command when you've left him in position with a "Stay!" command and you don't really want him to stay, but to wait for further orders. Try changing your command to "Wait!" when you're going to give him a following action command from any distance, even as you're training him from one room to another in the house or apartment. You'll be happily surprised at how quickly he catches on to the new regulations and responds to you.

TRAINING CLASSES

If you plan to enter your dog in the Novice Classes at an AKC show, a training class can be a help. You will be able to teach your dog perfectly well without a class to do all the exercises when the two of you are alone in your training area. The training class supplies, aside from instruction, the presence of other dogs and people, and the general noises and distractions that you run into at a show.

In a show, your dog has to perform the long sit and long down in line with up to fifteen other dogs, and the separation between dogs may be as little as three feet on either side. Besides which, you will no longer be standing alone thirty feet in front of him, but in a line of handlers with the judge and stewards walking about between you and your dog. However well he may have been trained alone, the possibility is very good that he will become unhappy and confused by all this hullabaloo, and try to get back to you. He may, in fact, decide that now is the time for sex or warfare, depending on who happens to be sitting on either side of him, and you will not only fail the exercise but incur the undying enmity of the other handlers. There are few things so little calculated to begin a warm friendship as your dog sniffing or snapping another handler's dog into a move and failure.

If you have become fairly adept at training, and have your dog's confidence completely, you can train him well enough in the stay so that he does not mind whatever new circumstances he finds himself in. In such a case there is no real need to attend a class, unless you want to see how other people are getting along with their dogs, and to get some of the feel of a show before actually going into one. If you are fortunate enough to have a few trained dogs in your neighborhood with accommodating owners, you can simulate the "other dog" atmosphere of the show stays without bothering with a class. Don't attempt it with untrained dogs, though, because chaos is sure to result. One badly fouled-up stay with other dogs leaping at him or romping about can set your dog's progress back a long way.

Because in a show you may find your dog sitting next to almost any breed, it's a good idea to go to a training class that takes all breeds. "Specialty" classes, all of one breed, are in many cases excellent for general obedience work, but they suffer from an artificial situation in the group stays. This lesson was bitterly learned by one of the authors years ago at the beginning of his training experience. Having trained a Cocker Spaniel in an all-Cocker class, he easily conquered the first show, when his dog took first place, and all was well in the stays. At the next show, however, the Cocker found himself sitting between a Great Dane and a St. Bernard. One look on either side convinced him that this was no place for a sensible Cocker Spaniel to be, and he lit out for hearth and home. His previous work in that show was such that he would have taken first place again, and the disappointment to his owner was considerable. So if you do find a specialty class most convenient, take the dog to a session or two of an all-breed class before entering a show, just to prevent unhappiness. Your dog *must* sit in the line according to the catalog listing; no judge will allow any exception, whatever the circumstances.

Training classes also offer benefits for the strictly home trainer. Unusual behavior problems can many times be worked out with ease by an experienced instructor, saving you hours of fruitless work and sweat. Again, the "other dogs and people" factor can be a valuable one, for a few sessions at least. Getting your dog to be obedient under all circumstances is the ultimate goal, and the presence of other dogs, particularly, is a circumstance that can best be met in a training class.

In most areas, there is only one class (if any) within a reasonable distance, so the choice is not great. But if you have a choice, try to select the best class by inquiring among friends who have trained dogs. There are, as with anything else, good classes and bad, excellent training directors, and almost criminally ignorant instructors. There are few tests of a good class that we can offer you other than the feeling of the class you will get after looking on at a session. Avoid, if possible, the class in which the instructor insists on absolute quiet among handlers and spectators. Noise and distractions may seem to shake the dog a bit at first, but he is not going to have respectful silence all his life, so why try to train him under those circumstances? Various instructors do use different teaching methods, so don't cavil at departures from the methods outlined in this book, but avoid instructors who radically violate some of the cardinal principles of successful training by using food as a reward, striking the dog with leash or newspapers, throwing leashes or chains to startle the dog into performing, using pinch or spike collars. Do look for an instructor who pays attention to your individual problems rather than running the class like a drill team.

SOME PRACTICAL APPLICATIONS

With or without show intentions, the dog who has received a thorough course in Basic and Novice training can be relied on to a great extent to conduct himself as a gentleman and a scholar. Even if his baser instincts at times seem to be getting the upper hand, his obedience training can be the tool whereby you give him further lessons in acceptable conduct.

One of the problems that almost always comes up with male dogs—mounting—can be easily controlled in the obedience-trained dog. When he shows the first signs of trying to mount your leg, or starting to molest guests this way, give him the sharp order "Off!" This command can be used also to keep him off the furniture, and from just jumping up on guests. Show him firmly what you mean by using his collar when you give the command, with authority in your voice but not with a punishing tone. Immediately, give him the command "Down!" and praise him heartily. He'll go along with you, as you've taken his mind off the original situation and off the correction by using a normal obedience command and the following praise.

Yard boundaries in town and country can be taught by using the recall. Let him run until he comes to the limits of your yard, then call him: "Mike, come!" Welcome him back with all due and appropriate praise and then let him run again. When he comes to the boundary call him again. Repeat this until he learns that he is not to go beyond a certain line without your express permission. If the recall lessons have been well ingrained, he will learn surprisingly fast.

The sit, stand, or down stays can be used to control his aggressions when people come to the door. Instead of sending him to his bed, let him come with you when you answer the door. Sit or down him a few feet from the door with the order "Stay!" If the caller is not a friend, let the dog stay there and watch what's going on. If it is a friend, keep the dog in position until coats are off and greetings made, or let him go at once to make greetings, if you like. The same treatment applies to the overly effusive dog; keep him at the down-stay if he tends to get too familiar with guests, or send him to bed if he persists.

One word of caution: Don't ever use the recall as a practical way to get your dog to you for a correction. If he has done something quite beyond the pale, *always go to him* to correct him. Make it a rule absolutely without exception that whenever he comes to you, either on command or of his own volition, you welcome him with genuine friendliness and save the reprimand for next time, or until a few moments later, when you can take him to the scene of the crime. It may be a bit difficult—you may have to say "Good boy" through gritted teeth—but do it. Put yourself in his place and imagine how happily or readily you would come to someone if there were a very good chance you would get sworn at and slugged when you got there.

FURTHER TRAINING

Where do we go from here in training? If you are out for obedience degrees, you will want to go on, but what is in it for you and your dog if the ring doesn't interest you? A great deal, we believe. Through further training, even more control and cooperation are established, and the dog can learn a great many more practical skills.

In Open work, for example, he learns to retrieve things, not just in play, but to retrieve what you tell him, when you tell him. He will learn to jump on command over the equivalents of walls and ditches. He will learn the "drop on recall," an exercise that has saved the life of many a dog. And he will learn to sit and down at the stay for an even longer time, in this case with you out of sight. All these things are highly useful items to add to your dog's repertoire.

In Utility work, the postgraduate course in obedience, he learns to work with you exclusively by signals, to pick out something of yours from among other articles by using his nose, to stand quietly while being examined by a judge (with you some distance away), and to elaborate his "jump on command" abilities.

Open and Utility work require a fairly sure understanding between you and your dog, complete mastery of all Novice and Basic work, and more patience, thought, and control than you have had to exercise up to now. But believe us, the result—a really well-trained dog who is a genuine companion, and a useful one—is well worth it.

CHAPTER 5

Open

"The purpose of Obedience Trials is to demonstrate the usefulness of the purebred dog as the companion and guardian of man, and not the ability of the dog to acquire facility in the performance of mere tricks." So says the AKC in its regulations for obedience trials. We might say the same about obedience training, and in fact we have from time to time in other chapters. Here we say it again, with the added proviso that it applies to *all* pet dogs, mongrel, half-breed, or purebred. The training that the dog acquires in the exercises comprising AKC Open work is such as to increase his usefulness to you, your pleasure in having him around, and his propaganda value as a dog. To explain that latter a bit, most dog owners feel that everyone else should have a dog, too, and are baffled by people who either hate dogs, are afraid of dogs, or who feel it would be just too much bother and trouble to own a dog. We have found that an obedience-trained dog can make some astonishing conversions in any of these groups.

In following the work in this chapter, we again recommend that you train your dog to show-ring standards, even if you never intend to go near a ring. None of the training will do you much good if you don't. A dog that does not drop on recall *every time*, not just when he feels like it, is little better than one that has never heard of the exercise. A dog that stays only most of the time is one that you can never feel fully confident in leaving outside a store off leash. Work for perfection and unfailing obedience.

HEEL OFF LEAD

This is simply an extension of heeling, and requires only more practice. In the show ring, you will do off-leash heeling in the figure eight for the first time, but there is no necessary difficulty in this. For practical use, off-leash heeling, including the figure eight, is a basic exercise. Well trained in this, your dog can accompany you through crowded streets and stores without the bother, to you, of holding on to a leash. The figure eight gives him practice in following at your side no matter how much pedestrian traffic you may have to duck around, and should be practiced. Work him, just as in Novice, through and around as many objects as you can think of, particularly people moving and people standing still. When he is this far along in training, try to heel him around other dogs (trained ones, of course) and even around cats, pigeons, or whatever other "livestock" is available to you.

The trained dog, when heeling, should concentrate solely on staying at your side unless the preservation of life and limb becomes the greater consideration. He should not be distracted by other dogs, cats, horses, motorcycles, fires, floods, or cyclones, unless they present an immediate danger to him or you. You can't, of course, ever keep him from noticing the distractions and looking at them, nor should you try, but a passing dog that merits a glance or perhaps a lip curl from him should never budge him from your side. Work on heeling until he is absolutely steady off leash.

DROP ON RECALL

The practical usage idea behind this exercise is that your dog should respond to your command (or signal) to "drop," or down, no matter where he is or what he is doing. He should, in particular, respond to the command or signal when he is running in to you on the recall—probably the most difficult of circumstances, as he wants to come in and be near you. There have been many cases of dogs' lives being saved through the drop on recall. Imagine for a moment your dog running to you from across a street and a car approaching at full speed. What would you do? Shout to him to go back? Or to look out? Not much good. But if you could shout or signal to him to drop in his tracks, you could avert the danger. And this is not the only practical application.

The first step in training is to introduce the drop signal. This is generally (and by AKC regulation for obedience trials) a raising of your right hand and arm, straight up, with fingers extended and palm forward, much like a policeman's "Stop!" signal. You hand can go as high as your shoulder or all the way up to arm's length, according to taste. The only requirement is that your dog be able to see your signal clearly. For nontrial work you can obviously do the signal any way you want to, but in trials there are only two ways accepted by the AKC, and it's just as easy for the dog to learn according to these standards. In the first, the raising of the hand to whatever height is the drop signal. By AKC regulations, in such a signal the hand must be *immediately* brought down, with any hesitation considered an extra signal.

In the second type of signal, the downswing of the hand and arm is the signal—clearly a motion indicating "down." Of course, to swing your arm down you must get your hand and arm up. But again, any hesitation while holding the hand up is considered an extra signal by the AKC. We like the first signal best, but it is up to you and your dog to choose the one that suits you.

Teaching him to respond to the signal is simply the introduction of another secondary stimulus to get the action you want. By this time, he should drop instantly on your voice command, either at heel beside you, close in front of you, or some distance away. Now you will begin to give the hand signal simultaneously with the verbal command, and keep it up until he realizes that one means the same as the other.

Put him back on leash for the first lessons. With him sitting at your side, on leash, swing your hand up in the signal and at the same time command him, "Down!" Swing your body around toward him as you give the signal to be sure he sees it. If he does not go down instantly you have the leash and collar there to make the necessary correction. Be very patient, for the upswinging hand may confuse or even frighten a dog. He may think you're about to swing at him, if you've done so in the past. Reassure him that all is well, but insist that he drop immediately, and then praise him. At the very start of training, you can keep your hand up in the air a few moments, and even wiggle it a bit to draw his attention, but the signal should quickly become a sharp raising and an immediate lowering of the hand. Repeat the command-and-signal training until you feel he has the idea, then try it without the voice command. If he does not drop immediately, get in a sharp leash correction. In most cases, the dog will have caught on quite well, but if you have difficulty, go back to the voice-and-signal a few times, then try it again with only the signal. Keep at it until he works well with the signal only—and insist on an *immediate* drop, not a slow and reluctant sinking to the ground. Be sure to use plenty of praise and patience. As a last resort, try dropping to your left knee, just as you give the command and/or signal. It's a powerful suggestion aid.

Remember, when you start this training, that a signal is really very simple for a dog to comprehend and comply with. It is, in a way, far more logical for an animal to understand body motions than human words, as well as dogs *do* manage to do that. But at the beginning, it is an entirely new idea for him, so bear with him if it takes time. And mix up the work. Don't drop him and then sit him back up many times in a row, or he will quickly get as bored with the whole thing as you will be. Do half a dozen drops, then heel some, then do a stay, then return to the drop training. It'll keep you both from ennui.

When he will drop on signal at your side, have him sit-wait and move around to his front, close in front of him. Give the command-and-signal a few times, then progress to the signal alone just as you did above. With you in front of him, there is the possibility that he may become confused by the whole business and try to come to you when you signal, particularly if you have been using informal sweeps of your arm to get him to come in recall training. It is a natural enough confusion on his part, so deal with it firmly and gently. Stand quite close to him, and reach down with your left hand, taking hold of the training collar just under his chin. Then give the command-and-signal, plus a combined snap down and push backward on the collar and his chest to remind him that he is supposed to go down, and stay where he is while dropping. Work this a time or two until he has the idea, then go back to command-and-signal only. Mix up the way you get him out of the down position, one time giving him the command to sit directly from the down, the next time telling him to stay at the down, walking around him to heel position, then having him sit. This makes him feel a little better, for you return and are near him at the familiar heel position once in a while rather than standing formidably in front of him all the time.

When he drops on the signal only, in front of you, move back about six feet, the full length of the lead, and begin again with command-and-signal, working up to signal only. Then, leaving the lead on, keep increasing your distance until he responds at a distance of thirty feet.

When he is reliable in his drop from a sitting position, go back to heel position, on leash, and repeat the entire procedure from the stand-stay. There should be no difficulty in this repeat exercise, but the dog's being on his feet sometimes brings up a problem of his trying to walk toward you rather than dropping in his tracks. If this happens, you will find it out while you are still close to him, and you can take immediate action. Go straight to him and take hold of his collar as before, with your palm against his chest, and push him firmly back and downward. Don't rush at him as you do this;

simply get to him quickly and make the correction. Any rushing or shouting or sudden grabbing at his collar will frighten and confuse him. Just be firm. Tell him, "No!" quite sternly as he tries to step forward, then give him a sharp "Down!" as you apply the correction. Don't, whatever you do, try to keep him from walking toward you by shouting, "Stay!" once you have given the down command and/or signal, or you will foul up things to a pretty pass, as you will see if you think about it.

With any of this preliminary drop-on-recall training, do not settle for wrestling your dog down to make him obey the command. If the addition of the signal confuses him or makes him fail to respond quickly, you cannot solve it by wrestling with him. Go right back to on-lead basic training in the down, and work up again until he drops instantly on the verbal command, then progress again to the signal work. The collar corrections we have given you are simply to reinforce the primary down stimulus in his mind, not to drag him down resisting and howling.

When you have trained him to the point where he will drop on your signal from the sit or stand position at whatever distance, you have already passed over the major hurdle that causes trouble for many amateur trainers. Impatient to get on with things, many trainers try to get a dog to drop while in motion before he is steady in the drop from the sit or stand. Naturally enough, the dog has at least as much trouble performing the exercise in motion as he does while sitting or standing still, and probably more. The inexperienced trainer then tries to make corrections while the dog is walking or running, despairs at the whole business, and at best ends up with a confused and unwilling dog who works imperfectly and wishes he had stayed in bed. At any Open Class you watch, you will see one or more dogs fail this exercise. Generally the dog slows down when he gets the signal and creeps, tail down, to the handler, looking afraid and sheepish. The reason, almost without fail, is that the handler rushed things too much. It is well worth it to be sure, completely sure, at every step.

The next step is back on lead. Walk with your dog at heel, then suddenly step back, calling him to come, just as you did in Basic training. This time, however, keep walking backward until the dog is in full motion toward you. Then stop quickly and give the command-and-signal for the drop. Your stopping will stop him, and the command-and-signal should drop him. If not, get in a quick correction with the lead. Then, after he has been down a few moments, walk quickly backward again, telling him to come as you step back. Go backward until he is in full motion again, then stop and have him sit in front of you as in the normal recall. Keep the lead ready to force the sit this time, for he may have caught on too well and try to drop again as you stop. Then send him to heel and the step is completed.

In giving your "Down!" command, be sure not to use his name. As we have explained before, use of his name tends to alert him for action— probably coming to you. A good sharp "Down!" alone will get the desired results in training.

There is in this part of the training an area of easy confusion for the dog, and it must be watched for carefully and prevented. If you do the drop every time, he will quickly come to think that it is now a normal part of the recall, and will try to drop every time you call him to you. To prevent this, alternate the way you do it, one time dropping him, the next time having him come in to a normal recall, with a sit in front. Keep at this until you are sure that he is working on your command only and not anticipating on his own.

Don't at this time try to get him to drop on the recall with the signal only. It is enough that he learn to drop while coming in to you. That is the major part of the exercise. Wait until the next step, which is the drop on recall from the sit-wait.

After he is perfectly steady in the drop on recall from heeling, leave him at the sit-wait with the "Wait!" command and walk to about ten feet in front of him. Call him in and when he is halfway, give him the command-and-signal to drop. Let him stay down a few seconds, then call him again for a normal recall. If all has gone well up to this point, there should be no trouble at all, for he has learned to drop while running in to you, and the slightly different circumstances should mean nothing to him. Otherwise go right back to the heeling drop to refresh him, then try it from the sit-stay again.

Work at the drop on recall until he will drop on a recall from at least thirty feet away. Drop him at varying distances from you rather than always halfway, and remember to alternate with straight recalls so that he works entirely on command. If, on straight recalls, or on what you intended to be a drop on recall, you notice him slowing down in preparation for a drop, start running backward and coax him to speed up and come in to you. Do not ever give him the command to drop unless he is coming in full tilt—it is a gilt-edged invitation to anticipation if you try to fool yourself or him. And he'll accept the invitation with pleasure. Don't blame him or remon- strate with him if he does try to drop without your command. He has learned that you want him to drop while coming in, and is only trying to do the right thing by you. It is to him just like the sit when you come to a stop in heeling; there he has learned to perform an action automatically, and he will try to do the drop without command. It is not bad work on his part, but actually too good an understanding of what training is about. If you realize this you will not be tempted to howl at him, but will simply continue patient training until he realizes that in this case he must act only on your specific command. Vary all drops with straight recalls until you are sure he works only at command. To be sure of it, try dropping him twice on a long recall. Keep mixing it up for steadiness. Also, mix up the drops and straight recalls with other work to keep it from becoming boring for both of you. Do a drop or two, then heel a bit, then do a straight recall, then a stay, another drop, and so on. Vary the length of time you keep him at the down, too, before you call him in. Otherwise he may get the idea that he is to stay down for just five seconds, then get up and come in to you. Do a drop and an immediate recall one time, then do a drop and keep him there thirty seconds the next time.

As you progressively increase your distance on the drop on recall, try it a few times with the signal alone. Work at it until he will drop by signal alone, and immediately. If he does not drop immediately, you can only go back a step or two in the training. It is absolutely essential that he learn to drop on one and only one command or signal; there is no effective correction we know of at the advanced stage. Certainly you should never rush at the dog and bash him or yank at him. Use only thorough preparation.

In a show you are allowed to give him either the signal or command for the drop, not both, and he should work at either. In out-of-ring life, immediate response to either is invaluable, for sometime you may want him to drop in noisy circumstances in which he might have difficulty hearing you.

THE RETRIEVE

The first consideration for the retrieve is that, like any other exercise, it must be performed every time, at command. You may hear or read comments that the "forced retrieve" is bad, a harsh thing to inflict on a dog. To us, "forced retrieve" means simply that the dog retrieves at command, every time, rather than as a playful act. As such, it is no more or less "forced" than any other aspect of obedience. Almost every dog from puppyhood on will enjoy chasing after anything thrown for him, and returning with it for another throw. His enjoyment of it is based in his prey instinct, the urge to chase anything that is "running" away from him. This is all well and good, and should be used in the retrieve training, but in itself cannot be relied on. By steps, the dog must be trained to retrieve objects not particularly congenial to him, like metal—and to do so every time he is required to.

The standard method is that of using a wooden dumbbell in training. The dumbbell is a good device, being, if well chosen, easy for the dog to pick up and handy for him to carry. And here the operative phrase is "if well chosen"! More dogs than we care to think of have been stalled permanently at this point in training, simply because the trainer gave no thought to the dumbbell and its selection. It may seem curious to you that we put so much emphasis on this, as the dog must eventually learn in around-the-house life to carry almost anything, but at this touchy point in training, it is indeed vital. We have seen dogs, long in training, who balked totally at dumbbell training—and who learned to retrieve within days when the right dumbbell was substituted for a careless selection.

For obedience-trial work, the AKC has quite specific regulations about the composition of a dumbbell: "The dumbbell, which must be approved by the judge, shall be made of one or more solid pieces of one of the heavy hardwoods, which shall not be hollowed out." And: "The size of the dumbbell shall be proportionate to the size of the dog." Why the specification of heavy hardwood we don't really know, as the object of this training is simply to have the dog retrieve something, and it would clearly demonstrate this ability if the dumbbell were made of papier-mâché. But there you are—that is the way the regulations read. Of course, there is no reason that your dog cannot pick up and carry, and retrieve, a "heavy" hardwood dumbbell quite as easily as a lighter object.

The next consideration, and the one that brings the most grief to many trainers, is the construction of the dumbbell. Many commercially available dumbbells are made, and bought, with little thought except that the item have a roughly dumbbell shape. Actually, it should be specifically selected for two factors: the height of the bar from the ground, and the distance between the bells (ends). The bells may be of two styles: cubical, like a box, or tapered toward the insides and the connecting bar. The height of the bar, determined by the diameters of the bells and of the bar itself, should be great enough that your dog can grab it without having to rub his nose into the ground or scrape the bottom of his jaw. Dogs don't like that a bit.

What height this should be for your own dog only you and he can determine. Remembering that the dog will try to grab the bar and hold it just behind the long incisor teeth, calculate just how far the bar should be from the ground.

Next, and really foremost in importance, is the distance between the bells. Your dog's ability to see beyond the bells is a consideration, as well as the fact that bells too close together can press on his lips. As a rough rule, the bar should be long enough to allow about one-half-inch clearance on either side of his mouth, or the stiff whiskers of some breeds. This allows clear and unimpeded vision. This basically simple consideration has been the downfall of countless dogs in training, who have been provided with dumbbells so short in the bar that the bells sit squarely in front of their eyes when they hold it. A dog, much as anyone else, likes to see where he is going; even sitting still he doesn't like to have his vision obscured by two large blocks of wood right in front of his eyes. Try it yourself, holding your fists up dead in front of your eyes and about two inches in front—see how much you would like running and jumping like that. Then move your fists apart until they are about half an inch beyond the outside corners of your eyes. There's a great difference, no? And that's just the way your dog feels about things. We have found that this one factor—a change to a longer bar—works wonders in solving retrieve problems in dogs who have been training with a poorly selected dumbbell.

Getting the right dumbbell for your dog may be a bit difficult, as the majority of commercial ones are made, at this writing, with no thought for the preceding considerations. The chances are somewhat better than ten to one that your local pet-supply department will have nothing suitable (the right length and height of bar for your dog in the right size and weight for him), if it has dumbbells at all. If you are a home craftsman you can turn one out on your lathe from a light wood, or a local carpenter should be able to make you one quite reasonably. Even without a lathe you can make a dumbbell from a dowel and two blocks of wood. Be sure, though, to glue the bar quite firmly into the blocks, since constant throwing onto even soft ground can loosen a bar very quickly. Be sure that the bar is sanded very smooth, as nothing will discourage a dog quite so much as a splinter or two in the mouth. The bells should be about half as wide as they are high, and more or less square. If you want to plane off the corners and sharp edges, go ahead, but don't make the bells round or octagonal, as this will make the dumbbell roll when you don't want it to. As a general guide to construction, look closely at the pictures in this book and follow the pattern.

As to appearance, we suggest that you paint the bells white for easier visibility in grass or elsewhere. Especially if you are working on bare ground, or if you enter a trial indoors with wooden floors, a wooden dumbbell is almost invisible to the dog unless it is painted white. We have seen more than one dog fail because he simply didn't see the dumbbell. Leave the bar unpainted, of course, and be sure the bells are quite dry before using it. You may see, or hear of, dumbbells whose ends are decorated to resemble dice, or with some other motifs. Whether or not you like that sort of thing, it is not acceptable in AKC competition. The regulations specify quite clearly about the dumbbell: "It may be unfinished, or coated with a clear finish, or painted white. It shall have no decorations or attachments but may bear an inconspicuous mark for identification." Again, we don't really know the reason behind the rigid specifications, except perhaps that some years ago exhibitors had an attack of the cutes, appearing with some bizarre dumbbell designs, and the AKC decided standardization was as appropriate in dumbbells as in other facets of obedience work.

With the proper dumbbell in hand, you should introduce it to your dog with the greatest of care. Carry it around with you during a few training days while he is practicing heeling, or learning the last stages of the drop on recall. Let him sniff it and look at it and generally get used to it before you try to work with it. When you are resting during training, leave it on the ground or on a chair and let him sniff and investigate it as much as he will. But don't let him chew on it in play. If he does, just pick it up, praise him highly, let him hold it a minute, and then take it from him with the "Out!" or "Give!" command. But never, now or later, let him think that the dumbbell is a toy to be played with or chewed up. It is strictly for business.

One day, during a rest period, hold the dumbbell in your hand and play with it yourself, rolling it around and tossing it up to get him interested in it. When he comes over inquisitively, offer it to him, saying, "Take it" coaxingly. If he does take it, praise him to the cumulus layers, let him hold it a minute, then take it from him. Then after a minute, try it again, this time with him at the sit-stay. If that works, consider yourself thrice blessed, for this is one of the trickiest points in training. A few dogs take the dumbbell from the beginning. Most don't. Some shy away, some clamp their mouths shut, some just plain cut and run at the very thought. On the assumption that yours is the difficult one, here is what to do:

Put him on leash at the sit-stay and loop the end of the leash around your wrist so that both hands are free to hold the dumbbell. Then, standing in front of him, reach down and push the bar gently against his lips, saying,

"Take it." Some few give in at this point, and open up to take the bell. If your dog does, push the dumbbell gently into his mouth and say, "Hold it." Leave it there a few seconds, then take it from him with the command "Out!" Increase gradually the length of time you have him hold it until he keeps it in his mouth for a minute or more before you take it from him. If he tries to drop it before you take it, keep one hand under his chin and the other on top of his muzzle, pressing only hard enough so that he understands he is to hold on to it until commanded to give it to you. If your dog accepts the dumbbell gracefully, you will have little or no trouble in getting him to hold on to it for as long as you want. The holding problems arise with dogs who refuse to take it from the first.

If he has simply clamped his mouth shut from the beginning, put the dumbbell aside for the moment and try working with a length of dowel, approximately the same diameter as the dumbbell bar and about the same length as the entire dumbbell. Perhaps there is something about the bells that bothers him; perhaps they are too close together, or it may just be the *fact* of them. But a dowel is just a stick, and there is no reason at all that a simple stick should bother a dog in and of itself—it seems almost a hereditary trait that dogs will grab sticks and carry them. Now, of course, it isn't really natural—you are forcing him to open his mouth and take the "stick," but you will find that the dowel will almost certainly work.

To introduce it, put your left arm across his back (you're working at his right side) and around his neck, then gently push the forefinger of your left hand between his lips and against his teeth. He will almost automatically open his mouth wide enough for you to slip the dowel behind his canine teeth as you simultaneously give him the command "Take it!" Hold it in place and gently tip his head up with your right-hand fingers under his chin, letting him hold the dowel by himself and praising him. As you feel him relax, release his head, repeating, "Hold it!", and then take it from him gently with your command "Out!" or "Give!" Give him abundant praise, let everybody relax for a few moments, and then try it again.

When everything seems to be going well, switch back to the regular dumbbell, taking everything slow and easy. It *will* work, if you go about it gently and in an instructive way. But if you force it too hard, a dog with a hurt mouth and a memory of bad experiences connected with the dumbbell can dislike it for years to come.

One of the major faults in training is the wrong attitude toward the dumbbell and the taking of it. Some people, knowing that the dog will

Left thumb and forefinger force the mouth open gently, while the dumbbell is inserted.

most probably have to be forced to take the dumbbell, make a personal contest of it. This sort of trainer crams the dumbbell roughly into the dog's mouth, grabs his muzzle hard to keep it shut, and then yanks out the bell with a cry of victory, saying in effect, "There, you obstinate beast, I made you do it, by golly!" Therewith is training loused up to a fare-thee-well, and the dog will have a reluctant attitude toward the bell for the rest of his life. It must be looked at as a triumph for the dog for having learned a new idea, and he must be shown that you think highly of him indeed for his new accomplishment. The bar of the dumbbell is not so nasty an object as all that—he will happily pick up and carry dirty twigs and branches—but it is the idea that he will object to at first, the idea of anything at all being forced into his mouth. But if you let him know from the first that it is a great accomplishment to take and hold something when you tell him to, you're on the way.

Above all, no matter how reluctant he may be at first to take it, he must never be allowed to associate unpleasantness with the dumbbell. Never, for example, follow the method you may hear of—choking the dog with his chain until he throws open his mouth in a gasp for breath, then shoving the dumbbell in.

Incredible though it may seem, we once encountered a woman having difficulty with this phase of training who would offer the dumbbell to her dog, then when he refused to take it would hit him a smart crack on the head with it. She couldn't understand why her dog got hysterical every time she brought the dumbbell out. Other trainers having trouble bang the bar against the dog's front teeth with considerable force, and with the same predictable results. Any of these procedures is repellent to any thinking person, and we doubt that you will ever try to use them; but keep them in mind as a reminder that the dumbbell must never become an object of unpleasantness for your dog.

One of the most extreme problems is the dog who cries and fights and tries to run away when the dumbbell is presented to him. This is almost always the result of a crude introduction, but it can happen occasionally with the best treatment. To cure it, take up the heel position again, this time kneeling with your left leg behind him to keep him from backing away, just as you did if you had a similar problem with the down. Put your left arm around his neck again, this time holding the leash, quite close to his neck, between the third and fourth fingers of your left hand—leaving the thumb and first two fingers free to apply to the jaw. Then, keeping control of him with your left leg, your left arm around him, and your left hand on the lead, give the command and put the dumbbell in, applying the gentle pressure to his jaw. Reassure him with your voice as you do this, for his reactions are purely from fright. Keep your left arm around the neck and use the left hand as before under the chin to keep his mouth closed, using your right hand on top of the muzzle, if necessary, to keep his head still and his mouth closed. Be as gentle as possible, use his name and praise as he holds it, and then take it from him.

In extremis, if for some reason you have a really serious problem with the dumbbell—if for example you have tried to teach him to take it by the wrong method—then you must examine your conscience and your training history for the trouble. No dog in the world objects to the dumbbell per se, or at least very, very few. Whatever the cause, if the problem is severe, you can only soft-pedal the training for a few days, then reintroduce the dumbbell gradually. Carry it with you while heeling, tucked under your left arm. After a while transfer it to your right hand and carry it with you for a day of training. Then carry it in your left hand while heeling. This may panic him and cause him to heel wide in order to get away from it, but just this once pretend not to notice his bad heeling. He may sit wide when you stop, but ignore it—reach down and praise him, letting the dumbbell touch him lightly. If he shies away, affect not to notice it, but keep up the heeling and the gentle touching until he realizes it won't hurt him. Then begin again with the training, being extra gentle this time. You may find it hard to believe, reading this, that it can ever be such a problem, but a dog really badly introduced to the dumbbell can panic at the mere sight of one. Careful introduction avoids the problem.

None of this really need be as grim as we may have made it sound. With the proper precautions and patience, teaching the dumbbell retrieve can go quite smoothly. We have, however, seen so much trouble with this single exercise, through faulty training, that we feel the major problems need emphasis. Slow and steady wins the race, as someone must have said, and the same applies to dumbbell training.

The one remaining major problem is the dog who takes the dumbbell readily enough, but tries to spit it out quickly. If you run into this, first check his mouth and teeth to be sure there is no soreness there that makes it painful for him to hold anything hard. If all is well in his mouth, then you can concentrate on forcing the hold by simply holding his mouth shut. You will find that this problem is much more common in smaller breeds, for the interesting reason that a small dog, to look at your face, has to raise his head nearly to the vertical. If there is a dumbbell in his mouth at the time, it will tend to roll back in his mouth and he will think he is about to be choked. Larger breeds need only hold their heads level, and the problem does not occur so frequently. If yours is a small dog, you can solve that aspect of the problem by getting to your knees, or even sitting with him when first working with the dumbbell. Later, as he learns to hold it, you won't have to bother with this.

Whatever your problems, or lack of them, continue the "Take it!" training until he first opens his mouth on command and accepts and holds the dumbbell, then actually reaches forward a few inches to take it from your hand. It won't take long if you work at it steadily.

With all the problems in the take and hold out of the way, you and he are ready for the next step: carrying the dumbbell while in motion. If he has been introduced properly to the dumbbell and now holds it without resentment, there will be no problems here. Give it to him, and from a position a few feet in front of him, tell him to come to you. Reach out with your left hand and put your extended fingers gently under his chin to remind him to hold on to it and urge him forward with praise and coaxing. Just one step is a victory. Take it from him and praise him extensively. Then continue until he comes to you with it, you walking backward, for at least ten feet. Then go back to the beginning and have him sit-wait with the dumbbell while you walk a short distance in front of him. Call him in, make sure he sits properly in front of you, take the dumbbell, and send him to heel. Increase your distance until he is coming to you at least from thirty feet away, carrying the dumbbell and coming to a proper sit, giving it to you smartly, and going to heel.

The third step involves his taking the dumbbell while in motion at heel. Walk with him at heel, with the dumbbell in your right hand. Bring it around in front of you easily and naturally (don't just pop it suddenly into his face); holding it an inch or so in front of his mouth as you both walk along, tell him to take it. When he opens his mouth, put the dumbbell in and let him hold it. Praise him highly, even if he didn't reach out for it. Then take it from him and come to a halt. Start up again and offer it to him again with the command while walking, this time holding it a few inches away and getting him to reach out for it. Keep at this, increasing the distance until you have it out in front of him as far as you can reach and he is almost jumping out to take it. Then, starting close to his nose again, offer it to him at a lower level. Get him reaching down for it, by easy stages, until you are holding it only an inch from the ground and he is reaching down quickly to grab it. This is not as hard as it may sound (except on your back), for if he has been trained well up to this point, grabbing for it will be automatic on your command.

Next, when he is reaching almost to the ground for it, actually touch it to the ground and come to a stop as you do so, commanding him, "Take it!" If there is any hesitation, guide his head down gently until he takes it. Then step backward immediately and call him to come. When he comes in, take it from him, and send him to heel. Do this a few times, then actually drop it just in front of him as you stop, and repeat the take, come, and heel.

Finally, from the sit at your side, throw the dumbbell out in front of you a foot or two and tell him to take it. As he gets it into his mouth, tell him to come, and insist that he sit squarely in front of you and hold the dumbbell until you tell him to give it up. Don't at this time try to make him wait as you throw the dumbbell. Make it as much fun for him as you can, with repeated coaxing and praise, until you see that he is going out eagerly to get it, and is enjoying the whole idea. Increase your distance until you are throwing it thirty or forty feet and he goes out rapidly to get it and runs back happily to you with it.

One thing you must insist on, even at this stage, is that when he goes out after the dumbbell, he must pick it up and return to you with it. As you get along in training, you will drop all extra commands until you have reached the point where a single "Take it!" as you throw is enough. If for some reason he doesn't take the dumbbell when he goes out, go right out with him and put it in his mouth, then run backward calling him to come. Once you have reached the stage where he understands what to do, don't stand and plead with him to take it if he has run out and just stands there looking stupid. This double command situation is one of the great temptations—it seems so much easier to tell him once again to take it, rather than going out and putting it in his mouth. Soon he will get the idea that he should go out after it and wait until you command him to pick it up—and it will show up in the ring. We will lay you eight to five that at any Open ring you watch, there will be at least one dog who goes out after the dumbbell, then stands there looking either at the dumbbell or at his owner, visibly waiting for the command to go ahead and take it. Don't let this happen to you. Insist that he get it with only one command. If necessary, put him back on the old thirty-foot clothesline so that you have him under control while solving this problem.

When he is going out to get it reliably, you can introduce the stay, thus establishing the final bit of control. Take hold of his training collar with your left hand and tell him, "Wait!" Then throw the dumbbell out. As it hits the ground release him and tell him to get it. Next time, hold him a few seconds longer, then longer the next time, taking your hand off the collar only when you are sure he is steady and won't break. Work on this until he will stay at least a minute after the throw, then race after it and bring it in to you. When he does that, you have a dog well and full trained in the basic retrieve.

To add practical value, and to get him used to taking, holding, carrying, and retrieving whatever you want him to, you can graduate now to various items other than the dumbbell. Try a retrieve or two with a rolled-up newspaper held together with tape or string. Then get him to carry light paper bags or baskets. Before you know it, you will be able to send him to fetch your slippers. Try just that: Point them out to him, telling him, "Get the slippers!"; keep it up until he understands and travels to wherever they are, locates them, and bears them back triumphantly to you.

One final word in this exercise concerns throwing the dumbbell. A surprising number of competition-obedience handlers don't know how to throw a dumbbell. Although this bit of esoterica is intended largely for ring-bound people, you will want to be able to control your throw in training, too, so a little practice is in order. The best technique we have found is as follows: Hold it by one of the bells, with your thumb on one side and the fingers on the other, holding it only tightly enough to keep it from sliding out of your fingers. Swing your arm back, then forward and up so that your thumb is on top when you release the bell, then let it simply slide out of your hand. This way it is difficult to put any backflip on the dumbbell. Backflip is undesirable as it causes the dumbbell to bounce wildly when it lands. The perfect throw is the one in which the dumbbell travels through the air like an arrow, landing flat and sliding if at all only a few inches from where it hit. Try this a few times before you work with your dog, until you can make it land, and stay, where you want it.

THE HURDLE RETRIEVE

Jumping is in the realm of fun for any healthy dog. Combined with the already learned retrieve, hurdle work, if approached properly, is something you can both enjoy. But as much fun as jumping randomly may have been for him, the first step is to teach him to jump a standard hurdle on your command. The height of the hurdle used in obedience rings has been set by the AKC as follows: one and one-half times the height of the dog at the shoulder, or three feet, whichever is less. The exceptions to this are a few of the large and giant breeds, who have some trouble in getting off the ground, or for whom the jump would be towering in a ring. Bloodhounds, Bullmastiffs, Great Danes, Great Pyrenees, Mastiffs, Newfoundlands, and St. Bernards are required to jump once their height at the shoulder, or three feet, whichever is less. At the other end of the scale are exceptions for many of the medium-sized and small dogs (for the breeds, see the AKC "Obedience Regulations" in the Appendix), who jump once their height at the shoulder or eight inches, whichever is greater.

Whatever the height required for your dog, don't get overenthusiastic and keep him working to try for greater heights. Some breeds can jump considerably higher than the specifications, but one crash down onto the top of a too-high jump can hurt a dog seriously, and once he's hurt you may never be able to persuade him to try it again.

In the Appendix you will find diagrams and instructions for building a standard ring-type hurdle. Basically, it consists of two braced uprights plus one six-inch board, one four-inch board, and enough eight-inch boards to make up the proper height for your dog. With these, any height from four inches, by two-inch steps, can be set up. If yours is a small breed you may need only one of the eight-inch boards. But even for the smallest, make your uprights the standard four feet, for that is what your dog will encounter at a show.

The home-training departure from the standard ring hurdle is that yours should be equipped to serve both as a solid hurdle (with the boards) and as a bar jump. There are several ways to make it serve as a bar jump: with the bar holder, spaced nails on the backs of the uprights, or a hole-and-pin arrangement on each upright. The details of all three are given in the Appendix under "Obedience Equipment." The bar holder is easiest to use, being actually a pair of iron (or even wood) pieces roughly in the shape of an "h" that fit over the top board and support the bar. Later, in the "Utility and Beyond" chapter we use a combination of solid hurdle plus the bar for particular purposes. But for the moment, don't experiment and ask your dog to retrieve over anything but the solid jump. Again, an accident here —hurting himself or having the bar come clattering down behind him if he touches it while jumping—can seriously get in the way of his confidence.

Whatever the size of your dog, begin jump training in gradual steps, starting with what is not even a jump for him. Put the four-inch board into the uprights (for the tiny breeds it is a good idea to have a special two-inch board to start with). Then, with your dog on lead and heeling beside you, walk up to the jump and step over it, giving a jump command as you do. "Jump!", "Hup!", or "Over!" are widely used commands for the jump, with "Over!" by far the most common, but choose what you will. With the single board in place, your dog will simply step over the obstacle.

Praise him mildly once he is over, saying "Good boy, heel," but do not overdo the praise in this case, since you are trying to create the impression that the jump isn't much of a thing at all—which it isn't if you start low. Walk a short distance away, then turn and come back over the jump as before. Repeat until you see the dog also thinks nothing of it. Then take

First step: Walking over jump with the dog at heel. Lead guides him over but is not hauling him.

Third step: Dog comes straight over jump to you. Note loose lead. The bar was omitted in these pictures for clarity, but we recommend that you use it from the first.

Second step: Dog comes over jump as you walk around standard.

With dumbbell, the dog comes to you over jump in a recall. Jump is raised later.

out the four-inch board and put in the six-incher. Go over this two or three times exactly as before, then raise the jump to eight inches.

At this point, size becomes a factor. Some of the small breeds need jump no more than eight inches, and this is as far as they need go. If yours is one of these, then follow us only so long as we talk about eight inches and then skip to the next step. In general, carry on with each step only so far as it applies to your dog's height and the regulations applicable to his breed.

At the twelve-inch level comes the first departure. After going over it with him a few times, then the next time, as you walk up to it, aim yourself somewhat at the right-hand standard. When you reach the jump, veer slightly to the right to go close around it, giving your dog the command to jump—and being very careful not to get the leash tangled with the upright or his legs. Swing your left hand, holding the leash, over the jump itself. Several things can happen here aside from his going over in good order. He may swerve with you and try to squeeze himself between your left leg and the upright, or simply follow you around to the right of the jump. If so, you can't blame him a bit, because the idea of sticking at your side is much more firmly entrenched than this new business of jumping. If this happens, stop, take him back, and approach the jump again, this time pulling him gently to the left with the lead in your outstretched left hand, and try to guide him over. He may then, or even at the first try, simply stand there and look at the jump, or sit down. This is unlikely if you have gone over with him enough times, but if it does happen go right back and go over with him half a dozen times more, then try again going around to the right as he jumps. Do not try to yank him over with the leash; this will sabotage all your efforts to date, as the jump becomes a hateful object to him. Simply keep at it until he realizes, all by himself, that the jump is nothing to fear.

When he does it successfully (and most dogs do the first time), call him to heel and walk ahead a bit, then turn around to try it again. Because most dogs think the whole idea is a great lark, the quick command "Mike, heel!" as he hits the ground may be needed to get his mind back on the fact that you are working.

After he has done this well a few times, heel up to about three feet from the jump and stop, making him sit. After waiting a few seconds, start up again with the command "Mike, heel! Over!" and then turn around to try again. The purpose of this is to let him know that he cannot just waltz up and jump, but that he must wait for your command every time.

A highly important cautionary word is in order at this point: Do not, at this time or ever, allow him to *walk* around the jump. Many of the tragedies of the show ring can be traced directly to this point. The trainer has, in moments of play and in pleasure that the dog is jumping well, sent him out over the jump and allowed him to circle around on his way back. Then months later in the ring, the dog, working well and enjoying it, circles around the jump without even dreaming that he is doing wrong. And there goes the show for that dog and owner. You must impress on him, from the very first times, that he always goes over the jump. This is so important that even in the first times over the four-inch board you should go over, walk away, and turn around, then come back over rather than circling around to approach it from the same side every time. It drills into the dog that over is the only way to negotiate that jump.

When there are no problems on lead at the eight-inch height, you can go on to retracing the same steps in jump training without the lead, heeling him up to the jump and over with your commands and an encouraging tone of voice. If you encounter any problems and need to go back to some work on lead, be sure to keep it loose. With a tight lead you can cause him to lose his balance, and that will confuse him more than a little, particularly if you cause him to stumble over the jump and/or hit it.

From now on, in fact, everything—even new steps—is done off lead. The next step is the "over and back"—teaching him the essential idea of going out, jumping over, turning, and coming back to you over the jump. Start with him toward the jump and step over with your right foot just as you give him the command to jump. As soon as he has touched down on the other side, call his name and give the recall command "Mike, come!", and step back several steps to give him room to get over the jump and take a few steps before coming in to sit in front of you. This step is just an extension, now including the jump, of the first steps in the recall training; and although he may be a bit confused the first time or two, he'll catch on quite quickly.

Don't try to make corrections off lead, because there's really no effective way you can do so. If he decides while off lead to come around the jump instead of coming over on the way back, your timing must be excellent here to stop him before he gets around. If you see him veering even slightly toward a path around the jump, jump over it quickly yourself, call him to you, and then get him over in the right direction at heel. Then put him back on lead for a time or two until he seems sure of what is going on.

When your dog is doing the "over and back" steadily off lead, you can introduce the dumbbell. Set the jump back at its minimum height—two or four inches—and have him sit at your side at an appropriate distance from the jump. You will know by this time how much of a run he needs, although with the minimum height it won't be much. Give him his dumbbell, tell him to hold it, and start right back with heeling over the jump, progressing to the "over and back" and to leaving him with a "Wait!" command, walking over the jump, and calling him to you. When he has come over the jump with the dumbbell, take it from him as soon as he gets to you, praising him highly, without worrying just now about a proper sit and delivery. That can be introduced slowly, as can the finish to heel position. Most important is that he learns that delivering the dumbbell to you over the jump is a pleasant experience, without too many corrections.

Keep a close watch for any tendency to run around rather than jump over, even if the jump is only a few inches high. Always stay within controlling distance until you're sure your dog fully understands what he's supposed to do, close enough to get in a correction if it's needed.

Another possible problem, as the situation is a new one to him, is his coming right up to the jump and then standing there looking confused about the whole business. Don't laugh at him, however funny it may seem, but step right over to him and lead him back to the starting point, praising him heartily to take his mind off the fact that he may have done something wrong. Give him all reassurances possible, then leave him to try it again. This time, stand halfway over the jump with your right foot over and your left foot behind. Call him again, and as he approaches the jump swing your left foot over as a guide for him. This will give him the idea. After doing this three or four times, leave him, take up 'the same position, and as he starts at your "Come!" command, swing your left foot over right away. Repeat this a few times, and progress to simply standing close on the far side. By these easy stages you will build up his confidence and he will get the idea.

When he comes to you successfully, with you standing close to the jump, begin increasing your own distance from it until he comes over the jump, dumbbell in mouth, and into a recall with you standing about fifteen feet away from the jump. Then, build up the height of the jump by two-inch intervals until it is as close as possible to his height at the shoulder, but don't try to take it to full height yet. And remember that this is not a one-day affair. All the work we have described so far should be spread out through several training sessions, mixed up with other work for variety, getting a little improvement and progress each time. Don't try to push him too hard, as jumping is tiring for a dog, and if worn out he will just sit down on you.

Now comes the first try at an actual retrieve over the hurdle. Take the height right back down to minimum; it is not the height that's important at all now, but the fact of his going over the jump to get the dumbbell. You might as well make it as easy and uncomplicated as possible for him when he's getting the new idea. Do a few straight retrieves well away from the jump—definitely not beside it, which could confuse him badly—just to refresh his mind as to what he is supposed to do when the dumbbell is thrown. Then, stand with him in front of the jump, just far enough away so that he can make a normal approach and jump, but no farther away.

Give him the command to wait, toss the dumbbell over the jump so that it lands just a little beyond where he will, then give him your retrieve command. Swing your left arm forward and up and move forward with him to help get him going. Step over the jump with your right foot and give him the retrieve command again as he goes over, with praise and encouragement. Really give him an excited talking-to as he lowers his head to pick up the dumbbell; then, when he has it in his mouth, step back over the jump and move backward, calling him to come, then jump. Once again, take the dumbbell when he reaches you, and worry about a proper sit and heel only as he becomes more confident.

Finally, just stand there, give him the command and signal, and send him out. Perhaps a time or two, take a step or two forward with him, but he should have the idea pretty firmly in his mind by this time. Repeat all this, gradually cutting down on the extra commands until he does a nice retrieve over the low hurdle with the single original command to wait, and the command to fetch. Any problems you run into will be the ones you have already encountered in the straight retrieve or in simple jumping; apply the necessary corrections to suit. But remember to insist, without exception, that every time he is sent out he goes over the jump both ways, and always comes back with the dumbbell. Begin to make the necessary gentle corrections to get him to sit straight in front of you and wait with the dumbbell in his mouth until you take it from him, and to go to heel—neither of these steps should be a problem, because he has learned them well and reliably in the retrieve without a jump.

When he is doing good, reliable work over the two to four inches, gradually increase your distance from the jump and the distance the dumbbell lands on the other side, until you are throwing from at least fifteen feet and the dumbbell is landing fifteen feet on the other side of the hurdle. Moving back from the jump for the throw is very important—he must learn to go over the jump even when he starts out at quite a distance from it. If he only knows to go over it when he starts out practically touching it—when its apparent size is such as to make it almost the only thing he can see— then he will refuse it sometimes when you stand a bit farther back.

As you increase your throwing distances, also increase the height of the jump until the boards equal his height at the shoulder. Then, start making your throws of the dumbbell a bit erratic, so that it lands to the left or right a few degrees rather than directly across the jump. This teaches him that no matter where it lands (and you will inevitably, due to nervousness or whatever, make a bad throw in at least one show), he must go over to get it and go over coming back. But be reasonable about how far off true your throws are—just somewhat to the right or left. Don't throw it 90° off to

At full height, a Weimaraner goes over thirty-six inches of jump, plus the bar.

your right and expect your dog to go over, get it, and come back over with it.

As you increase the height, you may begin to encounter a problem with your dog scrambling over the jump, rather than jumping it cleanly, using the top to climb over. The solution to this is a "bar" of sorts to go on top of the top board. It can be made of light cardboard tubing—the kind rugs come rolled in—or light plastic plumber's pipe, but definitely something light. Mark it like a real Utility high-jump bar with stripes of black paint or with black tape. Start with your jump quite low again, and put the bar above it on the "h"-shaped supports, or on nails or pegs in the uprights.

With the bar in place, the first time your dog tries to scramble or use the top board, presto! the bar will fall right away under him. The idea is not to scare him, but to supply poor footing at the top, thus encouraging him to go over clean rather than trying to climb. When it happens, at whatever height, reassure and comfort and encourage him to make light of it, pretending that it was all a most unfortunate accident, but that he shouldn't mind at all. Don't reprimand him. Let him figure out for himself that climbing isn't the right way. Then put the bar right back on and send him over again. He will put that little bit of extra effort into his spring and clear the whole apparatus. Later, once he has learned to clear his maximum height without touching, you can remove the bar and send him over a few times without it to get him used to the plain hurdle.

As a final caution, remember always that you are training a dog, not a jumping machine. He will inevitably make mistakes, especially in this exercise, as he is being asked to do a variety of parts of an exercise all without any but an original command. Be patient with him, correct the mistakes as they come up, as pleasantly as possible. Don't press too hard—jumping is tiring after a while. Keep it fun for him, no matter how "forced" the exercises may be.

THE BROAD JUMP

This exercise is considered by many inexperienced trainers to be the hardest of all to teach and perfect, yet it is actually one of the easiest if you go about it the right way. In a show, the dog is required to broad jump over a set of low jumps (see pictures on pages 150–51), the total length of which is twice that of the height of the high jump for the particular dog. Thus the greatest jump will be six feet (or twice the height at the shoulders for the special breeds mentioned earlier), and as little as sixteen inches for a tiny dog. The great problem in most broad-jump training is that the dog is pulled and lifted over the jumps to persuade him to get enough oomph in his spring to clear them; yet no dog likes this sort of thing, and the problems proliferate. We advocate the use of the "crib," which rather resembles the foot or side of a baby's crib. When the crib is in place, it helps your dog get enough height and thrust in his jump to clear the broad jump quite nicely, and all without having to haul him up and over in getting the idea across.

With good control of your dog—and you should certainly have that by now—and with both of you jumping together at the beginning, there should be no special problems. But don't get carried away. By now he will almost certainly have learned that training is fun, something that brings praise, and the two of you should be working together quite nicely. Again, jumping is tiring, so don't overdo your practice sessions. He'll get tired and bored and confused, and you'll get tired and irritable just because he isn't doing as well as you think he should, or when he was fresh. And things *can* deteriorate. Don't let it happen.

The practical background of the broad jump is that it teaches the dog to jump over such things as ditches and streams at command. As it is somewhat impractical to dig a series of ditches of graded sizes in the show ring, and equally improbable that you will want to spade up your lawn, the four-section wooden broad jump was developed for training and the ring. The construction of this, too, is described in the Appendix.

To begin training, set up the two lowest of the jumps close together, making a total width of about sixteen inches. Set the crib on the second jump at a low angle, about 30° off the horizontal. Then, standing ten feet in front of the first jump with your dog at heel, begin running toward it with him still at heel. As you reach the jump, give him your jump command and sail over yourself. As you go over, bring your left hand, holding the lead, up and toward the front, but do not try to pull him over. The hand and arm movement is something of a signal to him, letting him know that he should go up and out just as your arm moves. As soon as you land, back around to the right until you are standing even with the middle of the jumps, about two feet to their right. As you back, call him to come to you just as in Basic training recall from heeling. Finish by sending him to heel, and then circle away for another jump. Do this enough times that he realizes what is up, then you can progress to the stage of standing at the side of the jumps while he does the entire thing by himself.

If you should have really fundamental difficulty in his refusing to go over with you the first time you try it, don't try to haul him over. If he screeches to a halt, drop the leash and go on over the jumps yourself. Come around to him and reassure him that all is well. Remember that it is the unusual appearance of the broad jumps plus the crib that is holding him back. Take away the first jump, leaving only the second with the crib on it, and approach that with him. The remaining jump plus crib will then be no more than a low hurdle, and no dog who has mastered the high jump will have any problem. When he is used to going over that with you, add the first jump again, quite close, and go over both. Slowly separate them until there is a length element in the jump as well as height.

At an obedience trial you leave your dog in the "sit at heel" position at least eight feet in front of the jump, with a "Wait!" command. You walk to a position at the right side of the jumps, facing them with your feet about two feet from the jumps, and anywhere between the front edge of the first board and the far edge of the last one. On your command to jump, he should completely clear the jump, turn around, and return to sit in front of you as in the recall. To be facing the right way for him to come to you this way, you make a 90° right turn while he is in the air. After he sits in front of you, send him to heel. All this seems quite artificial, but it does teach broad jumping *under control*, not allowing the dog simply to jump and then scamper about.

For the second step, use the lead or not, as you wish and as your dog's comprehension and progress dictate. Leave him sitting at least eight feet from the front of the jump, give the "Wait!" command, and move to your position at the side of the jump. Turn your head toward him and give him the jump command. As you do this, swing your left hand in a large motion toward the high end of the jump, indicating the direction you want him to take. Just as he gets to the low end of the jump, give him another "Over!" command. Then, just as his front feet touch the ground, successfully over the jump, call his name sharply with the recall command "Mike, come!" You will have made your right turn by this time, and he will come in to you—he certainly knows what "Come!" means.

With the crib at its proper angle and height, you have eliminated before it started one nasty tendency of dogs learning the broad jump: to try to walk over or between the jumps. He *must* jump to get over the crib and so has no chance to yield to the temptation to walk over the low boards. The problem you may run into is a tendency to jump at an angle from left to right, or even to try to sneak between you and the jumps rather than clear-

Going over with dog
helps him get the idea.
The lead acts as a guide,
but note that there is no
force used.

Back quickly to the side
of jumps and guide
him around into a straight
sit in front of you.

Stepping into the jumps will keep him from jumping toward *you*.

The finished product: a clean jump as you stand beside jumps. Note "crib" in position.

ing them. If this comes up as he is learning, step right into the jump about a third of the way before you call him to come over. Then, as he does go over, step back out and into position to call him to you. This way he must jump straight, and obviously cannot do any sneaking between. As the problem diminishes, step less and less into the jumps at each succeeding try, until he does it well with you in your original position.

Now you can begin to increase the width of the jump gradually until it is up to the specifications for his height or breed. See Chapter IV, Section 12, of the AKC "Obedience Regulations" in the Appendix for the number of boards to be used for any length of jump. Use the raised crib again if he develops any tendency to walk over the boards as the distance increases. When he is jumping the specified distance with no trouble, and with the crib in optimum position, gradually lower the crib from one time to the next until it is lying flat on the jump. Keep him working at that distance, without the crib as an aid, until he is perfect in his performance.

LONG SIT AND DOWN

Here is an exercise of the greatest practicality, for it teaches your dog to stay where he is when you tell him to, even though you are out of sight for a few minutes. It is very handy around the house, and when you are out of the house. If you are going into a store where you cannot take him, you will be able to leave him outside the door while you shop, and there he will be when you come out again. Even if you walk him only on leash, it will be better for both him and you if he stays quietly in one position though he be securely tied to a tree or post.

The exact practicality of requiring him to hold one position, either the sit or down, rather than just staying in one spot, may escape you at first consideration. It would seem much more logical simply to require him to stay where he is, regardless of whether he changes his body position while you are away. Yet you will find that it is much easier, mentally, for a dog to stay in one spot if he must hold one position. Sitting up from a down position, or lying down from a sit, or standing, all are invitations to move about a bit while changing positions. These temptations lead from a slight straying to major movement, and the first thing you know he's off and gone. But if it is impressed on him that when he is left in a position he stays in that position until you come back, then all the temptations to move are gone.

The major consideration in training the handler-away sit and down is confidence. He must become confident that you will return. In the Novice stays he can see you all the time and knows you're not going to desert him. That he likes. But when you leave him at a stay and go out of sight his first thought will be, "Whoops, there he goes, better get after him and see what's up." This is entirely natural and is to be expected, for you two are after all companions and he wants to be near you. So proceed with care and patience in this training, remembering always that when he breaks he does it out of love for you and a desire not to be left alone.

The actual mechanisms of the sit-stay he has already learned, so the only new factor is your being out of sight. Do the preliminary training in your house, where there are familiar surroundings for him. Pick a room where no one else is sitting to distract him, put him at a sit in the middle of the room (facing a door), and leave him with a definite command, "Stay!" Make it an order, not a request, and walk away, stepping off on your right foot. Go through the doorway and out of sight for only a few seconds, then return to him and circle to heel position. Release him and praise him for the good work.

As soon as you are out of sight through the doorway, he may get up and follow you. It's wrong, but the motives are clear enough, and you should not treat it as disobedience. If he comes after you, bring him to heel position and heel right back to where you left him. When he is at the sit again, take hold of his collar with your left hand behind his neck (don't try to use it as a choke) and just as you leave him, give him a sharp snap backward with the collar as you tell him to stay. Tell him in no uncertain terms and swing your right hand around in a firm stay signal. Head out of the room again, but this time turn as you reach the doorway and return to him, praising him for a good stay. Repeat this three or four times, dropping the preliminary snap on his collar as it becomes unnecessary. Then, go just out of sight again, staying only a few seconds, and return to him. Keep increasing your time gradually until you are able to stay out of his sight for five minutes. You won't be able to do this in one or two sessions, or probably even in a dozen. Work at it slowly, and remember that you are not teaching him anything new, but slowly building his confidence that you will return to him.

Insist from the beginning that he not only remain where he is, but that he remain sitting. This is a little difficult to handle in the observation end, but you should be able to work it with a small mirror, or through the help of an accomplice peering in at a window or around a corner (from behind the dog, so that he doesn't know he's being observed) and signaling you if the dog breaks. When he breaks—and he will a few times, for it seems much more sensible to him to lie down and take it easy if you're going to be away for a while—return to him immediately and tell him quite harshly, "Sit!" with a sharp snap upward on the collar. Then leave him again immediately with a stern "Stay!"

After a few of these corrections he will grasp the thought that he is supposed to stay seated, as well as just stay.

When you can stay away five minutes in the house, you are ready to try it outdoors. But be sure that in the house you have been well and truly not only out of his sight but of his ken in total. It will accomplish little if you sit in the next room and breathe heavily for the five minutes, for he will know full well that you are there. You must really be "gone" as far as he is concerned, out of sight and smell and hearing.

Outdoors, sit him in your yard or in a field or wherever you have to work. Leave him just as in the house and get out of sight somewhere. Behind a car is not much good, as he will see your legs underneath and will be tempted to come over and investigate this new game you've thought up. Nor is hiding behind a tree very efficient, for he will probably see a leg sticking out and succumb to the same temptation. Go around the corner of a building if possible. Do a complete repeat of the inside procedure, starting with only a few seconds out of sight and working up to about three minutes. Then start increasing the distance you go to get out of sight as you work the time up to five minutes. Work until you are walking about a hundred feet straight away from him before slipping around the corner, and can stay for five minutes with no breaks on his part.

All is well up to now and you can begin to tempt him with distractions as he sits there. After you have left and are out of sight, have a friend or family member come into the training area and walk around, not too close to the dog, ignoring him. At this stage, don't make a break too tempting; just introduce the presence of someone he knows into the training area. As you progress, you can have your assistant walk closer and closer to the dog, and even brush right by him to test his steadiness. But work up to it slowly. Then try it with another dog or dogs. Try to get friends to bring their dogs over, even if untrained, and have them first walk around in his area after you are out of sight (but keep the dogs on leash unless they are trained!) and then try leaving him at the sit while the other dogs are already in the area and near him.

Every time you return to him, indoors or out, insist that he stay until you have definitely released him. When you come back to him and have circled to heel position, praise him but insist that he stay. Make him wait a few seconds before you release him.

The long down is handled in much the same manner, except that you need not go back inside for the start of the training. Leave him at the down outside, and work up until he stays at the down for at least six minutes with you out of sight. Be wary that he does not sit as you leave him or while you are out of sight. He has been taught that you want him to sit while you are out of sight, and he may change his position to what he thinks is the proper one. Just let him know calmly and firmly that now you want him to stay down when you leave him in that position.

One additional point to keep in mind is that six minutes is a long time for your dog, and he should be in a comfortable down position when you leave him. Just what the most comfortable position is for him is something you will have to let him decide. If you have trained him correctly in the down, with his rear slewed over, he will probably find that comfortable enough. But don't make the mistake you will see being made in the obedience ring, where handlers down their dogs and then wrestle them into a position the handler thinks is comfortable. The handler doesn't really know anything about it, and is only imposing on the dog what he, the handler, thinks of as comfort. Let your dog determine his own most comfortable posture, and he'll stick with it.

Here again, as we suggested in Novice, a training class can be helpful in getting your dog accustomed to sitting or downing in line with other dogs—and getting used to noise and confusion and people moving about while he is at a stay. If you found a good class for your Novice stays, use it again for this Open work. You can teach the stays perfectly well all by yourself if you never plan to go into a ring, but if you do have ring ambitions, try him with other trained dogs before chancing your money on an entry.

FINAL THOUGHTS

Having gone through all the work in this chapter, you have a dog who can not only qualify for his CDX (Companion Dog Excellent) in the show ring, but who can honestly be called trained. He is much more than basically civilized, as he can jump, retrieve, stay, and even carry packages for you if you are so inclined. There are further steps, in the next chapters, and we hope you will continue with your training—by now you will have found out that training can be fun if done the right way. But, believe us, you can feel proud of yourself and of your dog once you have attained this level of obedience.

We must emphasize again before closing this chapter the absolute necessity of progressing slowly and steadily rather than rushing through a skimpy training schedule. Every step must be built on the rock-solid foundation of perfect sureness of the ones preceding. If you do it this way, the path of training can be smooth and easy, and most of the problems we mention and give you solutions for will never come up. Without exaggeration, fully 50 percent of all training problems arise through haste and inadequate preparation before moving on to the next step. Don't fall into the trap of what seems the easy way out—a quick dab and a snatch of work. It is by far the hardest way of all. Training should be fun for you and your dog, and all the unpleasantness of sweating and snarling and shoving about is totally unnecessary. It should be, by this point, an act of cooperation and coordination between you and the dog, enjoyable to both and well done because you have learned together, the right way. Go to obedience shows even if you never intend to enter one. Watch the dogs. There you will see cringing dogs (although only a few anymore), unwilling workers, sloppy workers, and happy, cheerful dogs who do everything right because they don't know any other way. Decide for yourself which way you want to have your dog be. Then train him accordingly.

CHAPTER 6

Utility and Beyond

Utility work, if you have seen it in a competition ring, looks frighteningly difficult. Taken cold, it could be. But as a further step in obedience training it follows with no more necessary difficulty than any of the exercises that have gone before. There are, of course, considerably fewer dogs trained at the Utility level than at the Basic or Novice levels, for the additional training takes time and, most of all, a successful technique. According to recent AKC records, approximately one out of every four dogs winning a CD goes on to Open and the CDX. Again, one out of every four CDX dogs goes on to win a UD (Utility Dog) title in the most advanced classes. Thus only one out of every sixteen dogs who complete Novice goes on to the UD. Novice training as we have presented it to you is simple and rewarding, but almost anyone can get a dog to perform sufficiently well just to get by in a Novice ring by cajoling, pounding, hauling about, cursing, and sweating. Many trainers, unfortunately, do *just* get by, as you will see in shows. But Utility work is another sort of thing entirely.

To quote the AKC again: "The classification which has been adopted is progressive, with the thought in mind that a dog which can be termed a Utility Dog has demonstrated his fitness to a place in our modern scheme of living." A trifle high-flown, perhaps, but the germ of truth is there. In Utility work you will arrive at an entirely new concept of dog owning—as different from Companion Dog as that is different from simply having a dog around the house. Even as the highest AKC title is Utility Dog, rather than something on the lines of Companion Dog Super-Excellent, so is Utility work of a different order altogether.

Even though you never plan to herd sheep with your dog, or use him in whatever other occupations might be considered under "utility," you will see in this advanced work that your dog *could*, with a little work along the right lines, be trained to do just about anything except play chess. Even on that we wouldn't take bets. Some years ago one of the authors met a dog who could distinguish among the pieces of a large-sized chess set. By this time he may be beating his owner regularly. In any case, Utility work is as much a gateway as a goal: the Utility-trained dog is so much a working partner of his owner that it is no longer even a question of "obedience" as such. That is taken for granted. It is by this time cooperative learning for use and enjoyment.

SCENT DISCRIMINATION

At first look, scent discrimination may seem difficult, but it is, in concept and practice, a very straightforward process. The actual use of the dog's nose is nothing unusual—you could do much the same yourself, taking into account the relative powers of your dog's nose and your own. If you were asked to pick out from among five identical objects the one that had been rubbed with Limburger, you would have little trouble. Your dog will have no more difficulty, for any article that has been touched by you carries, to him, just as strong and identifiable an odor. In this training, you are not teaching him to smell, but getting across the idea that the object that smells of you is the one to be retrieved from among others.

In the obedience-ring test of scent discrimination, each handler brings a set of ten identically shaped articles, five each of leather and metal, no more than six inches long and each numbered prominently for easy identification (see the section on this exercise in the AKC "Obedience Regulations" in the Appendix). You should be completely familiar with these regulations before you begin scent training.

The box or carrying case containing the articles is given to the judge, who picks out one each of metal and leather to be used in the exercise. The ring steward then puts the remaining eight articles on the floor or ground about fifteen feet in front of the dog and handler, roughly in a circle and with each article at least six inches from any other. Dog and handler do an about-face, with the dog at heel and facing away from the articles. The handler scents one of the selected two to get his scent on it, and then it is placed by the judge in the circle with the others. Turning, the handler sends his dog to find and retrieve the article. It is a suspenseful moment, for the dog goes out and worries about among the articles, sniffing along at one after another until he finds the right one, grabs it, and runs back to his handler with it. Some examine each article quite carefully, even if they have happened to sniff the correct one first, making sure there is not another with a stronger and fresher smell on it. Some pick up the right article immediately they come to it, ignoring the others. Either way, it is fascinating to watch a dog at this work, and even more so to know that your own can and will perform the exercise.

The "scent articles" used in the ring, as commercially available, come in a variety of sizes and shapes. Some are like miniature leather or metal dumbbells, some are simply small tubes or cylinders of leather or metal. The best we have seen, and the type we recommend, are made in the shape of orange crates without sides and with ribs at opposite corners to hold the ends together. These as well as the other types can be bought in sets with attractive carrying boxes, or you can make them yourself from aluminum, leather, and dowels. You'll need six each of metal and leather, each set numbered from one to six, the sixth being used as a practice article only and not for the ring. You should also have at least three similarly shaped articles of wood—easy to make with squares of plywood and dowels—to provide a training link between the wooden dumbbell and the new scent articles in the beginnings of teaching scent discrimination. Your dog is already quite used to having your scent on the dumbbell, and using the interim wooden scent articles helps bridge the gap to full scent discrimination with the metal and leather articles.

Homemade or bought, the advantage of the "open orange crate"-type construction is that such an article will not roll about if walked on and/or kicked by the dog while working; more importantly, no matter how it falls, one of the bars is always in the air for easy grabbing and carrying. It is thus much easier for your dog while in training. We have had considerable discussion on this point with various manufacturers of obedience equipment, whose majority opinion is that "an article is an article." Their feeling, and we mention this because you may hear it from other sources, is that the trained dog must eventually learn to scent-discriminate among, and work with, almost any shape; so why should he be pampered with specially designed articles? The answer is simple enough: During this training as during any other, you must make it in the beginning as easy as possible for your dog. Let the hard work come later. It is rather like jump training— you can either face your dog from the beginning with a full-sized jump and tell him to flaming well jump it, or you can work him up gradually from the lowest jump. However relevant it may be to the above discussion, the fact remains that even though several designs are stocked by many dog suppliers it remains difficult to locate identically shaped articles of wood. Instructions for manufacture at home, with illustrations, are in the Appendix.

There are methods and methods of training in scent discrimination. Most involve one way or another of pulling the dog away every time he tries to pick up the wrong article from a pair or group, until he gets the idea. It seems much simpler to arrange the training situation so that the dog *cannot* pick up the wrong article even if he tries, thus eliminating corrections that can easily be interpreted by the dog as reprimands for having picked up anything at all. To this end we ask you to construct one further piece of equipment, the article board.

From a piece of heavy rubber matting—like those used at dog shows and in apartment-building lobbies—or plywood, or an old piece of carpet, cut a three- to four-foot square to use as an article board. Then fasten four of your metal articles, four leather ones, and two wooden articles on to the "board" in a random arrangement, keeping the articles well separated. The "orange crate" articles suit particularly well to the article board as they can be fastened by a loop of string or wire around the lower bar. And the old piece of carpet is an especially good material for the board if you are doing your preliminary training inside, for it is less conspicuous visually to your dog, and when he walks on it, as he will, it will feel much the same as your regular rug. Whatever articles you use, and whatever your board material, fasten the articles so that they seem to be lying on the board. One trainer to whom this board was hastily described tried screwing broom-handle clips on to a board and then clipping the practice articles on. Naturally enough training faltered, for the articles were raised inches above the board in a forest of spiky miscellany and the whole affair had no resemblance whatever to a set of articles lying on the ground or floor. The article board does introduce an artificial note, but properly handled it is minimal and unimportant. When you have made your board and fastened your articles to it, let the whole apparatus air off for a day or two outside, and after that handle it only with pliers or tongs; never touch it with your hands, bare or gloved.

While the board is being de-scented you can begin to accustom your dog to the three practice articles, one of each material, that you have not fastened to the board. Beginning with the wooden article, first give it to him to hold, then let him carry it at heel, then have him do a recall with it, then a short retrieve. In short, a repeat of your dumbbell training. The idea is to get him used to first carrying it and then retrieving it, just as he did the dumbbell. When he retrieves the wooden article well, go through the same procedure with the leather article, and finally with the metal. This last may cause some difficulty, for many dogs object to the feel and taste of metal in the mouth. Some go to quite ridiculous lengths to avoid picking up metal, as happened at one obedience show held in a chilly, drafty armory. A small Poodle in Utility found and retrieved the leather article in good order and then was sent after the metal one. Finding it, he picked it up and dropped it immediately—it had gotten cold in the chilly air—and pushed it all the way, with his nose, across the floor to his owner. You may, of course, encounter somewhat less picturesque trouble if your dog simply rebels at taking a metal article in his mouth. In introducing the metal articles, a dog often accepts them much more willingly if you let him feel your fingers in his mouth as you insert the metal. One "bridging" technique is to make it a point to give him, from a metal spoon, some food he particularly likes. If you start this sort of thing when he's a young puppy, the metal problem will probably never come up, but it can help even an adult dog to overcome his distaste for metal in his mouth.

When he will do a short retrieve with any of the articles well in sight, find yourself a patch of moderately tall grass, just tall enough to hide the article when thrown, and do longer and longer retrieves with the article falling out of sight into the grass. If the first out-of-sight retrieve puzzles him—if he goes out but can't seem to find it—go right out to the article with him and stand close to it, encouraging him with your voice to find it. Don't actually point it out to him. Your standing there will make him look in close circles around you until he spies it. Then let him know he has passed a minor miracle, for the impression you want to give him is that you didn't really know where it was and that he did true and noble service in discovering the thing.

Somewhere along the line he will very likely start using his nose to locate it, and this is all to the good. But if he does all his searching by eye, don't try to think up some way to get him sniffing, for it will do more harm than good. That part comes later. Keep at this until he hunts and finds even an article thrown far, but keep things straightforward. Don't succumb to the temptation to make it nearly impossible for him, just to see if he can do it, or try to make him use his nose to find a well-hidden article. Discouragement comes easily at this stage, and he must never be allowed to become discouraged. After a few instances in which you have to go out and point or actually pick up the article, he is going to sit back and realize,

"Okay, smart guy, you're so much better at this than I am, you just do all the finding from now on."

If you are forced to work inside at first, the long throw into tall grass will have to be replaced by throwing the article so that it lands behind chairs or tables or any other inside obstacles. The work will go just as well inside as out but takes a bit more patience and ingenuity. Inside or out, work the routine with all three articles until you are satisfied that he fully understands that he is to look for, find, and retrieve the article, whatever the circumstances. Then you can begin to work with the article board to instill the idea that one article from among many is to be selected and retrieved, and he will figure out for himself that the correct one is the one with your smell on it.

Do not, whatever you do, fall prey to the temptation to try him out in a discrimination before you use the board. There you have all those articles, just sitting around if they haven't been put on the board yet. And it's terribly easy to think, "Well, I'll try it just once, to see if maybe he won't do it." Believe us, he won't, and you're in for trouble.

The function of the article board is to prevent trouble brought about by corrections after the fact. The unscented articles are fastened to the board and cannot be picked up. This is correction enough in itself to the dog—he will discover shortly that only the one *with* your scent can be picked up. Otherwise, not using the board, you will have to correct him time and again as he tries to return to you with wrong articles picked up. Such corrections are no good, and do definite harm, as we point out later.

With the article board, the greatest care must be exercised in regard to unwanted scent. Your body smell gets around astonishingly easily, and before you begin to work with the board it might be a good idea to read over, in Chapter 9, "Tracking and Advanced Tracking," the discussion of scent and how it acts. A great deal has been learned in recent years about body scent and its properties—just by stepping over the board you'll leave a little of what we call "artificial scent," a light scent which drifts off your body and away, and onto the board, but which disappears fairly rapidly. When there's direct contact, when you touch something, you leave "natural scent," a much heavier and longer-lasting type. Handle the article board with tongs or pliers once it has been assembled and aired out. True, it's impossible to keep *every* hint of scent off it, but the less that gets on it, the easier it will be for your dog during this beginning scent-discrimination training.

Observing all these cautions, put the article board down in your training area and let your dog become familiar with this new piece of equipment. Put him on lead, and heel him up to it, around it, and even over it—just him, not you, to prevent your down-drifting artificial scent from getting on the board. And be informal about it, too. Let him go to it and sniff the articles.

Then, with him by your side, off lead, stand about fifteen feet away from the board. Give him the usual wait command and throw your practice wooden article so that it lands two or three feet in front of the board. Send him to get it with the command, "Find it!" It's just a retrieve, which he can do perfectly well now, but when he gets to it, reinforce the whole idea with praise. Time it well, and as his head just tips down to pick up the article, tell him, "That's it! Good boy! That's the way!"

The movement of your arm as you throw, the article flying out and landing, all will probably rivet his attention on that article, but there is always the possibility that he may run right beyond it and start poking about among the articles on the board. Don't make any correction; let him sniff, and encourage him with "Find it!" and "Fetch!" He simply won't be able to pick up any of the board articles. Even if you have to go out to the area and gently point out the correct article to him, the correction will have been made.

Probably you won't have this problem, but whether you do or not, praise him mightily when he picks up the right article and brings it back to you. Don't insist on the proper sit and heel, but keep it fun, keep the working conditions happy as you introduce this whole new idea. Repeat it again with your metal and leather practice articles, going through the same procedure. But don't overdo this and other early scent-training sessions.

Finally, throw the article directly onto the board, starting again with the wooden one, working as before until he picks up the right one unerringly. If your throwing arm is good enough so that you can land the article on the board every time, all well and good. If you miss, send him anyway. The practice is all to the good. When it does land on the board, he will have to use his nose definitely for the first time, as he may not have noticed exactly where it fell. Here again, let him sniff to his heart's content, using only a gentle reprimand well timed if he insists on trying to pull one of the fastened "wrong" articles off the board. Use a *very* gentle reprimand, softly, "No, Mike, *that's* not it." It's possible you have, yourself, somehow inadvertently scented one or more of the "wrong" articles on the board, or he may just be confused—all of which means you haven't done the preliminary training thoroughly enough. Do *not* let him get the idea, through a sharp reprimand, that picking *something* up when you've sent him is wrong. It could set back your training quite a bit. Walk out and show him the correct article, moving it a bit, and encouraging him to take that one. Enough of this and he'll get the idea—you will have reassured him that, despite the confusing appearance of the situation, one of those articles is the right one and can be picked up and brought back to you, and he will learn all by himself that the right one is the one that smells of you. Be very careful when you are doing this bit of assistance not to touch anything on the board but the right article.

The next step, once he is retrieving the thrown article of any of the materials, is to leave him at heel facing the board in the sit-stay position, go out to the board with an article, and place it on the board. Return to him and send him to get it. This first time may confuse him a bit, but if he hesitates to go to the board, swing your arm at it and take a step or two with him to get him in motion. What with the progression of this training, he will probably not hesitate a moment, for he has learned first to get the articles, then that what he is to get will be found on the board—so he will go to the board and begin hunting.

When he is actually at the board, let him sniff around as before, giving the correction if necessary, until he happens on the right one and grabs it. Keep a sharp eye yourself on the one you left there, and when his nose passes over it, redouble your encouragement and commands to find it. That will give him just the extra confidence he needs if, having found the familiar scent, he isn't quite sure whether to try to pick it up. When he brings it back to you this time, give him high praise. Repeat with all three articles until he has a thorough understanding of what to do. Then remove the two wooden articles.

With all this in hand there comes your, and his, first true scent find. Get him in heel position facing *directly away from* the board, and leave him at the sit-stay while you go to the board and place the practice article. Return to him and get both of you turned around to face the board. Then send him to the board to find it. This is all exactly as before, except that he didn't see the article placed, and there should be no confusion whatever. Repeat with the two articles until he is sure of his smelling and finding.

Even at this advanced stage he may try to pick up a wrong article. If so, it is very likely your fault. Examine your aseptic procedures carefully, for you may have unwittingly scented one or more of the fastened articles. If so, no blame to him for trying to pick one of them up. If you can't imagine having done anything wrong, you probably did anyway, so don't fight it. Call off the training for a day and give the board a good airing overnight. Then begin again the next day and be even more careful than before. Scent-discrimination training takes time in any case, so one lost day makes little difference.

Work at the board until he never makes a mistake in selecting the right article to bring to you, and shows complete confidence in going out, sniffing over the lot, and grabbing the right one. When you place the article, be sure to put it in different spots on the board—it will do precious little good to anyone if he has simply learned to pick up the article in the upper left-hand corner. By this time you will be a fairly experienced trainer, and we probably don't have to tell you anything so simple as that, but the things some people do in training are peculiar, to say the least. Always remember that this business of training isn't just a cut-and-dried, follow-the-rules proposition. You've got to think about it to get anywhere. And think the right way.

Once he is steady at board work, take the articles off the board and let them "cool off" a day or two, and give yourself and your dog a rest from the training. It's easy to overwork your dog, particularly when you think you see rapid progress. He can get what is literally "nose fatigue" by overworking his scenting mechanism. When you are ready, take the now loose articles with tongs and scatter them around in a small circle, arranged much as they were on the board. Better yet, ask someone in your family, or a friend, to arrange the articles for you.

Then, with your dog at heel, stand facing away from the articles about fifteen feet away. "Scent" the practice article by holding one of the bars firmly in one hand, and don't overdo it. At trials some years ago it was common to see handlers rubbing every part of the chosen article, trying to insure that it was heavily scented, and you may still see this. But it really isn't necessary. By holding the article, your scent gets quite thoroughly onto it, and rubbing won't help. You'll be able to tell quite quickly from his work whether or not you have scented the article well enough—you may want to hold it a moment longer if he seems confused.

Leave him at heel, go out and place the article among the others, return, swing around, and send him to find it. Very probably he will do it just as before and will return to you with the proper article.

The dog gets the scent. Note the scented article lying near board.

The dog goes first to board to smell all the articles.

He finds the scented article—the one he can pick up.

At a later stage in training: All articles are loose, but by now he will touch only the one with his handler's scent.

As he searches among the articles this first time, you must keep a very sharp eye out for a mistake. Be absolutely sure you know which one is the right article, for you can imagine the harm done if you gave him a correction while he was in the act of picking up that right one. But if he tries to pick up a wrong article, here is where your board training pays off again. Just as he reaches for it, give him exactly the same gentle "No" you would give for trying to take a wrong article from the board. He will have made mistakes before, and by now he will know full well that that "No," friendly though it may be, indicates that he is on the wrong track. If he desists, all well and good—encourage him to find the right one. If for any reason he continues with the wrong article, go out to him and let him know that it is the wrong one. Again, gentle and friendly, no harsh reprimands. Keep in mind that, no matter how wrong he may be, he thinks he is doing right in picking up whatever article he does select. If he thinks he is doing right, a strong, loud correction will give him a pretty poor opinion of everything about the training situation—here he went out and got the thing as you told him to and now you're hollering at him. What is he going to do?

Generally, if mistakes are made at all, one or two corrections will get him back on the right track and training can proceed. If not—if there seems to be real confusion in his mind as to what to do—the only thing you can do is go right back to the article board and work with him until he *never* tries to pick up the wrong article. Then return to off-board work and proceed as before. Work off board until he can and will find and retrieve the wood, the leather, and the metal article without error.

Now you are ready for the real test: a mock-up of the show procedure, in which you yourself do not know which is the right article. For this you need an assistant. Putting aside your practice articles, you will have five of each of the two kinds of articles—leather and metal, by AKC rule—all un-scented, in some sort of box. Give your assistant the box of articles and ask him to take out one of each kind with the tongs, lay them aside, and spread the remaining eight in a small circle in your training area. Make sure he understands the necessity for care in avoiding scenting the articles himself and the importance of arranging them carefully.

Then, facing away from the articles, leave your dog and pick up one of the two working articles. Hold it tightly in your hand for as long as you've found is necessary to scent it, as you return to your dog. Have your helper carry the article out to the others on a clipboard or with tongs, or in any other way not touching it, and place the working article among the others. Then turn and send your dog to find it, giving him lots of praise. Repeat the procedure with the second article, again with praise, for he's accomplished a major breakthrough.

If there are any mistakes, it is up to your assistant to catch them immediately and let you know so you can get in a correction. Along with your lecture on the dangers of careless handling of articles, impress on him that he must be very sure of which article is the right one, for here as before a correction at the wrong time is extremely harmful. Handle any mistakes as before, with a quiet "No" and further encouragement if it is necessary. Work at this practice until you can do the complete show routine—sending him out with no further commands or encouragement after the initial command to find it for each article.

If your dog makes a mistake or two even at this point, give him a chance to straighten out. You've made mistakes even in things you've been thoroughly trained to do, and he is no better than you are. But if the mistakes become many, the only solution is a return to the board and further intensive training until all is corrected. This may seem a tedious path to glory, and it won't be necessary if you have taken all the preliminary training slowly and carefully. But it is an unfortunate truth that the temptations to rush training, particularly at this advanced level, are mighty. You may have done so, and now you'll suffer for it. But buckle down and go back and start all over at the board. The second time will do it, and then it will be done.

DIRECTED RETRIEVE

The directed retrieve is really quite a simple exercise, although it may sound formidable at first that your dog is to go pick up one of three gloves at your command and return it to you. This exercise is only a mild extension of a regular retrieve of the dumbbell; in an obedience ring, you will be facing the glove the judge has directed you to send him for, and you also signal to him with your hand and arm to make sure he is going in the right direction to start. Take a look at the "Obedience Regulations" in the Appendix for a detailed description of the exercise as it must be performed.

Your dog has by now become accustomed to going out to bring back to you any number of things. Thus introducing him to the idea of getting a glove is easy enough. The gloves used in the ring exercise are specified as "predominantly white cotton work gloves." Once you have the gloves, give them a good washing before you ask your dog to carry them, to soften them and make them more acceptable and easier to pick up and carry.

The left hand moves out by dog's head and points to the proper article in the directed retrieve.

Then the training begins, again in easy, progressive steps. Get your dog to take a glove and hold it (which for a dog trained to this point should cause no problem) and to give it to you on command, then to carry it as he walks at heel beside you, and then to run out after it when you have thrown it in front of you as you are heeling with the glove in your hand. When he gets to this point, have him bring it back properly, just as he did with the dumbbell, give it to you smartly, and then finish to heel position.

For the next step, have him sit at heel, give him the "Wait!" command, throw out the glove with your left hand, and send him for it. Then leave him sitting at heel position while you go out and drop it, returning to heel to send him for it. In other words, this is the retrieve he already knows so well, with the difference that a glove is used rather than a dumbbell and a signal is given to indicate the direction of the glove.

You might run into a slight problem if he finds the glove such a soft, floppy, and amenable object that he wants to shake it and toss it around. You can cure this by taping all the fingers together with adhesive or masking tape, so that the glove becomes, in effect, a larger and softer bar of a dumbbell. If the problem develops, try taking and holding the taped glove with him first, then walking at heel, and work your way back up to the retrieve. Then, untape just one finger and work with the glove that way, continuing one finger at a time until the glove is back to its normal condition.

With all this in hand or, more properly, mouth, begin to teach your dog to turn while you are in place so that you can face away from the gloves in a ring, and on the judge's order, turn to face the glove he has designated for the dog to retrieve. The procedure is an oddly artificial business that seems to have nothing to do with the real world, but that is the way it works. You face away from the end of the ring where the three gloves are dropped by the judge or steward, then when the judge tells you which one he wants retrieved, you turn in place with your dog to face that glove. Go back on lead for this training, get him seated at heel position, then turn around to your right 180°, gently urging him to get up and walk around you, staying at heel as you turn, then sit as you stop turning. He won't understand all this at first, but he does have the background of turning with you in the scent-discrimination exercise, so it's not completely strange to him.

The gloves are designated "One," "Two," and "Three," starting with the left-hand glove at the end of the ring. Turning to face One it is clearly easier to turn to your right, as it's less than a full about-turn. Turning to face Two is usually more easily done to the right, but turning for Three can be done about as easily to the right—a turn of over 180°—or to the left. A turn to the left is as easy to teach as to the right, except that here you don't spin around in place, which would require your dog to back around to stay in heel position. Try it, and you'll see that you can maneuver to the left around your dog, with him doing the turning in place, until you face the direction where glove Three would be in a ring, placed as per the regulations.

He will now turn with you to face whichever of the three gloves you want him to retrieve, and will retrieve a glove you have thrown out. The transition to directing him to one of two or three gloves is quite simple. Start with directing him to one glove only, leaving him at heel with the wait command and going out about twenty feet to drop a glove. Return to him, then kneel right down beside him. Swing your left arm and hand out along on his right, toward the glove, ending up pointing directly at it, and give him the retrieve command. You should have no trouble at all with this, but if he betrays any confusion—you haven't thrown it but gone out and dropped it—encourage him if necessary by starting toward the glove with repeated urgings to him to go out and get it. Continue this, reducing the kneeling until you can stand normally, bending only slightly to swing your left arm to show him the direction to the glove.

Now come two gloves, and the essence of the exercise. If you are working by yourself, leave him at the sit and go out with two gloves, dropping one about twenty-five feet away from him and somewhat to the left, and the other about the same distance away, somewhat to the right, with a distance between the gloves of, again, about twenty-five feet. When you return to your dog, you will both be at one corner of a roughly equilateral triangle, with the two gloves at the other corners. As you face either of the gloves, the other one will be 60° to one side or another, and it is difficult for the dog to be confused about which one you want him to retrieve, particularly when you give a strong, definite signal toward the one glove.

Still, problems *can* occur. He may have a tendency to go for the glove you dropped last, which is not unnatural, as you've just had him get a glove you've just dropped. If so, move in closer to the line between the two gloves, so the angle is greater. If necessary, keep it up until you are very nearly standing between the gloves, and he will then have no chance whatever to go to the other one. Then work back slowly, repeating the exercise, until you are in the original position about twenty-five feet away from the line between the gloves. If you do encounter this difficulty, and have to move closer and then back, remember to keep the training sessions reasonably short, and not tire him out with repeated directed retrieves.

When he is completely reliable—when he will go to either the left or the right glove and retrieve it—then you can introduce the third glove, halfway between the other two and in the middle of a line between them. Leave him at the sit, go out and drop all three, return, and send him for any of the three. The angle between the gloves is now considerably smaller, and it is possible that some slight confusion may occur here, but the angle is still about 30° and it is hard for him to mistake your clear direction signal. If the problem does occur, the corrective procedure is the same as before: Move a little closer to the center glove to increase the angle and reduce the chance of confusion on his part. Then, when any confusion clears up, go back to your original position and send him, at random, for any of the three gloves. Once again, though, be careful not to overdo this training. Keep it to no more than a half-dozen retrieves at any one session.

Finally, with a friend, assistant, or helper, practice the actual exercise. Stand with your dog seated at heel beside you, and ask your assistant to drop the three gloves in a line behind you, with the center glove about twenty-five feet directly behind you and the other two each about fifteen feet away from the center one. Ask your assistant to designate glove One, Two, or Three, and turn with your dog to face that glove, remembering that One is the left glove, Two is the center glove, and Three the one on the right, always.

If you've worked along carefully, step by step, in your training, this is a simple exercise. If there are any problems still, you might try, after giving the direction signal, moving out a few steps toward the designated glove, giving your dog encouragement and even repeating the direction signal to be sure that he understands that he is to go out to the glove you're facing. We doubt you'll ever have to bother with this, but, as with all training work, think through whatever problem you may encounter, and go back a few steps in the training, if necessary, to overcome it. Be sure in your practice that you randomly mix up the numbers of the glove to be retrieved, and don't go along One, Two, Three, or your dog could come to expect this pattern.

DIRECTED JUMPING

This is one of the most impressive things to be seen in obedience work, for in it the dog goes away from his handler and then comes back over one or another jump, widely spaced, as specified. It is a considerable advance over the hurdle retrieve, where the dog sits directly in front of a solid hurdle and has the simple task of jumping over it and back. For the first time your dog must go away from you with nothing specific to do other than simply moving away until he hears your command to stop. Then he must do, not always the same thing, but first one and then another, in response to one of two signals. Because directed jumping is impressive when done well, it has acquired the reputation of being one of the hardest exercises to teach. It isn't. Perhaps we should say it is only as hard as you imagine it or make it. It is rather like calculus, appalling to contemplate without preparation, but easy enough providing you have the proper mathematical background.

Training in directed jumping breaks down into three stages: teaching the bar jump, teaching the "go," and teaching the directed return. Of these, the easiest and procedurally the first is the bar jump. For this you need the jump, which is easily made of two four-foot standards and a two-inch-thick bar. The bar you already have if you were with us through Open; by the same token, your dog will be accustomed, from Open training, to going over the bar on top of the solid hurdle.

The procedure with the bar is almost exactly the same as with Open training for the solid hurdle. Start your dog out, on leash, with the bar set very low (about half his shoulder height) and go over it with him at heel. Then progress to stepping around as he goes over. Then send him over and back on lead and finally off lead. Work up the height until you have reached one and a half times his shoulder height, as with the solid hurdle. For the details of the training and corrections, reread Chapter 5, "Open," on jumping. Even if you trained in Open with our chapter, go back and read it again and follow the methods step by step. It is all too easy to forget details of procedure if you went through them months ago.

Having become accustomed, in Open training, to going over the bar, it may never occur to your dog to go under. At the very least, the concept of going over the bar will not be new to him—all that will be new is the fact that the space underneath is not now blocked by the boards. If he does try to go under any of the times he is on leash you can instantly restrain him and there is no problem. If, as the height goes up and he is off leash, he tries to go under, the problem is minor. The solution is the same one we have given you for every exercise: Go back to on-lead work and concentrate on that until the idea of going under the bar is as foreign to him as walking fences at night and screeching at the moon. The chances that this will come up are really quite small, but if it does, go right back. It's no reflection on anyone.

Step two is the "go," or "sendaway," in which at your command the dog goes in a straight line away from you until you instruct him to turn and sit. This is a totally artificial situation—as is the entire directed-jumping exercise—and it requires intelligent cooperation on his part, and an excellent basis in training. He is to leave you, walk or run about forty feet away from you, turn and sit, and then at your instructions swerve out of his way on returning to you to go over a jump just because it is there and you tell him to. Therefore, be patient, and expect mild confusion as you train for this exercise.

Getting him to "go" can be accomplished in one of two ways. Try the simpler way first—it might work with your dog, and avoid a lot of on-lead training. Put a favorite toy or some other familiar object about ten feet in front of him, then return to him, and from heel position tell him, "Go!" and swing your arm toward it, even starting out yourself toward it, all with great enthusiasm. Then, just as he reaches it, call his name enticingly, "Mike," and as he turns to see what you want, give him a "Sit!" command. Go to him and praise him immediately. If he wants to pick up the toy or other article and bring it to you—which is natural enough considering his past training—don't correct him. Just get across the basic idea of going away from you on command, turning, and sitting. If this system works, try putting the toy farther away, and calling his name with the sit command well before he gets to it, increasing the distance of toy and command until he is going out at least forty feet in a straight line before he turns and sits. By then, the idea should be getting through to him, and you can start again at a shorter distance without the toy or article, working your way back up to the forty-foot distance.

If your previous training in distant control has been good (here, again, we repeat that each exercise is built on what comes before; he *should* be thoroughly trained to sit at a distance under all circumstances, and you have no business starting Utility training unless he will), you should have no problem with the sit at a distance, but you might have a little trouble getting him to turn around precisely and face you. The correction is simple: Go out with him on the shorter sends, and as he is turning, make a gentle, encouraging correction to let him know that you want a sit exactly facing you.

Whatever you do, always *go to him* after each sendaway and sit, to praise him. *Never* save yourself steps by calling him back directly to you. You are going to be teaching him that that is exactly what you don't want him to do—that he must always, after a sendaway, go up to and over one or the other of the jumps. If he has never been allowed to come directly to you after a sendaway, your dog will never be in the situation that you see at trial after trial in the Utility classes—in which the dog confusedly comes straight back to his handler between the jumps and, of course, completely fails the exercise.

If the "favorite article" technique doesn't seem to be working, try it a different way. Put him on lead, and *without* a heel command, start running forward, commanding him instead to "Go out!" If you sound happy and playful, he will go along and forge ahead of you. Then, with delicate and careful timing as he is about to come to the end of the lead, call his name enticingly, with an upward lilt to your voice, just as he's about at the end of the lead ahead of you.

Be sure to do this with the snap on the dead ring of the collar; naturally, the last thing you want is to have the collar tighten and choke him if he for some reason doesn't pay attention to your call. Calling his name should make him turn, and just as he does, give him the sit command, if necessary using the lead gently and going to him to put him in the sit position. Do this a few times until he gets the idea that the "Go!" or "Go out!" commands mean to start running in front of you. Then take him off lead and try it again. Think it through here. He may very well have the idea that the command "Go!" means he is to go out just about six feet, the length of the lead, and then turn to face you. Logical enough. So, off lead, if he shows this tendency, keep going with him and urging him on until he grasps the idea that "Go!" means to keep on going until he hears otherwise. Repeat the "Go!" command as necessary, but then, as training progresses, cut down on the repeated commands and encouragement until he starts up at a single "Go out!" command and continues in a straight line until you call his name and tell him to sit.

The final step, sending him over the jumps, requires you to have a fair amount of space in which to set up the training situation. Your hurdle and your bar jump should be set up about eighteen to twenty feet apart and in line with each other end to end. There should be at least forty feet of clear working space on a line between the jumps and at right angles to them. For the city dweller this may be a bit of a problem, for it dictates a training area of about thirty by forty feet, but there is simply no way around it—there is no abbreviated way to do the exercise. If you are really strapped for space, look into the facilities of any training classes in your area. Most training directors will let you use their facilities during training sessions if you pay the regular class fee.

With your jumps set up, place yourself and your dog about twenty feet from the jumps and on a line running between them. Send your dog from you so that he passes between the jumps as he goes, and turn and sit him twenty feet beyond them. Call to him, "Mike, over!" and point vigorously at one jump with the nearest arm and hand. As you move your arm and give the command, run to your side of the jump and encourage him to come to you over it. As he comes, back up enough so that he has room to land and come in to a sit, then send him to heel. There should be no difficulty with this part of it, for he knows the jumping idea quite well, and he has come to you over the jump many times. But if for some reason he just sits there, you will have to back a half step. Send him in exactly the same way, then move before you call him so that you are directly across the jump from him. Call him to you just as in Open training. Then work your way slowly over until you are calling him from the sendaway position. Work this procedure with both jumps, alternating them. Do not get him used to going over one jump more frequently than others or you may have trouble, for on the sendaway he will tend to turn and face that jump.

When he is doing this well, cut down your movement gradually after the original jump command until you can stand where you were when he left you and he'll go to the jump, over it, and come in to you. As he jumps, turn in position to face the jump so he can come straight to you and sit straight.

Work from the beginning with both jumps, sending him a few times over the solid hurdle, then a few times over the bar, so that he doesn't get the idea that one is more important than the other. Also, when you have reached this point in training, change ends from time to time to have the bar jump on the right sometimes, and sometimes on the left. When you change ends, be sure to change the bar jump to have the bar always on the side of the uprights away from the dog, so that if he happens to hit it, it will fall off the nails or pegs and not bring down the entire jump. Nothing in the regulations states on which side each jump is to be placed, so you may run into either placement—solid jump on the right or left. Mix it up, therefore, in your practice.

When the dog will go out between the jumps and come back in to you over either jump on your command and signal, you have finished the training, and need only practice to get him and you sharpened up. Try the ring procedure several times. Get an assistant to act as judge, and stand with your dog beside you in position in front of the jumps. At your assistant's command, "Send him!" send the dog away. Then have him come in over whichever jump your assistant designates. Face yourselves straight again,

The dog is commanded and signaled, "Go!"

The handler runs partway out to show dog what she wants him to do.

He is sent on his own for
the last part of his run.

At the command, dog
turns and sits.

Having walked back, the
handler commands and
signals dog to take one
of the jumps.

then send him again, and at your assistant's order have your dog come in to you over the other jump. Then rest for a bit and try it again. In practice by yourself, mix up the work so that the dog does not come to expect a pattern of alternation. Send him out and have him come back over the bar jump three times in a row. Then do it over the solid hurdle twice. And do the same sort of thing with the assistant giving you orders—a dog is quick to realize differences in situations, and it is quite possible that he will work perfectly when you and he are alone, and then will expect an alternation when a "judge" is present. Don't let him get "ring wise" or you will run into trouble when you do go into the ring.

The one remaining problem you may run into is an erratic sendaway once you have started working regularly with the jumps. Almost without fail this will be your fault, the result of having sent him out to come back over one jump or the other most of the time. At shows you will see the result of this: the dog who goes out and circles halfway back to sit directly in front of one jump, usually the solid hurdle. And the judge inevitably instructs the handler to send the dog over the other jump. Result? Failure, probably, although we have seen dogs recover from the situation. You need never run into it if you insist on a straight sendaway and mix up your jumps from the first. But if you do, for whatever reason, have the trouble, it requires only your insistence that your dog go out straight every time.

SIGNAL WORK

Working in response to signals is another accomplishment that impresses the uninitiated onlooker a great deal, and for no good reason. It is as easy for the dog to learn as is working at verbal command, if not actually easier. Signals, after all, are a more basic means of communication than words. It is, when you think about it, more surprising that a dog can learn to work on spoken commands than on signals. If you keep this in mind and forget how impressive it looks, you will have no trouble at all in training your dog in signal responses.

The signals you will use in the signal exercises performed in the obedience ring are: heel, stand, wait, sit, down, come, and go to heel. Simply, here they are, defined:

Heel—a smooth forward motion of the left hand in front of the dog's head, at arm's length as you stand erect, regardless of the dog's size.

Stand—a smooth motion of either hand, waist-high from right to left, palm extended toward the dog, stopping in front of but not touching the nose. Clearly a demonstrative signal to stay.

Stay—a sweep of your hand, across with your right or slightly forward with your left, and then back toward the muzzle.

Wait—a motion similar to the stay signal, except that it is carried on to the left of the dog's nose before returning the hand to a normal position. The stay signal stops directly in front of his nose; the wait continues on past in a small sweep.

Sit—a forward scooping motion of the right or left hand and arm from a normal hanging position at the side, the hand moving in a quarter-circle with the palm forward and upward until the forearm is nearly horizontal, with the fingers pointing forward.

Down—either raise the right hand to shoulder, head, or full arm's-length height, then return it to your side, with the raising being the signal; or raise your hand and then sweep it down and forward, with the downward sweep being the signal.

Come—swing right or left hand out from side to shoulder height, then around to opposite shoulder.

Go to heel—depending on which way your dog goes to heel, the signal is a quick motion of the right or left hand around in the proper direction.

The first step in training is the signal for heeling. In this case you do not progress from command-and-signal to signal alone, but begin again on leash and work with the signal from the first. Here you will see one of the great benefits of the system we have been asking you to follow all along: starting off at heel always with the left foot, leaving your dog at the stay always on the right foot. When you begin your heeling signals, starting off with only a signal, your dog will be so accustomed to moving off when he sees your left foot go that he will in all probability start right up the first time.

Put him at heel at your left side, leash on and in your right hand, and step off, giving the heel signal as you do. If there is any hesitation on his part, give him a gentle snap with the lead to get him in motion. He is no longer a novice at this business, and the slightest snap on the lead, if necessary at all, will get him going. Heel him a way, halt, start up again, halt, and continue working until he fully understands the heel signal, then work with him off lead until he is steady at it.

The next step is a review of your "drop" training on signal. Leave him at a sit, walk out in front of him, and drop him on your signal. Return to him, have him sit, heel forward a bit, give him the command-and-signal to stand, then to stay, and walk out in front of him and drop him on your signal. All this is training done before, and any problems that arise should be corrected by the methods already outlined in the appropriate chapter.

The stand in signal exercise is done with the dog and handler heeling at a normal pace. Use the same signal you did in the Novice stand for examination to stop him as you stop, and in a standing position. Then use the "Wait!" signal to keep him in place as you walk away to go to the position where you will turn and drop him by signal at the judge's direction. If necessary, go back on lead for a short refresher training period, working with just the signals and corrections, without commands.

The drop on signal from the stand is nothing new, but when your dog is down, sitting from that position on command is a new item to him. After downing him as you face him, and on lead, hold the lead in your left hand and give the command "Sit!", simultaneously taking a half-step forward, bringing your right arm and hand forward and up in a sit signal. The lead comes up with the left hand, of course, and you can bring your right hand up under the lead to give it a slight snap or slap to give the dog the idea that you want him to get up into the sit position. Sitting on command and on signal is nothing at all new—all he has to learn is getting to the sit from the down position. For a dog trained to this level in Utility, it should just be a matter of simple on-lead demonstration, then going off lead and working on the signal alone. But even with this experienced a dog, do it step-by-step. When he has understood that the sit signal plus the step forward plus the upward slight snap on the lead plus the command all add up to getting up and sitting, abandon the signals one at a time. First eliminate the command, then the use of the lead, then the step—until it takes only the upward swing of your hand to get him to change position. Only then work on it at a slightly greater distance, until he will do it at least forty feet away.

The final steps are the recall and the go-to-heel signals, and both are worked from a command-and-signal status to signal only. In both cases, the signal will remind him of the motion of your hand in using the leash in your original training, so the transition should be very easy for him. Then you are ready to try the complete exercise. Sit him at heel beside you, start up with the heel signal, and heel around with turns, about-turns, fast and

slow, and a halt or two. Then, on one straightaway, give him the stand signal and stand beside him a few seconds. Then give him the wait signal and
walk about thirty feet away from him and turn to face him. Give him the
down signal, then after a few seconds the sit signal, then the recall signal,
and finally the go to heel. And there you have it, as simple as that.

If possible, go through the routine a few times with an assistant signaling
the parts of the exercise to you (read the AKC rules on this quite closely so
that you and your assistant understand which parts the judge gives verbal
orders for and which parts he signals to you). Be very sure that your dog ignores the signals and commands of the "judge" and is working only at your
signals.

Through the point of leaving him at the stand and walking away there
should be no problems in the final exercise, except of course the ever-
strong temptation to give him a "Heel!" command as you start up each time.
Trouble can arise with the succeeding signals, and it will be your fault—
sloppy signals that confuse your dog. He may, unless you execute it carefully, mistake the raising of your hand for the down, and sit, so differentiate
clearly between these. Be sure that your down signal is a quick raising of
the hand without any outward motion, and that your sit signal is a definite
forward scooping motion. And in the sit signal, watch that your hand starts
immediately forward and up. Do not swing it back a few inches to get
momentum, as is natural and as you will see quite often in the ring. At that
distance it isn't likely, but your dog just could see that preliminary backward motion as a signal to go to heel. He might try it, and then all would
be over with you. Also be careful of confusion between the sit and the
beginning of the come signal. Improperly executed, the movement of your
right hand up to the beginning position for the recall signal can look quite a
bit like the sit signal, and he might stay there confusedly at the sit instead
of coming in to you. Make all your signals clear and distinct, and be sure
that he knows every one and never mistakes them.

When he does the show routine perfectly, work in variations so that he
does not come to expect the same sequence every time. Although it is
always done in exactly the same order in the show, and you could pass if
your dog knew only that order, that is not the point of the thing. The idea
is to have a trained dog who works at specific signals—not just one who has
learned a circus routine and proceeds from one part to the next at any old
signal from you.

The "heel" signal: At the forward motion of the hand, the dog starts forward. Note that handler started with left foot.

The "down" signal: Hand is well up. From any distance, the dog cannot miss or mistake this.

The "sit" signal: Here
with left hand, at the
highest point of the
signal.

The "come" signal:
Hand is brought around
horizontally to this
position.

LONG STAND FOR EXAMINATION

As a further exercise in control, the stand for examination as practiced in the Utility obedience ring is excellent. When your dog does this well—stands still for three minutes while you are twenty feet away, and allows himself to be thoroughly gone over by a judge—you can be quite sure that there will never be any unpleasant incidents along the line of aggression, in the ring or out. And remember that what he is doing, he does strictly on command. It will have no effect on his use as a watchdog around the house or as a protector of your person or property.

He already knows the one-minute stand for examination, and the progression to four minutes off lead (one minute longer than is required in the ring), with you twenty or thirty feet away, is a simple one. Give him some on-lead work as a refresher, then, off lead, move farther and farther away each time, staying longer as you move out, until he will stand there for four minutes without moving. Correct any breaks or movements just as you did with the Novice work in stand for examination.

The examination you must do, at the beginning, yourself. Leave him at the stand-stay in your training area, and stay twenty feet in front of him for about two minutes. Then walk normally toward him, and as you approach him repeat, "Stay!" to keep him steady. In Utility, the examination can be considerably more thorough than in Novice, so get him accustomed to more of a going-over than a simple touch on the head, shoulders, and hindquarters. The AKC specifies: "The judge will approach each dog in turn from the front and examine it, going over the dog with his hands as in a dog show judging, except that under no circumstances shall the examination include the dog's mouth or testicles."

Run your hands over his head and look at his ears. Run both hands down his shoulders and down his front legs, inside and out. Repeat all this, standing on both sides. Run your hands down his back, over his haunches, and down his back legs. In other words, get him used to whatever sort of "breed show" examination a judge in Utility might conduct. Then walk away from him and return to your position in front. Stay there for another minute, then return to him, going around to heel position, wait a moment, then release him and praise him highly.

After putting him through an ordeal of this sort—and it is a strain—let him rest before you try it again. Do not do the full stand for examination more than two or three times during any training session. Then, when he submits to your examination without your having to repeat "Stay!" to him as you do it, take the final step to examination by another person. Put him at the stand-stay off leash and this time step out only six feet away and watch closely for any sign of a break as your assistant approaches the dog and goes over him thoroughly. Then increase your distance until you can stand the full thirty feet away while your dog is being examined. Have your assistant approach the dog from any direction, coming up to him both fast and slow, and vary the time of the examination; have him examined almost immediately after you leave him and then keep him standing for more than three minutes; next time, have him stand for at least three minutes prior to the examination; plus variations in between. In the ring, all the Utility entries will be lined up and left at the stand at the same time, and the judge begins at one end of the line and works his way down, examining as he goes. If your dog should be first in line, he would have an examination and then the long wait; if last in line, the long wait would come first. So be prepared for any combination of waiting before and after the examination. When you've had one helper do the examination, try to get several other people outside your family to conduct examinations, to get your dog accustomed to the idea of anyone at all being able to examine him once you've left him at the stand in this situation.

Again, be particularly careful that you do not strain the dog's patience and strength. Standing still for three or four minutes can be very tiring. Try it yourself, standing at solid attention without so much as moving your eyes, for four minutes. Then you'll have an understanding of what your dog is doing for you, and won't be tempted to overdo it.

BEYOND UTILITY TO CHAMPIONSHIP

Although there have been championships in breed shows since dog shows began, obedience dogs could for decades get as far as the UD title, and that was it. Dogs with UD titles could continue to enter the Utility and Open Classes, and many did, but there was no recognition of the really superb obedience workers other than a growing collection of ribbons and high scores. And a UD was a UD whether he had managed to get through three qualifications with passing but relatively undistinguished scores after many tries—not really bad in itself—or had sailed through with absolutely top performances.

Then, on July 1, 1977, the AKC established the title of Obedience Trial Champion, to recognize top obedience dogs who could win first place in a minimum of three Utility and Open Classes, and acquire a total of one hundred points, the points depending on the number of competing dogs in the classes. A complete description of the tough requirements for an Obedience Trial Championship is included in Chapter 6 of the "Obedience Regulations" (see Appendix).

As one of the best possible advertisements for the breed as obedience dogs, Golden Retrievers completely swept the field in early accomplishments in this area. The historic first, OTCh Moreland's Golden Tonka, won her championship just twenty-three days after the competition was established. The second was a Golden, and the first dog with a combined breed championship and obedience championship was also a Golden Retriever. Then, just to sew up the dominance, yet another Golden established somewhat later what will probably be a permanent record by winning an obedience championship in just *two days,* in two shows and four classes, Utility and Open.

Other breeds have completed their obedience championships—a total of thirty OTChs were awarded in the first year of competition; if you really feel like working at it, there's no reason your own dog could not eventually earn the proud title. Absolute precision in the exercises is an essential— Tonka, for example, won two scores of 200 on her way to the first obedience championship, and 200 scores are rare indeed, meaning that the dog did every step of every exercise without the slightest fault. But even more important is the *way* the dog did things, and the dog and handler together.

Here speaks the AKC: "The performances of the dog and handler in the ring must be accurate and correct and must conform to the requirements of these Regulations. However, it is also essential that the dog demonstrate willingness and enjoyment of the work, and that smoothness and naturalness on the part of the handler be given precedence over a performance based on military precision and peremptory commands."

It is certainly worth trying for precise performance, for ribbons, and for first prizes, but you will achieve them only if your dog is indeed a happily working dog. No dog ever won a ribbon or a prize by slinking through its exercises, clearly doing what was required but just as clearly doing so out of fear or as the result of harsh discipline. If you qualify in a number of classes but consistently *just* make it, or place in the ribbons but never first, it is well worthwhile asking the judges what it was that kept your dog's scores low. By firm AKC regulation the judges may *not* give you their score sheets on which they have noted the problems that caused them to mark you down, but many judges are pleased to cooperate and discuss with you where you went wrong, if they're not too tired after a long day of judging and if you ask for constructive criticism, rather than approach them in an argumentative, challenging mode about why your Mike didn't do as well as all those other dogs of clearly dubious ancestry who scored above him.

But most important is the pleasure the dog takes in his work. If that is the major comment a judge, or other people at ringside, can give you, go back, don't worry so much about precision in performance, and work on that element alone. Go right back to the Novice exercises, and make it the most important thing that *he* enjoy it, that you work as a team.

HOW TO BE HAPPY THOUGH ALMOST PERFECT

It has been the particular pleasure of the authors, when showing their own dogs in obedience, to be stopped by spectators outside the ring after a competition with comments on how happily the dog worked, how much he seemed to enjoy being in the ring and doing the exercises. Win ribbons or not, qualify or not (and, Lord knows, we have been in more than once and not qualified, so don't despair when it happens to you), the dog has worked happily and willingly. This, we maintain, is the goal to be worked for. If you've read through these chapters, the way to that goal should be plain enough—it rests mainly on thoughtful handling and mainly on praise. Your dog will forgive you almost anything if you are kind and gentle with him, and if you praise him for what he has done, even if all the work was yours. In this chapter on advanced work we have not emphasized it at every turn as we have in others, for you are by this time an experienced trainer, or at least we hope you are. It should come to you naturally at this point.

Remember: Always praise him, understand him, make excuses for him, and he will love you for it and work his heart out. Treat him harshly and the game is up. Particularly in this advanced work, when the frustrations can be immense, keep a tight control over your temper, think out everything from his angle, always give him the benefit of the doubt, and remember that any mistakes he makes are mistakes you taught him to make. Do that, and you will have a happy working dog who will bring you not only private joy but compliments at ringside—a far greater reward than any ribbon, prize, or trophy ever devised.

CHAPTER 7

The Obedience Ring

Competition in the show ring is the ultimate proof of the training of your dog, and of your ability to work together. For successful work in the ring, the AKC awards the titles CD, CDX, and UD, which the dog then wears after his official name in the records, plus the highest award of Obedience Trial Champion (OTCh), which comes before his name. He may be Slugger to you, but on the books he'll be Rajah von Scharnhorst, UD, or perhaps even OTCh Rajah, a scholar and a gentleman, with all the rights and privileges appertaining thereto. Ideally, the titles are awards signifying a certain level of training, even as a college degree is nothing of itself, but an indication that you have supposedly learned a few things. Unfortunately, even as in human affairs, the pursuit of titles at times becomes an end in itself to some dog owners and handlers. Dogs are brought into the ring when the handler hopes and prays that the dog may sneak by with a barely qualifying score. As a result, we have seen some shockingly bad dogs "working" in the ring, a procedure that reflects little credit on the handler and in fact justly merits seething looks from other handlers whose dogs are going to have to sit next to the flighty pooch. We hope, if you go into the ring, that yours will be there just to show how well trained he is in comparison with all those louts.

Shows come in two varieties, point and match, and these too each have two forms. Titles are won at point shows, and match shows are more or less just for practice. An obedience trial may be held of itself, usually sponsored by an obedience club, or as a part of either an all-breed or specialty-breed show. In either case the show may be benched or unbenched. "Benched" means that there is at the show a specific stall for each dog, in which he is kept when he is not in the ring. At an unbenched show you keep the dog with you wherever you go about the grounds. Depending largely on the season, a show may be indoors or outdoors; if benched outdoors, the benches will be under tents and the whole affair looks at times like a medieval fair with banners flapping from the tent roofs.

Match shows also come in all the varieties found in the point show, except that rarely will a match show be benched. The two special divisions of match shows are "OA" and "OB," AKC designations that tell you something about what will go on at the show. An OA show is held by a club trying to get AKC permission to hold a point show, and the procedure is exactly that of a point show, except that the results don't count toward a title. OB matches, on the other hand, are held strictly for the fun of it, under only loose AKC supervision, and may have additional classes such as "Beginners" and "Graduate Novice." For your practice, experience, and fun, one kind is just as good as another. We do recommend that you enter a match show or two before trying for a title. It will give you and your dog invaluable experience in ring procedure and handling.

ENTRIES

Most dog shows and obedience trials are handled by one of the many superintendents who operate in various areas of the United States. Some trials are handled by obedience clubs directly, who do everything themselves: the superintending, equipment supplying, and all the paperwork. From one or the other you obtain your "premium list" and to them send fees and filled-out entry forms. Premium list is dog jargon for a booklet that gives the date and location of a show or trial, the classes offered, judges' names, entry forms, and various miscellaneous information.

The best source of information on dog shows with obedience trials included, and separate trials, is the AKC's official publication, *Pure Bred Dogs/American Kennel Gazette,* which comes out monthly and contains a list of all shows and trials upcoming for several months. A subscription is a handy thing, but if you write to the AKC (51 Madison Ave., New York, N.Y. 10010), they'll send you without charge the show-listing pages from the most recent issue of the *Gazette.* There you'll find, by date, the names and locations of shows and trials, along with the name of the superintendent, or the name and address of the show secretary. Ask the secretary or superintendent for the premium of the show or trials you're interested in, and ask to be put on the mailing list, which he or she will probably do in any case.

When you get your premium list and decide to enter, fill out the form and ship it off with your check. Entry fees, which change from time to time, usually upward, cover everything: your admission (but not guests or family, who get separate tickets at the entrance), the bench (if there is one), and the dog's appearance in the ring.

Most shows "close" two weeks in advance of the show date, which means that no entries can be accepted or canceled after the closing. During the week before the show, you receive your entry ticket in the mail along with the program, which gives the ring number for your class and states the time judging begins.

When you make out your form, the question is which division of the class to enter, Novice A or B, Open A or B, or A or B in Utility if the class is divided (sometimes there is only one Utility Class, sometimes not). The distinction between A and B in Novice is that in A only the owner of the dog, or a member of his immediate family, may handle the dog in the ring. In B, anyone may handle, including professional handlers and/or trainers. But despite the first-glance appearance of that, we have found that Novice B is the best place to enter if you're trying for one of the four first places (and who isn't?). The way it actually works is that dogs being handled by their owners often work better than those handled by a professional who has no close contact with the dog. So you have a better chance for a ribbon and a prize in B.

In Open, the A and B distinction is the same, with the addition that dogs already having either a CDX or a UD may still compete in Open B. All of which will throw the beginning Open dog up against stiff competition. Here our recommendation is definitely Open A as the best chance of coming in among the winners. Also, in any of the classes, your choice may be dictated by who is judging. But more on this later.

In Utility, if the class is divided, here again the clear choice is Utility A, for in B you will find the dogs who have already won their UDs, and the ferocious competition of those dogs working on points toward the obedience championship.

Match shows are something else again. Very rarely if ever will a superintendent run one of these. The sponsoring club is in charge of all arrangements, and entries are made when you bring your dog to the show. Entry fees are substantially lower at match shows, and the entire atmosphere is one of informality. Finding out the where and when of matches can be a difficult procedure. Among dog people there seems to be a sort of jungle tomtom system inaudible to the uninitiated—word of match shows appears quite mysteriously out of the air. Sometimes the managers of match shows mail notices to people known to be seriously interested in obedience, sometimes culling names from recent show catalogs. Many Sunday newspapers run a "Dog Calendar" of upcoming matches, trials, dog shows, etc. Otherwise, it always seems to the tyro to be "Joe told me about it." Until and unless you get wired into the circuit, check with dog friends, with local breed and obedience clubs, or with the AKC to find out what matches are going.

AT THE SHOW

Before you even get to the show, make sure you know the hours of admission and of your particular ring. Admissions stop at a certain hour, and you won't get in after then, even if your dog doesn't go into the ring for several hours afterward. Check carefully the advertised hours of your class, and try to be there on time. Note especially the "closing hour" of the show—some shows require that all dogs remain on the grounds until a certain hour of the afternoon (generally 3 P.M.) even if the dog has finished completely with all judging much earlier. Don't try to sneak your dog out early, hidden under a blanket in the back seat, for some shows take up the entry stub when you leave. If you've snuck out early and your slip is among those missing when the roll is counted at the AKC, you are in for some sharp questions and possible suspension. The best policy to follow with this, as with all AKC and show regulations, is compliance with the rules, however unjust and pointless they might seem. The AKC's rules are made for a reason, and, believe us, the organization has a great deal of experience in detecting evasions. After having overseen several hundred thousand show entries, they know every dodge you or we might think up, and then some. They are an eminently fair bunch of people, but when they have reason to crack down, they do so, and hard.

If you're at a benched show, you'll need a couple of items of equipment for your dog. First is a bench chain, a handy device about three feet long with a snap at each end and two loops, each about a third of the way from each end. At the back of each of the wooden stalls (for the bigger and middle-sized breeds at shows), on the "floor," there is a sort of ringbolt to which you fasten the end of the bench chain, usually by slipping an end through and fastening the snap on to one of the loops. Some pet-supply departments have them, but they are sold at a booth at almost any benched shows. Don't worry about getting the right length—just tell the salesman what breed you have and he'll supply you with the right one and instructions on its use. And don't use your leather or canvas leash as a bench chain; it is much too easily chewed through by a lonely dog. Something in the way of padding for the bottom of the bench is not a strict necessity, but it's nice for the dog to have an old blanket or something similar to lie on.

Dogs are benched by group and breed—all Cocker Spaniels together and so forth. When you get to the show, ask the way to the section of your breed—obedience dogs are benched right in with the "beauty" specimens of the same breed—and find your bench number. Put him on the chain, make him comfortable, and leave him in peace until just before you're ready to go into the ring. He may be lonely and upset the first few times he's benched and you go away, but leave him be. He'll get used to it. Nobody will mind his howls (just wait until you get an earful of your first benched show!) and probably nobody will bother him. If he's an especially trusting and friendly type, various children and strangers may pet and fondle him, but there's nothing you can do about it unless you sit right with him and fend off social climbers. It's just one of the perils of the benched show. No matter how friendly he really is, if he's one of the larger breeds he'll be left alone. Few people, other than masochists and those suicidally inclined, go along sticking their hands into the large dogs' benches.

Benching arrangements for the really tiny dogs are somewhat different. For one reason or another, including that of preventing grubby poking fingers, little dogs are benched in small metal enclosures, completely closed in by a sort of heavy metal mesh. There you don't need a bench chain, and you can snap the catch of your bench and go off, sure that he won't be bothered by anything but stares and pre-ring nerves.

At a benched show, dogs must be "on their benches, in their show rings or exercising rings, or enroute thereto or therefrom, during the advertised hours of the show's duration" according to the AKC. For obedience dogs the "enroute thereto" can be stretched to include some preliminary practice work before you go into the ring, and nobody will mind. But in general, keep him on the bench. At unbenched shows the dog stays with you on leash. For outdoor unbenched shows there is a handy gadget on the market, looking much like an overgrown corkscrew. This you can sink quite firmly into the ground and attach the leash to. It's more of a convenience than anything else, to keep you from having to hang on to the leash all day. It's definitely not a good idea to hook him to a stake and leave him alone, for anything that happens during your absence will be entirely your own fault for leaving a dog unattended. People at unbenched shows are some-times quite careless about walking about with their dogs on loose leashes, and conflict might easily result.

Many outdoor shows, and all indoor ones, provide fenced-in areas where your dog can relieve himself without littering the grounds. There'll be an area for males and one for females. Water is always supplied at shows, with a spigot somewhere or other with arrows directing you to it. You may want to bring your own bowl, but at larger shows one or more of the dog-food companies will supply composition bowls. The dog-food people also supply at many shows buckets of their brand of food, and you are free to take along a bowl or two for your dog.

THE RING

Your Obedience number, as distinct from your bench number, deter-mines when you "go on" in the obedience ring. Soon after you get to the show and get your dog settled and benched, check with the steward of your ring to let him know your dog is present and to get your armband with your number on it. At an unbenched show, of course bring your dog along with you to ringside. AKC regulations require that dogs be judged in catalog order, but if there is some good reason your dog can't be judged when it's his turn, you can make arrangements *in advance* with the steward at the ring entrance, who will ask the judge for his approval. You may have been tied up in bad traffic, for example, and your number may come up just as you've gotten to the ring and your dog may be tired from a long ride. Stewards are very understanding about this sort of thing, usually being obedience handlers themselves, and all judges have been in the ring themselves. Nobody will insist that you march straight in on arrival. But once your number has been passed, don't expect any special concessions from the steward as far as time of showing goes—the people who are ready on time have priority over you. If the class is large enough to be broken up into several sections for the sits and downs (AKC rules allow no more than fifteen dogs in each section), you may even be in a completely different section from the handlers with numbers directly before and after yours. Except for the actual placing of the dogs (in strict catalog order insofar as they are available) for the sits and downs, order of appearance is pretty flexible.

When you are ready to go in and the steward gives you the okay to enter the ring, march in, get your dog settled at heel by your side on a loose lead, and wait patiently for the judge. When he has finished marking down the scores of the last dog, he'll come up to you and ask if you understand the rules of obedience. You should be able to give him an unequivocal "Yes" (be sure to read and understand *all* the AKC rules as printed in the Appendix). If not, now is the time to ask questions. Don't be afraid to speak up if there's anything at all you don't understand about ring procedure or the regulations. Once you've started off there should be no further comment to the judge unless you haven't been able to hear a command or have misunderstood one. And be sure you understand that, once in the ring, you *must* go through all the exercises, no matter how badly you may do in the opening ones. You might want to go hide, and the judge might wish he could boot you and your unready dog far out of the ring, but you've got to finish what you started. And that includes the later sit and down.

We assume that you've brought your dog to the ring completely trained and ready to display his prowess under any circumstances. If so, and you're shooting for a prize, there are a good many tricks of handling that can help you improve your score, things that are not really so much tricks as principles of good handling. One of the first of these is observation at ringside before you go in. By watching the routine the judge puts the dogs through, you will be more prepared for the turns and halts in heeling, for where the stewards will stand for the figure eight, for which direction the judge will ask the dog to go on the recall. Almost all judges run every dog through exactly the same pattern; your preparation for the parts of the pattern will help allay your nervousness, which in turn will make the dog feel better about things in general. Will this in mind, here is a detailed description of what happens in the ring in Novice, along with some handling pointers.

NOVICE

Heeling: As soon as you've answered the judge's "Are you ready?" he'll start you off, commanding, "Forward." From this point the routine is up to the judge, but as we've said, he usually follows the same pattern for all dogs. There will be a few right and left turns, about-turns, one fast, one slow. Be prepared for the judge who asks you to stop directly from the fast—some do. And watch for a stop only two or three paces after you've started—some do this, too. Give your dog plenty of lead, enough so that you won't pull on him inadvertently on right or about-turns. Many judges take off for that as "guiding the dog." Hold the leash so that it hangs loosely. The AKC says: "The leash may be held in either hand or both hands, providing the hands are in a natural position. However, any tightening or jerking of the leash or any act, signal or command which in the judge's opinion gives the dog assistance shall be penalized." One of the most common mistakes you will see in the ring is a handler with his leash slightly tight, usually quite unwittingly, and particularly you will see an unthinkingly tight lead on right turns and about-turns. Keep it loose! Keep your head up and don't watch to see if your dog is there. If he is, he is; if he isn't, there's nothing you can do about it. Have confidence in him. Nothing in the rules requires you not to look at your dog but if you are unsure of him and keep looking for him it may upset him. The judge can in fact deduct points for too much anxiety, as the rules hold the ideal performance to be "working as a team," and in this, continued anxious checking on your dog's position has no part.

Keep moving at a smart pace except in the "slow." A creeping pace doesn't help the dog a bit. It in fact tends to make him unsteady and not sure whether you're about to stop or not. We've seen more than one handler moving so slowly at supposedly "normal" pace that when the command came to "slow" it wasn't possible to go any slower without stopping. Usually this sort of handler goes through an elaborate pantomine of going more slowly, but in fact doesn't slow at all. It means a certain deduction in the judge's book.

Float into and out of the fast and slow, increasing and decreasing your speed over three or four steps. And float to a halt, from either normal or fast. Sudden, sharp changes of pace or halts throw your dog off and cause him to lag or overshoot. Put yourself in his place for a moment—imagine yourself walking at the left of a friend at a good pace. Suddenly he stops. How much chance do you have, without any warning, of stopping dead beside him? And you, we like to believe, are smarter than the dog. True, some dogs have been able to master a sudden stop, but their heeling is uncertain, hesitant, because they are constantly watching their handlers for some small clue that a screeching halt is coming.

Remember to swing your right leg around on left turns, and your left on right turns. Make your corners as square as possible and make your about-turns to your right but don't spin around on your heel or you'll find your dog lagging. The first few times you're in the ring you'll probably be so nervous you'll forget you ever read these paragraphs, but practice the pointers at home and they'll become habit. Remember that you are allowed a "Mike, heel!" each time you start up from a halt, but at no other time. Don't use any other command or signal or encouragement. And don't praise the dog until the judge has said, "Exercise finished"—then give him plenty.

Figure Eight: The two stewards come into the ring and place themselves eight feet apart, facing each other. With the judge standing at one side of their axis, bring your dog around to the other, facing him, about two feet from the center of the axis. Don't set yourself and wait for the judge and stewards to accommodate you—wait until they're in place and then position yourself. You may start around in the figure eight in either direction, but as you're going around the stewards, give them enough clearance so that neither you nor the dog has to brush against them. Watch this particularly with the left-hand steward; we've seen many handlers, particularly with large and bushy-haired dogs, trying to make a precise tight turn and forcing their dogs into the stewards. The judge may ask you to halt anywhere in your circuit, in the middle or behind one of the stewards, so be prepared for a halt anywhere, although you'll rarely see a halt anywhere but between the stewards.

Stand for Examination: After the judge has given you the "Exercise finished" to complete the figure eight, he will ask you to hand your lead to one of the stewards and then tell you, "Stand your dog and leave when you are ready." You may either stand him on command or pose your dog in a comfortable and steady position, taking a reasonable time to get him set. Place him facing the judge, and when you're ready, you're allowed to give command or signal or both. Here it is a firm "Stay!" and not a "Wait!" Walk forward about six feet and turn to face your dog, without further word from the judge and, as usual, don't stare at your dog. Keep it casual.

When the judge has completed his brief examination, he'll walk away and tell you to return to your dog. Walk around to heel position and wait for the "Exercise finished." Then finish whichever way you like, by heeling the dog forward a few paces to a sit and a release, or simply by releasing him from the stand-stay. It is really quite a simple exercise, and fewer dogs fail this or even lose points on it than any other of the Novice exercises.

Heel Off Leash: From the same starting point as before, you'll be started off in probably exactly the same routine you followed on lead. Do everything as carefully as you did on lead. Here is where the problem of the dis-interested or runaway dog can come up. It's a sure sign of shoddy training and unreadiness for the ring, but it does happen, so here's what to do (but if it happens to you after training by this book, you're on *our* list forever). If the dog lags and wanders a bit, keep right on going where the judge tells you. Don't lag, yourself, in hopes he'll catch up, or pat your leg, or talk to him. That's an automatic failure for the exercise. Don't even look down or around for him—if you're handling properly you won't know until some ringside friend tells you whether your dog was with you all the time. If he really lights out for the far country, the judge will let you know that he's running out of the ring, so call him back and wait for the judge to decide whether to boot you out of the ring or just flunk you. A second time is sure disqualification, so don't worry about what to do on repeats. Our advice, if your dog repeatedly runs out of the ring while heeling, is to turn in your uniform and take up needlepoint.

Recall: Get your dog sitting at heel where the judge tells you. He'll ask if you're ready (and be sure you are), then tell you to leave your dog and walk to the other end of the ring. Tell the dog to wait (this is one time you may, and should, use both command *and* signal) and walk away confidently without looking back. Looking back won't help a bit if he isn't sitting there quietly, and if he is your look is tantamount to an engraved invitation for him to break and follow you. When you get to the spot to call him, turn around and face him. Be careful with your arms. Don't swing them around or suddenly fold or unfold them as you're turning or once you've turned. The dog could interpret that as a signal to come, and it would serve you right.

When the judge tells you to call him, wait a few moments if necessary to be sure you have the dog's attention, then sing out loud and clear. We've seen too many people lose this exercise simply because their dog didn't hear the command in a noisy indoor show. Don't bellow, though. As the AKC says: "Loud commands by handlers to their dogs create a poor im-pression of obedience and should be avoided. Shouting is not necessary even in a noisy place if the dog is properly trained to respond to a normal tone of voice. Commands which in the judge's opinion are excessively loud will be penalized." That "excessively loud" is clearly a matter of judgment. A judge rightly enough will calculate that if *he* can hear you clearly (and the judge may be standing back of or near the dog), then the dog can. If your command is a little louder than required, don't worry; but if it is loud enough to make the judge flinch and heads turn two rings away, you are in for trouble. Don't make any inadvertent signals as you call—quite a few people unconsciously lean forward as they give the command. Some judges don't mind, but others count that as a signal and lacerate your score, even if in your own heart you know it was unthinking "body English."

If by some horrid mischance your dog *doesn't* come when you call him, it's all up with the two of you. Don't call him again until the judge directs you to. There's always the chance the dog is thinking about other things and the command will sink in after a moment or two. If after, say, five seconds the dog shows no signs of coming, look over to the judge and wait for some word or signal from him. He won't let it go on too long.

When the dog has come and heeled, and the judge has said, "Exercise finished," the steward gives you your leash and you then leave the ring to wait for the long sit and down. Don't make any comments or ask any questions of the judge then, unless he stops you to make a point or two. Many thoughtful judges take time then to give you pointers on handling, or to tell you how your dog did; but let him take the initiative. As you leave the ring, check with the steward on how many dogs there are to go before the long sit and down, so that you can be at ringside when called.

Long Sit: When you come into the ring the steward will show where your place is in line. Get the dog seated, then take off his leash, stuff it into your armband, and place the works about three feet directly behind your dog. The armband is at the rear so the judge and stewards can tell quickly which dog goofed; and the leash stuffing helps keep the armband upright. You may have to wait a minute or two until all the dogs are assembled— there always seems to be one laggard. If so, you'll know best how to handle your dog. If he's very steady, just let him sit there and wait until things begin. If he tends to be nervous, heel him forward a few paces, then back around to position to keep him from getting bored or flighty from sitting too long. It's quite legal, as long as you're set and ready when the judge asks, "Are you ready?" of all the handlers in the line. When he says, "Leave your dogs!" give your dog the usual command-and-signal (this is another place in Novice where *both* command and signal are permitted), and walk across the ring to the line the judge has designated for handlers. Again, don't look back, and watch your arms as you turn. Stand as still as you can, but play it cool and casual. When the judge says, "Return to your dogs," walk back with all the other handlers at a normal pace, and don't get ahead of the crowd. If you are ahead it just means you will have to stand at heel that much longer waiting for the end of the exercise, tempting your dog to get up, or lie down, or whatever. Wait until the "Exercise finished" before you so much as look at the dog, then give him plenty of praise.

If your dog has gone down during the sit there's nothing you can do; if he gets up and comes toward you, let him come. A steward may take hold of him, or he may be allowed to come all the way to you. In either case, stand quietly until the exercise is finished, then go back to position for the long down. Let the stewards handle any misdemeanors such as wandering or sniffing another dog, unless an all-out fight develops. We've never seen that happen, so don't worry about it.

Long Down: After you've released him on returning from the long sit, he may move from position when you praise him. If so, get him back into a neat sit-at-heel position in line with the other dogs and handlers, and when the judge gives the command "Down your dogs," give your dog the command or signal, or both, to get him down. Keep in mind that the regulations do not allow you to touch either him or his collar to get him down— he must go down on command and/or signal. A surprising number of exhibitors seem to be unaware of this, and a surprising number of judges let them get away with it—placing their dogs in the down position, or urging them down with snaps on the collar. You shouldn't have to do this, so don't. Nothing in the rules prevents you from giving more than one command or signal in the ring, but we'll be ashamed of you if you have to.

Then the judge will tell you to leave your dog, and you walk across the ring just as you did in the long sit. Turn and face your dog, and again, don't stare at him. Just relax, at least as much as possible. The three minutes you stand across from the dog will seem the longest in your life—they seem endless even to the judges and stewards, who have nothing at stake—but once you've got back to him, it's all over. If you've done well, it's a "leg," one of three you need for your CD title. And maybe even a ribbon.

Once out of the ring, it won't be long until you know your score if it's a one-section class. Otherwise you'll have to wait until all the sections are finished. After the last of the sits and downs, the judge and stewards add up all the scores and call the four winners into the ring for presentation of ribbons and prizes, plus all the dogs who achieved qualifying scores. Although it is not an AKC requirement, many clubs give out dark green "qualifying score" ribbons to qualifiers. The judge announces to the spectators the placings and their scores, hands the winners their ribbons and prizes, and then tells each qualifying handler the score he and his dog made, so you'll know right away how well you did. If you're not called into the ring, it means you didn't make it—but by then you'll probably know it anyway, because your dog will have quite obviously fouled up on one or more exercises.

Problems and pointers: If you don't hear what the judge is telling you, in a noisy armory or on a windy field, let him know about it quickly. He'll speak up. And if you mistake right for left, or something else, bear up. All judges are former handlers and have been in your position once. They know you're probably nervous and will do their best to help you along within the rules.

One of the major problems that can arise in the ring is anticipation. The dog comes when he hears the judge say, "Call him," or starts up to heel when the judge says, "Forward." There's little you can do about it on the spot—if he anticipates any command even before the judge gives it, there's nothing you can do. You can forestall it, or cure it, by having a friend act as judge when you're practicing, giving the judge's commands loud and clear and in as commanding a tone as he can. Wait for varying lengths of time between the "judge's" commands and your own, until you are sure the dog is working on your command alone.

Between exercises in the ring, heel your dog around with you without pulling on the leash or his collar. Although it is permissible to lead him from one exercise to another, it is a sign of bad training if you have so little control over him that you do have to use the collar or leash. By the time you get to Open and Utility it is forbidden by the rules, so get used to controlling him without the lead.

OPEN

Up to now we have been writing for the complete Novice who has either never been to a show or who is having handling problems in Novice Class. By the time you're ready for this section on Open, you will have been in at least three shows and will have watched Open procedures in the other rings. So we'll leave out the detailed description of what goes on in the ring and concentrate on handling and behavior pointers.

Heeling: All off leash, including the figure eight. The same principles apply as in Novice off-lead work.

Drop on Recall: Use either command or signal, following our explanations in Chapter 5 (signal when it's noisy, command if visibility is bad). If you use the command, watch for unconscious body motions; some judges mark you off for them. In using the signal, be sure that your arm goes up and comes right back down in a sharply defined signal. Some judges look leniently on a long-drawn-out hand waving, wherein the signaling hand stays up in the air for several seconds until the dog reluctantly complies. Some mark you complete failure for this, calling it a double command if your hand stays up in the air. Be sure you understand whether the judge wants you to drop the dog opposite him, or on a signal from him. If it's opposite him, determine from your knowledge of the dog when to give the command or signal. If the dog takes a step or two before dropping, time your command so that he does down directly in front of the judge. Watch this point in training—he should drop immediately. Some judges count several steps between command and drop as complete failure. For the reasons behind this, see again the practical applications of the drop on recall, as set out in Chapter 5.

Retrieve on Flat: Be sure the dog is settled and given a firm "Wait!" before throwing the dumbbell. When you throw, throw carefully and well with a technique developed by the practice outlined in Chapter 5. Be careful with your hands when the dog comes in with the dumbbell; anticipatory motions on your part might cause him to drop it before the judge says, "Take it." If your throw has gone really wild, say, out of the ring, let the judge move it if he sees fit. He may not, and if he tells you to send your dog after a bad throw, it's nobody's fault but your own. Don't ask him for a second throw; if he thinks it's in a very bad position, he'll either move it or give it to you to throw again.

Retrieve over High Jump: Again, settle your dog well, and be *very* careful of your throw. If it lands where the dog can see it from where he sits, he has every good reason to go around the jump to get it. Try to get it just a few feet ahead of where he will land when he goes over. In case he gets the dumbbell and stands looking at you across the jump, wait for the judge's instruction before giving a second command.

Be sure you know the correct height of the jump for your dog as specified in the regulations—the steward will probably ask you for it as you enter the ring. If your dog does not jump the maximum height, or is not one of the "excepted" breeds, the judge will probably measure your dog at the shoulder to be sure that the jump is set to the correct height. It will be set up before you begin heeling, so be sure that it is set up right. The numbers painted on the high-jump boards tell you if the number of inches is correct. If there seems to be anything wrong, ask the judge to have it corrected when he asks you if there are any questions. Don't save it until you come to the jump, and above all don't hesitate to ask if there's any doubt at all in your mind.

Broad Jump: Be sure you know the proper measurement here, too. It's not too easy to tell the width of the jump just by looking, but you'll be able to see if it seems radically out of order. If so, speak up loud and clear. Remember: It's "a distance twice the height of the high jump as set for the particular dog." That may not need reemphasis for you, but we've seen more than one handler come into the ring thinking it was twice the height of the dog at the shoulder. You can get that impression if you read the regulations too quickly.

In fact, a close rereading of the regulations for this exercise might be in order; we've seen misunderstandings over almost every sentence of the AKC's rules for the broad jump. One of the most common is about the handler's turn while the dog is jumping. First of all, the turn must be made while the dog is in *midair,* not before he takes off or after he lands. This is very specifically spelled out in the regulations. Just why the insistence on turning while in midair we don't know, but that's the rule.

The turn must be a right-angle turn. Here is a point open to the interpretation of the judge, some holding that it means just that, exactly 90°. Others allow you to turn more than 90° to face your dog, whichever way he comes in to you. Our advice is that you make an exact right face in training and train your dog to come in to you properly. You're almost sure to run up against one or more "90° right face" judges in Open showing. Our feeling is that they're closer to the letter and spirit of the rules than the lenient judges, so you have no squawk if you're marked off for over-turning.

Long Sit and Down: Here everything from Novice applies, except of course that you will be out of sight of the dog. Don't let your curiosity get the better of you when you're away with the other handlers. The dog knows pretty well where you've gone and he may be straining his head around, watching the place where you were last seen. If he catches a glimpse of you peeking around a corner it'll give him every encouragement to come to you as if it were a game. Stay out of sight.

UTILITY

It is surprising, but even on this high plateau of obedience there are still serious and basic handling mistakes made, and evidences shown of grossly improper training methods. Check over your own handling carefully to see if any of these applies to you.

Scent Discrimination: One very curious thing about scent discrimination is that, although the regulations call for five articles of each kind, some handlers use six. In the commonly available article sets there are usually six of each kind, but in these cases the sixth article is intended as a spare and practice article for training.

Watch how you scent the article. Holding and squeezing it applies plenty of smell, but rubbing it vigorously heats the surface by friction and changes the character of the scent. And you can't put it in your armpit, for example, to give it a real whomp of smell, for the rules say "hands only." Train that way, and do it that way.

Once you've given your scented article to the judge, he will place it among the others, return to your general area, and instruct you to send your dog. You may either turn around with your dog at heel and stop with him sitting at heel, and then give another command to send him out for the article, or turn and simultaneously give the command "Find it!" so that the dog turns with you and then runs right out to the articles without stopping at heel. We think the latter method is slightly better, but the choice is up to you and how it works best with your own dog. And although the regulations allow you to give your dog a fresh whiff of scent "by gently touching the dog's nose with the palm of one open hand" before you make the turn, we strongly recommend that you don't. You'll see many handlers doing this in the ring, but all it does is load up your dog's nose with a strong whiff of your smell and could possibly confuse him if he retains that smell when he gets to the first, and almost certainly wrong, article. If he doesn't know by now what you smell like, and what an article smells like that you've touched, you're both in big trouble, and shouldn't be in the Utility ring anyway.

Directed Retrieve: You are the most important part of this exercise—you and your handling. If you turn properly and crisply so that your dog faces the correct glove, if you give him a good, clear, unmistakable signal that he is to go get the glove you're facing, your dog has no reason to achieve anything but perfection in this exercise. And remember that you may *not* touch your dog to get him into position; you must make the turn and he must be with you, so that when you stop, both of you are facing the correct glove. If you turn poorly, or if he overshoots or undershoots the turn so that he isn't facing the way you are, there's no way you can correct him. You can only hope that by a really good direction signal you get things straightened out.

Signal Exercise: Make your heeling signals sharp and clear. After the heeling part, you are allowed by a sort of unwritten agreement to wait a moment or two between the judge's signals for each part and your own signal, to be sure you have your dog's attention. Don't stretch it out too long or you may be marked off rather heavily on general principles. Again, make your signals as sharp and clear as possible, and make them brief, just as in the drop on recall. The AKC specifies that the finishing parts of the exercise—the stand, leave, drop, sit, recall, and finish—must be done in exactly that order, so you can profitably rehearse that sequence in your ring preparations.

Directed Jumping: We have seen more dogs come to grief in this exercise than in almost any other. The reason is, without fail, thoughtless training. At the ring you will have seen it yourself: Dog after dog will, when sent out, either edge toward the high jump or actually circle around and sit squarely in front of it. And we'll bet you've never seen a dog circle to sit in front of the bar jump. The reason is simply that through faulty training the dog has come to expect always, or most of the time, to be sent over the solid jump first. This is less a handling problem than one of training, but we mention it again here as in Chapter 6 because of its importance. *Always* mix up the sequence of the jumps in training, and insist that the dog go out straight to the sit. If he sits squarely in front of the solid jump, most judges will ask you to send him over the bar jump, and then it's up the spout. Even if you run into a lenient judge, what happens when you send the dog out the second time?

Group Examination: Handling errors are few and far between in this simple exercise. Be sure only that the dog is well set and comfortable before you leave. Take your time about it. For some reason dogs break far less often in the seemingly more difficult stand than in the sits and downs.

RUNOFFS

If you really have an outstanding dog, whose work is such that you finish in the ribbons, you may become involved in a runoff for one of the placings. If so, your dog and the other dog or dogs who have tied in score will be put through one of the exercises in your class to break the tie. In Novice and Open it is the heel free, or heel off leash. "All or some part" of the exercise is specified, but a runoff is usually completed quite quickly, often with no more than a bit of heeling, an about-turn, and a bit more; with both dogs doing it at the same time it is generally quite quickly apparent which one has the edge. All we can tell you to do is relax—tension and nerves will only upset your dog and, unless you're in a runoff for fourth place, you're already guaranteed one nice ribbon.

In Utility it is the signal exercise, and here the judge often goes through the whole exercise in order to compare how well the dogs do the stand, drop, sit, and recall before making up his mind which one wins the runoff. Again, just relax, and do it as you would at any other time.

HANDLING IN GENERAL

The operative word here is *relax*. Far easier said than done, but try at any rate. Time and again dogs who have worked perfectly in practice cover themselves with inglory in the ring and their handlers never seem to understand why. Largely it is because in practice the handlers are relaxed, but once in the ring they tighten up and make mistakes themselves. Nervousness and tension are transmitted to a dog somewhat faster than the speed of light, and the dog's work suffers as a result.

Be very careful about one thing: motions that might be interpreted by a strict judge as extra signals to the dog. As an example of this, take the handler we know who was once knocked out of first place in a very tight class because he came to a very military halt when heeling in Novice. Every time he halted, his heels came together with a bang, and the judge took off a point or two each time because of the possibility that these bangings of the heels might have been signals to the dog to stop and sit. They weren't, but the judge has to mark on appearances. He obviously can't go up to the handler and ask, "Were you trying to cheat, or was all that stuff unconscious?" Watch especially for a forward lean when calling the dog either in Novice or Open, and for a sideways jerk of the head or body when telling him to heel from a sit in front of you. True, none of these will fail you, but you may lose points.

One word that we hope is unnecessary: Don't try to cheat. Cheating is reprehensible in any sport, and there's the additional thought that in obedience one very seldom gets away with it. Judges as a whole are a lynx-eyed lot, and their ears are finely tuned to the softest of whispered extra commands even at the far end of the ring. Additionally, there are quite often plainclothes AKC types loitering about at ringside keeping an unobtrusive eye on things. Don't risk a lifetime suspension for an extra point or two.

In the ring you are not allowed to correct or discipline the dog in any way. If you do, the judge may fail you or even throw you out of the ring. If your dog has fouled up really badly, all you can do is take it with a smile and resolve to work on that point in further training. Although nothing is said about it in the rules, remember your training and praise the dog when the exercise is finished, even if he shamed you and your descendants for three generations to come. Displays of temper toward the dog are one of the most unpleasant things you can see in a ring, and they make no sense at all. The dog won't learn anything if you yank him about spitefully, and you'll lose points in the eyes of the spectators—they know full well whose fault it is if your training hasn't been good enough.

Match shows are something else again, as far as correction goes. Because they are largely for practice and are much more informal, many times the judge will let you go through an exercise again if the dog has made any serious mistake. The second time will be strictly for your benefit, though; you'll be scored on the first try. Don't hesitate to ask the judge for a second practice try. Unless he has a heavy schedule of dogs to get through, he'll probably okay it. Here again, though, serious corrections or disciplining are frowned on. Just take the dog through the exercise again so that he doesn't get ring wise and realize that he can never be corrected while in a show ring.

SCORING AND TITLES

In each of the three classes, you must qualify at three trials, under a different judge in each, with a score of 170 or more, having received more than 50 percent of the points for each exercise. It is technically possible, although difficult, to win more than 170 points and still not qualify, if you've done exceptionally well in all the exercises but one, and received just under 50 percent of the points for that one. But if you are called into the ring among the qualifiers, you've got it locked, for that time at least.

Because of the fact that each of your legs (as qualifications are called) must be under a different judge, watch the premiums carefully to be sure you don't enter under a judge who has passed you. Usually show-giving clubs stagger the assignments of judges in a show, if possible. One judge will have Novice A and Open B, another Novice B and Open A, unless there is a separate judge for each division of each class. If you've worked successfully under one judge at another show, you generally will be able to enter the other section—this consideration will outweigh other reasons for a choice between A and B within a class.

When you have made your three legs, just sit back and wait for the certificate to come through from the AKC. It's an automatic process and calls or letters to the AKC won't help at all. They have hundreds of registrations and championships and titles to contend with every day of the week, and though it may take a little time yours will come.

JUDGES AND JUDGING

Judges come in all shapes and varieties: male and female, old and young, helpful and grumpy, strict and lenient. Exactly the same work may get you a leg under one judge and a failure under another. This, however, can be applied only to marginal performance, a pass in one case with 171 and a failure under another judge with 168. It can be safely said that if you and your dog do your work well you will pass and with good scores. If the judge is hyperstrict he will be so with every dog in the ring, and it won't affect your chances of winning a placing. For the most part judges are eminently fair and helpful, and the score you get is the score you deserve. Remember always that the judge is the absolute authority within the ring; argument with his decisions does you not a whit of good. If you think you've been done wrong, there's nothing in the world you can do but vow never to show under that judge again. Human nature being what it is, there are the rare few judges who have forgotten that they themselves were ever handlers, and if they've had a bad breakfast that day you'll be marked off for blinking your eyes. All judges *were* handlers once, and even a first-time Novice judge has probably put several dogs right through to Utility, so he or she has had plenty of experience being a handler and perspiring under the flinty eyes of a stern judge. Still, a few—fortunately, few—have been judging for so long that they've forgotten what it feels like, and so can be unfair. We say this not as a slam at judges—the authors are both obedience judges themselves—but to prepare you for the facts of ring life: you may run into one of them. If so, take it as best you can, for there's nothing you can do about it. The AKC regularly reviews the qualifications of its judges, and word gets around with lightning rapidity in the dog world if a judge seems really out of line. It will catch up with him, and it's just unfortunate that you had to be in the way before the ax fell. But until the day of judgment, the AKC gives its judges the widest possible latitude within the regulations, and there's little use in trying to appeal a decision. You can, if things really rankle, write to the AKC about it. They will take note and investigate.

Don't, however, take these statements and turn them against the many strict but fair judges you will run into. We know many judges who judge by the letter of the law, who are as helpful as possible to handlers, extremely considerate, but who insist that your performance be what is required in the rule book. These, we feel, are the real backbone of obedience; the too lenient judge is not really helping anyone.

Remember, in all obedience, that dog shows are a sport. Exercise sportsmanship at all times, and go into it for the fun of it. Obedience should, after all, be enjoyable for you, for the dog, and for the spectators at ringside. Have fun.

CHAPTER 8

Brace and Team

By definition strictly for two-dog people, Brace work is primarily a ring-competition endeavor. Even if you have two entirely noncompeting dogs, parts of Brace work are handy as practical training, in particular the heeling and figure-eight work. Too many times people with two dogs have problems with them on the street—one goes one way, one goes the other, and leashes, arms, and legs get tangled about until the owner looks like a multilimbed East Indian idol with the hiccups.

In the ring (and there are no titles awarded for Brace, only prizes and ribbons) the exercises are almost exactly the same as in Novice Class, with both dogs performing each exercise at the same time. The dogs walk shoulder-to-shoulder at heel, they stand for examination side by side, both come in at the same time on the recall, and they sit-stay and down-stay together. In order to begin Brace work, both dogs must be fully trained in Novice work (though they need not have titles). Brace training consists simply of teaching them to do the work together.

As heeling together is the first exercise to learn, you must determine which of the two dogs is to heel close beside you and which is to take the outside position. This can best be done by observation—walking along with them, get them both at your left side with one in close to your left leg. If the other constantly crowds and tries to get closer, try them with positions reversed to see if they are happier that way. If both want to walk close to you, you will have to make an arbitrary decision on the matter. Perhaps you will want your older dog to work closer to you, or if one works just a little better and is a mite sharper, perhaps you will want him to work on the outside. It is the outside dog who will have to make the most adjustments to the new situation: walking faster on right and about-turns, slower on left turns. Probably the sharper dog will be able to learn this better.

The second consideration is what to call your dogs. If you want only to do a bit of Brace heeling for street use, the problem of names won't arise, but in the ring you will find that their own names may not serve. "Asafoetida, Blankinsop, heel!" is an awkward command, and even with shorter names, the one called first may react to his name and start off a beat or two before the second dog. About the best solution is to use an accommodation name for both, one that they will learn to recognize as the attention-getter in Brace work. If both are males, you can simply use "Boys" and your command will be "Boys, heel!" or "Boys, come!" If this strikes you as a bit cute, you can use anything at all that appeals to you, just so it is distinctive—a word they can come to recognize as applying to them.

The third item is the tandem chain, used quite commonly in ring competition. This is a chain with a snap at both ends and a ring in the middle, the chain being just long enough to keep the two dogs together without making them crowd each other. When each end is snapped to a training collar and the leash is snapped to the middle ring, both dogs can be guided by one hand and leash, but the tandem is not used until later in training. In the competition ring, Brace dogs may be shown either unattached (which requires two leads for the heel on lead) or coupled with the tandem chain, and in competition the tandem chain may not be shorter than six inches. The decision on which route to take is up to you and your dogs.

With names and positions decided, you can begin to work on the Brace heeling. The tandem chain should very definitely not be used at this point, for, with it, it is very nearly impossible to correct one dog without also snapping the other, a circumstance that leads only to confusion compounded. Start out with a leash in your left hand to control the outside dog, and one in your right for the inside dog. Either can thus be corrected separately in the heeling. It takes some getting used to, this working with either or both hands, and there is no way in the world you can practice except on the dogs, so concentrate on your coordination and you will soon learn to control two almost as easily as one.

Get the two of them sitting side by side, and put yourself in the proper place to the right of the right-hand dog. With leashes in hand (your right hand held to the left so that any corrections on the inside dog come from the proper direction, not from across your body) give them the heel command and start off. Use your leads for whatever corrections need be given: gentle snaps to urge either one forward or back to keep them even with each other and with you. Such verbal corrections as you may have to give, give gently. Here is where control of voice and emotions are absolutely essential, for if you shout a correction for something at one dog, the other will hear it too and wonder what he did wrong, even if the correction was prefaced by the name of the erring dog.

Go through the entire Novice heeling routine, with fast and slow, turns and about-turns, and halts. Remember on the turns that the outside dog has to move either faster or slower to keep the line straight. Give most of your attention to him, as the inside dog has to do little more than what he has been doing in individual Novice work. Such corrections as are necessary for the inside dog are generally in the nature of holding him back slightly if you slow a bit on turns to make the work easier for the outside dog. Keep at the work until you can go through the entire heeling routine, including the figure eight, and both work perfectly.

Now is the time to introduce the tandem chain. Keeping the dogs both on their separate leashes, hook the tandem between their collars and do some heeling that way until you are sure the idea of the chain between them, tugging on them occasionally, does not bother them. Then take off the leashes, snap one on to the ring at the center of the tandem, and try heeling that way. Remember that a leash on the tandem cannot be used for correcting an individual dog, but can be used only for gentle guidance of both. When they work well that way, take the leash off entirely and work them through the heeling routine off leash.

The go to heel is again taught at first with two leashes. In this exercise, the "around" heel is far easier for them, but if individually they know the "left" heel, they need only learn that they must accommodate each other as they make a wider swing to your left to get into position without fouling each other. Work on them with the two leashes until they do it well, then go to tandem and one leash, and then tandem alone.

In teaching the Brace stand for examination, you can either pose them both or let them walk into the stand, whichever they have done in individual Novice work. The stand is done off lead, but if the dogs are being shown coupled throughout (and you can't change it from one exercise to another—it's either unattached or coupled for all exercises), they will do their stand with the tandem chain attaching them.

The Brace recall is taught with the tandem on from the first, for by this time they will be used to working with it. Put them at the sit-stay, and stand about ten feet in front of them. Give them the recall command and as they approach you, begin to run backward just in front of them. This way

The tandem chain. With the leash snapped to the center ring, both dogs can be gently guided.

neither will forge ahead of the other and both will come to you on an even keel. Keep moving backward, even if only a few steps, until they are even; then stop for them to come in to a sit in front of you. The original ten feet does not give them enough room to become seriously entangled even if they are clumsy about it at first. The greater probability is that they will come in fairly well the first time. As they get used to it and work together, increase the distance you stand in front of them until they do a thirty-foot recall in proper order, without your having to go backward to straighten them out.

The long sit and long down require hardly any extra training. The only difference in the situation is that they will be sitting or lying closer together than would be the case in the Novice ring. Be sure that your tandem chain is long enough so that they can sit without getting in each other's way too much.

For any serious corrections in any of the exercises, at whatever time, go back to individual leashes. Any tugging on the tandem will be felt by both dogs, and the dog who is doing right at the time will become confused if he feels snaps on his collar. And with that you have it. Brace work can be a great deal of fun, and it is impressive to watch in the ring, for two dogs working well together are somehow more than twice as appealing as one. It is, true, hard and extra work, and you'll never have an engraved certificate to show for it, but the enjoyment can more than make up the difference.

TEAM

Team obedience is strictly for demonstration and ring competition, having no application to everyday life unless you happen to be one of four inseparable friends who take their dogs everywhere with them. In Team work, four handlers and their dogs go through a variety of exercises from Novice and Open, all in line and all working much like a drill team. Here again there are no titles, but there are sometimes quite attractive prizes in the ring. At this writing, the majority of dog shows do not have Team competition, but interest in it is growing. It may come to be, if not an every-show affair, quite common.

The ideal team would consist of four handlers of the same sex, hair coloring, and general build, with four very similar dogs of the same breed. As these circumstances are a bit hard to come by, there are teams of very nearly every nature, with varying sexes and sizes among the handlers, and four different breeds of dog. If you contemplate organizing a team, try to have dogs of the same breed, but even that is secondary—although a team comprising a Great Dane, a Chihuahua, a Poodle, and a Doberman might strike a more comical note than would seem proper.

Ideally, in getting a group together to practice Team work, you should have five people with their dogs—an extra in case of sickness or other inability to make a show. In practice and performance each of the five members of the team should work each of the four positions; thus, in case of enforced absence, any four can make up the team without the necessity of extra practice. If all five are able and willing to make all the shows, there will have to be a rotation of the "off" man. Team work can of course be done with only four people and their dogs, but the fifth member is a good idea as insurance.

When you choose your team members, if you have any choice at all, you will have to consider personalities, but this is no different from any other

Not a Brace or Team exercise—but an example of what obedience training can accomplish. (Photo by Abbie Rowe—Courtesy National Park Service)

line of human endeavor. The team members will have to work together in close cooperation, they must be able to learn the equivalent of close-order drill, and they must be able to work amicably with each other and under the orders of the captain of the team. Actually, Team work is far more a matter of training the human participants to work together than it is of work with the dogs—everything the dogs do they will have done already in individual training. All they have to do is learn to follow their handlers' instructions while working in a group. For the dogs it isn't difficult—almost all the team troubles and problems are human.

The first training is done entirely without your dogs. Once you have gotten the team together, appoint a captain. Under the direction of the captain, the team begin to learn the field movements all by themselves. The first steps are difficult, for unless you have four veterans of ROTC or army service or something of the sort, you will have to start out instructing your members in the basics of close-order drill, walking in a straight line, turning in unison and column, and all the other niceties of common drilling.

The first order of business is to get everyone into line, as at a review or inspection. The proper spacing for the line, with or without dogs, is one arm's length. So, working from the left-hand man, the one on his right should raise his left arm and adjust his position until his fingertips just touch the left-hand man's right shoulder. Then the third man does the same, and so does the fourth. For purposes of drill and identification, the man at the left of the line is No. One, and the others Two, Three and Four to the right. However the line is facing, left-hand is No. One. This is a bit hard for your team members to grasp at once, but if you about-face the line a few times and explain it, all will become clear. When the line becomes a file, one man behind another, the man in front is No. One in every case. In the course of a few turns the No. One position will switch back and forth rapidly from one end to the other, but this way works out best, we have found.

All this preliminary drilling and lining up is simple enough. If you do it in your backyard, the neighbors will think you have either gone quite mad or are drilling up a small army for an insurrection. But bear with it—there's worse to come.

When your team is in line at the proper spacing, and you have decided who is to act as captain (the captain may work in any position), you can begin your first marching. At the captain's command, "Forward," everyone steps off, left foot first, and moves forward until the command "Halt." People totally inexperienced in drilling will wander off course, lag behind, or forge ahead. But these matters must be straightened out at the beginning, and the team must work until it can walk as a line across the yard, keeping a straight line. Instruct everyone that the left-hand man, No. One, will set the pace, and that each other team member is to guide on him: look to their left to make sure the line is straight as they are walking, and when they halt. At each halt, have the members raise their left arms to check spacing. Do this, as a matter of fact, at each halt for quite a while. After some practice, everyone will be working together and each man need only check the straightness of the line and the spacing by looking out of the corner of his eye at the man on his left, and will be able to maintain proper pace and space without giving it too much thought.

At first there may be more trouble than you might imagine, unless you were a drill instructor in earlier days. People who have spent all their adult lives walking quite comfortably and competently will suddenly develop severe cases of noncontrol when asked to walk in line with others. Also, some people are incurably right- or left-footed; they simply cannot walk a straight line to save themselves. Keep at it, though, and do not try to progress to more complex maneuvers until your four members can walk abreast across your training area in good order.

With this in hand you can introduce the about-turn. As all four walk across the field, the captain commands, "About-turn!" and all members turn in their places and walk in the opposite direction, again maintaining the straight line and spacing. If you want to work out a regular bit of footwork on the order of army drill procedure, fine, but any sort of thing will do as long as everyone turns at the command word "turn," not on the "about." It is a good idea to work on that a bit—the captain giving the "about" part of the command several times to catch the unwary, before giving the complete command, "About-turn."

Then more complicated movements come in. Here it is a very good idea to have your fifth member act as drill master, issuing the commands as a judge would. If you have only four, the captain will initiate all commands. In the ring, the judge gives commands to the team just as he would to an individual handler in Novice—forward, slow, halt, fast, about-turn, right turn, left turn, and so forth—and the fifth-member drill master is a help in getting the team used to working to external orders.

The left and right turns are easy. At the command "Right turn!" each member turns to the right in place and steps off in the new direction. From walking abreast, the team is then walking in file. At the command "Left turn!" each member then turns to his left and steps off, and the team is back in line, walking abreast. To get some semblance of order in these movements, you can only practice and practice again until your members work together.

All of these maneuvers can be a great deal simpler if everyone keeps in step, but this is sometimes too much to ask. They can be done if everyone is walking normally, but if you are interested in real snap and precision, get a copy of any army, ROTC, or other close-order drill manual and study in it the proper way of executing each movement. From it you will learn how to control things to a fare-thee-well, with commands given on the proper foot and turns much simplified and more orderly. Or recruit an army veteran friend from your neighborhood to show you the basics.

As your team develops competence in the drill, switch positions so that all members can work in each position. The captain should of course be able to work in any of the positions, and the captaincy should remain in the same hands except when the usual captain is the "off" man in the five-man setup. Everyone, though, should learn to call the commands and act as captain.

Having gotten your team working smoothly together, you can now bring the dogs into the act for the first time. But, caution: Don't succumb to the temptation to bring them in earlier. If you bring your dogs in when the humans are still stumbling over their feet, it will make for great difficulties. Bringing the dogs in is the easiest part of all, for all they have to do is follow their handlers at heel, just as they have always done. Work at first on lead, for the dogs are accustomed to working alone. There will be a little confusion when each dog finds himself not only at heel but with another handler practically at heel beside him, but a very little work cures this; soon the dogs come to accept the novelty of the situation.

With the dogs at heel, go through all the routine the team has practiced up to this point. If each dog is a good, steady worker, there should be no problems, except of course with the handlers. Drilling alone and drilling with a dog at your side are different things, although not all that different. By the time the handlers get used to it, the dogs will be veterans of the game, and you can go through all the routines again, off lead, switching places from time to time so that each dog gets used to working in each position.

If one dog member of the team is a little lacking in his training, or if one suddenly begins to get his feet mixed up, the whole team must go back on lead until that one dog is straightened out. For some curious reason, the other dogs have a tendency to repeat any mistakes made by one dog, and so all should go back on lead to prevent this contagiousness until the erring dog has been straightened out by lead corrections.

When dogs and handlers have gone through the drill to this point, leave the dogs aside again. The next maneuver, the column right and column left, is easy in the watching but more difficult in the doing. It is performed when the team is walking in file, and at the command "Column right!" the No. One man turns right and steps off. No. Two follows in his path, forward until he comes to the spot where No. One turned, then turning himself, and so on for No. Three and No. Four. Then the Team is moving off to the right, still in file. The overall mechanics of the maneuver are not difficult; it is the timing that takes a bit of work. When No. One is making his turn, he necessarily slows his forward motion a bit, and No. Two is strongly tempted to slow down before he hits the turn to avoid running into No.

One. Trying to keep things neat, he piles up No. Three and No. Four behind, like freight cars in a collision. When the entire file has turned, the spacing has stretched all out of hand. No. Two, and each man behind him, must practice going into the turn at full speed—nobody will step on anyone else's heels.

Put all the members through this exercise in each position, and mix up the work as you go along until everyone can perform without trouble. Run a full routine in practice (this is not a show routine, just for practice): forward, about-turn, left turn, column left, right turn, about-turn, column right, right turn, halt. That will bring you about back where you started, and if everyone has gone through it well, you can get your dogs at heel and go through the whole thing again.

By the time you have gone through all this and stumbled over your own feet and everybody else's and turned left when you should have turned right and committed all the other basic sins of drilling, you should be in a properly humble mood and sympathetic to any mistakes your dog may make. Insist, though, that he heel properly all the while you are going through the drill—that he keep his mind on his work. Particularly while walking in file, watch for attempts to sniff the dog in front of him. Another dog walking only three or four feet ahead may be interesting in the extreme, but yours must pay attention only to keeping strictly at your side. But go easy on the corrections, just as you have done all through training. It may be a bit easier for you now, when you just might find him working better than you.

The figure eight in Team work is a fairly complicated and grandiose affair. In brief, five "stewards" stand in a straight line, each eight feet from the next. This sort of cooperation from five other people in your training may be a little difficult to arrange; five stakes in the ground, or five boxes, or five of almost anything will do for the initial training.

Each dog and handler stand between two stewards, all in line and facing the same way. On the "judge's" order, the team begins the figure eight in unison, each handler taking the left turn first. It looks complicated, and it *is* impressive to watch, but it is really nothing but four separate figure eights. The critical essential is unison and timing, which means that in practice the team leader must be at either the right or left end, and each team member must keep his or her eyes open to be sure everyone is doing the circles at the same time.

Practice it first without the dogs. Team member No. Two watches the leader, No. Three watches No. Two, and No. Four watches No. Three. It is really not hard to learn quite good precision with four people just making a simple figure eight around five stewards in practice; and once that is mastered, the dogs will keep pace.

The stand for examination is done off lead, and all dogs should be gotten into the stand by the same method. They *can* all be posed by their handlers, but Team work is meant to be smart, snappy, and done in unison. Therefore, a much better impression is given if all four are seated at heel in line, brought forward a pace or two to the stand in unison, and given the stay command-and-signal in unison, with the four handlers walking out together to their positions.

A steward or stewards may collect the leads after the on-lead heeling, or you can make quite a military production out of the stand if you like, looking somewhat like a canine version of the Changing of the Guard at Buckingham Palace. By AKC regulations: "In all exercises except the Drop on Recall, the teams have the option of executing the judge's commands on the team captain's repeat of the command."

A Keeshond team, ready to go, in uniform.

Thus, once the judge has ordered, "Stand your dogs and leave when you are ready!" you can put the Changing of the Guard into effect, and it is quite impressive. The team members unsnap their leads in unison, the captain steps out in front and walks down the line collecting leads, makes an about-turn, and returns to his own heel position, handing the leads to the steward when he is finished. When he is back in place, the captain orders the handlers to stand their dogs, and then to leave them.

Although all the rest of Team work is normal Novice work, the drop on recall is substituted for the normal recall because it is more visually interesting, and Team work in the ring is designed for this. It requires individual drop training, of course, but it is the rare team that consists of dogs trained only to the Novice level. In the ring, all the dogs are left together, with the handlers walking together across the ring and turning together to face their dogs. Now comes the first time the dogs do a part of the exercise separately. One by one, on the judge's command to each handler, the dogs are called and dropped without further command from the judge or from the team captain. The entire team should use either command or signal, and the ideal is to have all four dogs drop so that they are in a precise line at the down. This takes more than a little preparatory work, but each individual team member should know just how long it takes his or her dog to drop after the command or signal, and time things on the drop so that all four will be in line. Then all four are called in together and finished together.

The long sit and down exercises are, even with the Team, identical with individual work. The only practice involved is timing on the part of the team members, so that they give their command-and-signal at the same time, leave their dogs, and walk across the ring in line, stop and turn at the same time, and return to their dogs again in line and circle to heel together.

And there you have Team work. It takes, as we have said, long and hard work, most of it on the part of the handlers in learning to work together as a team even before the dogs are brought into it. Team work is, however, rewarding and fascinating to watch. Some breed Teams have even gone to the lengths of having special uniforms made up to add to the picture. Others simply decide on, say, dark pants or skirts and white shirts to give the appearance of uniformity. Others dress as they please. It is, however, the precision and work that count, so don't hesitate to try making up a team even if the thought of informal uniforms leaves you cold. It's fun.

CHAPTER 9

Tracking and Advanced Tracking

Tracking, in a brief definition, is the dog's use of his nose to follow an invisible path of scent to find an object or person—exactly the sort of thing you've seen in old movies about escaped prisoners or lost children, with the sheriff's hounds baying along the trail. For most people, tracking is at once simplicity personified and the greatest of mysteries. Actually, it is neither of these. Almost any dog can be trained to track quite respectably (mind you, we said *almost* any dog). Once you have mastered the principles, tracking is easily understood. The training and the work are enjoyable, both for handler and dog, and although almost all lost-child and escaped-convict tracking is left to professionals, it just could be of practical use to you one day. They may laugh when your Poodle sits down at the trail of that lost child, but oh when he starts to track!

For the most part, though, tracking is an end in itself. It is a source of considerable pride if your dog can use his natural-born nose the way it was designed. Also, a purebred with or without any other obedience titles can earn a TD (Tracking Dog) title at AKC Tracking Tests. And don't *you* laugh at the Poodle mentioned above. Although the Sporting and Working breeds take most TD titles, in one recent year several Poodles received the title, as did a number of terriers and, so help us, a Pomeranian.

Done the right way, teaching your dog to track is easy enough, even if it does take time. If he has already done Utility work or its equivalent, he has the idea of smelling things out from scent discrimination. And even without a UD, there isn't a dog in the world who doesn't use his highly developed nose for his own purposes. Male dogs on their walks sniff everything vertical nearby to see who else has been there recently; very young puppies

223

race about the carpeting with their noses down, following scents; and you've certainly come home to find your own dog fascinated with sniffing the soles of your shoes to find out where you've been and what interesting new smells you're bringing home for him. But your dog should know retrieving fairly well and be under good obedience control before you try to start tracking training, as you will see when we get into the instruction. Aside from that it's wide open.

Above all, tracking is enjoyable. You and your dog get out into the fields and are exposed to sunshine and fresh air. You both get exercise whether you like it or not—and a great feeling of accomplishment when things begin to click. There are few greater thrills in dog owning than the first time you see him actually loping along a track, nose down—and he'll get a kick out of it too.

THE THEORY OF TRACKING

Exactly what happens when a dog follows a scent trail no one really knows. There are many theories, among them one which holds that the dog is able to follow a track by holding his nose half in and half out of a path of scent in the air—getting his directions at turns in the track by the way his nose slides out of the scent path. This sort of thing would imply a sharp border to a scent path, which, as far as anyone can tell, doesn't exist. Yet a dog *will* tend to follow one "edge" of a windblown scent, so far as we can tell. We don't really know.

For that matter, no one really knows even what smell itself is and how it works. The other senses we know a good deal about, but smell in humans, dogs, or whatever remains obscure.

With our own relatively weak human noses we smell. We get good smells and bad ones. After a fashion we, too, can locate the sources of strong odors. Thus far we can see into what goes on when a dog follows a track, but really little further. Our smell location is almost entirely on a trial-and-error basis. Comes a good smell of steak, we know it comes from the kitchen. Comes a smell of escaping gas and we check the stove, the heater, and all other likely sources until we hit a strong patch. Sometimes, by poking about a bit, we can even track down an elusive smell, good or bad, by casting about with our noses until we stumble on the source. But following the path taken by an odor source is largely beyond our comprehension.

Imagine, if you will, some strong smell that appeals to you particularly: steak, fried fish, or whatever. Then imagine again that someone has gone ahead of you in an open field with a platter of whatever it is, walking at random, making turns and twists for a quarter of a mile. Half an hour later, it's your job to follow the path that person took and end up wherever he laid the platter down. Pretty difficult to imagine even how to start. And that's the job that faces a dog in tracking.

Without knowing exactly what smell is, we have found out quite a bit about how it operates, and how a track is laid. When a person walks across a field, some of his personal smell is left on the ground by his shoes. More of it descends from his body (this smell-stuff, whatever it is, seems to be heavier than air) and is left on the ground and in the air where he has passed. It stays there or thereabouts for a surprisingly long time. Really good tracking dogs have been known to follow a track as much as a week old, under good conditions.

On a still, calm day, the scent stays pretty much where it was laid, getting fainter and more dispersed as time goes on. Heavy rain will wash it away, but a light shower may actually freshen it. Winds will push it this way and that. Later in this chapter we will go more thoroughly into the effects of winds and terrain on a track. For the moment, though, suffice it to say that a track, once laid, is astonishingly enduring and can be followed by a trained dog even if half a dozen different tracks and scents have been laid over it more recently.

Nor does a track have to be over grass or dirt, although an open field track is somewhat easier for a dog to follow. Late one night in London, one of the authors was walking with a constable and a police dog on patrol, when the constable offered to demonstrate street tracking. The author walked away, turning several corners, and about six blocks away went down the stairs of a basement entryway to a house. After some fifteen minutes the experiment seemed a failure. Starting up the steps to find the constable and offer consolation, the "criminal" heard a low, warning growl from the top of the stairs and stood very still, until the constable came up to put his dog back on lead.

That is routine work for a well-trained police/tracking dog. The scent *was* very fresh, but the dog had tracked over nothing but concrete and asphalt, across streets where cars and busses were passing and belching odors from their exhausts, and over sidewalks where other late-strolling pedestrians had left their scents after the "criminal" had gone by.

This power of distinguishing is one of the most interesting and baffling factors in tracking. The dog without question follows a specific, to him identifiable, scent—not just a strong smell of indeterminate nature. Not only that, but he can distinguish readily between two tracks, one older than the other, laid by the same person. He even seems able to detect the difference in strength of smell between one footstep and the following, for a tracking dog seldom backtracks. Put a dog on the middle of a trail, and he will head in the direction the tracklayer went, rather than where he came from.

The falling air scent of a person comprises the greater part of the track, contrary to popular mythology. A trained dog can follow a track laid by a person wearing rubber-soled shoes, galoshes, or rubber hip boots for that matter. Leather shoes, well impregnated with a personal smell, will leave a slightly stronger track by their contact with the ground, but leather shoes are far from a necessity, except in early training. Some dogs even track with their heads quite high in the air, giving the appearance of going for a casual stroll, with none of the B-movie business of snuffling along the ground and baying hideously. They work on the higher body smell left hanging in the air. Others do work with noses close to the ground, but here it is less the influence of the smell of the shoe leather than the fact that the heavier odor tends to collect at ground level and leaves a stronger track. So if you plan to work the other end of this business, don't bother to include gum-soled shoes in your escape budget. It doesn't do a bit of good.

One item that popular opinion and the Sunday supplements have largely right is the effect of water on a track. If a tracklayer crosses a fast-running stream he will confuse a tracking dog, but only momentarily. The air currents above moving water tend to carry scent right along with them. If the dog comes along a few hours later, however, the scent that was left above the water may be in the next county by that time. There is also the fact that anyone crossing more than a minor stream without a boat handy swims across, leaving little or no scent. But if the tracklayer exits from a stream directly across from where he entered, he might as well not have bothered. The dog and his handler, when faced with a track that ends at a stream, simply go across and see if a track is to be picked up on the other side. In a serious case, as with a lost person involved, the dog and handler will cast up and down the far side of the stream for a mile or more to find the spot where the tracklayer came out.

When a dog is about to begin a track, for business, pleasure, or competition, he has to get the scent he is to follow. The stock scene of giving the dog a shoe or other article of the tracklayer is quite valid in the business cases. It tells him what to look for, and then he is shown where the track begins, or set to looking for a track. In pleasure and competition tracking, the tracklayer scuffles around a bit at the start of the track, leaving an area well impregnated with his scent, and the dog is given this area as his clue. From then on, he is on his own. If he knows what he's about, and you've trained him well, he'll get to the end of the track through sleet and snow. All the theory in the world won't do him or you a bit of good. Let him have his head and be ready to move fast behind him.

TRACKING EQUIPMENT

The special equipment required for tracking training is quite inexpensive. You need, first of all, a tracking harness. This is much like a regular walking harness. The main idea of the tracking harness is to put the strain of pulling at the tracking line on the dog's chest. A walking harness does this to some extent, but a real tracking harness is better, if it is at all possible for you to lay your hands on one, or have one made.

Second, you should have a tracking line, twenty to forty feet in length with a marker twenty feet from the snap—a loop or knot in the line to let you know when the dog is twenty feet in front of you. The most practical tracking line is lightweight webbing, but you can also use a length of nylon clothesline with a snap on the end. Some people prefer this, but the nylon line gets tangled up much more easily than webbing, and it will tend to slip through your hand when you are trying to control a fast-tracking dog. The twenty-foot marker complies with the AKC regulation for a Tracking Test, in which the dog must be at least that distance in front of you.

Next, two track flags, which are easy enough to make. They should be of quarter- to half-inch dowel, approximately four feet long and sharpened on one end for ramming into the ground. On to the other end fasten a square of some material—the bigger the better, up to eighteen inches square. These two flags are used to mark out the beginning of your practice tracks. They are important for two reasons: It is highly essential that you remember exactly where the track goes, and they will get the dog used to working next to flapping flags if he ever tracks in competition.

Half a dozen "turn stakes" also come in handy. These are easily made from green bamboo garden stakes, three to four feet long, available at any garden store. Again, sharpened at one end—and on the other a small bit of bright material wrapped around tightly (not flapping loose, as in the starting flags) so that you can see them at a distance in a green field. These stakes are used to mark the turning points in practice tracks—visible to you, but to the dog looking just like something growing there. Fortunately for training in this case, dogs are color-blind, and are not likely to notice the colored material at the top, be it even blinding red. But the stakes themselves should be green, or close thereto. Color-blind or not, the dog does see varying shades of white, gray, and black, and a white dowel used as a turn stake will attract his attention.

Finally, you need an article for the dog to find at the end of the track. Generally, this is an old glove. A glove is ideal; it is small, hard to see lying in grass, and probably had been soaking for years in your scent. Other articles are all right if you've given all your old gloves to the Salvation Army.

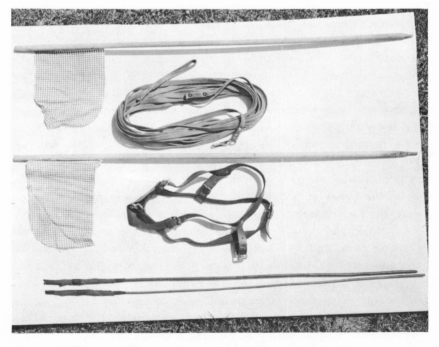

Tracking equipment: two flags, tracking lead and harness, and turn stakes (you may need only two of these).

An old sock rolled up isn't bad; some use an old wallet or even a cheap new one from the dime store, thoroughly scented before using.

In the final analysis, none of these things, except the article, is drastically necessary for the early stages of tracking training—the dog can be trained at first using a normal collar and a lead, no flags at all, and not a stake in sight. But we wouldn't guarantee it. The first day or two out in the field, you might want to try it with just a collar and short lead to see how things go before putting money into harness and tracking line. We don't recommend it, but if you want to try it that way, go ahead. Where we say "harness" in the first stages, read "collar"; but if it's a training collar, be sure to fasten your snap on the dead ring so your dog isn't choking himself when he strains to pull along the track.

THE FIRST STAGES

The harness and line will be new items to the dog. If he's well trained, and pretty well resigned to various kinds of foolishness from you, he may not react to them at all. Find out first, though, before you start to work. Operate just as if he were a puppy with his first collar, letting him get used to the thing before you strap it on him. And then let him romp and play a bit with the harness on, to get accustomed to it. Next step: Fasten on the tracking line, and let him drag that around a little. When you're actually tracking, you'll find it impossible to keep twenty to forty feet of line off the ground, and in fact you shouldn't try to. So let him get used to the idea of all that line dragging behind him and at times snagging on things. Here we don't anticipate any trouble, as most dogs work quite happily as soon as a harness is put on. But if you have one of the rare problem cases, just stick with it, slow and easy and cajolingly until he gets used to it.

Once he has gotten used to it, the harness should be kept strictly for business. Put it on him when you are ready to start work, take it off when you take a break, and take it off as soon as you have finished working for the day. To him the harness should mean that the time for tracking has come—when he has it on he is to work, and no nonsense.

As soon as the dog doesn't mind the harness and line, you are ready for the first step. This is the point that to most people seems hardest of all, but it is actually the easiest. All his life your dog has been using his nose for his own diverse purposes: to identify friend and foe, to see where you've been by sniffing your clothes and shoes when you come in. Now you're going to almost trick him into using it to follow a trail. Perhaps we can best explain by using you as an example.

Whenever, in the past, you've wanted to find a bakery, you've gotten there by means of addresses and signs in the window. And at the same time you've undoubtedly mouth-watered at the wonderful and unmistakable smell of fresh bread, cakes, and rolls. Suppose, now, that you were blindfolded and led down a strange street in which there was a bakery with an open door. Think you could find it? You could, and without straining a bit—yet you've probably never thought of trying to find a bakery by smell alone.

This is pretty much what you're going to do with your dog now. From visual finding of something with your smell on it, along a strong trail of your own odor, you're going to nudge him into scent finding. Remember: You're not teaching your dog to smell—you're just teaching him a new way to use the talent he's had all his life.

At the beginning, it's a big help if you have someone else along with you in the field to lay out the flags and stakes you'll use for the track you'll lay, but it isn't essential. If you can manage to start training with another handler, the two of you can reciprocate in stake planting. If an assistant does all the handling and placing of stakes, they won't have your scent on them and the dog won't be tempted to try to retrieve them. But again, it's not strictly necessary, so if you have to do your initial training alone, go to it.

Select an open field somewhere, as big as you can find. This will be a problem for urbanites, but a little judicious investigation should turn up a promising area not too far from where you live. Ask at farmhouses and the like; if you can establish your bonafides and make an interesting story of tracking training you should be able to get permission to use an empty field. But whatever you do, and this we cannot emphasize too strongly, take care of that field like a putting green. Any littering or damage will end your use of it, and ruin it and the entire neighborhood for anyone else who may want to use fields for tracking, picnicking, or other activities.

If you have a choice, pick a flat field with no trees and bushes, and with grass about ankle high. At least avoid as many obstacles as possible, and keep an eye out for such natural hazards as low-lying brambles, poison ivy, and other bucolic flotsam. Before you go field hunting, we recommend a reading of the section on "Scent and Tracks" (pages 255–58) so that you'll be able to avoid some of the worst barriers to tracking success.

When you have the field in hand, take a good reading of the prevailing wind. This is best done not with the traditional wetted forefinger raised, but by dropping some dried grass and chaff to see which way it blows. This bit of advice may seem superfluous if you're an old woodsman, but you'd be surprised how many city dwellers can't tell which way the wind is blowing until their hats go rolling down the street to leeward.

Set up shop on the downwind side of the field, about thirty feet from the edge—and don't let your dog play about in the field before you settle down to work. Plant your first flag in the ground. Walk thirty yards straight into the wind and plant the second flag (in a Tracking Test, the flags are always thirty yards apart). Then walk back straight along the line to the first flag and the dog. Get your article ready and you're off.

This day, and all through your beginning, we recommend that you wear leather shoes, despite our introductory remarks about leather vs. rubber. True, to a trained tracking dog it matters little whether the tracklayer has been shod in rubber or leather. But a leather sole does leave a slightly stronger scent along the ground, and you want to throw every advantage to the dog in the beginning. So stick to leather at first, if you can.

With the dog at heel beside you—you on his right and the starting flag on his left—throw the glove about halfway to the second flag. Send him for it, harness and all, and shower him with praise when he retrieves it for you. Then throw it out a little farther and send him again. Keep this up until he has retrieved it a time or two from as far away as you can throw it.

Pick a command now to use for tracking, the most logical being "Track!" or "Seek!" or "Go find!" The first few times you throw the glove out, use your retrieve command, and then for a few times use the two commands together: "Mike, fetch! Track!" Then switch to the tracking command and use it only when your dog is in the tracking harness and down to the business of tracking.

All this, of course, presupposes the dog to be trained in the retrieve. If for any reason you are trying to teach a dog tracking who does not have the basic obedience training preceding this chapter, we can only refer you to the appropriate chapter of this book, in this case "Open," and tell you to go back a step and teach him to retrieve, starting with the dumbbell. And of course learning the retrieve depends on the dog's knowing the sit-stay, so if yours is completely untrained at this point, back you'll go right to "Basic Training." Rare indeed is the handler who tries to train his dog in tracking before anything else, but if it happens to be you, this is as good a place as any to point out again that all training, including tracking, is built up pyramidally on the foundations of the work that has gone before. We don't mean to say that he must be ring trained, or even obedience trained as we define it; but to follow our method of tracking training he must be able to do a controlled retrieve of one kind or another.

If the dog is well up on his retrieve, you may at this point run into a momentary problem with the flags. Some few dogs, of almost any size, will be put off by the flapping. If it happens to you, don't try to force him to retrieve by the flags until you've heeled him in a figure eight around the flags to get him used to them. Then, give him a few retrieves away from the flags, slowly working him back until he goes out right by them without minding. After this, change your flags to a new location before starting work again, as this area will be well churned up with scent in all directions.

As soon as the dog has done the few retrieves as far as you can throw the article along the line of the flags, you are ready for the second step: beginning to lay a heavy path of your own scent leading to the article. Have him sit and stay just back of the first flag. Walk directly past the second flag about ten feet, drop the glove (and be sure he's watching you do it—make a production of it if necessary), and walk back directly to him. Snap on the line and be sure it is lying free and unkinked on the ground behind him. Don't try to carry it coiled up, cowboy-style, in your hand. Then give him a command to lie down, having placed him first so that when he goes down his nose is close by the first flag. This means little in actual practice at this time, but it is the pattern for future tracking and you may as well start establishing it now.

Putting him down at the start of the track is done to get his nose close to the beginning of the scent. Some trainers and handlers advocate going further: actually holding the dog's head down so that his nose is millimeters from the ground. We don't like this procedure, largely because it is totally unnecessary. There is plenty of odor a few inches from the ground where the dog's head will normally be at the down; forcing his head down for, say, thirty seconds is an imposition on the dog just at the time when you want his wholehearted cooperation.

When he has been at the down for a few seconds, take hold of the line about six inches from the harness, and as you give him the command to get the glove, urge him along in the right direction. Do anything within reason to get him moving out after the glove. Fling out your free arm in the proper direction; begin yourself along the route; give him the command again and again coaxingly; guide him a few feet by the harness. Generally, after having gone through the free retrieve along the track and having seen you go out to drop the glove, he will charge right off to get it this time.

Once he's going, let the line slip through your hand and stand still while he gets the glove and returns to you with it. Next time, clamp down on the line just slightly so that he has to pull a very little as he's going. If he's so well leash trained that a slight pressure stops him, encourage him to go on, and on successive tries increase the pressure as he goes out, until you have control of the situation. But don't make it too hard for him, and don't force him to a dead stop yet. Just get him used to the idea of pulling against the harness as he goes after the article.

Increase the distance by ten-foot steps until you are going out 100 to 120 feet to drop the glove. Stop calling his attention to the fact that you are dropping it. At that distance a dog's sight is not too good anyway, and at 100 feet about all he will know is that you went out with the glove and came back empty-handed. When he goes out on these longer retrieves, let the line slip through your hand until you feel the twenty-foot knot, then begin to apply light pressure and go along behind the dog. Vary the distance between you from twenty feet to the end of the line, depending on how fast he is going out. When he gets the article and runs back to you with it, praise him highly each time, of course, then take it and go along with him back to the starting flag—being careful yourself to walk back along the straight-line track, no matter if he wanders beside you off the track.

By the time he's going out 120 feet for the article, he may already have started using his nose to find it. In most cases he will have, so you must be careful about your handling of him and the line. Important: Don't restrain him or call him back to you if he does not go out exactly along the line of the track as you've laid it. Even into the wind, and particularly if there's any crosswind at all, the dog may be working a scent that has blown a good distance away from where you walked. As long as he's going approximately in the right direction, let him go. He may in fact travel in a wide semicircle from starting point to the article. If so, let him go. It is of the greatest importance at this point that the dog not become discouraged about tracking—and nothing will discourage him more than your pulling him off a track that he was happily and correctly following.

At this point, too, it would be well to reemphasize the essential fact that no dog in the world can be coerced into learning tracking. Tracking is, more than any other thing he does, a gesture of goodwill from the dog to you, and he'll only learn it on a foundation of obedience and respect. Aside from that, it's fun for him when he's handled correctly—as witness the fact that every puppy in the world loves nothing better than to chase things and find them. But the dog absolutely cannot be forced into tracking. Just about the first time you scream at him, or belt him, he's going to turn in his uniform and head for the showers. And if anyone thinks he can make a dog track by gritting at him, "Smell, dammit, smell!". . . well, we hope he never offers his dog's services when we get lost in the woods.

Therefore, if your dog seems to be having difficulties on these first easy retrieves, the only solution is patience, praise, and a willingness to think out the difficulties and to go back over each step until the dog has the idea down. If you run into trouble, sit down and ponder on where you made the mistake; *he* hasn't made any mistakes in training. Whatever you do, don't try to rush tracking training. Take each step slowly and don't go on to the next until you are absolutely sure that your dog has mastered the one in hand. Too fast progression may only confuse him, and then you've had it.

If the dog is beginning to use his nose on the longer straight runs—and as we've said, most of them will have—you'll run into a few minor points in handling aside from the temptation to pull him off when he's not searching dead in your footsteps. Among them is the problem of what to do with all that line. One of the most common mistakes of the beginning handler is trying to keep the line too short, and in the air. If the dog is loping along after the article, you should be working twenty feet or more behind him. Unless he's pulling quite hard, part of the line will be on the ground. Then, suddenly, he will seem to lose the scent, and will circle around trying to find it again. He will in all probability come right back up to you as he searches for the scent. When he does this, don't try to keep the line straight between you and him. Just hold on to it wherever you were holding when he stopped going straight ahead, and let it lie on the ground. He'll walk over it and won't get tangled up. Then, when he's off on the trail again you can either let him take up the slack himself or close it up a bit yourself. If you try to keep pulling it in as he wanders, it will almost inevitably get fouled up in his legs, and then the panic is on for fair. Just let it lie. This takes a bit of practice and self-control, but you'll catch on almost as quickly as he does.

The other greatest beginner's mistake is a feeling of horror when he does circle back to you in looking for a lost scent. The immediate reaction is, "Lordy, here he comes—he'll get a great big fresh whiff of me and then the track I laid will seem like nothing to him." It isn't so, for some reason we can't fully explain. Even if he brushes right by you, getting a really ripe noseful of just the scent he's looking for on the ground, it won't confuse him. He'll just ignore it. Probably it's because he knows full well *you* don't have the glove, and he knows that the glove does lie at the end of that older scent trail. Whatever it is, coming near you or passing behind you on the track won't bother him at all. He'll hunt until he finds the original track, put his nose down, and off he'll go until he finds the glove.

When he does do this circling to refind the track, stand right where you were when he lost it. Play out the lead if necessary, and let him cast around until he comes across it again. If you yourself move about with him, chances are you will both wander away from the track, and you will lose it. In the early stages, it is vital that you remember where it is, and give him help and encouragement in finding it again. With you standing still and letting him cast around you in a circle, he is certain to cross the track again at two points, and will pick it up more surely.

What you've been doing all this time, walking back and forth over the same path, is laying down a really powerful path of your own odor. Each time you walk over it you reinforce it until it has become the dominant impression the dog receives as he runs out along that line to get the glove. Every time he goes out along the right line his nose is filled with your scent. Then, the first time he's not sure by sight where the glove is—and wanders off the true, trying to find it—the great light will dawn. By that time the two factors, the glove and your scent along the ground, will be closely joined in his mind. He'll hunt back until he finds the scent trail, follow it, and lo! there is the glove, giving off a slightly stronger scent of you to lead him on the last few feet.

The moment he first makes the connection is monumental—when he first puts his nose down and begins sniffing the trail. It is one of the greatest thrills of dog owning and training. And from that moment on, the procedure of tracking training is simply one of extension of that discovery of his, and practice under increasing amounts of difficulty.

THE FIRST TURN

Provided you have the space in your training field, you should continue your straight line tracks until the dog will go out 200 feet to find the article dropped there by you, working with his nose all the time, and retrieve it without fail. When he can do that to your satisfaction (and that is probably as far as you will get on your first training day), you are ready for a turn in the track.

This first turn is probably the most critical point in tracking training. Until now your dog has been going out in a straight line, and over a track laid and relaid by you as you walk back and forth along it, first to drop the glove and then to go out with him to find it. Even assuming he has made the vital connection between the retrieving and the smelling, you should be aware that he is still doing only what amounts to a long retrieve in a straight line. Now he is going to go out over a once-laid track, where the scent will be considerably lighter, and the glove isn't going to be right at the end of the straight line. He is likely to become confused when he passes the turn going straight ahead, and runs out of scent without coming to the glove.

To help him, start with a fresh track laid crosswind. This first turn will be on a separate day, so the old track shouldn't confuse him, but if you're using the same field, still try to avoid the old track. Put down your flags, and if possible have an assistant walk out about 200 feet beyond the starting flag to put in a turn stake. Wait twenty to thirty minutes to let his track cool off a bit. Then, with your article in hand and the dog waiting by the first flag, walk out along the line until you are ten feet or so from the turn stake and make a right-angle turn *into the wind*. If you're working alone, simply plant the flag as you make the turn.

Making the first turn into the wind will give your dog considerable help in catching on to the idea. As he works out along the original crosswind track, he will quite probably be working downwind of the track, following the edge of the odor—but of course he may not. Always allow him and his nose to be the judge of how he tracks. As he gets to the end of the familiar straight line, he'll get a slightly stronger scent as the wind blows the scent from the article and from the short right-angle track back across the first leg.

To help him further, scuffle up the ground after making the turn in laying the track, and shuffle along a bit scuffing your feet as you go after the turn. Leave the article only about fifteen feet along the new leg. Then go straight ahead thirty or forty yards before you turn again, making a large rectangle of your path, coming back to the line of the starting flags well away from the straight long first leg, and around back to your dog. This makes his first one-turn track also his first single-scent track with a definite pattern to it, the scent getting fresher and newer as he follows the track/trail in the right direction. All your practice tracks from now on should be made this way.

Down your dog at the beginning of the scent, right by the first flag, then give him the command to get the article. He'll go sniffing along the path until he comes to where you made your turn and probably keep right on going a few feet before he realizes that the scent has stopped dead. Then comes your first real handling in tracking, for now you must control him via the line while he learns that all tracks do not invariably go in a straight line in this best of all possible worlds.

This takes a bit of skill and practice. When he comes to where you made the turn (and this is the purpose of the stakes—so you'll know exactly where the turn is), you should be twenty to forty feet behind him on the line. He will be pulling hard on the harness, and when you see him over-shoot the turn you can bring him to a halt with not much extra pressure on the line. However, and heed this most carefully, be *absolutely sure* that he is well beyond the turn and off the track before you bring him to a stop. A vagary of the wind may have blown your scent ten or twenty feet ahead of where you actually turned, and he may still be working a legitimate scent even if he is that far past the turning spot.

When he finally has run out of scent, either directly at the turn or beyond it, he will appear confused for a moment, or he may immediately begin to circle, or "cast," to find out where the scent went. If he appears confused, it is because he didn't find the article at what, to him, is the end of the track. Be sure to urge him on encouragingly here. Coax him with the "Find it!" command. This keeps him working, and lets him know that it's perfectly all right that he didn't find it where he expected to. Otherwise, if he walks out to the end of that straight line, finds nothing, and you just let him stand there, he may think he's gotten a bad shuffle this time around.

Most dogs, running out of scent, *will* begin to cast for the track. Whether he moves in a circle toward or away from where you know the new leg to be, stand where you are and let him cast, acting as the center of the circle he can move in by not letting any more line out. In casting, the dog will do one of two things. He may go around a half circle the wrong way, come across the original straight-line track, and follow it again to the turning point. If he does this, let him go along, not moving yourself unless you are standing right where he wants to go. When he comes to the end of the

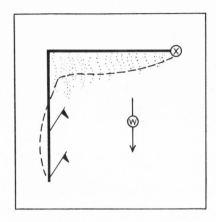

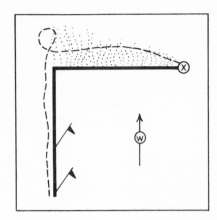

Dog (*dashed line*) making turn with
first "leg" into wind.

Dog casting for turn with first "leg"
downwind.

Dog's path with diagonal wind across
track.

Dog casting for turn, with no wind.

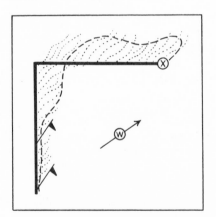

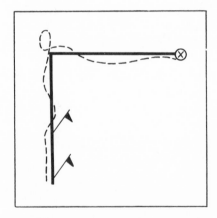

These possible paths indicate how a dog may work apparently far off the actual line
of the track under varying conditions. It is vitally important *not* to insist on his
following right in the footsteps of the tracklayer. He can't and won't do it.

scent again he will probably stop a little sooner in his overshoot, and may
even repeat the whole performance. Keep letting him have his head and
eventually he will try a circle in the other direction and hit upon the second leg. He may of course turn the right way in the first place and get right

onto the track again. In either case, remember that the scent of the second leg may have been blown about a bit, so don't be too adamant about where he should or should not get onto the track. He'll pick it up, or the edge of it, and follow that along until it runs out, this time at the article. As he searches for the second leg, keep encouraging him with the command, his name, and an occasional "Good boy" to keep him happy and working. And of course when he comes across the article and brings it to you, smother him with effusive praise.

Again, there is the rare dog who simply can't seem to grasp the idea at first that there can be a turn in the track. If he passes right over the new leg several times without realizing that it is the track, or if he simply gives up when the first leg runs out on him, go right up to him and gently lead him to the turn and then off in the right direction until you both happen upon the article. Point it out to him if necessary, tell him to retrieve it, and then make a gigantic fuss over him as though he'd done the whole thing all by himself. If you have gone slowly and carefully in your training up to the first turn, being sure that he is actually using his nose, your chances of running into such serious first-turn trouble are small indeed. And if you do run into it, leading him through the turn a few times will solve it.

Having gotten over this second major hurdle in tracking, you then proceed to make the second leg longer and longer until he can infallibly negotiate the turn at 200 feet and go along the new leg another 200 feet. But be absolutely sure he has the turn well mastered—do the "turn plus fifteen feet" several times before starting to increase the distance. He may overshoot and cast about for the scent every time, but you will know when he has the idea well in hand.

Surprisingly enough, no matter how often you have done it, your dog will probably not automatically turn in the direction you've been turning unless his nose tells him to. By this point in training he will be well convinced that you're a pretty sly character, albeit lovable, and he wouldn't put it past you to make the turn in the opposite direction one of these times, just to confuse him. So don't worry about his cheating. Even if he comes within a time or two to take the turn easily, count only your blessings and look not the gift tracking dog in the mouth. It means only that he's getting good at the business quickly.

He may even shortcut the turn quite sharply, changing direction toward the glove well before he comes to where you've been making the turn. Again, it's his nose that's dictating his actions, not any real foreknowledge that thither lies the article. If he does do this, check your wind direction to see if perhaps the scent from the second leg mightn't have blown back along the first leg, allowing the dog to find the turn many feet before you actually made it. The wind, in fact, may be blowing the stronger scent of the article right along to the first leg. If so, the dog will take off in a direct line for it. The only solution for this is a careful check of wind direction to make sure that it is not blowing diagonally from the article back across the first leg.

As the dog goes along the straight second leg, or even in the middle of the first, he may lose the scent even without a turn. Just why this happens to a dog we don't really know, but it does happen. Again, the handler should allow the dog to circle at the end of the line, encouraging him with commands and praise to cast until he finds it again. Here you can be specially helpful because you know when he has come across approximately the right place to pick up the scent again. When he reaches the spot, increase your praise and make your commands more urgent so that he will know there is something of significance about that area. He'll probably pick it right up again and be off. It may happen several times on the straightaway, but keep him at it, and have patience.

Sometimes, right in the middle of a hot track, the dog may stop cold and appear to forget not only what he is doing but even why in the world he's out in the middle of a big field wearing a harness and a forty-foot line. In the middle of a training session he may go cold at the very beginning of a track. In either case, try taking hold of the harness and leading him along the track for ten or twenty feet, urging and commanding him, "Find it!" This may snap him out of it. If not, take him back to the start, take a break, lay a fresh track out to the article, and try to get him started off again. If that doesn't get him going, the only solution is to give it up for the day. He may be just plain beat. There may be something in the wind that bothers him—perhaps a nasty odor blowing in from the next field. There's no way to know, so take his word for it that he can't or won't track anymore that day and pack it in. Come back next day to another field, if possible, or a few days later to the same place. But think about it in the interim, especially about whether you may have been overworking him. Overtraining can be fatal in tracking. If he gets bored, you're finished, so keep him working only as long as he seems happy about finding that glove.

There are two disciplinary problems that crop up not infrequently in the field in the middle of a track. He may see an appetizing bird or rabbit or other denizen of the woods and take off after it. The solution to this is to stop where you are and let him fetch up short at the end of the line, with you standing still as an anchor. Don't snap or jerk on the line to make a correction—he's following his most basic natural instincts, and it's only a misdemeanor. And you definitely don't want any misbehavior corrections associated with the harness and tracking line. The other, and really quite minor, problem is the dog's relieving himself while on a track. These natural functions can't be controlled to any extent when the dog is exposed to bushes just made for leg lifting, so let him finish and then put him back on the track. Insist on this—some dogs want to halloo around the field in triumph after so wondrously complicated an accomplishment as wetting a bush, but bring him up short with the line and put him right back to work.

MORE TURNS

When you've progressed to finding the article 200 feet beyond the turn and the dog is doing a steady and sure job of it, you are ready for the second turn. The procedure here is exactly the same as with the first turn. Again, if you can have someone else place the stake for the turn, well and good, but do it yourself if necessary.

Again, drop your article about fifteen feet beyond the turn. Continue in your squared pattern, returning to the rear of your dog. When he comes to the second running out of scent he'll have had experience of turns, so he won't be confused. Use your handling experience and let him cast until he has found the way, and he'll get to the article. When he's sure of his second turn, keep increasing the distance until you're dropping the article 200 feet beyond. This will make a total track of 600 feet—and you'll develop strong legs in the process. Several hundred yards out and around with the article, then another several hundred yards behind the dog as he goes out and returns. What with something like half a mile of walking on each two-turn track you do, there's not too much danger of your overworking the dog. You'll probably be willing to call it quits before he is.

At this point we might insert a cautionary word about progress and overworking. As we do not attempt to give you a day-by-day schedule of steps and work, it is easy to get the idea that tracking is something that can be learned in a weekend or two. It isn't so. Particularly if you live in the city and can work at it only on weekends, it will take you several months before your dog is tracking well. The rule here, perhaps even more than in any other work, is: Take it slow and easy. He cannot learn more than a little each day, and it is far better to get that little well established than trying to push on to new things. Work with him an hour at a time, at most. If it is a cool and pleasant day and you are in the country anyway, it won't hurt to put in two one-hour sessions, well separated. But give him plenty of rest, and try not to work steadily for the hour; take a break at the half-hour. That way he will be fresh and willing, and your progress will be good. But, again, don't expect it to be sudden and easy. It takes time and work, and nothing else will do it.

On all the tracks, from the very first one hardly farther than the second flag to the 600-foot two-turn tracks, always keep in mind the vitally important fact that the dog's nose is better than yours. This may seem ridiculous, but it's something that even experienced handlers forget at times. Either the handlers do know just where the track is and can't believe that the dog is really working way off there, or they don't know and can't quite believe that the track was laid that way. In the beginning, even when you know where the track is and your dog seems to be way, way off, let him have his head until and unless he has gone a long way in a completely wrong direction and obviously isn't working a track. Later, when you're following a track that you haven't seen laid, you have to be completely dependent on your dog's nose, and not at all on your own common sense.

At one AKC Tracking Test, we watched a really heartbreaking example of the pitfalls of knowing more than the dog about the track. One handler, who had trained for months and had an excellent dog, was put on a track. The starting flags made a line pointing directly between two large, close-together trees about fifty feet in front of the flags. Sure enough, the dog put his nose down and started loping directly out toward the gap between the trees. His handler, however, was convinced that the track couldn't have been laid between those trees. As the dog headed toward the trees, the handler held him back via the line and urged him to cast for a turn. The dog cast around a bit, then headed straight for the trees again. Once more his handler pulled him off and told him to cast. Again it happened, and when he was pulled off for the third time the unhappy dog agreed, in effect, "Okay boss, I'll go somewhere else." He turned to the right and made off in that direction. All of which made his handler very happy until the judge's whistle shrilled to let him know that he was far off the track and had failed.

When he got back, one of the judges asked him, "Why in the devil didn't you let that dog go between those trees?" The awful truth dawned, and great oaths were heard in the land. It was hard on him, but it was an object lesson never to be forgotten by the spectators. When you're working with your dog, keep this story in mind—and remember that the dog's nose is a good deal better than yours.

THE STRANGE TRACK

The third and final hurdle in tracking is the switch from your own long-familiar scent to a track laid by someone else. We call this latter the "strange" track simply to differentiate it from all those going before that were laid and relaid by you. Here it is absolutely essential to have an assistant who is willing to work with you and your dog. It is also helpful to have a third person to place the flags and stakes.

You will be ready for the strange track when your dog can follow your own track at least 600 feet, through a minimum of two turns, and do a very respectable job each time. If you have room in the field, practice with even longer "self" tracks and more turns to be sure your dog knows his job before going to the strange track. At an AKC Tracking Test, the track will be between 440 and 500 *yards*, and it is worthwhile working up to this distance before making the switch. A little later in this chapter you'll see sample diagrams of tracks laid to get the maximum distance out of a moderate-sized field—so you may be able to lay a longer track in your field than you think. You can, of course, go through gates into adjoining fields. For the effects of gates on windblown scent, see the later discussion of "Scent and Tracks" (pages 255–58).

Once you are ready, the switch of tracks is a simple extension of all your training to date. Keep the dog in the car, or at least somewhere well away so that he can't see what's going on. After determining the best work area, ask your third party to lay out a long track, starting with the flags and marking the turns with stakes. He should be wearing rubbers or rubber-soled shoes for this to cut his track down slightly, but it isn't strictly necessary. If you have no third party to work with, your tracklayer himself will have to go out to plant the stakes as he makes the turns.

Your tracklayer for this strange track should ideally be a stranger, not a family member, friend, or anyone who has worked with you in the training. This may be difficult to arrange, but you can often' enough persuade a friend to ask a friend to spend a nice day outdoors with a plentiful supply of

(1) Arranging the lead before the start. Dog is down at the starting flag, getting the scent.

(3) Dog makes the first turn, short of the turn stake. The model here is the country's first UDT Great Dane.

(2) Dog starts, while the handler pays out the line. These snow pictures illustrate that tracking is not confined to spring days.

(4) Victory. Dog returns with glove in mouth.

food and drink and the opportunity of an interesting new experience watching a tracking dog at work. Clearly, a family member will do in a pinch, but get as "strange" a tracklayer as you can. And be quite sure you explain fully and carefully exactly what you need done. One of the unfortunately true maxims of tracking is, "It's harder to train a good tracklayer than a dog."

With the track plotted, flags and stakes in place, you begin on the strange scent almost exactly as you did with your own. Your tracklayer begins by scuffing around at the first flag to leave a good patch of scent, then walks out into the wind about twenty-five feet beyond the second flag to drop the article, holding it in his hand as he goes, to apply his scent to it. After he has dropped the article, he should continue to walk along the path of the longer track you have plotted, then circle well around, behind and away from the starting flag.

As soon as the tracklayer has gotten off the field (be careful that he doesn't come near the dog afterward), take the dog to the starting flag and down him so that his nose is in the middle of the heavy patch of scent made by the shuffling at the flag. Start him off with the usual command, and help him by leading him by the harness toward the second flag if necessary. If he seems to have the idea right away, start paying out the line and let him go. If he is puzzled at not finding a strong trail of your scent, encourage him forward by commands, pointing and leading with the harness—right up to the article, if required. Ninety-nine percent of all dogs who have been carefully trained up to this point catch on with little trouble. By this time he has gotten used to the fact that the article he is to find lies somewhere out along the line of the flags. Even if your scent isn't there, and tricky as he knows you to be, he'll take a sporting chance and start out along that line. Then, somewhere along the line he realizes that this new scent filling his nose is going right along with him, and the second great light will dawn. Lo! other scents than yours can lead to the article!

We have seen very few dogs trained up to this point who cannot make the switch. If yours is slow to get the idea, it means only that the strange scent is confusing him, and that he needs your help to make the connection. Have your tracklayer start over again at the first flag and walk out along the track carrying the glove. You walk out along directly behind him, lagging by eight or ten feet. This lays down a combination of your two scents, and when you put your dog down now on the combined track— yours and the tracklayer's, which leads to the article with only the tracklayer's scent—the idea will begin to get through to him. Then try the tracklayer's track again, without your own scent on it.

When he makes the first unassisted find on the strange track, make a great deal of fuss over him. Even if you've had to lead him right up to the article and build a large sign over it with neon arrows, praise him each time he gets it. Then the first time he gets it all by himelf, really let out all the stops. Give him to understand that he is the most loyal, intelligent, trustworthy, kind, considerate, noble, talented dog in the surrounding seven counties. He'll get the message. Then give everybody a rest.

It is possible that with a really acute dog you may run into an overshoot problem. After all, there is for the first time a track, however much lighter, leading right past the article. In the excitement of following this new scent he may try to lope right past the article and follow the track the tracklayer left when circling out of the field. It does happen. If it happens to you (and you're luckier than you realize if it does), you can use the lead to snub him up just as he passes the article, and call his attention to it. If he's stopped cold by the lead, and you give him the "Find it!" command, he'll stumble on the article in casting. Continue to apply this correction as often as necessary, for it is essential that the dog find the article rather than follow the track to its end. If the problem continues, ask your tracklayer to carry a turn stake out with him and plant it just off to the side of the track, where he has dropped the article. This lets you know exactly where it is, and you can start to slow down your dog with the tracking line as he approaches the article.

When you are sure that your dog has a thorough understanding of the new circumstances, you can have the tracklayer go out progressively to 100 feet beyond the flag. Then introduce one turn with a short second leg— then longer second legs, then on to two turns and more. Don't try to go too fast, but be sure the dog is doing a very good job before adding more distance or another turn.

In tracking the strange scent, you will use the same handling techniques you used on your "self" tracks. If he loses the track momentarily at a turn or on a straightaway, snub him gently with the line and encourage him to cast until he has picked it up again. And always keep in mind the prime dictum about his nose being better than yours.

THE BLIND TRACK

Though this will be the first "real" track for you as the handler, it is no harder for the dog than the ones directly before. For a blind track, ask your tracklayer to go out into a fresh field, put down the starting flags, and proceed to lay a long (600 feet or more) track with at least two turns, without putting down any turn stakes. Here, of course, is where you must have an understanding tracklayer, for he must himself plot a good track that will not confuse your dog with too-close turns, overlapping scents, or scents splashed along walls or bushes. The tracklayer should proceed as before, leaving a strong patch of scent at the starting flag, a strong track to the second flag, and then step out along the track. You yourself must not have any idea where the track goes, so sit in the car with your dog until the tracklayer signals from a distance that all is in readiness.

When you bring your dog up to the first flag for this track, do everything just as you have done it before. Take your time, make sure the harness is on properly, talk to the dog encouragingly, and try to keep his enthusiasm up. Then down him at the first flag, give him a minute to get the scent well in his nose while you're straightening out the line, and start him off.

Stand beside the first flag paying out the line until he is past the second flag and obviously on the track. If he seems confused before getting to the second flag, let him cast for the scent at the end of your line, but don't let him get beyond the second flag until he obviously is working the track. It is very nearly impossible for us to tell you how to know when your dog is really working—by this time you will certainly know. Once he is beyond that second flag, do your utmost only to keep going along with him, without trying to guide him with the line. From there on out, the track may go 100 yards straight or it may take a turn twenty-five feet beyond the flag, or do almost anything else. Only the tracklayer knows. If at any time the dog seems to have lost it, stand still and let him cast at the end of the line, but don't try to encourage him in any particular direction from that point. The track may take a turn there, or go straight ahead. And don't assume that a turn must be to the left because you saw the tracklayer coming from the left as he returned to the car. The article may be there, but there may be any number of curious turns before you get there. We keep repeating this advice to the point of monotony only because it applies to such a common mistake, even with experienced handlers. You won't really understand how easy it is to try to guide the dog until you're out in the field yourself, but once there you'll find the temptation at times near irresistible. Don't do it.

If the field you are working is a particularly bushy one, or even if not, the line may become tangled and snagged somewhere as the dog is casting for the scent. If it happens, work the snag loose, calling encouragement to the dog as you do so. If you've been keeping an eye on things properly, you'll know which way he was headed when he was stopped by the snag. This is one of the few times you can somewhat guide the dog—when he starts up on being freed you can encourage him with the line to continue in the same direction. But don't insist if he wants to go another way. He may have been at a turn just then.

When he passes this test, do another one with a colder track. Wait twenty minutes after the tracklayer finishes before putting your dog on. Then try one that is half an hour old. Work him up until he can pick up and follow a blind strange track that is at least two hours old; this is the maximum for AKC Tracking Tests. Once the dog has successfully followed several such tracks by the same tracklayer, switch again to someone else. Test your dog with a variety of tracks laid by a variety of people—men, women, and children, light and heavy individuals. He'll thus learn to follow all sorts of different scent trails, and get used to different degrees of crushed grass and overturned or disturbed earth in the tracks of people of different weights walking in different manners. For an AKC Tracking Test, prepare your dog for anything; you'll have no advance information as to the sex or other characteristics of the tracklayers to be used in the test.

ADVANCED TRACKING

Up to this point the dog, however well he has been working, has followed only what are essentially simple, straightforward tracks. They have started at a well-defined point, gone in a stated direction, and traversed only ordinary ground. Before a dog can truly be called a tracking dog, he must be able to work under considerably more difficult circumstances. He should, for example, be able to find and pick up a track in an unmarked field. He should be able to follow one person's track even when it has been crossed, before and after, by other people. He should be able to track across a stream, and along and across a road.

Difficult as these tasks may sound, they are only a few of the conditions that might easily be met in a "professional" track—one in which you used your dog to find a lost person. A lost child or adult may wander aimlessly in circles in a field, crossing and recrossing his own track. He may stumble through thick undergrowth, crawl over a stone fence, flounder through a marsh or hundreds of yards down the middle of a shallow stream. A fully trained tracking dog could handle all of those contingencies, and would have to be able to if he were to be of any practical use.

Advanced tracking training is started right back at the beginning of regular tracking training, with your own scent and your own article, but this time with difficulties and complications introduced as you go. Don't start throwing in complications with a strange blind track; instead, follow the logic of all training: Take simple steps to make everything easier for your dog.

Multiple articles are the first complication, but before they are employed you must introduce your dog to distractions near the track. Up to now he has faced a barren field, with nobody around once the tracking has begun. Now you begin to introduce off-track distractions. This is clearly a group effort, and you will probably be working with an obedience or tracking club, but such training *can* be arranged with a group of friends.

Start right back at the beginning, leave your dog at the first stake and walk out a short distance with your article, dropping it so he can see it. But this time, have one or more people walking about and talking on both sides of the track, but being careful not to cross it. After you've made a production of dropping the article, return to your dog and command him to start out after it. It's possible he may become confused here but not too likely, because if he's been in the obedience ring, he's done ordinary retrieves and probably scent discrimination with a judge and stewards standing about, as well as other people and dogs clustered at ringside. His concentration should be quite good enough to carry him through this distraction, even if he uses his nose on this very short first "distraction" track.

Then try people *and* their dogs with them, the dogs of course firmly under control, and have your dog track/fetch past them. Work up the distance as he gains confidence. Finally, take out the article and do not let him see you drop it, so that he is forced to use his nose and experience to sniff right along the track, past all the distractions, thus doing his first real tracking job under these conditions.

Now you can begin to introduce turns and several articles; but cut down on the distracting people and dogs, as there is a limit to the cooperation you can expect even from fellow tracking trainers. Take out an article and make a turn into the wind, not a right-angle turn, but perhaps 45°. Test him on this one until he is steady. Then you are ready for the second article, which will come as a major surprise to him, as he is very much used to going out, finding a single article, and calling it a day, at least for that track. Go drop your first article somewhere after the first turn, then drop yet another article after the second turn.

After he has found and delivered the first article, make much of him; then put him right back on the track with another command, "Track!" Expect mild confusion, but stuff the first article in your pocket and lead him gently along the line toward the second turn, gently urging him, "Good boy, track! Find it!" until the idea sinks in. If he really has trouble comprehending that there is more than one article, try again from the start. This time, leave the second article just twenty to thirty feet along the second leg of the track, so you can practically lead him to it after he has found and given you the first article. Then increase the distance from the first to the second article as he gets the idea.

Very soon he will be confident about it all and will continue searching along the track, expecting to find any number of articles anywhere. For tracking dogs, this becomes a wonderful sort of game; and you will hardly have to praise him as he finds each article, because his joy at finding each will be so apparent. But put in the praise, too, anyway.

Then come "cross" tracks, which you should start out the correct way. Have someone walk back and forth across the path where you intend to make your own track, give the cross track ten to twenty minutes to cool off, then lay your own track and send your dog along it. Having worked not only with your own scent but with those of strange tracklayers, there is a slight possibility he might suddenly find the strange cross track and want to start off after it. Just urge him along the right way, with understanding. After all, you started him working with your own scent and then asked him to switch to strange scents, so it's a natural-enough mistake on his part. But you probably won't have much trouble with this.

Then reverse the procedure. Lay your own track, and have at least one strange track laid across it, fresher. Go through the same procedures, starting again with a very short track of your own and dropping an article in plain sight to teach him that the track he starts on is the track he is to follow, no matter what distractions, cross tracks, or other elements he may find along the way. Have several people cross a track you have already laid as you get along in the training, including several cross tracks laid anywhere along the line, after one or more turns. Work each step carefully and easily, always ready to go back to an earlier stage where he wasn't confused if you have trouble with any step in the training.

UNDERBRUSH, ROADS, STREAMS, AND FENCES

Until now, you have presumably been working with all these new complications in a reasonably clear area, but not necessarily a nice flat open field. Variations in terrain—slopes, mild hills, and valleys—are no particular challenge to the dog in advanced tracking work, but actual obstacles are something else. Really advanced tracking work, simulating genuine tracking conditions, must prepare the dog for whatever he might encounter in a real-life tracking situation. Few lost individuals or escaped criminals (however slight the chance that *your* dog will encounter such a situation) are accommodating enough to walk neatly about a flat or irregular field. Therefore, in advanced tracking, your dog must learn to follow a track laid through bushes and trees; across roads and streams; and over, under, or through fences and hedgerows.

To teach stream crossing, find if possible a shallow stream about ten feet across. Have your tracklayer wade through it and proceed ahead directly he gets ashore. (By this time you will have realized that your tracklayer must be willing, patient, and durable—preferably a spouse or other indentured person.) When the dog comes to the edge of the stream, he will try to cast in both directions along the bank to find a turning that is short of the edge. Not finding it will confuse him, so you must lead him across the stream to where the track begins anew and put him on it with encouragement and commands. Don't insist that he plunge right in when a track comes to an end at a stream. If he learns to do that he will ignore the very good possibility that a tracklayer may have turned off without crossing.

When he confidently picks up a track leading straight across a stream, have the tracklayer walk ten or twenty feet down- or upstream before going ashore again. When the dog gets to the far bank and finds no track, encourage him, or lead him, to cast upstream and down until he finds it again. It is a surprisingly good general rule to assume that lost individuals, if they do not go directly across a stream, will wander downstream rather than up. Whatever the reason for this—perhaps it is the path of least resistance— you can concentrate on tracks picking up downstream from the entry point without prejudicing the dog's training, with only an occasional upstream restart.

Roads can be confusing to your dog, because even a seldom-used country road has the scents of exhausts, gas, oil, tire tracks, or soft surfaces churned up by passing vehicles. Getting across a road is mostly a matter of repetition of the stream technique; the clear scent runs out on one side of the road, and the dog must be taught by gentle urging that somewhere on the other side the scent will pick up again. Be careful in your road training to work on gently snubbing your dog up with the tracking line, so that he doesn't simply dash across a road, once having learned that tracks do lead across them. Teach him by gentle demonstration that your holding him back is never a correction, but that you are doing it just as another part of training. The real purpose, of course, is his safety.

Fences and hedgerows are still another problem, because in various wind conditions the tracklayer's scent (yours or a strange tracklayer's) can do odd things at these obstacles. A strong wind from one side may plaster the tracklayer's scent all along the front of the windward side of a solid fence, leading your dog to follow along in that direction with a fully legitimate scent trail going that way. Before long, though, the scent will weaken and evaporate, and you bring him gently back, with urgings and your track command, to the point where your tracklayer (or you) crossed. It may be necessary actually to lift your dog across the first time or two, as this is something entirely new to him; however, after a few demonstrations that a track doesn't always go along a straight open field, but may indeed actually go over a fence, he will get the idea. If you have problems, start a track near a fence and go right back to the short article retrieve so that he gets the idea.

Open fences are somewhat easier, as a strong crosswind is less likely to carry a false trail of scent downwind from the crossing point, and your dog can go right through or under the fence, hot on the trail. You'll have a little trouble with the tracking line here, another case where your dog must understand that snubbing him up short temporarily is not a correction. Once he's gone under, hold him back briefly while you yourself manage to get over the fence, feed the line through, and then start him off again.

Underbrush can be another severe complication, because with any wind at all the tracklayer's scent can be plastered all over every bush in the vicinity where he passed. Be absolutely sure to allow your dog full freedom in investigating every trace of smell until he decides which way it is that the true track goes. It may require some gentle urging on your part, as *you* know where the track is in the early stages. But handle it gently, and don't pull the dog off what appears to him to be a perfectly good scent pattern. He'll work it out.

In any of these situations, if you run into real trouble and confusion, be prepared to take your dog back a few hundred feet, or even a few hundred yards, to a spot where the track is relatively simple. Keep clearly in mind yourself where the track is good before the point of confusion, then take him back and start him over. That may restore his confidence and concentration and get him past the obstacle or complication. But also consider the possibility that you may have been overworking him by the time you got to the complication. Think of yourself working on various mental problems, and how after a while things just seem to go blah. The same thing can happen to your dog and tracking, so give him a little time off, a day or two, and then start him out fresh and the problem may solve itself.

In many of these "complication" tracks, you will have laid the tracks yourself to make it not too difficult for your dog, but now comes the time for a "strange" tracklayer again. (Don't make the mistake of having as the first strange tracklayer one of the people who helped you in the beginning to make "cross" tracks that your dog was to ignore.) Work up with a strange tracklayer's scent from short tracks with multiple articles to longer tracks with obstacles and complications introduced one at a time. Particularly in the early tracks, carry an item belonging to the tracklayer with you, stuck in your belt, so that if at any time the dog appears to lose the idea you can let him have a sniff of the original scent to remind him of what he is supposed to be doing.

The final stage is your dog's finding the tracklayer at the end of the track, after having found and given to you a minimum of three articles belonging to the tracklayer. It is particularly effective if the tracklayer proceeds to a field of fairly high grass and then sits or lies down halfway across. When the dog stumbles across him it will come as a considerable surprise and he will in all likelihood set up a considerable commotion at this curious turn of events. Encourage him to make a racket when he has found the tracklayer. If it should happen to be a large dog and a small tracklayer, we recommend that you discourage the dog from trying to retrieve in this case. Whatever happens, the dog will certainly not stroll unconcernedly past a body lying in his path, and will let you know that he has made a world-shaking discovery. On the next track of this sort, though, make sure that he finds only an article and does not try to go on to find the tracklayer. He must not be allowed to get the impression that he has graduated from articles to people. Mix it up for him, using the "lost person" find only occasionally.

At the beginning of these last variations, you should set him searching for the track while it is very fresh, but put him on older and older tracks until he can pick up one that is at least two hours old. When he has reached this point in tracking, and can pick up a two-hour-old scent, either from the beginning or middle, and follow it unvaryingly to the article, he is a veteran tracking dog and there is little more you can teach him.

SCENT AND TRACKS

When you have worked at tracking for a while, the behavior of scent will become clear to you through experience. What we know about it has been learned in just that way—by watching dogs work tracks under every possible condition, and theorizing a little.

You can best visualize the actions of scent if you think of it as being a slightly heavier-than-air gas, very easily blown about by the wind, yet sticking tenaciously in part to everything it touches. Imagining, or describing, the actions of something invisible (scent) in something else invisible (air) is tricky, but we can outline very generally some of the actions of scent under various wind and terrain conditions.

Scent of course travels with the wind. This is not meant to say that it travels wholly and bodily with the wind—rather that a breeze stretches it out from its starting point over considerable ground. In a crosswind there is a diffused broad path of the tracklayer's scent stretching between where he walked and the limit of the windblown area. Dogs generally work the downwind "edge" of such a diffuse scent—maybe the "front" is slightly stronger—perhaps because they do, as the theory holds, like to work half in and half out of a scent path.

But beware of being too sure of this "downwind" idea and trying to impose it on your dog. Particularly if the wind or breeze is light, the passage of the tracklayer's body through the air can stir up eddies and currents and actually leave airborne scent somewhat upwind of the actual track where he walked. Let your dog work where he wants to and is most comfortable. After all, *he* is doing the smelling and the tracking, not you.

And beware, also, of trying to impose on your dog the concept that he must have his nose to the ground, snuffling along that way. Some dogs work with their heads in the air, at least part of the time, and perhaps much of the time. This is particularly true in such cases as a newly mown field, where the smell of the fresh cutting is so strong that even you can smell it; so imagine what a nose-down exposure to this means to the dog's sensitive nose. Again, and again, let him find his own way of working. Don't impose your own notions on his expertise.

Hills have a sometimes devastating effect on a track. If the wind is coming at all into the hill, across the track, it tends to lift the whole track up and blow it uphill and even across the top and into nothingness. Hitting a hillside seems to accelerate a wind, and an angle somehow lets it "dig

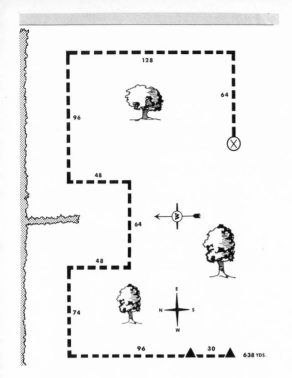

Four examples of good tracks laid
in different fields under varying wind
conditions.

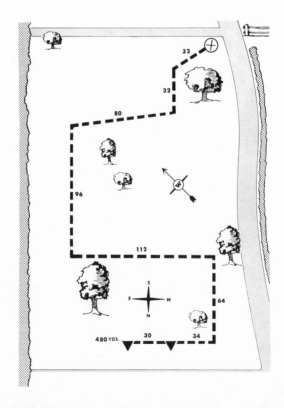

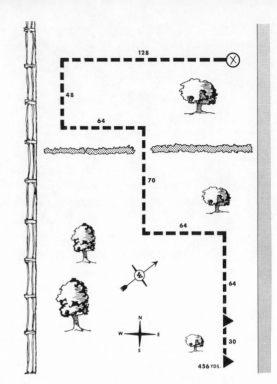

Each track is AKC regulation length or more, and makes excellent use of the available fields.

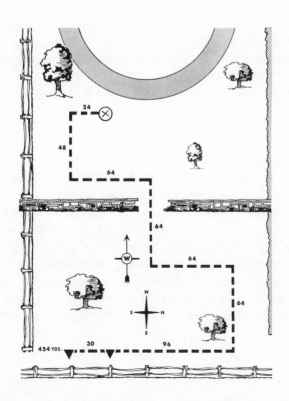

under" a scent and obliterate it for the novice dog. So avoid this condition if possible.

The corresponding valleys, however small, also can work havoc. Scent tends to collect quite heavily in a small valley (here we mean even only a few feet deep) and roll around like mist. If a track several hours old crosses a small dip like this, you may see the dog casting about quite confusedly within the dip as he explores the extent of the rolling scent. After a bit he will find the slightly stronger track and go off again.

Even the time of day affects a track. In the morning, when the ground is cooler than the air, a track lies very low to the ground as the ground absorbs heat and almost sucks up the scent too. Conversely, in the evening when the ground is giving off heat to the air, a track tends to rise as it gets older, and you may find that a dog that normally works with his nose right to the ground will be tracking high, head in the air as he follows the track.

Keep all these factors well in mind when you are laying tracks for your in-training dog, and even when he is more advanced. The central idea is never to try to confuse the dog. Make it as easy as possible for him as long as possible. Only when he is fully in command of the situation and you are sure he could track the Devil himself over burning coals should you deliberately introduce confusing factors of wind and terrain. And be sure that your assistant-cum-tracklayer has a good working knowledge of this "Scent and Tracks" section before he goes out to lay track for you.

The diagrams of tracks under varying circumstances should be of help to you and your tracklayer. Study them carefully before you lay your tracks, and adapt the principles we have discussed to your own chosen fields.

AKC TRACKING TESTS

These are hard things to find. About the only way to find out when and where a test is to be held in your vicinity is through the AKC—either by a mail request or through the current issue of *The Kennel Gazette*. As Tracking Tests are hardly ever run by professional obedience superintendents, and never at shows, notices are rarely sent out. It's up to you to find out when and where.

Even when you manage to locate one, you've only started. To enter a test, you must have a letter from an AKC tracking judge certifying that he has examined your dog and considers him ready for a test. This, of course, involves finding such a judge. Here again, the AKC is the only answer.

They will give you, on request, the names of tracking judges in your area. Then it is up to you to contact the judge, persuade him to come out in the fields with you, and put your dog through a tough track. If you pass his inspection, and there's no reason you shouldn't if you've followed this chapter and don't try to jump the gun with a partly trained dog, he will give you that precious letter, and you're ready for a test.

Armed with the letter, you apply for entry to a test you've found, and if it isn't full, you're ready to go. As for the test itself, there's little we can tell you except to relax. Most dogs fail their first test, even very well-trained dogs. This, we are convinced, is because 95 percent of all handlers freeze up into unmanageable masses of raw nerves when they step out onto that fatal field for the first time. It can easily happen to you, too, so don't sneer until you've given it a try.

A test track will be considerably easier than the hardest tracks you've encountered in this chapter. It will be quite a straightforward one, over generally simple terrain—440 yards long at least and not more than 500 yards, with at least two turns. If you keep cool and let your dog use his educated nose, you'll breeze right through. But don't count the prize money yet. Tracking titles are among the most coveted in obedience, because they require long and hard work, and they testify to an understanding and cooperation between dog and owner that cannot be surpassed in any obedience ring, even at the OTCh level.

Tracking is growing constantly in popularity, despite its difficulties. Not too long ago, even after years of Tracking Tests, there were perhaps no more than 300 dogs in the country with TD titles. Now, that many are awarded in a single year. Tracking is one of the most enjoyable and rewarding areas of obedience training, and we hope you can find the time, the space, and the cooperative assistants to give it at least a try. There's nothing quite like that first time you set your dog down at the starting flag to begin on a strange track, under real competition conditions—and know that it's he, not you, who'll be doing all the work, the most natural work in the world for a dog, with you just going along for the ride. Or the walk.

CHAPTER 10

Training Problems

Because every dog is an individual, and especially because every trainer is an individual, problems in training inevitably arise. The major cause of problems, as we hope you have seen from reading the other chapters of this book, is the trainer. It is an easy thing indeed to go wrong in one phase or another of training, as we well know from our own beginnings in training. Despite all the cautions we have given you, all the admonitions to go slowly, to take each exercise carefully step by step, the temptations are great to skip a thing or two, to think, "Oh, nonsense—my dog just doesn't work that way," or, "I can skip that bit of work, for my dog's much smarter than average." If you have followed every step in every exercise in every chapter, you are the exception among human beings. If you haven't, then the problems you have with your dog are highly likely to be due to your deviations.

This is not to say that training is as rigid as all that. We would be the last to advocate a mechanical approach to training, because your dog is not a machine, and can't be trained by one-two-three rules and regulations. What we do say is that the variations from good procedure that the great majority of amateur trainers make are those that complicate training. Your variations may have worked out extremely well. But the fact that you are reading this chapter on problems indicates that at least some of them didn't. It is those we are concerned with here.

You may also be coming to this chapter with problems originating in your own training methods, or in methods of friends or other trainers that have not worked entirely well with your dog. In such a case, we recommend that before going any further you turn back to the chapter covering the particular exercise you are having trouble with. Read over our method and explanations regarding that exercise, compare them with what you have been doing, and you may well find a solution right there. In a great many problem cases, complete retraining is the only satisfactory answer, and you may find that it is the answer in your case.

In the examination of problems that follows, we repeat much of what we have said in other sections of this book—and for good reason. Most training involves learning to think about your dog in a new way. The more times we indicate to you the right way to think about him, the more likely you are to accept this, and to put it to practical use. We know from personal experience that a student trainer can not only hear an explanation, but even see the proper method work on his dog—and turn around a few minutes later to repeat his own private method that has resulted in weeks of failure. Much too often, training problems degenerate into a contest of wills, with the trainer thinking, "This is the way I've been doing it, and my dog is bloody well going to learn it my way, because *I* say so!" If this can happen, and it can, then a mere exposition of method in a book will be far easier to either ignore or wrongly adapt.

To the point: If you are having problems in a specific exercise, it is simply and flatly because you have been doing something wrong in your training procedure. Somehow, you have done it wrong. What you must do now, rather than look for a specific answer in this chapter, is to take a look at exactly how your dog is doing things wrong, and then sit back for a long think about it—about why he does what he does, or doesn't do what he doesn't. And leave out answers like "He's stubborn" or "He's stupid." The only acceptable answers are ones that point to faults in your teaching.

The final major ingredient is confidence, your confidence that your dog can learn whatever you're trying to teach him, and that you will be able to work out a way to teach it to him. To the beginner, it can seem miraculous that anyone can teach a dog to walk beside him without hauling on the leash, and to sit quietly at heel when he stops. Even to a relatively advanced trainer, it may seem improbable that he will ever really be able to teach his dog to pick out by smell one of several articles in a scent-discrimination exercise. But obviously it can be done.

Over *ten thousand* obedience titles are awarded by the AKC every year, which means that over ten thousand dogs have learned the necessary exercises and done them successfully in three separate obedience trials. Ten thousand handlers and owners have trained their dogs to do these things, and there is simply no reason for you to believe that you can't. If you can sit down with yourself and say, "*Of course* my dog can learn to do a simple thing like walking at my side, and *of course* I can teach him to do it!" then you'll do it, and he will. And every progressive step along the way will follow.

That confidence is one of the hardest things to teach in a class situation, and therefore even harder to get across in a book, but believe us, it works—sometimes too well in classes. There isn't a class trainer who hasn't taken an apparently uncontrollable dog out into the middle of the ring and, with a few minutes of gentle instruction, coaxing, praise, and minor corrections, had the dog heeling as smartly as a professional and sitting firmly at heel, to the total astonishment of his owner, who can only believe he has witnessed some sort of magic. Then it is the instructor's difficult task to dispel the "magic" idea and get across the fact that the big secret is his confidence radiating down the leash to the dog like a message on a telegraph line. That and, of course, using the right methods. *You* can do it. Believe it.

In each of the following sections, we discuss the probable reasons for the major problems that arise, the way you may have been thinking wrong about the exercise, and give some general pointers on correcting the problems. But from there on it is up to you to apply your own mind constructively.

HEELING

The major difficulties encountered in heeling are those of position—total failure to get the dog walking more or less alongside in some sort of fashion is almost beyond the bounds of possibility. Thus we will assume that your dog heels to some extent. The first thing to examine, if your dog heels out of proper position, is why. Here there is usually a good and simple reason. If he lags, for example, there is a very good chance that he does so in order to be able to make the turns and about-turns without being constantly corrected. Behind that lies the very good possibility that you have been making your turns without any warning to him. You should slow slightly before any turn, or halt to let your dog know something is going to happen. If you haven't been doing this, then he will have trouble making the turns sharply, and will have been getting correction after correction to no avail. So now he lags behind to be able to see what's going to happen.

Much the same applies to general problems on the turns—inability to make them with you. If you've been giving him no warning, you can't expect him to move smartly with you. Slow down slightly before any turn. If he has trouble even then, corrective measures are in order. Swinging wide or crowding on any of the turns means that you need a little more gentle guidance with the lead in practice, more talking to keep his attention. Use very light snaps on the collar, with the lead attached to the dead ring, and each time tell him what you want him to do, with an encouraging, instructing tone of voice. Swinging wide on left and about-turns means that you should guide him around the turns in practice. You have probably been trying to get him around using the full length of the leash. This allows him to swing wide like an aerocar at an amusement park. But if you take hold of the leash close to his collar and bend down to guide him around, he will have to stay close. On the about-turn, be sure first that you aren't doing some sort of fancy footwork or kicking up your heels, which he is trying to avoid by going wide.

Heeling Wide: Look for the reason he wants to walk at a distance from you. A woman trainer's swirling skirts often make a dog heel wide. You may have been too harsh with left-turn corrections and he's trying to escape your prodding knee. When you've found the reason, eliminate it and apply gentle snaps on the lead to urge him back in closer. Don't keep up a steady pressure on the lead. If you've made it quite comfortable for him to heel normally right at your side, he won't heel wide, so think it through. He's heeling wide for a reason. Urge him in with your tone of voice and *gentle* corrections, and praise him as he gets closer.

Crowding: The reason may be overinsistence on your part, too harsh corrections on wide heeling, or even a timid nature on his part. Guide him gently away from you with your left arm held stiffly, not bent at the elbow, with gentle snaps away from your side. Don't look down at him as you heel and make these corrections—he may be trying to stick close so he can see you better all the way up there, and make eye contact.

Snapping at Heels: Generally done in the spirit of play, this nevertheless needs fairly severe leash corrections, followed by praise. Don't kick at him with your heels, for you may either hurt him, or even convince him further that it is a game.

Biting at Hand or Leash: This is active rebellion, and for some good reason. It may have been a harsh or too-sudden introduction to collar and lead, or your whole training attitude may be too harsh. Lay off for a while, then try gentle reintroduction. If the habit persists, apply a strong rebellion correction (see "Basic Training"), but don't be vindictive. Let him know you won't stand for it, then continue calmly with the training.

Refusal to Change Gait: Generally this means that you give him no warning by slight anticipatory slowing for the "slow," slight anticipatory speeding for the "fast." Always "float" into a change of pace. This may solve it. Otherwise, insist with a few snaps on the leash; don't haul or tug him.

Refusal to Move After Halt: You may have emphasized stay training too much. You may be moving off on the wrong foot. Be sure there is no confusion in his mind, then snap him forward sharply when you start up.

Trying to Get at Other Dogs, Sniffing Ground, Sniffing Stewards on Figure Eight: This stems from probably no reason but inattention. Insist quite firmly on work. Demand his attention.

Good Work On Lead, Bad Work Off: A rerun through leash work is indicated. It is very possible you have been tugging on him on lead, rather than snapping for corrections. You may have gone off leash too soon. Redo your leash work until he does all work with the leash slack. Then work for a while with the leash hanging loose at your left side to let him know it is still there. Then try him off lead again.

Good Work Off Lead, Sloppy Work On: This problem occurs not infrequently with city dogs. To them, the leash means going outside for a walk or a romp, while heeling off leash is always work. One solution is to do some on-leash heeling practice in the street every time you take him out. Another one is to snap the leash on the dead ring of his training collar when you do on-leash heeling in the Novice ring. You can't use the leash for corrections anyway in the ring, so it makes little difference to you which ring it is snapped on to. But to the dog there is an entirely different feeling about the collar, even when the leash is slack. A third possible solution is the use of an entirely different type of collar for street walks. It is less desirable than simple insistence through practice on good work when you want it, but if the problem is severe, the dog will readily learn that one collar, a leather one, means freedom, while putting on the training collar means strict work, on lead or off.

In General: The major overall error in training that leads to bad heeling work is tugging on the dog to get or keep him in position. A constant pressure on his neck teaches him nothing but resistance. Make every correction a quick snap and an immediate release, plus praise, and he will soon learn that there is nothing to pull against, and that it is far more comfortable to stay in the right place.

THE SIT

Sitting is an easy-enough thing for a dog to do. He certainly does not have to learn any new skills in order to sit, so you can be quite sure that problems in the sit can be traced back to faulty training.

Refusal to Sit: This stems probably from not enough on-lead work. If on-lead he resists strongly, bracing his feet against you, and you cannot get his rear down without a fight, try surprising him. Heel along, and as you slow to a stop, give a sharp "Sit!" command. Get your left hand down behind his rear and bring your right hand up with the lead, before he has stopped moving. Thus he does not have time to brace himself at the stand.

Sits Wide, Ahead, Behind, In Back, or In Front: Very likely he is trying to escape too harsh corrections. Start teaching the sit all over again, using the surprise technique outlined above. Be gentle in your corrections and be sure to praise him each time. The essence of the idea of teaching a straight, close sit is to get him down right in his line of travel, close at your left side, before he has a chance to make a mistake.

Sits and Then Stands: You've not put enough emphasis on staying where he is. Also, this may stem from his anticipation of starting up again, if you have been a little too harsh on forward yanks when you start. Insist that he stay sitting at your side, and counteract his anticipation by staying at the halt for as much as a minute before you start up again.

Keeps Moving After Handler Halts, Then Sits: Probably there has been no warning from you that you are about to halt. "Float" into the halt, taking one or two slightly slower steps before halting. To correct, hold the leash close to his collar and be prepared to give a sharp backward snap as you halt. Don't use the full length of the lead. When coming to a halt, be sure you stop on your right foot and bring your left foot (the guide foot) up to it as the last in motion.

Refusal to Sit After Halt from Slow: You may have been overcorrecting on his attempts to sit when your pace was slow. Also, your practice "slow" may be too slow—it need only be a slow stroll as contrasted to the brisk pace of "normal." Don't make your "slow" a funeral step. Correct the refusal to sit with the short-lead snap.

Refusal to Sit, or Crooked Sit in Front on Recall: This generally means that he is anticipating the go to heel. Each time he refuses to sit, or sits crooked, begin walking backward. When he is straightened out, stop with a sharp sit command. Don't attempt to correct with hands or feet. Do the backward step as many times as necessary, until he straightens himself out or sits of his own accord.

Swings Rear Away on the Heeling Sit: This generally results from trying to correct or force the sit, with the right foot brought around in back. He is trying to get his rear away from you for some good reason. Correct this by using your left hand on the outside of his haunches as you come in to the halt. Don't try to correct it after he is down—start up again and this time get him straight on the way down.

Refusal to Stay Sitting on the Long Sit: Generally this is due to inadequate preparation, and nothing else. Go back to the beginning, have him stay sitting a minute or two at your side, then longer while you stand directly in front of him, then move away slowly. If you establish the habit thoroughly close to him and on leash, the problem will not occur when he's off leash. Long before you go off leash and/or any distance away, he must thoroughly understand that he cannot leave the sitting position under any circumstances until you release him. Don't progress in the training when he just barely, with luck, stays for the required time. Be sure there is no question of his understanding it.

THE DOWN

Widespread misunderstanding of how to teach a dog the down causes quite a few problems. We suggest that before looking at the specific difficulties, you read the section on "Teaching the Down" in the "Basic Training" chapter.

Refusal to Go Down: This results from trying to force him down with a leash or your hand. Try "lifting" him down as outlined in "Basic Training." That way he has nothing to fight.

Cries or Panics When Forced Down: The answer lies in the definition of the problem. "Lifting" him down involves no force, and he will not dislike it. Try that method.

Refusal to Down Unless at Heel: When he has learned the down with you at his side, the new situation—you in front—may confuse him. Go back to the side, then slowly move around to the front on each successive try, still crouching and helping him down by lifting his legs. When you are in front, one hand on his back and one holding both legs will get him down without a fight, if you have worked enough at his side.

Refusal to Stay Down Without Your Hand on Him: Probably you have taken your hand away too fast. When he is down and your hand on his shoulder is holding him there, take it off for only a second. Next time, take it off for a few seconds. Work slowly to longer times. Also, you may be making the mistake of straightening up too soon—your rising will tempt him to rise. Straighten up only when he stays down unassisted, and then do it by gradual stages—don't just shoot up.

Goes Down Only with Collar and Lead: You have probably been depending on the collar and lead to hold him or force him down. Use your hands and body as described in teaching the down. Once he has learned it, you can dispense with the collar and lead, and do more downs using hands and body only. Then he will not differentiate between collar on and collar off.

STAND FOR EXAMINATION

Almost all the problems in the stand for examination occur in the examination segment. Some few dogs are so very timid by nature that they require hours of careful, slow exposure to other people; others have unfortunate aggressive streaks and require hours, too, of slow reeducation. For the most part, though, problems in the examination result from a too hurried introduction to the idea.

If you have trouble with any of the facets of the examination, start your stand training all over again. Go back to the first stand-stay, and work through standing in front of him while he stays, standing at his side, and standing in back of him. Be absolutely sure before you try an examination, even by yourself, that he is firm in the stand. This may take weeks, but it is essential. Then proceed again to examining him yourself.

When he is perfectly steady under your own examination, have a friend stand by as you examine your dog. Have the friend stand quite close after a time or two, and make a casual business of showing your friend how to go over the dog. Then, have the friend put his hand gently on your dog at the same time you have your hand on him. Gradually, work up to the point where the friend can examine him gently while you stand at the dog's head without touching him. Then remove the leash and repeat as above with the friend doing the examination, until you can stand at least six feet away after you've given the stay command and your friend or a stranger can examine your dog with no problems. The idea is to make it casual and easy. A good many of the problems found in the examination result from a too formal approach to the situation, wherein a handler expects his dog to undergo a full examination as soon as he has learned to stand and stay. Go about it slow and easy.

Moving as You Walk Around to Heel: This can be tricky, for the dog will almost always try to watch you as you walk around. The problem can be solved by a retraining in the stand-stay, wherein you get him to stay as you stand at lead's length away in any direction. After a while he will come to ignore you as you stand away, and will stand steady as you come around. Another angle is that your body may be brushing him as you come around, or you may be dragging the leash across his head or face. If caution in this does not solve the problem, we suggest that you go back yet again for some intensive retraining. Begin with the sit-stay and walk around him several times, holding the leash beside his head as your axis. When you can do that, do the same at the down-stay, not only going around but stepping over him as we described in "Basic Training." Keep at it, repeating your stay commands as you move around him or over him, until he is steady, no matter what you do. Then begin again on stand-stay work, and he should be confident that he can stand still as you go around without any harm coming to him. Then you should be able to progress to a steady stand-stay off lead.

Sits as You Return to Heel: This is generally the result of confusion on his part, and needs only patience to correct. He is accustomed to the idea of sitting at your side when you are standing still, and is simply trying to do the right thing by sitting when you get to heel position. As you come around, block his sit by putting your left hand just in front of his rear leg. Another possible reason, if you have been teaching him to sit directly as a release from the stand, is that he may be anticipating. Make him work at command only, by standing for as much as a minute after you return to heel, and before you let him sit.

THE RECALL

Some of the most maddening problems of all can arise in the recall. It seems a simple-enough thing for a dog to run to his owner, yet in the ring you will see every possible variation of foul-up. Perhaps one of the most common is the lagging dog, the one who stays where he is left and then comes when he is called, but at roughly the rate of reluctant molasses. Almost without exception, this can be traced to that cardinal sin, calling the dog to make a correction. As we have explained before, one can hardly expect a dog to come in gaily and fast if there is a chance he will be hit or shouted at when he gets there. The less frequent cause is tugging and hauling on the leash to get him to come in the original recall training. This is one of the common-sense ways of training that are terribly wrong, for if you give a dog something to pull against, he will pull against it. If you try to tug and haul him to you, he will tug and haul in the opposite direction for all he's worth. It all goes back to the very basic philosophy of training with the leash and training collar—using snaps on the leash. A quick snap and a release gives the dog nothing to fight, and several snaps accomplish far more than a steady tug. However, in recall training, even the snaps are to be left as a last resort.

If you have been doing either (be honest with yourself), then there is nothing you can do but resolve never again to call him in for a correction and never again to haul him in with the leash. The damage is done, and it will take time and patience to undo it. You must now reestablish happy relations with your dog. Put him at a sit-stay, go to the other end of the leash, and crouch there facing him. Call him to you in the friendliest voice you can muster. If he doesn't move, don't touch that leash! Call him, cajole him, sweet-talk him, roll on the ground, clap your hands—anything at all to get him to come to you of his own accord. When he gets there, praise him as you've never praised him before. Don't insist on a sit, or a go to heel—just get him to come to you. Keep working at that, day after day, never giving him a correction, but cajoling until he comes to you happily on your first call. When he has done that a dozen times, begin to use the leash as a guide, not as a correcting device. Guide him in straight, and after a few times tell him to sit as he gets in front of you—but make all your moves gentle and friendly. Persuade him to sit, as one friend to another. When he does that with no help from you, progress to the go to heel to finish the exercise. But go slowly, praise him at every step, and do not try to insist on precision and accuracy for quite a while.

When he is coming in well, and if he still does not do it at a full run, speed him up by running backward, away from him. Call him, and if he does not begin to run immediately, run backward as fast as you can, running in a crouch and calling to him to hurry up as you do so. The sight of you receding will make him step up his pace to get to you before you fade into the distance, and he will start to run. Keep that up until he runs from the first.

Refusal to Stay: There are many variations on this theme, from walking after you as you leave through getting up just before you call. All reflect sloppiness in the stay training, and the solution is a redoing of that. Go back over it step by careful step, not rushing it this time. Be sure there is no question of his staying when you are three feet away before you try going four feet away. It is the only solution. One further problem may be in your handling if he always breaks, say, just when you turn around after leaving him. Check carefully to see that you are not swinging your arms as you turn, or after you turn, for such motions can look to him like signals to come.

If this problem occurs mainly in the show ring and not outside it, look into the possibility of confusion with the heeling that he has just completed in the ring. In Novice, you have heeled first on leash, and then off leash, and from that you go right into the recall. Every time you have started off, he has been supposed to go with you. Now you start off quickly again, and he may be confused, even if you have given him a firm "Wait!" command. After you have finished heeling and are in a position to leave him for the recall, make a little break for him. Within reason, you don't have to slam right into the exercise. The judge will ask if you are ready, and only when you say, "Yes," will the exercise begin. Take a few seconds, steady yourself, and let your dog get comfortably settled at heel before you say you are ready. It will take his mind off the heeling you've just done. Then, after the judge's command to leave your dog, give him a firm "Wait!" command with a strong, definite signal—and the problem may be solved.

If you've done early training using the "Stay!" command when you don't really want him to stay but to wait, you can try changing your command (and signal) in the recall. Telling him to wait rather than stay when the problem is that he doesn't stay may seem illogical; but consistent use of "Stay!" when you want him to remain there until you return, and "Wait!" when you're going to want him to do something else, can clear up any confusion in his mind.

Refusal to Come, or Breaks and Runs: Here, again, the reason is that he does not want to come to you. Examine your training to find out why, and then go through the procedures outlined above for slow recall.

Running Straight to Heel: This is a natural enough thing for him to try, for it is a sensible shortcut. Why bother to sit in front for a moment if he is going to end up at heel every time? You may have been sending him to heel too quickly on the recall. Try, on leash, having him sit in front of you for as much as a minute before he goes to heel. If he tries to go straight to heel even on leash, you must snap him back quickly as he heads around to the side, but praise him just after you snap! It is essential that he think of it as a regrettable accident, not as a correction coming from you.

Curving on Recall: This is a frustrating problem for which we cannot offer much of an explanation. Most dogs come in, at whatever speed, straight. Some, for reasons known only to themselves, take a curved path as if they were avoiding an obstacle. Any number of methods of correcting this have been tried, including practice recalls in narrow alleyways or passages, and using a fishing reel to take up line fast enough to haul the dog in straight. These have very little success, if they work at all, for as soon as the dog is called without them, he curves again. Some very few dogs never do lose this curious habit, but many can be cured by the backward running method. If you stand still and call him, he will almost seem to plot a curved course that will bring him to you. But if, as soon as you call him, you begin to run backward away from him, this calculated course doesn't work out, and he will tend to straighten out and make directly for you, for he doesn't know where you will be when you stop. Try that if you have a curve problem. Chances are it will straighten him out.

The many other recall problems—stand in front, refusal to go to heel, crooked sit at heel, and others—are almost all the result of confusion on the dog's part. He is not sure what you want, and you must show him patiently with the leash, guiding and snapping him around and into proper position. Most of these minor problems require only a firm but gentle insistence on your part that he does what you want him to.

DROP ON RECALL

Most of the problems in this exercise result from inadequate training in the plain drop, or down. Refusal to drop, slow drop, sit instead of drop—these can only be worked out by going back to your down training. Do it all over again until your dog drops on your command from any position, at any distance, and in any direction from you. Only when he drops promptly *every time* while he is stationary in any position (see Chapter 3, "Basic Training," for drop training) should you try to drop him in motion. Then start again with the drop on the recall from heeling, and work up to the drop on the straight recall. We have found that this is the only way to correct the drop problems, for these problems are invariably the result of hurried and inadequate preliminary training.

Drops Before Command or Signal: You have probably been training him too rigidly in dropping at a certain distance from you. If you always drop him ten feet after he starts coming, he will quickly learn that that is the place you want him to drop, and will try to accommodate you by going down without a command. Retrain on the drop, this time dropping him sometimes immediately after he starts coming, sometimes only just before he gets to you. And of course mix it up with nondrop recalls, to teach him that he must not go down except on command or signal. Whatever you do, don't try to fool him by slipping in a quick command as he slows for an unordered drop. It fools nobody. If he has started to drop by himself, always call him in to you and finish that recall without a drop. Don't chastise or correct him. Just keep doing it until he comes all the way without trying to drop, then restart the dropping at various places. A variant of this problem is the dog who has become accustomed to the idea of dropping in front of the judge in a ring. Train him out of this by having a friend stand close to the line of the recall and insisting that your dog come past the "judge" either with no drop at all or dropping him well after he has passed. Only by re-creating the actual situation can you solve this one.

Signal Problems: These may result from faulty training in one of two ways. If your dog drops on your signal only if your hand is held in the air, chances are that you timed your corrective command wrong when you were doing the original training. If you gave a signal, then shouted a command when he did not go down, you should not be surprised that he has learned that he is to go down after the signal hand has been in the air for a few moments. Retrain him on the signal, this time giving the command simultaneously with the signal several times. Then try the signal alone, and if he does not respond immediately, go right back to the simultaneous command and signal half a dozen times, and then try the signal alone again.

The other possible mistraining involves simply holding the signal too long. If in training you have taught him that your hand going up in the air and staying there means to drop, then he will have learned just that. You must retrain, using simultaneous command and signal, this time shooting your hand up and bringing it right back down. Work until he responds to that; don't try to make a visual correction by keeping your hand up in the air, perhaps even wiggling it, if he doesn't drop at once. At any failure to drop when your hand flashes up, go back to the command-and-signal a few times, then back to quick signal alone, and so on until he responds to the quick raising of the hand rather than its presence above your hand.

THE RETRIEVE

Running after and bringing back a wooden dumbbell is not a thing that should logically put a strain on any healthy dog. Yet something that is so natural for a dog causes endless problems for trainers. The reason is largely a faulty and overformal approach to the situation, an approach that does not allow the dog to enjoy things.

First, though, we refer you to the "Open" chapter for the discussion of the proper construction of the dumbbell for your dog. If you have been training with the wrong dumbbell, using the right one will work wonders. Take care of that first. But assuming that you have been working with a properly constructed dumbbell all along and are having the most serious common problem—refusal to take, hold, or carry the dumbbell—our suggestion is that you go right back to the basics of retrieving for a complete retraining.

If your dog is frightened of the dumbbell, if he runs at the sight of it, or just stares dumbly when you tell him to get it, or goes out to it and just stands there, something has gone radically wrong somewhere, and applying patchwork corrections will probably not do much good. Instead, put the dumbbell aside for the moment. Your first job now is to establish the fact, for him, that simply going after something, anything, is fun and won't hurt him. Take a favorite toy of his—a ball, a stick, anything at all—and play with him. Throw it to him, at him, from him, urging him to chase it and get it and bring it back to you. This must be done entirely in play, with no atmosphere of formal training or compulsion. You must simply romp with him and slowly get him to the point of retrieving things you throw. Don't make any attempt to make him stay as you throw it, or come in to a sit when he brings it back, or anything of that sort. Just get him retrieving again.

Next step, reintroduce the dumbbell. As you play with him, throw it from you and urge him to get it. If he is still unhappy about it because of his past experience with it, chase it yourself. This may take hours of patience and running, but in the end it will work. Throw the dumbbell, and say to him in an ~xcited tone, "Get it!" Then take off after it yourself at a run, urging him to come along with you. Make a contest and a game of it. If the problem is serious, you will reach it first and get it yourself a discouraging number of times. He may in fact just sit and watch you apathetically. But if you persevere, calling to him and competing with him for the privilege of retrieving the dumbbell, he will break down finally and try to get it first. Then you have won a great victory and you must praise him highly for it.

When you have done this for a while, after he has relented and is chasing it with you, slack down your own attempts to get it. Don't do it suddenly, but one time run just a little slower so that it is an easy victory for him. Slowly work down until he is going out all by himself to get it. Don't expect to get to this stage in one day, or two, or even three. Take it very slowly.

Now that you have shown him that retrieving is fun after all—that you are not going to be an ogre about it any more—and that the dumbbell is nothing to be afraid of, you can begin to reintroduce the retrieve. But gently. With him at a sit, put the dumbbell in front of his mouth and tell him to take it. If he doesn't, get his mouth open in the manner we have described, and put the dumbbell in, but do this as gently as you possibly can, praising him and talking to him all the while, and then take it from him promptly. When you've done this, throw the dumbbell and get him to go get it, to keep in his mind that everything is still okay. Then with him back beside you, repeat the "take it" lesson. Do it again, then throw the dumbbell for him in play. Keep up this alternation of work and play with the dumbbell, never correcting him or doing anything but very gently forcing him to take the dumbbell, until he opens his mouth for it. That, of course, calls for even higher praise.

From this point, go right through dumbbell training as we have outlined it in the "Open" chapter, progressing from a take in the air to a take on the ground and to the final retrieve. You must, however—we will say this yet again—you must go about it slowly and gently and make it as much fun for him as possible.

You may have far less serious problems in the retrieve, but difficult ones nonetheless, we discuss below.

Waiting for Second Command: The problem is just that, as we described it in the "Open" chapter. The dog goes out fast to the dumbbell and stands there, waiting. What he is waiting for is a command to go ahead and pick it up. The only reason he does that is that he has learned to do so in training. In training, when he goes to the dumbbell and stands looking at it, you must go out to him, put it in his mouth, then get him back with you to the original position to deliver it to you. Then go back to the shortest possible retrieve, just a few feet in front of you. There he will either pick it up immediately or at least you are in a position to make the correction without moving your feet much. Then throw it only a very little bit farther. And then only a very little bit farther again. Progress very slowly to a long throw. The mistake that is commonly made is that of doing the long throw too fast. The trainer will say, "Ah, he does it fine when I throw it only three feet in front, so now he must understand." Then he throws it as far as his arm will serve, and the dog goes out to stand and look at the dumbbell again. Increase your distance only a foot at a time—the idea is to put it over on the dog. If you increase the distance slowly enough, he will be retrieving successfully at thirty feet before he realizes it. But whatever you do, don't give him a second command, or you'll be right back where you started. The foot-by-foot progress seems tedious, and it is; but going a foot at a time will take only thirty throws until you are at the thirty-foot distance, and that's not so wearing.

Sudden Unwillingness to Take Dumbbell: This does not happen often, but it can be terribly frustrating if it happens to you and you don't know what has occurred. Check to make sure that the dumbbell has not become fouled in throwing and rolling along the ground. A fouled dumbbell is repulsive to a dog. It may be so slightly tainted that it is only apparent to his nose, but sufficient to make him reluctant to pick it up. Just in case, wipe it well with a damp rag and let it air a day or two before trying again. In any case, suspect at once some change in the dumbbell; don't chalk it up to sudden stubbornness in your dog.

Dropping or Playing with Dumbbell: This traces back to insufficient practice in simply holding it. Take him back over the ground, giving it to him to hold, and then have him hold it for several minutes as he sits by you and heels with you, ending with a short recall so that he can deliver it to you. Simply holding a properly constructed dumbbell in his mouth for several minutes absolutely cannot hurt your dog—he is able to breathe and swallow and everything else, so you must simply convince him, by working up slowly from a short hold to several minutes, that he must hold it until he delivers it to you.

Overeagerness, Refusal to Stay: If you have this problem, you may consider yourself lucky, for there are legions of trainers who wish only that their dog would be so eager to go after the dumbbell that they would have trouble restraining him. This problem sometimes results from a playful retraining, in which the dog comes to like the idea of retrieving so much that it is difficult to make him stay when you have thrown the dumbbell. The best solution is putting him back on leash. Take a short hold on the leash, and throw the dumbbell. If he charges after it, you can snap him back into position. Then release the leash from his collar and send him for the dumbbell. Go from that to holding lightly on to his collar at the back of his neck to restrain him—but be careful in both cases not to be harsh about it. If you do, he may lose interest in retrieving altogether, and there you'll be, ready for the third round. Another method is to interpose other exercises. Put him on leash and throw the dumbbell not far—about six or seven feet—and then start up at heel, making a quick turn in either direction, then another turn and another until you have come around quickly back to position. Then release him and send him for it. This gets across to him that he is to work only at command. The short throw in this case is to make it easy for him to see the dumbbell and to remember, once you are back in position, that he is to get it. Then try the same thing off lead, holding lightly on to his collar until you begin to heel. Another time, you can give him a down command, and then a sit, before you send him. Finally, send him only after a wait of as much as a minute—without any other exercises in between—to keep him in mind of the fact that he is to work only at your orders.

THE HURDLE RETRIEVE

One of the most serious problems in this is going around the jump. It results almost without fail from having allowed the dog to go around it in early training, and in play. It is, however, an almost universal error of training and extremely easy to make; once done, it is difficult to undo. But it is important that you realize, when you are trying to solve the problem, that he is going around the jump not out of spite, stubbornness, stupidity, or any unwillingness to take the jump in both directions—but simply because he doesn't know any better. In early training, when jumping was great fun, he went cantering around it with your full permission. Now, when you are throwing the dumbbell and all relations are warm and friendly, he goes around it again. Whatever you do, don't shout or scream at him or chastise him for it. What you must do now is convince him that under no circumstances can he go around the thing. The answer is retraining, but first investigate the possibility that differing circumstances may be causing it. Not infrequently, a dog who has been working extremely well on the home training grounds will, at a show, suddenly go around the hurdle. This is the result of the dog's failure to generalize his training from the specific (your training hurdle) to the general (any hurdle he is faced with). If this seems to be the situation, don't go back over all the training, but do do some practice work in several different situations—and if possible with a different hurdle. Take your own hurdle from the backyard and set it up in a park if you can, or in a country field. Also, set it up somewhere inside where there is room. If possible, work with a training-class hurdle. The dog who has had the idea that his instructions to jump apply only to a hurdle set up in your backyard will soon learn after practice work in different locales that he is to go over any hurdle you point at, no matter where he finds it.

If the problem occurs in your training area, too, then retraining is the only way out. You can never completely erase from his mind that he can go and has gone around it, but an intensive new course will help a great deal. Foolish though it may seem, the dog who can jump full height must be taken, on leash, back to the basic step of jumping over the single eight-inch board with you, then over and back, and from there up to full height and regular work again. This time, on leash or off, never allow him to go around.

Climbing Over Jump: For some dogs it's simply easier under normal circumstances, and you have to convince yours that it really isn't. Set up the bar according to the instructions in "Open," either with nails or the iron holders. Then when he tries to scramble over he will knock the bar off and soon learn to clear it. Remember, though, that the idea is not to frighten him with the falling bar, but to convince him that the footing is not so good up there. If the falling bar should frighten him, go back for a quick refresher course by lowering the hurdle-plus-bar and letting him clear it a few times, then build it up slowly. When he is clearing everything at full height, remove the bar.

Refusal to Jump At All: Look for a good reason. His feet may be sore, or his legs. You may be working on too hard a surface, or one that is too slippery—change or pad it somehow. Another thing to check is what he can see as he sits in front of the jump. If his view over the top consists of nothing but sky, he may just possibly be worried about what's on the other side of the jump: pit or precipice or solid ground. We've seen it happen. No matter how many times you've gone over it with him, he may be much happier if he can see trees, or a wall, from his spot. Try repositioning the jump. If none of these measures applies, it may mean that you have been trying to drag him over the jump with the leash—a not uncommon training

method that leads to many difficulties. The only real solution is again retraining the right way. Take him right back to the first steps and slowly
follow the procedure in our "Open" chapter.

Refusal to Jump with Dumbbell: Check first that it is not too heavy for
him, and then that it is otherwise properly constructed for him. Quite often
a dog who can be trained to retrieve and carry a wrongly designed dumbbell will refuse to jump with it; the bells in front of his eyes make jumping
difficult if not impossible. If this has nothing to do with it, go through a
quick jumping retraining while he is carrying the dumbbell, walking over
the jump with him as he holds it, progressing to over-and-back holding it,
and to a recall over a low hurdle holding it. Then start off again doing a retrieve over a low hurdle, and work the height up slowly.

Jumps Over, Refuses to Retrieve: First of all, it may mean that he does
not see the dumbbell when he lands. Practice your throw until you have it
well under control, then in training throw the dumbbell so that it lands just
a foot or two in front of where the dog lands in going over. Keep doing that
until he retrieves well, and only then throw farther. If this is not the
problem, examine the possibility that here, too, the dumbbell may be
wrongly constructed for him. Otherwise, the solution may be strong drilling in the retrieve on the flat. Work at this until he retrieves without fail,
then begin hurdle work with a very low jump—hardly more than a flat retrieve. Work his distance up very slowly.

Picks Up Dumbbell, Does Not Return: This may be caused by a fear of
jumping with it, in which case check the construction of the dumbbell and
go through the retraining outlined above under "Refusal to Jump with
Dumbbell." It may also indicate severe corrections on your part concerning
the return—you may have been too harsh with him about sitting straight,
or about dropping the dumbbell. If so, do a retraining from the beginning,
with gentle handling. Otherwise, the chances are his work in the flat retrieve is not steady enough. Go back over that thoroughly, then begin work
again with a very low jump.

THE BROAD JUMP

Broad-jump problems are often quite severe, for the situation is a highly
artificial one, and the long jump is nowhere nearly as natural for a dog as a
high hurdle. If you have trained, or tried to train, your dog without the
"crib" described in the "Open" chapter, we strongly recommend that you

make one and retrain with it. Its use almost automatically solves most problems involving clearing the jumps.

Inability to Clear Jumps: Check first your dog's physical condition, and then the surface he has to land on. Here, particularly, a slippery surface throws a dog off. Then go back to the beginnings and work with the crib and only two jumps making up a short broad jump. The crib will force your dog to get height into his jump, and then he will be able to clear the required length.

Refusal to Jump Off Lead: This probably means you have been using the lead to pull him over, a common mistake. Go back through a proper re-training, then try him off lead again when he will do the jump with no lead corrections at all. If this does not help, work up from a short jump, going over the jump yourself with him at your side, on lead. You should try as long a running jump as necessary, up to six feet. From that you can go to jumping with him off lead, and then letting him jump by himself.

Running to Left of Jump: A fairly rare problem, but easily solved with leash control. Use a longer clothesline on the full jump, and keep it short enough to be able to control him.

Jumping Toward Handler: Step into the jumps before calling him to jump. Step in about a third of the way the first time, then gradually step in less until you can stay outside of them and he is jumping straight.

Refusal to Stay Until Command: This comes from overtraining in the jump. Leave it alone a few days, and concentrate on firm wait training. Then start again with a very short jump, which allows you to be close to him while he is staying, in position for a quick correction if he breaks. Work up to the full jump and leaving him ten feet away, only very slowly.

Goes to Jump, Then Stands: This is another second-command problem. It almost always means that in training you have been giving him a second command to jump as he gets to the first board. The only solution is retraining, leaving out the extra command. Never expect your dog to do anything in performance that he hasn't been doing in training—and always expect him to do in performance what he *has* been doing in training.

Does Not Come Around Quickly After Jump: This is a very common problem, traceable to the fact that it is simply easier for him to keep on running in a straight line after landing, rather than swinging around quickly. If he is jumping well and confidently, put him back on lead and insist that he come around to you fast and sit straight. It is almost always as simple as that. Don't be ashamed to go back on leash even if he is a fantastically good jumper—it is the only way you will teach him to come around fast.

The first few times, send him over, and just as he lands give him the sharp command "Mike!" to get his attention. This normally gets him to turn and come to you, but if it doesn't, quickly add the "Come!" command, with praise as he turns to you. The lead is only to catch him up short if for some reason he doesn't respond and keeps going on out straight. Don't snap him with the lead just as he lands, as it can throw him badly off balance and possibly injure him.

DIRECTED JUMPING

The problems here can be divided roughly into three parts: the sendaway, the bar jump, and the direction signals. Of these, the sendaway offers the most trouble, for it involves a totally unnatural concept for the dog: going away from you at command. Also, because of its difficulty, and the patience needed, it offers the greatest chance for a lost temper, which founders the training quite effectively.

Refusal to Go Out: If when you send him your dog simply looks confused or takes a step or two and then stops, it is due to insufficient instruction on your part. Remember always, when he looks confused, he *is* confused. Put the leash back on, give him the "Go!" command, and then run along with him thirty or forty feet, then call him and step backward to bring him around. Give him the sit command when he has turned himself around, then praise him and go to heel position to try it again. Only by patient repetition of this will he get the idea. It may seem difficult to get across to him that you do not want him, at the command,. to run alongside you, but rather to go out himself. But if you work at it and watch his reactions and encourage his being out in front, you will be able to make him differentiate. Some dogs have been taught the sendaway when their handler throws them an article to retrieve, then calls them to halt before getting there, and by being pulled away on a long rope, around a pulley or in the hands of a confederate. These methods are sometimes effective, but we have found that they are no substitute for basic insistence on the dog's going out unassisted, for no reason except that you tell him to. Going out with him again and again and yet again may get to be a colossal bore and seem to get you nowhere, but it eventually shows results, and good ones. Keep at it, urging him to keep going in front of you. As he begins to take the first tentative steps away, don't be afraid to keep repeating the go command and pointing with your arm. Later you can cut down on the extra commands. But whatever you do, don't try to keep him moving by running at him to scare him away. That will destroy your friendly relations and ruin your other work.

Refusal to Go Out Straight: Often this is a result of the rope-and-pulley training. It gets him there, but in his attempts to resist the pull of the rope he pulls to one side or the other and follows a semicircular course on the way out. Retrain by going with him, time and again, and urge him on to a faster pace. This will counteract the circular trend. It can also result from training in a limited space, in which he always ends up the sendaway in a specific spot. Much as in the curving recall, he learns to plot a curved path to the ultimate destination. Somehow find a larger space to work in, and send him farther and farther, until he realizes that a straight line is the easiest way to do it.

Turning to Sit in Front of a Jump: This can be the result of sending him over one jump too often. Frequently, a trainer begins directed jumping with only one jump, the solid hurdle already built, figuring to build the bar jump later if the dog masters the sendaway. Thus the dog always tends to circle to face the solid hurdle. If the dog has learned his mistaken lesson too well, it can be unlearned by working again with the jumps—sending him between the jumps and then very far beyond, fifty or sixty feet, without having him return over the jumps, but going to him and then sending him back between them. If he never knows whether he is going to be stopped near the jumps, or if he is going to be sent over at all, he will lose the tendency to circle to face one of them. One caution, though: Do not ever call him back to you between the jumps to save the labor of walking to him and sending him again; always go to him or he will get the idea that coming back between them is okay.

Tries to Jump Going Out: This is a logical thing for a dog to do, for in Utility training he will have strong memories of being sent out over the hurdle after the dumbbell. Even if you have laid a firm foundation of straight sendaway work, he may try it the first times you work between the jumps. To curb this tendency, stand with him squarely between the jumps and send him away, then walk back to a normal position to call him over either jump. Next time, stand with him only a few feet in front of the midline of the jumps, and send him, then walk back to call him over. Work back slowly to a normal sendaway position, and he will have become gradually accustomed to going out between them. Then the problem should be solved.

Walking Under Bar Jump: The slight change of situation, from being sent over and back on the bar jump to being directed over it sometimes causes confusion. Try sending him out and directing him over the bar set very low. Gradually work it up to regulation height, and he will have relearned the bar-clearing idea in the new circumstance.

Inability to Clear Bar: If he can clear the solid hurdle at the regulation height, he can clear the bar. Some dogs, though, have a hard time learning to make as much effort. Some even change jumping styles for the bar. This rarely occurs with a dog who has learned the solid hurdle with the bar on top, but the dog who has been introduced cold to the bar sometimes finds it hard to realize that the bar is as high as it is. In most cases, the problem can be overcome by slow and patient retraining on the bar. Take it down low again and work up slowly, never raising the bar until he has no trouble at all gauging the distance and clearing it. Too sudden raising will throw him off, for he has been used to taking the spring required for a lower position, and the different height of the bar is not as apparent to him as is raising the solid hurdle. You must almost fool him into making the extra effort, by successive raises of no more than two inches at a time. If you want to go to the trouble of fixing your jump standards so that the bar can be raised one inch at a time, so much the better. What you must do is create in his mind the idea that the bar hasn't really been moved up, but that he has mistakenly jumped a little too low. Then he will put out the slight extra effort needed to clear it easily. It may seem improbable that you can fool him that way, but you can.

Another minor possibility is that he simply can't see the bar well. If in training you haven't bothered to paint the bar in the regulation black and white stripes, do so at once. That specification is not to make the bar attractive, but to make it as visible to the dog as possible. Be sure the bar is as thick as the regulations call for: at least two inches in diameter—again, for easy visibility. Don't try to use an old broomstick or anything like that, or he may have trouble seeing it, and consequent difficulty in gauging his effort.

A third possibility is a misconception on your part of the function of the jump command. Some trainers have the idea that the command "Hup!" or "Over!" or whatever they use is a command to the dog to jump right then. With that idea in mind, you *can* train your dog to take off as he hears the word. Unfortunately, some dogs are trained that way. Thus, you may be mistiming the command and making him take his spring too early or too late. The idea of the jump command is that when he hears it he is to go over either the obstacle directly in front of him (as in the hurdle retrieve) or over the one you point out, no matter how many steps he takes before he gets to it. If you have trained your dog, either consciously or unconsciously, to leap when he hears the word, go back and *un*train him in that particular. Get him to go over jumps with only the original command given when you send him—let him decide by himself how to gauge his leap. In fact, in the ring, you may give only the original command and/or signal when you order your dog over either jump at the judge's discretion, and the dog must run from his sitting position ten to twenty feet to the jump.

Ignoring Directional Signals: This generally stems from a too quick introduction to the idea. Go right back to basics. Send him out, then walk to one side until you are facing him across one jump. Call him to you across that jump, pointing vigorously outside it. Then heel with him back to the center position and send him out again. Walk over to face him across the other jump, calling him over that as you point outside it. Gradually cut down your walking, but very gradually, until you need only take a few steps toward the desired jump as you direct him. Then cut down to a very vigorous signal. Only after he is completely sure of what he is doing should you cut down to the arm signal alone. Taking an arm direction is an entirely new concept, and you must explain it to him clearly and patiently.

SCENT DISCRIMINATION

The most common problem in scent discrimination is a simple general confusion on the part of the dog. Because of mistaken ideas on how to teach discrimination, the handler often creates in the dog's mind the impression that nothing he does is right, and so the dog just gives up trying. The specific villain in this case is a correction for picking up the wrong article. You must keep uppermost in your mind in this training that *whatever* article the dog picks up, he thinks that is the right one. When you correct him you give him the idea that even picking anything up is wrong, and deep confusion sets in.

If you have been training him by any other method and are having trouble, we recommend strongly that you stop, make yourself an article board as described in the "Utility" chapter, and begin again with that. It is the only way he can be prevented from picking up a wrong article without strong corrections from you.

Assuming, though, that you have trained with the article board and are having trouble once off the board, the probable fault is that you went off the board too soon. One or two mistakes in the articles are natural, but continued mistakes off the board after good work on it indicate that you should make another board and go right back over the training. There are any number of specific ways the dog may demonstrate the fact that he is confused about the idea: he may simply stand near the articles, circle them without going near them, kick at them, refuse to go out at all, go out and run away, or even wet on the articles. Anything of that nature means that he is not sure what to do, and the only solution is to go right back to throwing the scented articles near the board, then progress to the board, to fix the idea well in his mind.

One special caution: When you begin to work off the board, be extremely careful that you are sure which article has the scent. It is far easier than you might think to place an article in the group and then lose track of it when you are back in position to send him. Even assistants who place an article and whose eyes never leave the circle can become confused. It needs only one correction when the dog has picked up the right article to set training back a great distance. So watch it with great care.

Picking Up Article Next to Proper One: This happens fairly often, and results from having your articles too close together. Even if your dog understands fully what to do, he may pass his nose over a wrong article, and just as it is passing over he may get the scent from the right article only an inch or two away. If he grabs, he grabs the article right under his nose, which is the wrong one. It is not his fault at all—so work with sufficient distance between articles.

Refusal to Walk Between Articles: This usually results again from too close placement of the articles. If only two or three inches separate the articles, he won't be able to walk among them without stepping on them and perhaps stumbling. Have a minimum of six inches between articles. To cure the tendency to be afraid of stepping on them, try working for a while with the articles well spread out; a distance of two feet between articles is not too much until he learns that it is all right to walk between them. Then reduce the distance.

Insists on Picking Up One or More Specific Wrong Articles: Suspect immediately that scent has somehow gotten onto them. If it is only one, remove it for that training session. If more than one, leave all articles to air a day or two, outside if possible, before trying again. Remember that scent moves in mysterious ways, and give your dog the benefit of the doubt. A strong correction on a wrong article that does have your scent is just as bad as a correction on a right article.

Refusal to Pick Up One Type of Article: This generally requires only patient insistence on your part. Put the article in his mouth, time and again, and insist that he hold it and then walk with it. Almost always the problem is with the metal article, and this may require more patience, but persistence and praise will solve it. With metal articles, one thing to watch is temperature. If you are working outside in cool weather or inside where there is a cold draft along the floor, the metal articles will be colder to the touch than the others—and cold metal in the mouth is not pleasant. When teaching him to carry the metal article, warm it by holding it and rubbing it before giving it to him. This will make him less reluctant to take it. In the ring, the metal article you have scented will be warmed from contact with your hands, and he will take it then, too.

Dropping Article: This may simply be inattention on your part to sufficient "hold it" training with each type of article, or it may be a reflection of wrong corrections. If he has been corrected frequently after picking up an article, he will be reluctant to hold on to any article, and will tend to drop it. The solution for either problem follows from the cause.

Smelling in Wide Circles Around Articles: This may not even be a problem, although you may think of it as one. If he goes out to work at the articles, and first, or even in the middle of working, strays away to sniff the ground, stones, the jumps, or anything else, he may simply be working extra hard to be sure the right article is not somewhere outside the circle. If this extra sniffing is within certain limits, don't do anything about it—it might just save the exercise if, one time, the article is placed a little away from the circle of other articles, since extra sniffing is much preferable to giving up if the article is not right in the circle. But if he goes too far afield, retrain by going back a step or two, letting him watch you place the article in the circle, and give him the idea that it will always be found near to or in the circle.

Ignoring Some of the Articles: This will result if you have been placing your article, in practice, always in one section of the circle. Go back a bit and work in practice with the scented article placed in various parts of the circle.

Sudden Confusion After Good Work: Not infrequently, a dog who has been doing faultless work in scent discrimination will seem to lose confidence in his ability. Often, this confusion can be traced to another exercise you are working on. If, for example, you are having trouble with directed jumping and have had to give him continued corrections, he will lose confidence in his ability to do anything right. Human though that sounds, it does at times happen to dogs. The answer is to build up his confidence in his scent work by going back a step, although you need not go back to the board. Set out the articles, and throw your scented article only a short way, then send him for it. Throw it farther on successive tries, until you throw it among the other articles. Then proceed to placing it with him watching, and with him facing away. A brief refresher will rebuild his confidence. Incidentally, this occurrence should give you pause about whatever other exercise you are teaching at the time—if your corrections in it have been so severe and frequent, and your praise so lacking, as to cause him to lose confidence in his ability, you had better sit down and think things out. Something is going wrong in your training.

SIGNALS

About problems in the signal exercise we can actually say very little, for almost any signal problem you can name results from the same old vice of insufficient training and too rapid advance. Slow reactions to signals follow the pattern of slow reaction to the drop signal as discussed earlier. Absolute nonreaction results either from insufficient preparation or too hurried progress from command-and-signal to signal alone. If there is confusion between signals, we can only advise you to practice your signals until they are sharp and very distinct—concentrating on distinguishing between the sit, down, and recall.

Inattention on the latter part of the exercise is sometimes troublesome. If his gaze and attention wander around as he stands, sits, or lies at some distance from you, he can't see your signals. Sometimes this can be blamed on nothing but a basically scatterbrained nature. Whatever the case, don't call to him, whistle at him, or otherwise make noises to get him to look at you, and don't wave at him. Noises and motions are far more likely to make him break from his position than anything else. As soon as his attention wanders, run away from him. That may seem a curious thing to do, but not only is your movement away going to catch even a wandering eye, but your slipping away as soon as his head is turned will make him want to keep an eye on you. If the cause is just boredom, it is only when he is sure you will stay put, hooting and waving, that he will look around for diversion. If you make him uncertain of your whereabouts when he looks away, you'll find that his attention will stay riveted on you.

DIRECTED RETRIEVE

Dislikes Holding Glove: The cotton work gloves used for this exercise often have a fuzzy texture when new, and some dogs object to holding this sort of thing. Wash the gloves several times in hot water to get the nap off, but don't use soap, bleach, or fabric softener.

Plays with Glove on Retrieve: This floppy thing is a natural for a dog to toss about in play, but if it has been introduced as an article in obedience training, he will probably regard it as such. The solution here is our suggestion from the original training. Tape all the fingers and the thumb together with masking or adhesive tape, and even go so far as to roll it up to make a longish cylinder with the tape. But don't cover it completely with tape so that none of the cotton shows through—just enough tape to make it no longer floppy. Then it becomes a soft object to hold in his mouth. Release the rolling and the fingers one by one as you concentrate on showing him that you want him only to pick it up and carry it calmly.

Breaking as You Turn: This is probably caused by your trying to progress too quickly, combined with a highly commendable eagerness on his part to run on out and do what you want him to do (which is to retrieve the glove). Go back to holding him lightly in place with your hand on the collar until he understands fully that he is to turn and wait for further command. If necessary, go right back to on-lead work, and simply concentrate on steadiness.

Problems with "Taking the Line": Some dogs go out quite smartly and then seem to become confused once away from you, searching around until they find any glove. Again, backtrack in the training, making sure that your arm and hand are pointing absolutely directly toward the proper glove and that your dog is looking along the line of your hand and arm. If necessary, go back to the point of starting your send closer to the line of gloves, until there is no chance at all that he can confuse which one you are sending him for. Then work your way back to the proper distance of about twenty-five feet from the line of gloves.

Doesn't Turn Properly with You to Face the Glove: Forget working with the gloves for a while, and concentrate on this point alone. Don't fall into the trap of allowing him to turn not quite right and then correct the error by faithfully following your "line" signal and getting the correct glove. Go back on lead and simply practice turning—right, left, around—any amount from a few degrees to a complete about-turn, guiding him gently with the lead until he understands that he is to stay smartly at your side—no matter which way you turn or how far—and end up sitting straight at heel. He'll think it is one of the most ridiculous things you've ever come up with, but be patient and he'll be patient with you, and will humor you by going through all the turns again.

Remember, though, that in competition, you are not allowed to touch your dog at any time. Work at it on lead, and then keep working off lead once he's gotten the idea. Don't try to help him along by nudging him about with your foot or pushing him into place with your hands. Get him to do it *properly* on lead, and he'll do it properly off lead.

PROBLEMS IN GENERAL

There are, naturally and unfortunately, many more minor problems than those we have covered in this chapter. To cover all problems in detail, and even to give detailed attention to all the major ones, would require an entire book on problems alone. So what we have done is give specific advice on those that we have found occurring most frequently.

It may well be that the particular problem driving you to the brink of distraction has not even been touched upon. If this is so, we can only ask that you read carefully the section of the book devoted to the exercise that is causing you trouble. Compare the methods given there with what you have been doing. Try to isolate the problem—put in words what he doesn't do, or doesn't do well enough. Then sit back and think hard about it along the lines we have indicated throughout this book. Sometimes the reason for a problem may not occur to you for days—this has happened to us enough times. Confronted with a particularly tricky problem, you may cudgel your brains for hours trying to find a logical explanation; then two or three days later the solution may spring into your mind like a flash of revelation. Thus we counsel patience and a layoff of several days if something is really going wrong. Put yourself in your dog's place as much as you can, and ask yourself what your reaction would be if you were being treated as you have been treating him.

Above all, in cases of nonperformance, ask yourself if you have really been demonstrating to him what you want done. If you have been simply telling him to do something and then trying to correct him into doing it, you'll have had very little success. Remember that the dog won't even know there's a lesson going on if you are not teaching him—if you are standing on your ego and insisting that he do something he doesn't understand.

Whatever you do, use as your guides to analysis and retraining the basic psychology of the dog and the philosophy of training as we have outlined it, and the psychology of your own individual dog as you know it. The dog has feelings, he has dignity, and he is capable of infinite response to the proper inducements. He is not a machine, but a living, responsive creature. He remembers things for a long time, but keep always in mind that he does not have a "connective" memory—you cannot correct him today for what he did yesterday, nor can you correct him now for what he did two minutes ago. Unless an action of his carries either a penalty result or a pleasure result, it will have no meaning for him. And the penalty or the pleasure must be immediate. All corrections must be made at the time of the fault, and they *must be followed by praise.*

On that note we will end this chapter, for there is no one thing in obedience that even approaches the importance of praise. We cannot say it too often. Praise him when he does right, and praise him when he does wrong and has been corrected. Praise him to keep him happy. Praise him to keep him working. We know how hard it can be to fully grasp the idea of praise after a correction, to accept it as something basic. But there it is, the one and only way to have a happy working dog, and for that matter, a working dog of almost any nature. Do it.

CHAPTER 11

Feeding and Health

The feeding and health problems of puppies and grown dogs are areas in which you will encounter a great deal of pontification and nonsense. Feeding, particularly, is rife with old wives' tales. Both fields, however, need only the application of a little common sense, backed by some of the facts we will give you, for easy understanding.

We firmly believe that your dog should be fed according to a sound nutrition-diet plan for his health and development. The diets and schedules you will find later in this chapter are what we, and many other dog owners, have found best for our own dogs. But none of this is to say that you can't do it differently and have a perfectly fine and happy dog around the house. Uncounted millions of dogs lived, grew, and prospered for thousands of years before the advent of scientific feeding and balanced diets, and many thousands now alive and healthy have never known any diet but table scraps and leavings. Lest we seem to paint too rosy a picture of the results of thoughtless feeding, we must also point out that millions of dogs have suffered shortened and unhappy lives through neglected feeding. However that may be, it has been our experience that a dog whose feeding is planned with a modicum of care has a definite edge in health, vitality, and longevity over the dog haphazardly fed. We feel that edge is well worth the small trouble involved.

PUPPY FEEDING

The first rule applicable to puppy feeding is that you can give him solid foods as soon as he will take them. The average age of acquisition is three months. At that age puppies happily eat, and should get, solid food. If you should happen to get a pup two months old, he can eat solid food too. Much younger than that it becomes a special case beyond the scope of this chapter, but you are not likely to encounter the problem.

When you do get the puppy, find out from the breeder or former owner what he has been feeding. If the pup comes to you in good condition—as indeed he must, or you shouldn't have taken him—the diet he has been getting will keep him that way. Follow the breeder's diet, but with a cautious eye to padding of the list. With only the best interests of the pup at heart, many breeders will supply the buyer with a fabulous list of condiments the like of which the pup has never seen. Some feeding lists include, for example, baby foods. Such foods are if anything too rich in vegetables and other nutritional items meant for humans, and short on meat. Baby foods are fine if you can afford them and if you supplement them with meat, but they are an unnecessary expense.

Rather than take you through a maze of possible diets—and there are many—here is one we recommend for the young puppy. First meal: milk and Pablum or dried cereal; second meal: milk and any good canned soft dog food; third meal: canned food plus a small amount of starchy filler (dried bread or kibbled biscuit, moistened with milk, water, or meat broth); fourth meal: fresh meat with fat.

You can also take your veterinarian's advice on the puppy's diet, and we strongly recommend this. If his advice on what to feed is different from ours, your best bet is to stick with him. Especially if your puppy has any specific problems, follow the vet's advice quite religiously. There are, as we will later point out, good vets and poor vets. It is unlikely that you will ever get harmful advice on feeding from a veterinarian, but then again you might just have bad luck. Just keep your eye out for patent nonsense. General rule: Trust your veterinarian as you would your own doctor, because he knows a good deal more about your dog's health than you will learn from this book or any other.

The prepared dog foods that we recommend for feeding—the soft canned foods—are almost all scientifically compounded by experts. In general, you are safe in buying canned foods distributed by major packers and companies. This is not to say that many of the canned foods put out by small specialty companies are not excellent, but you are on the safer side, until you know more about it, if you stick with the companies of known reputation. And this, incidentally, does not mean just companies with large advertising budgets. Among the reasons we recommend prepared foods is that they are an economical feeding for the puppy and grown dog. Table scraps may seem the cheapest way to feed, but this is, in a good many cases, simply false economy. Particularly if you have a medium-sized or a large dog, you will find yourself not just giving him the true leftovers, but sneaking in extra amounts at cooking time, so an adequate amount of scraps will be left over for feeding. And bingo! there goes the food budget—you're feeding him at human costs.

The prepared foods may seem to you like fairly unappetizing messes, but to the dog they are generally tasty. Don't make the mistake of anthropomorphism, which is a nice word covering most of the aspects of thinking of your dog as a person. Dogs just don't have the same tastes, preferences, or food prejudices as humans. Aside from that, their senses function differently, and to the dog a can of dog food is a mixture of a dozen different smells and tastes. You get one smell: dog food. He gets a dozen smells from the components, and thinks of it differently. This may seem improbable to you, but consider for a moment that humans, at least some of them, can be trained to do almost as well. The famed "noses" of the perfume industry can tell at a whiff all the ingredients of a perfume, plus the approximate amounts of each; and many organic chemists have trained themselves to do almost as well with malodorous chemical compounds. The dog has a long head start on them. To him that smell of hash is actually an interesting blend of food odors, and he'll pitch in.

Along this line, we might say also that some of the "meal" dog foods are also excellent for feeding. We generally recommend that you don't feed them such foods when they are too young, but when the pup has reached, say, three months, he can quite profitably eat the meal foods, moistened with water, milk, or meat broth. Here again, what to you is just dry-looking gravel is to him a mélange of quite attractive things.

This is not to say that dogs don't have preferences in foods. They do. One dog will, for no reason known to man, court starvation rather than eat some foods. Some adamantly refuse to touch one particular brand of prepared food that thousands of others guzzle with gusto.

There is, in fact, a famous television incident involving a prepared dog food. On a local show the producers somehow neglected to try the advertised food on the actor dog before the commercial. When he was led on camera, the dog sniffed it once, circled it, and then pointedly lifted his leg on the bowl. This reaction is hardly a common one, occurring, we suppose, only with the more demonstrative television dogs, but it does illustrate the fact of definite likes and dislikes. If your puppy really takes a strong dislike to one particular type of food, don't force it on him. Try another brand, and then another until you hit one he likes. If he turns up his nose at all prepared foods, and the vet certifies him as well, then he is just being finicky. Put one brand in front of him at several meals, until he gets ravenously hungry. He'll eat.

In addition to his milk, meat, starchy filler, and prepared food, give him dietary supplements. Bone meal is good for the puppy and helps his growth. Any good commercial mineral supplement also helps, as do vitamin supplements emphasizing the A and D vitamins. We recommend these supplements even if you are following our recommended diet for your pup, and especially if you are planning to feed him scraps, or all canned food, or any other diet. In using the supplements, follow the label regarding amount to be administered according to the size of the pup. Better to overdo slightly; it is difficult to overdose, as the body tends to throw off superfluous minerals and vitamins.

Most puppies seem ravenously hungry all the time. They gobble their food as though it might be the last meal. But some few present eating problems that can be worrisome to the owner. If you are faced with a puppy who doesn't eat, or eats listlessly—and you have established through trying that it isn't just that he doesn't like some particular food—you should suspect illness of some sort. Judge what to do by the pup's general behavior. If he is otherwise happy, alert, and active, it may just be a phase. Pups have them just like human children. If he mopes around the house and is generally unhappy about things, then noneating is likely to be an indicator of one illness or another. Not eating, in itself, won't do any harm to a puppy, but if he has fasted for thirty-six hours, take him to your vet for an examination. Once the vet has examined him and given you advice on the situation, follow that advice about periods of noneating. But the first time it is indeed far better to be safe.

A good general approach to number of feedings for a puppy is to assume that he needs four feedings a day at the age of two or three months. The puppy's stomach is small and cannot accommodate the large quantities eaten by an adult. To insure good growth and health, food should come into his system regularly. Puppies, like children, are growing every minute and must have the materials available for continued growth. It is a well-accepted maxim that "If you don't get it into them the first year, you won't get it into them"—meaning that the pattern of growth, health, and development is laid firmly then and little you do afterward has much effect. Within that first year, the first few months are again predominantly important. So feed your pup right up to the eyeballs with everything nutritious you can, and watch him sprout.

As he gets along in age, the number of feedings per day can be gradually reduced until he is eating just one meal, probably the late evening meal. Another very general rule, assuming you are starting at three months, is to knock off one daily feeding every three months until at one year he is eating once a day. This is, however, only a very general rule. If he seems lackadaisical about any of the four early feedings, and consistently refuses or only nibbles at one, cut him down to three right away. Feed him, in fact, only as often as he wants to eat. This is good physically, and also psychologically, for if you allow him to turn up his nose at a feeding every day of his early life, he can easily get into a finicky mood about the whole business of eating.

Approaching it from the other end, his feedings definitely should be cut down at about the stated intervals. Even if he relishes and gobbles four meals a day at six months, cut him down to three (with more in each), and so on. Many dogs stay at two meals all their lives, getting table scraps as they are available. But the balanced feeding plan of one meal a day is preferable. Among the reasons for this is that it establishes a good pattern of once-a-day elimination at a fairly regular time, which is considerably more convenient for you as the owner. Another is that this is the pattern of the wild dog, or any wild carnivore, and the dog is built to operate best that way. The wild animal makes a kill, wolfs his stomach bulging with food, and then rests and sleeps until it is time to get up and prowl again. Often, of course, the wild carnivore eats at much longer intervals than one day, but the once-a-day schedule of your civilized pet is a concession to your convenience and his small degree of removal from the wild state.

The amount to give at each feeding is something only you can judge. What with wildly varying sizes of breeds, different basic appetites, and different puppy sizes with a breed, any fixed schedule of amounts is illusory at best. The best rule is to feed him what he will eat. Once you have decided what your puppy's diet is going to be, try him with an overlarge amount the first few times—more than you can imagine him eating at one sitting. He will eat his fill and then waddle away. Take note of how much he put away and judge the next feeding accordingly, giving him that much plus a little more until you have a good idea of how much he will hold each time. Continue this practice throughout his life, adjusting the amount given to the amount taken, except in special cases of sickness or treatment of obesity.

Tidbits and between-meal snacks for the puppy should be avoided if you have the willpower. The temptation, as we know full well, is great to offer the cute little pup just a nibble of cracker, or a piece of doughnut, or any other snack, just to see if he likes it. He will, never fear, and once the habit is established he will be on the cadge all the rest of his life. It can get to be an annoyance to you and your guests, and it will foul up his diet and quite possibly make him unpleasantly fat. What he puts away in the form of snacks leaves less room for his calculated diet—and human snacks are generally of the fattening variety. But if you hold an iron hand over yourself from the first, and give it to be known that he eats only at mealtimes, he'll never get to know what he's missing. It's hard, but try. A little restraint at first can pay off large dividends in his later life.

ADULT FEEDING

Under normal circumstances your dog will be able, as an adult, to ingest and profit from almost anything you give him, including almost all of the items forbidden by rumor and custom. Milk, for example, will most definitely not cause worms in him, any more than it does in you. Raw meat will not cause worms any more than cooked (which is not at all), nor will it make him savage or vicious. If you feed him nothing but raw meat, he will thereby suffer from an unbalanced diet and consequent malnutrition, and he may get irritable and touchy. One item we do recommend against is pork in quantity. Pork, particularly pork fat, is an extremely rich meat, and if fed in large amounts can easily overburden a dog's system. If you feed it, use moderation. There is also the minor danger than humans tend at times to be somewhat less careful about cooking meat for a dog than for themselves (although this won't apply if you just feed pork scraps from your table). Thus the familiar specter of trichinosis raises its multiple head, along with a highly unpleasant condition known as toxoplasmosis, both resulting from underdone, infected pork.

One highly prevalent superstition concerns raw eggs and the dog's coat. People go to considerable expense to feed the pup or the grown dog raw eggs, sometimes two or three a day, in the vain hope that a glossy coat will result. There is, unfortunately, nothing to it. If there were, we would all be swallowing raw eggs ourselves and could throw away the hair tonic. It just doesn't work. Neither will garlic or onions have any effect on intestinal worms. A clove of garlic a day may keep the vampire away, but intestinal worms yield only to specific medication. A sulfur block in the drinking water does nothing at all for the dog's health, adding only a dubious decorative note to the drinking bowl, no matter what "scientific" claims you may read on the boxes of sulfur blocks in pet shops. In short, what you feed him simply nourishes him. If he needs medical treatment, give him medicines prescribed by your vet.

On the positive side of the ledger, beef and more fresh beef can do him nothing but good. Beef is the best source of protein, and good beef muscle cuts can be bought relatively cheaply if you shop for the sections low in human demand. Horse meat is also a good protein source, but rising relative prices of horse meat have lost for it the protein-per-dollar advantage it once had. Organ meats are also very nutritious. Some of them tend to be considerably cheaper than table cuts for humans, and dogs love them. You may be repelled by such items as hearts, lungs, and the like, but your dog will probably love the variety and taste, and he couldn't care less where it comes from.

Beef bones are almost without exception good for dogs, especially the heavy long and knuckle bones. They will chew all the meat scraps and gristle off the bones with great pleasure, and then chew some more for fun and mouth exercise. Sometimes, the bone will disappear bit by bit. Once in the stomach, bones of whatever variety are rapidly dissolved and digested. The dog's stomach acids work things over with a gothic ferocity, rapidly reducing almost anything to digestibility. This, incidentally, is why you should not worry if your dog wolfs his food without seeming to chew at all. From the hereditary necessity to eat and run, the dog has developed the habit of gulping large chunks, chewing only enough to make a given mouthful somewhat manageable and to lubricate it with saliva. All the digestion goes on in his highly durable and efficient stomach.

PUPPY HEALTH

The health of a puppy is at times a baffling business. A pup's life seems fraught with a multitude of dangers, but contradictorily, puppies seem to have an incredible hardihood and resistance to human and bacterial mistreatment. The major areas that will concern you in caring for your puppy are: feeding, preventive shots, worming, and disease. As this is not intended to be a handbook of veterinary care, we give you in each area simply good general rules to follow.

The first major question you will have to attend to in the consideration of your puppy's welfare is which vet to take him to. It is a difficult one to answer. There are, as we have said before, veterinarians ranging from excellent to downright poor. The balance is fortunately quite far to the high side, but this does you little good when it comes to choosing your vet. You may live in an area where there is only one vet, and there you have no choice. In larger communities there are likely to be several within a small radius of your home, or you may be willing to travel quite a distance if you can find an exceptionally good vet.

The best possible answer, albeit the obvious one, is personal references. The breeder of your pup will tell you vociferously enough who he thinks is the best vet in your area. Other dog owners will be glad to give you advice. Quite frankly, we can tell you little more. Use pretty much the same criteria you would in choosing your own family doctor: a good manner (with dogs), a willingness to discuss symptoms and treatment without mumbo-jumbo and a retreat into lofty professional hauteur, a gentle touch with his patients. You can make some sort of evaluation from the veterinarian's premises; anything really run-down and shabby hardly speaks well for the owner. Even if he treats only animals, the premises are a reflection of the owner. But don't rely on gleaming tile and shiny instruments either. Some of the best veterinarians we know function in totally unimpressive (but not run-down) offices and small clinics, whereas some ensconced in glittering array we wouldn't trust to treat a mild headache. But whatever you do, look into the matter beforehand—don't wait until the last minute to phone frantically around the city with a sick puppy on your hands.

The next major matter is that of preventive shots against distemper, hepatitis, rabies, and leptospirosis. Distemper is a prevalent disease of dogs, and many thousands of unprotected puppies are lost each year in heart-rending circumstances due to this ailment. Fortunately, persistent work by veterinarians and veterinary researchers plus a widespread vaccination program have reduced the once general menace of distemper. Still, it is a substantial danger, and we cannot too strongly recommend protection, for your susceptible young puppy can get distemper without even being near an infected dog. Until eight to ten weeks of age, puppies are pretty well protected against distemper by antibodies contained in their mothers' milk; preventive shots are seldom given before then. Assuming you have gotten your puppy at the recommended three months of age, the breeder or other seller will probably by then have had an initial shot given. Find out in detail exactly what was given and when; if possible, get the slip of paper veterinarians often leave to certify what shot has been given.

Aside from special distemper vaccines, there is now a combined distemper-hepatitis-leptospirosis-rabies vaccine. If your vet doesn't mention it, you might ask him about it. If for some reason it is unavailable, ask for the specific hepatitis vaccine in addition to distemper protection. Hepatitis is an insidious disease in that a puppy may suddenly die of it without his owner's ever having known that the pup was sick.

About rabies little need be said. This horrifying affliction is still very much with us—to the extent that any person bitten by an unknown dog, even in an area which has not known a case of rabies for decades, must go through a painful and expensive series of treatments rather than risk the irreversible ferocity of a fatal rabies infection. When the biting dog is identified, most localities require that he be held for examination for some period until it is certain that he is not infected with rabies. If your dog can be proven by a veterinarian's certificate to be fully protected, you may not have to go through this. In certain areas of the country the rabies problem is much less serious than in others. If you live in one of these areas (the nearest public health officer can advise you on this) and your dog never comes into contact with strange dogs, the danger is minute. But even in this case we recommend vaccination. The rabies shot for your puppy gives protection for one to three years, depending on the type of vaccine, and should be repeated at regular intervals for full protection.

Leptospirosis directly affects the kidneys, and can result in crippling uremia or death through uremic poisoning Vaccines now offer good protection, either separately or in one of the combination shots. As with all other preventive shots, don't ever believe that there are "permanent" shots, once and forever. Follow your veterinarian's recommendation on regular booster shots, shots either individually or in combination.

These four diseases are major threats to your puppy's life—and all are preventable. The preventive shots usually are given in a certain order, at specified times in the pup's growth. This should be left in the hands of the vet, for only he can judge whether your puppy is old enough to begin the course of treatment, and whether he is in the proper physical condition.

Again, as we have said about every aspect of dog care, it is possible that your dog could live to creaking old age without ever coming near a vaccination needle. Millions have. But we feel the chance is not worth taking. The time and expense involved in protection seem very small as against possible pain and death of a well-loved animal.

Worms of various varieties are also a particular problem of puppies. There are roundworms, hookworms, whipworms, tapeworms, and others— the most common being the first two. Diagnosis of worm infestation in your puppy is something which should be left strictly to your veterinarian, as should worm treatment. We recommend against commercial worming preparations for two very good reasons: You are completely unqualified to diagnose the presence of worms in your dog's system, and you as a layperson are quite likely to give the wrong preparation or give it in the wrong way. Most veterinarians do a stool examination of any puppy under their care as a matter of course. They are equipped to do the right thing if worms are found.

A serious infestation of roundworms, the most common variety, generally shows itself in the puppy through a distended abdomen (regardless of feeding), occasional diarrhea, dull coat, and general listlessness. You may even see tiny white worms in the stool, or occasional vomiting of worms. If these signs appear, take the pup to the vet. If possible, consult him on the phone before bringing the pup in, for the vet may want you to starve the puppy for twelve hours or more before he sees him. This allows the vet, if he finds worms, to begin treatment right away; otherwise you would have to bring the puppy back after a starvation period. The reason behind this is that various of the worming chemicals can react quite adversely on the pup if he has any food at all in his stomach or intestines, so he must be brought to the vet totally empty.

Puppies do not, incidentally, just automatically have worms, even of the most common kind. Many, many dogs go through life without a worm to their name, so don't give a pup a worming just on general principles. In some areas of the country, though, some worms like heartworms are particularly prevalent during certain seasons, and preventive drugs are available. Consult your veterinarian on this possibility, but in general if your pup is healthy and happy and shows no sign of problems, forget about worms unless there's good reason to do otherwise.

In general, the healthy puppy is characterized by all the familiar outward signs of playfulness, alertness, bright eyes, good appetite, and healthy coat.

The first signs of illness you will see in your pup are the reversals of these. If his appetite falls off sharply, suspect illness. If he becomes listless, if his eyes are dull, or his coat seems coarse and dry, something is wrong. Continued whimpering or moans of pain are obvious trouble signs. In addition, two very reliable indicators require only a little more watchfulness: the puppy's temperature and the condition of his stool.

A normal puppy's temperature varies between 101° and 102.7°. A cold wet nose means nothing, incidentally, nor do cold ears. A cold nose does not indicate health, nor does a warm nose indicate the presence of fever. You will, in fact, notice that your pup's nose is warm when he has been sleeping. So discount ears and nose as temperature indicators. We recommend that you keep in the house a good rectal thermometer to use as an additional check if you suspect illness. It will help you and the vet to know if the pup's temperature has been high. Using a rectal thermometer appeals to some people not at all, but it is a simple matter and one that can be gotten used to with little difficulty. The major problem is getting a puppy to hold still for the necessary minute. Shake the thermometer down (you must have seen doctors or nurses do it—it's the flip of the wrist that does the trick), lubricate the business end with salve or butter (be sure you have the rectal-model thermometer), and insert it a little more than halfway into the anus. Be sure to keep hold of the protruding end throughout, as a wiggly pup might get away and smash even a strongly built thermometer. Keep it in for a minute, then wipe the end off with cotton or tissue and read the temperature. This part seems to baffle large numbers of people, but if you settle down to it you'll find you can read any thermometer with a very small amount of practice.

The puppy's stool is also a very good general indicator of health. Keeping a check on this is easy enough during the first paper-cum-housebreaking days; later on you will just have to watch. A firm, normal-colored stool indicates, but does not assure, good intestinal health. Variations are the signs of trouble. The character and color of the stool will vary with diet. The main thing to watch for is any radical change while the dog's diet remains the same. Persistent diarrhea and loose stools indicate that something is wrong. Constipation is important to watch for, as it may indicate illness or may be caused by a blockage of the puppy's stomach by something he has swallowed when you weren't looking. Blood in the stool warns you that something is wrong. While none of these conditions indicates anything specific to you, a good description, along with a temperature check, goes a long way in helping your vet with his diagnosis.

TEETHING

At approximately four months (slightly later for the smaller breeds) the puppy begins to lose his milk teeth and grow a permanent set. This process causes his gums to become sore, and he may show other symptoms: a slight fever, occasional vomiting, or diarrhea. He may cut down on his eating during this period. It is advisable to have your vet check him at this time, even if you strongly suspect all the symptoms point only to teething troubles. Unless there is a growth abnormality (failure to lose a milk tooth and resultant crowding of the growing permanent tooth), there is little indeed you can do for the puppy at this time. He will chew on things in an instinctive attempt to loosen the milk teeth, so it is a good idea to let him have something to chew on other than your shoes and furniture. An uncooked beef bone is fine for this. Don't tug him about in tugs-of-wars in an attempt to help the process—he'll do what's necessary all by himself. Just keep an occasional eye on his gums to see that all is going well and that there are no double-tooth situations. Don't be alarmed, incidentally, if a pup's erect ears flop down at this stage, or at any other ear curiosities. Teething affects ears in a curious way. It's only temporary.

THE FEMALE PUPPY

There comes a time in every female puppy's life when she shows conclusively that she is indeed female. The average age of the first season is eight months, but it may occur anywhere from six months to a year, or even later. Thereafter she will probably have a season quite regularly at six-month intervals, each period lasting about three weeks.

From the age of six months on you should keep a careful eye on her for indications. Sometimes she will show it by an increased activity and affection, but this may be hard to judge in a happy and already affectionate pet. A preliminary swelling of the vulva area can often be seen, and more frequent urination is another common sign. If she is outside among other dogs much of the time, you will be tipped off by a sudden increase of interest in her by male dogs—interest not only in her but persistent and noticeable intense interest in wherever she has been, especially where she has urinated. Otherwise, you may not know it is upon you until she first begins to discharge and spots rugs and floors.

The primary action you must take, once she has come into season, is protection against males. If her habit is to run free outdoors, she must be kept behind a good high fence during her season—and be sure the fence is a good one, because the leaping abilities of an amorous male are marvelous to behold. If possible, or if it is your usual habit, let her outside only on leash, and be prepared to fend off precipitous advances from males. In a large city apartment you will have little trouble with males trailing her to her lair, but in a house you will find that the news gets surprisingly far around the neighborhood and you will be besieged by unwelcome and noisy dogs from the surrounding counties. There is nothing so attractive to the male nose as the scent of a female in heat. Males can track her from far away by such abstruse means as her in-season smell carried away from your house on the feet of another male. So be prepared.

To keep the inside of the house from being spotted and soiled by her vaginal discharge you can either confine her or use one of the commercial sanitary pads and harnesses. Confinement is probably the best answer if you have a room to spare, but the commercial pads with harness or dog panty will do the job quite adequately. They're a bother, both to you and her—and to some people highly ridiculous—but they work. Don't despair; it will be over in a week or two, and then you are safe for another six months.

If, by some unpleasant happenstance, she is caught by a male either before you know she is in season or during a known heat, you have fairly well had it. Your veterinarian may be able to induce chemical abortion if he gets her early enough, but the method is far from reliable. You may just have to resign yourself to puppies of half-unknown ancestry, to be handled in the best way possible. If yours is a mongrel, you may even have pups better looking than their mother, and you may like them. But if yours is a purebred and she is caught out by a different breed or a mongrel, don't despair. The old wives' tale about a mixed litter ruining her for future breeding is total nonsense. Each litter she has is a thing unto itself and has positively no effect on future litters.

Spaying is, of course, one way out. A "whole" female will be subject to seasons and the need for cleanliness and protection every six months, and some people find this bothersome in the extreme. If you find it so, and have no plans for breeding her, spaying may appeal to you. But we generally recommend that you wait until after the first season, for two reasons: First, the heat problem may be very slight with her; second, as you get to know her better you may change your mind about wanting to have a pup of hers. One thing you should disregard completely about spaying, however, is the possibility that it will make her fat, vicious, disaffected, or whatever else you may hear. Most of the folklore about spaying is based on false cause-and-effect assumptions. If an unspayed bitch gets fat, nobody remarks on it, but if it happens to a spayed bitch, spaying is assigned the blame. Many vets prefer to do the spaying operation at the age of six months, because the operation is relatively simple at or about that age. An older bitch, particularly an obese bitch, runs considerable risk, but if your bitch is up to two years old and in good physical condition, you can quite safely have the job done by your vet. The fact that she will no longer go through the minor physical changes, and no longer experience the mating urges, may have some slight effect on her weight and disposition, but it would be a chancy thing indeed to attribute any particular characteristic to spaying—she might well have got that way unspayed.

ADULT CARE

Once your dog has reached adulthood, his health, aside from continued good feeding, is a matter of incidents, as with the adult human. The adult dog falls heir to many of the ills and minor sieges of humans. To guard against these you can only exercise the same cautions you would with yourself: feed him sensibly, allow him to get plenty of rest, keep him clean, and watch for danger signs of illness. Look for any change of disposition, lack of energy, pain symptoms, dull eyes, dull coat, radical change in eating habits. Aside from incidents of illness or accident, your main concerns in his care will consist of grooming and attention to his ears, teeth, skin, and nails.

Under grooming, perhaps the major item is bathing. This, though surrounded by its own lore, is simple enough. We recommend that you do not bathe your dog until he is a year old, for a variety of reasons—central among which is the high susceptibility of puppies to bad colds and possible pneumonia. If he gets dirty as a pup, wet a towel with witch hazel or rubbing alcohol and clean him off that way, being careful to keep it out of his eyes. But after a year, bathe away. You may hear that any bathing at all is bad for a dog's coat, and to some extent that is true. A good soap-and-water scrubbing will wash away some of the vital oils of his coat, but it will do no more permanent harm than sensible washing of your own hair. The rule here is moderation. If he is bathed at reasonable intervals, the oils will replace themselves. Bathe him when he really needs it, and between times wipe the occasional mud off his feet with a rag and use the witch hazel or rubbing alcohol to clean up minor dirt on the coat.

When you do get to the actual bath, we recommend that you bathe him just as you would yourself—with warm water and a gentle soap. The standing cartoon subject of the household dog avoiding baths like bubonic plague is based very little on truth. That comes from senseless plunking him, wiggling and howling, into a tub of water. If your dog is well obedience trained, you will have no trouble getting him into or making him stay in the tub. Introduce him to the idea just as you would to a new obedience exercise—gently, with praise and coaxing. Make him stand or sit and stay while you wash him. Soon he'll get to think quite favorably of the whole business. When you're through, dry him thoroughly with a rough towel. That he'll like without reservation—to him it's just one prolonged petting.

With a short-haired dog, you never have the bother of clipping, and with most long-haired breeds, clipping is seldom necessary. The exception to this latter occurs in very hot weather, when some long-haired dogs can benefit from the removal of part of their coats. This sort of thing is taken care of ordinarily by the natural process of seasonal shedding, but civilized domestic dogs get their shedding cycles fouled up by living much of the time under artificial light. So if yours seems to suffer a great deal in the heat, have him clipped. "Sculpture-clipped" breeds such as Poodles, Bedlingtons, Kerry Blues, and Sealyhams are real problems unless you give it a good deal of study and become handy with the clippers. All of these breeds live quite happily without ever seeing a clipper. Artistic clipping is done solely for aesthetic values. If you plan to go in for that sort of thing— and it does make for a more attractive dog in most cases—we recommend strongly that you have the original clipping done by a professional and learn how to do it by watching. Charts and instructions such as you will encounter more often than not result in a botched job and a literal shaggy dog in the hands of a rank amateur. But once having seen what to do, and with clippers in hand, most people can handle things quite well. Warning, though: Don't try to do it with scissors. If you're going to go to all that trouble anyway, invest in either electric or manual clippers.

All dogs, long-haired or short, benefit from regular brushing. Any hairbrush or special dog brush works well. Long-haired breeds need brushing and combing on a regular basis to control mattings and "rats" in their hair, and to keep them comfortable and neat. It requires no more technique than taking care of your own hair. Even though the short-hairs don't often develop mats and rats, regular brushing keeps the coat sleek and healthy. In addition, it keeps your house a lot cleaner, for the loose hair of normal shedding ends up on the newspaper instead of all over the house.

For the dog, brushing becomes a very enjoyable experience. Just as in towel drying after a bath, it is like prolonged rubbing and petting. Teach a small dog to stand quietly on a table, or a large dog on the floor, while you brush him, and the job will be that much easier.

Care of the teeth is a subject of some contention. You may hear or read recommendations that you brush your dog's teeth at some regular interval, but we cannot hold with this particular bit of anthropomorphism. The major menace to dog teeth is tartar, a hard brownish deposit that may build up, particularly around the base of the teeth. Tartar in itself is no particular danger, but it often causes objectionable mouth odor and increases the possibility of cavities and decay. It is easily removed by your vet with a tartar scraper. Although you can acquire one of these yourself, we don't recommend that you work on your dog's teeth with one unless you're a dentist. It takes a knack and practice. What we do recommend is that you check your dog's mouth at least once a month for heavy tartar deposits, and for loose or broken teeth. These latter naturally require professional attention, but the chances are very high that he will never have any tooth trouble. If he has bones to chew on, he will help keep his teeth free of tartar.

The care of your dog's nails is something you may very well never have to bother with. City dogs who are constantly running and walking on pavement tend to keep their own filed by contact with the rough cement. Country dogs who are largely outdoors grow long, strong nails and, in fact, need and use them in getting around. It is the house dog, city or country— the one who spends most of his life on floors and rugs, or sleeping in the corner—who needs nail care. Having no opportunity to wear them off, and no earthly need for them—he will in fact lose traction on floors and linoleum if his nails are too long—he must have them kept short. Keep an eye on his nails—or better, an ear. If, as he walks around the house, you hear a continual clicking, his nails may be too long. In serious cases of neglect, where no attention at all has been given them, the nails may even grow around and bend under the pads, causing pain and unwillingness to walk or run. The latter case is strictly a job for the veterinarian, who may have to anaesthetize the dog while he does some fairly major surgery on the nails. But normal care is easily handled at home with a special nail clipper. There are two very good kinds of clipper: one a heavy nipper called an "end cutter" when it is a regular hardware tool, looking somewhat like a pair of pliers, but with heavy straight parallel blades at the ends of the jaws; the other is a sort of guillotine arrangement with a sliding blade. You can learn to use either quite readily.

When you do the clipping, proceed with caution. Within every nail there is a quick, and it may extend farther down into the nail than you think. This quick is visible but extremely hard to describe. Once again, we have to refer you to the vet, if only for an instructional session in the recognition of the extent of the quick so you can avoid cutting into it when you clip. If you can't get this instruction, the best way to go about it is to clip each nail very cautiously, taking off only the very tip, and do it regularly. If you clip too far in, you will hit the quick, which is a very painful experience for the dog. You may even cause the nail to bleed. This in itself is not dangerous, unless you have whacked off a mighty chunk and the bleeding is copious. In such cases a styptic pencil is of some use, or you can control bleeding with a bit of cotton soaked in hydrogen peroxide. Most minor nail bleeding takes care of itself through capillary closure. Just be sure to keep the dog off his feet for a few minutes, and off rough surfaces for a few hours, to let the healing take place.

No matter how carefully you do it, your dog will probably never accept nail clipping as part of his normal life. It is a mildly traumatic experience but you and he will just have to make the best of it. Be gentle, and firm, and clip away with a firm hold on the leg being worked on. Though traumatic, the experience will not damage his psyche permanently if you go about it the right way, with great caution and snipping off only the smallest bit of the tip at a time.

One of the major problems you may encounter, this one somewhere on the borderline between grooming and basic health, is the familiar fleas and other skin parasites. The symptoms of these hardly need explanation: excessive scratching and biting at the skin. As far as we know, almost every dog in the world has fleas at one time or another. It's just one of those things, and no sign of slovenly care on your part. Lice are a little less prevalent, and the same goes for ticks. When you see him scratching and biting at himself, it may be just a skin rash, but investigation will either establish that or rule it out. More likely it will be the parasites, and treatment is in order. There are antiparasitic dips and rinses that can be used in conjunction with a bath, and many of the commercial flea and louse powders are highly efficient if worked well into the coat and onto the skin. Follow the label instructions carefully when using either dips or powders, especially keeping the stuff out of the dog's eyes. And be very careful when buying powder or dip for your dog. Be absolutely sure from the label that it is intended for dogs and other animals that lick themselves; otherwise he might just lick up a lethal quantity of something poisonous. That's one sure way to end the flea problem, but not the best. The "flea and tick collars" you see widely advertised can be beneficial. If your dog or pup begins suffering, it is worth trying one. But if the problem continues, go back to regular treatment. In serious cases, the dog's bedding and the area around his bed or crate should also be treated with an anti-flea powder to get rid of any which may be lurking there, and then thoroughly washed before re-use.

Ticks you will have to look for, and should look for. Every week or so, and in particular immediately after a run in the woods or high grass, go over your dog's entire skin area carefully in a strong light. With a short-haired dog you may feel ticks under the hair as slight lumps, but long-haired dogs require laborious examination. Even if you've never seen a tick before, you'll know what it is the moment you find it: a smallish, bean-shaped item that looks for all the world like a watermelon seed, stuck by one end, the head, to the dog's skin. The old saw about holding a lighted match near the tick is not a very effective method of tick removal, quite aside from the danger of burning the dog's hair or skin. The best method is to soak a small wad of cotton with alcohol, then squeeze out alcohol all over the tick and the surrounding area. Hold the soaked cotton right over the tick for about a minute. The alcohol treatment dazes the tick and makes it lose its grip in the skin, where it has its jaws buried; then it can be extracted whole. Grasp the tick as close to the dog's skin as possible with tweezers and work it out slowly, moving it gently from side to side to feel if the jaws have released. Then douse the skin area again with more alcohol as an antiseptic. If you simply haul the tick out, you may leave the head inside the skin, where it can cause infection or even a nasty cyst. If the first alcohol treatment hasn't loosened it enough, douse it again. It'll come out with patience and careful treatment.

Attention to all these things—and they take little enough time—will result in a healthy, happy, and attractive animal to have around the house and call your own. Regular inspection of teeth, nails, and skin takes little of your time, bathing is a short process when necessary, and regular brushing is more of a gesture of affection for the dog than a chore. Keep at it, and you'll have a pet and companion you're proud to own, and not just another scratching, shaggy, messy dog.

HOME NURSING AND FIRST AID

A sick or injured dog is far harder to care for than a human, largely because of lack of understanding and cooperation on his part. You can't tell him that he must take his medicine, or hold still, or rest for a while. At best, home care for your dog is a compromise with what should be done, for fortunately dogs are so resistant to such things as infections that it generally works out all right.

When you have a sick dog at home who has been prescribed for by your veterinarian, you will probably have to give him pills or liquid medicines. This can be difficult. For liquid medicines, there are two ways to go about it, depending on the temper of your dog. The first, and better, is to have a member of the family hold the dog's mouth open while you pour a spoonful of the medicine in. Then close the mouth and hold the muzzle high while you gently stroke the dog's throat. This keeps the medicine in, and the stroking promotes swallowing, and then it's all over. If he's really obstinate about it, determined to keep his mouth shut come flood or fire, you can still get the liquid into him. In this second method, with his mouth firmly closed, pull out his lower lip until you have made a small flesh pouch and dump the medicine into that. Then close it up quickly, concentrate on keeping the mouth shut and the muzzle high, and stroke the throat. The medicine will go right in through his teeth and he can't help swallowing it. It can turn into an almighty struggle, even if you have help, but here again your basic obedience training will pay off if he will sit and stay at your command.

Pills are something else again. For these you will have to get his mouth open somehow. Try using the lip-squeezing trick described in the "Open" chapter, for making him take a dumbell. When you have the mouth open, put the pill in as far back on the tongue as you can get it, and then raise the muzzle and stroke the throat. If you get it far enough back on the tongue he won't be able to help swallowing it. But keep his mouth closed for a minute or two, and watch carefully that he doesn't hold it and later spit it out. As an alternative, you can try poking the pill or pills into his food. Chances are very good that he will, in the course of eating, take them right down without knowing they were there.

First-aid treatment may be called for in the case of accidents. For this we recommend the following be kept in a handy box or your medicine cabinet: gauze, iodine (or any other good antiseptic), mustard powder, a good commercial burn ointment, witch hazel, and cotton. Also, keep handy a bottle of milk of magnesia as a mild cathartic, although this is for general and not emergency use. Anything else you keep around as a standard remedy should be on the advice of your veterinarian, as his will be the responsibility for your dog's health and care.

The roster of serious things that can happen to your dog includes: broken bones, serious cuts or bites, burns, poisoning, car accidents, heat stroke, electric shock, and foreign-object swallowing. Here is a brief course on what to do until the veterinarian comes.

Broken Bones: When you suspect a break, put a restraining gauze muzzle on the dog before you handle or attempt to move him. This is for your protection, as a dog who is injured and in pain may snap at anything that moves near him, and may blindly bite you when you attempt to move him. To put on a gauze muzzle, take a strip of gauze about two feet long (and two or three inches wide) and pass it around the middle of the dog's muzzle, making a single half-knot under the muzzle. Then pass the ends around in back of the dog's neck, there making a bow knot, firm but easily released by you. Be sure it is a bow that can be released in a hurry. In an injury case, he may want to throw up. You'll have to keep a close eye on him all the time he is wearing a tight gauze muzzle. Otherwise he could quite conceivably strangle with his mouth clamped shut. Make the loop around the muzzle tight enough so that he cannot get his mouth open, and the loop around the neck just tight enough to insure that he cannot paw or slip the muzzle loop off over his nose. He won't like it a bit, but it won't hurt him—the gauze muzzle is standard veterinary practice when treating a dog who may bite, and may save you both a great deal of trouble.

If the broken bone is in the leg, which it will be in 95 percent of the cases, he will take care of keeping it off the ground all by himself once he has recovered from the initial shock of the mishap. It is all right to carry him away from the scene if there is any good reason to. Otherwise leave him there until he recovers enough to limp away himself. Then get him to the vet. Once he has recovered and is on his feet, remove the gauze muzzle, as the danger of fear and pain biting is almost entirely over, and he will feel better with it off.

Car Accidents: Here you may not have gauze handy, so use a necktie, or a strip torn from shirt or skirt. Apply the muzzle immediately before you attempt to move the dog. One added value of the muzzle in this case is that it removes any temptation on your part to give him water—and you should never give water after an accident, in case of internal injuries. Always suspect internal injuries and bleeding until you know different, and treat him with according gentleness. If at all possible, leave the dog where he is; if you have to move him try to find something flat to slide him onto. A wide plank will serve for a small dog; a piece of plywood for a larger one. Usually, though, nothing of any use is ready to hand in such cases, so even your coat or a blanket or car robe will help. Somehow, as gently as possible, get the dog onto it, and use it as a litter. The idea behind this is that he should be moved, internally, as little as possible. The safest position is the one in which he falls—broken bones can easily gash flesh and rupture veins and arteries if they are moved about within him, and movement will aggravate internal injuries. Keep the movement down as much as possible, consistent with getting him to the vet as quickly as possible. In case of serious bleeding, see the discussion in the next section.

Cuts and Bites: The major danger here is bleeding, not infection, although this can be guarded against too by the application of a mild antiseptic. Serious bleeding on the head, neck, or body can be stopped only by the direct application of a pressure bandage. On the body or head, strap on a pad of gauze as tightly as you can. Make the pad thick so that the pressure of the strap of gauze around the body or head presses the pad well into the wound. It will be painful for him, but control of blood loss is more important. On the neck, use your good judgment about pressure to be used on the pad. Major cuts or openings in the legs can be treated with a tourniquet if bleeding is serious. A slow flow should be pressure-bandaged, but a serious spurting of blood, meaning that a major vein or artery has been cut, is more easily controlled with the tourniquet. To make the tourniquet, take a strong strip of anything—gauze, strip of shirt, or whatever—and wrap it once around the leg above the wound. Then, after making a half-knot, tie the loose ends around a stick. Twist the stick until the band around the leg is tight enough to stop the bleeding or cut it down from a spurt to a slow flow. Be *very* careful when using a tourniquet—loosen it every few minutes to allow the blood to flow a little, then tighten it again. Otherwise, with all blood flow to the limb shut off, serious complications

can set in. If a spurting wound is in some awkward position where you simply can't use a tourniquet, you've no choice but to apply a pad or wad of
cloth and press hard.

Poisoning: This specter that haunts every dog owner presents no precise
symptoms to look for. But if you suspect for any reason that your dog may
have been poisoned, through spoiled food, accident, or deliberate action
(he may vomit or exhibit nausea and stomach pain), search quickly to see if
you can locate what he may have taken in. There may be an open can or
bottle of something, or something may have spilled on the floor where he
could get at it. If you're lucky enough to find what appears to be the
poison, read the label instructions carefully, and note whether vomiting up
the poison is recommended. Some caustic poisons should *not* be vomited
up, as they'll do more harm coming back up than if they remain in the
stomach and are treated there. But most poisons should come right back
out if possible. If you haven't any idea what it is, get your dog to vomit.
Immediately give him mustard and water as an emetic, and once he has
thrown up, give him as much milk as you can get into him. To make the
emetic solution, mix three tablespoons of mustard powder (not bottled
mustard) in half a standard drinking glass of warm water, and pour it into
him. It may be a real struggle, but it might save your dog's life, so force it
in until he vomits. That will help get some of the poisonous substance out
of his stomach, and the milk will help dilute what's left and generally
soothe his system. Then, of course, get him to your vet.

If you don't know the specific antidote for the poison he's taken, or don't
know what poison it is, you should have in your dog's medicine cabinet a
substance known as Universal Antidote, which you can have made up by a
pharmacist. The formula is two parts activated charcoal, one part light magnesium oxide, one part kaolin, and one part tannic acid. Universal Antidote
is a dark gray powder that is inert and can be stored for a long time. A
pharmacist is unlikely to have it on hand, so don't think you can rush out
and grab a bottle.

After the dog has vomited, mix four heaping tablespoonsful of the antidote with a standard glass of warm water, stir well, and get as much of it
as you can into him. It is not really a *universal* antidote, but it is the closest
thing to one, and can be very helpful against many poisonous substances. If
you haven't had Universal Antidote prepared in advance, you can quickly
make up a partial home substitute for it. The formula is two parts finely
crumbled, heavily burnt toast (for the charcoal), one part very strong tea
(for the tannic acid), and one part milk of magnesia (for the magnesium

oxide). Mix about half a cup of the tea with half a cup of milk of magnesia and stir in crumbled burnt toast until the mixture is a thick liquid. Get as much of it into him as possible—add a little milk if it is too thick for him to swallow easily. But remember that all these treatments are no substitute for a vet's attention. Poisoning is not a matter for amateur treatment.

Burns: The treatment of minor burns for dogs is much the same as for humans. Apply a good commercial burn ointment to the affected area, and do not cover it with any bandages. Keep a close eye on him to see that he does not attempt to lick the ointment off. If he is suffering considerable pain, apply the gauze muzzle before you begin to treat him; this also prevents him from licking off the ointment. Application of ice first will help considerably in holding down later swelling and scarring if the burn is not widespread and the skin is not burned open. Hold an ice cube against the burned spot, or rub the ice cube over the burn if it covers a somewhat larger area. Keep this up for ten minutes or so, then let it dry and apply the ointment. For an extensive or serious burned area on any of the legs, another good immediate treatment is holding the leg in a tub of ice water. Very difficult to do, but if you can manage to keep the leg in a tub or any other container filled with as much ice as you can get in it, plus the water to make sure the cold gets to all parts of the burned area, you stand a good chance of holding down tissue damage.

Electric Shock: This is almost entirely a hazard of house dogs, particularly younger ones. It usually results from chewing on a lamp cord or other electrical wire. With any luck, the only result will be a burned mouth, bad enough in itself—and this should be left strictly for the veterinarian to handle. House current will rarely knock a dog completely out, but if it does, remove him with caution from the wire and cover him with a blanket to keep him warm. If he seems not to be breathing, by all means try artificial respiration. Such cases are rare, though, for the biting that gave him the shock and burn usually causes a short circuit, blowing the house fuse and saving his life.

If you happen not to have read the section on electric cords in the chapter on raising the puppy, we will repeat our advice here. You simply can't keep a watchful enough eye all the time to keep him away from lamp cords, so coat every light cord in your house with something bitter-tasting that will discourage chewing. Musterole, citronella, or any of the commercial "Keeps Dogs Away" items will do the trick. It is well worth the trouble, for we have seen puppies and older dogs with badly burned mouths from chewing on light cords. It isn't pleasant to see.

Swallowing Foreign Objects: Most dogs, particularly young ones, swallow a few solid objects that aren't good for them. If you see something going down, apply the mustard-and-water emetic immediately—but only if what you saw didn't have any sharp edges. He might get a sharp object down successfully, but coming up it could rip his throat. If the emetic doesn't get it, only the vet can, and anything he swallows probably won't do him any harm once in the stomach. It'll just sit there, and may even pass out through the intestines—but a vet's care is advised. As an example of the quite incredible things a dog can swallow and get away with, consider the case of a Doberman belonging to one of the authors. Over a period of nine months, unbeknownst to anyone, he managed to swallow five twenty-two-inch chrome training collars. He showed no sign of it, being as happy and active as any dog could be, and was discovered in his secret vice only when he was actually seen to take the fifth one down. Several weeks later, after some fruitless attempts to get the chain regurgitated (during this time no one knew the other four had gone in the same way), he was operated on and out the five chains came from his stomach, weighing a total of a pound and a half. He recovered, and lived happily ever after.

Heat Prostration: In the summer, this happens to quite a surprisingly large number of dogs. Mostly, they are city dogs who are out of condition and slightly overweight, and who suffer through a city heat spell. If this happens to yours, bathe his head with cool water, keep him quiet, and feed him very lightly until he recovers. From then on, keep him quieter and in general cut his feeding down until the heat is over. In particular, don't allow him to exercise just after a meal—it works much on the same principle as the human rule about not swimming for an hour after eating. He must rest while he is digesting his food. If you have a really serious case dump him up to his neck in a tub of cold water, as cold as you can get it, and keep him there until his breathing improves. You can also give him two or three drops of aromatic spirits of ammonia in a teaspoon of water to bring him around. Then keep him cool and quiet.

As a last thought, and as a good general rule in all these emergency situations: Don't panic. Easy to say, and sometimes hard to do, that's true. But keep your head in case of accidents, and move swiftly and gently. Except for the muzzle, treat the dog as you would an injured human, and you stand a good chance of pulling him through.

CHAPTER 12

Travel, Tricks, and Other Matters

Someone once said, "You can either travel comfortably, or with children." This can apply equally to travel with a dog. Dogs are a little easier to travel with in that they do not have to be amused with license-number games and similar diversions, and they are very often better behaved (there are very few UD children or equivalents). Dogs are a little harder in that overnight arrangements are considerably more difficult. With suitable preplanning, some basic training for your dog, and a few facts, however, taking your dog along can be quite a smooth operation.

Almost all traveling with dogs is done by car, and if you plan a long trip with overnight stops, your first problem will be finding a place to stay. Fortunately, this problem has been partially solved by a booklet entitled "Touring with Towser," compiled and distributed by the Gaines Dog Research Center. The booklet lists several thousand hotels and motels (plus major hotel and motel chains) across the country and in Canada, covering most communities of any size, that accept dogs. Write to the center (250 North St., White Plains, N.Y., 10625) enclosing one dollar, and they will send you a copy of the latest edition.

"Touring with Towser" is periodically revised to include new establishments and to delete listings that have changed their policies on dogs. This latter is unfortunate, but hotels and motels are constantly dropping off the "Dogs Accepted" list because of unpleasant experiences with dog-owning travelers. In an earlier edition of the booklet, Gaines noted sadly:

> It is significant that almost every hotel and motor court we questioned had at one time or another accepted guests with dogs. In many cases, where a hotel

or motor court has a "No Dogs Allowed" policy, the management explained that they had been forced to take this stand because of their unfortunate experiences with badly-behaved dogs and irresponsible dog owners.

This was written long enough ago that motels were often called motor courts, but it is as true today as then. To make yourself, and your dog, welcome, and to keep things right for other owners and dogs, Gaines suggests the following:

Dogs will continue to be welcome at hotels and motels only if dog owners keep their pets from causing damage and disturbing other guests. To do so, owners need only follow a few basic rules:

- *Always* keep a dog on a leash in public areas.
- *Never* take a dog into a dining room, lounge or to pool side.
- *Never* leave a dog alone in a room unless crated.
- *Walk a dog* far from lawns, flower beds and public areas.
- *Never* permit a dog to sleep on beds, chairs or bed spreads, always bring canine bedding along.
- If a dog should damage motel property, volunteer to pay any costs.

Dogs with obedience training obviously will be more welcome as hotel or motel guests than dogs with little or no training. Responsible owners realize this and keep their dogs under control at all times.

As obedience training is what this book is all about, we hardly need add our concurrence to those last comments. But note that if you are planning a definite itinerary and writing or phoning ahead for reservations, you will find your answer considerably more cordial if you include the information that your dog is obedience trained. Hotel and motel managers are perhaps more alert to the advantages of obedience training than any other group of people in this country, having had experience with trained and untrained dogs. If the manager knows in advance that your dog is obedience trained, this can easily make the difference in acceptance or rejection of reservations when he thinks his place just might be filled anyway.

Additionally, the fact that an establishment accepts dogs does not in any way mean that you will be condemned to a run-down, shoddy fleabag. We have stayed, with dogs, in motels that boasted wall-to-wall carpeting, free television and radio, tiled baths, and all the amenities. As to hotels, little more need be said than that many of the major hotel chains (Hilton, Sheraton, Ramada, etc., as noted in the Gaines booklet) have a generally welcoming attitude toward dogs. True, there are also more modest places that accept dogs, but you will find that you will be able to stay in hotels and motels that are as good, or as bad, as the one down the road that can't abide dogs. (Note, however, one curious statewide restriction, in case you don't send for "Touring with Towser"—which quotes the law: In North Carolina it is *illegal* to keep a dog in a hotel room!)

Even having found a place that will take your dog, you still face minor problems. In a hotel or motel, what do you do with your dog when you go out to eat? Gaines's (and our) advice against leaving a dog alone in a room should be heeded—for other reasons than you might think. It isn't just the possible lonely howling or destruction that might result, but consider the fact that maids and other hotel service people quite routinely let themselves into rooms on their duty rounds. A lonely dog could dash out the door and be killed or disappear. Or a maid could be bitten, which could escalate your trip expenses more than somewhat. The collapsible "crate" we describe in Chapter 2 is an excellent solution, particularly if it has in it familiar bedding to keep your dog from feeling lonely and howling while you're away.

If you can't be bothered with a crate, then only you can answer the question of what to do, depending on whether your dog will get lonely and raise a great commotion if left alone for hours in a strange room. Remember, though, that even a dog who is well adjusted at home may surprise you in a hotel or motel room. There are people constantly going by, voices coming from the corridor and adjoining rooms, and things go bump in the night. Room service is an obvious answer, or eating in shifts. But if you must, at least let him have some sort of nest of familiar bedding, and put the "Do Not Disturb" sign on the door. Let the desk know where you can be reached in case he starts making a racket. And hope for the best.

We have found that motels are better for traveling with a dog, largely because of the convenience in exercising. In a hotel you have to get him down in the elevator (some hotels ask you to use a special service elevator with a dog), through the lobby, and out into the street when he has to relieve himself. At a motel, on the other hand, the outside is just beyond your door. In addition, some motels have grounds for limited free running and exercise. If your dog is well enough trained that he will not run out of bounds (be very sure of this before releasing him in strange territory), this can be a considerable advantage—always provided the management doesn't mind.

Some few dog owners, for lack of dog-accepting establishments, blithely put up any place and leave the dog locked in the car for the night. We cannot condemn this sort of thing too highly as senseless cruelty. Leaving a dog alone in a car for eight or more hours is cruel enough in itself, but you run the constant risk of trouble. If the windows are open to any great amount, he may get out, no matter how well trained he is. If the windows are closed, he'll suffocate. Drunks, for some reason, seem to gravitate to cars with dogs in them, and if one sticks his arm through the window to pet the "nishe little doggie" and gets a chunk taken out of him, you alone are to blame for the damage. Otherwise sober but mentally retarded louts sometimes take their evening pleasure by poking sticks through even the slimmest window opening to torment a dog who cannot get at them. Other stalwart citizens will pound on the car and shout at a locked-in dog for the diversion of seeing him bark and race around in frustrated anger. True, there is a minor risk of this sort of thing even when you leave your dog in the car for a half-hour's shopping in broad daylight in your hometown, but it is as nothing compared with an overnight stay in strange territory. In short, don't. There are enough places around the country that take dogs that you will always be able to find one reasonably near.

En route, a large cardboard box lined with papers at the bottom is a good idea for a puppy or an unhousebroken dog. It prevents damage to your car when he has to relieve himself or if he gets sick, and can be used in the hotel or motel room at night. For the older dog, you should have a small kit of supplies, which can be carried in a canvas flight-accessory bag, a small suitcase, or even a fiberboard dime-store doll's suitcase. Put in a few cans of his regular food, cans of evaporated milk if he gets milk in the mornings, a pan for his food and one for water, and a favorite toy or bone for him to play with at night. Include also a blanket or something for him to sleep on if he is accustomed to it at home. The familiar smell of his own blanket will make things easier for him, and will make the management much happier than if you used their sheets or pillows.

No matter how well trained he may be, it is an excellent idea to have a tag on your dog's collar at all times in case he wanders or runs off and is lost. A stamped metal tag is best, but you can make your own from a leather or imitation-leather luggage tag. A good form for the tag is: "If Found, Please Telephone or Telegraph Collect. Reward." Give your name, phone number, and full address, including the state. If you are on a long trip, it is a good idea to give, instead of your name, the name and address of a friend or relative at either end of the trip. That way anyone who finds your dog will be able to get in touch with someone immediately—and you will be able to check with occasional calls to find out if someone has located him.

Further, your dog should have a certain minimum of training for travel. Housebreaking is essential. Novice-level training in heeling, coming, and staying are very handy in this as in other aspects of dog owning. Beyond these, there are two special things he should learn: to stay quietly in the car until he is released, and always to sit and stay just outside the car when you let him out. A dog who wants badly to get out of a car, as you may have learned, is a force to be reckoned with. If he scrambles and leaps out of the car as soon as the door is opened at a stop, you may yourself be hurt or at least shaken up, and he just might get himself badly hurt by running out into traffic. Train him quite firmly that he must sit quietly until given permission to leave. Also, with leash on it is simple to train him to sit quietly after leaving the car, until he is released. This too may save his life. Insist on it at all times, traveling or at home, and riding with your dog will be more pleasant, not to say safer.

Car sickness can be a difficult matter, for some few dogs never seem to get over an aversion to long trips in cars. If you are starting out on a trip with a dog who has never ridden much, we suggest you introduce him to the idea in stages, as we have outlined in the "Pretraining" chapter. In addition, if he is fed only at night he will have less chance of throwing up in the car. If the problem is serious, see your veterinarian, who may be able to give you something in the way of medicine. Don't try dosing him yourself with aspirin, tranquilizers, or seasick remedies. Keeping him in a cardboard box minimizes the mess in the car, if he is small enough, but if yours is a large breed and the problem is serious, you can only arm yourself with rags and fortitude. Some dogs just get sick in cars.

Traveling through various states, counties, and cities, you will run into a bewildering variety of dog regulations and laws. In the car you will have little or no trouble, but once you step outside you will find that some localities are highly restrictive about dogs. Whatever the law in your own community, many cities and towns are very strict about allowing dogs off leash, and in stores, restaurants, and groceries. Keep him on leash whenever he is out of the car, and find out first whether it is permitted before you try to take him into any store. Also, for general convenience, take along a health certificate signed by your vet, and if possible a rabies certificate.

If you're taking him trailering or camping, once again we recommend

"Touring with Towser," which has lists of helpful publications on trailer parks and campgrounds that include any restrictions on dogs.

BY TRAIN OR PLANE

Railroads vary considerably in their regulations regarding dogs accompanying passengers, so be sure to check the line you will be traveling on. As a general rule, dogs are allowed to accompany owners in private Pullman space such as compartments. Getting on and off the train in these cases, the regulation generally is that the dog must be either in a carrying case or on leash and muzzled. Even in the private space, the rule sometimes is that a muzzle be worn, for the protection of porters, trainmen, and conductors. It is pretty much up to the conductor whether this rule is enforced, but the rule is there, so always carry a muzzle with you. We have found conductors and trainmen almost always cooperative and helpful about dogs on trains if you give them half a chance, and you will probably have no trouble at all if your dog is well mannered about things.

If you and another person are planning to travel first-class anyway, you will find that it is surprisingly inexpensive to take private space. The extra charge above the cost of two ordinary Pullman seats is small, particularly if you travel by day. Look into it if yours is a family trip, for the convenience of private space in traveling by train with a dog is considerable.

In nonprivate space, some lines allow certain dogs to accompany owners on coaches but not in first-class space. The reasons behind this curious distinction we have never been able to fathom, but be that as it may, such is the general rule. By "certain dogs" we mean that it is up to the conductor whether or not your dog gets on the coach with you. Dogs in carrying cases are seldom barred, providing they don't make a great fuss, and dogs on leash up to a reasonable size may be welcomed. But the larger varieties are almost always relegated to the baggage compartment, unless it should be one of those lines where the back end of the rear car is set aside for large dogs, bicycles, and other impedimenta. The conductor may himself be a dog lover, but the passenger across the aisle may be one of those people who are frightened out of their wits by anything bigger than a Pekingese, and the conductor has to operate by the rule of the greatest good for the greatest number. Some lines require that dogs be carried in the baggage car but allow you to feed them and take care of them en route. Here, of course, a crate is an absolute necessity even if the railroad doesn't happen to require it, as tying up a dog on a lead and leaving him alone in a baggage car would be unthinkable. For all train travel, check ahead on individual regulations. Don't just show up at the station with your dog.

As to air travel, we can only tell you to check with the particular airline you're planning to use. Most will allow one very small dog in each cabin, small enough to fit comfortably in a special travel kennel/crate sold to you by the airline, which is only 7½ inches high so as to fit under the seat in front of you like hand baggage. Special arrangements must be made in advance because of the "one dog per cabin" rule.

A larger dog must be taken along as "baggage," either in a special larger kennel/crate that the airline will sell you, or in a sturdy, well-ventilated crate of your own which meets airline specifications. In addition to the cost of the shipping kennel, if you buy one, the airlines make a fairly standard flat charge for the dog's passage, and the dog rides in the baggage compartment with the rest of the luggage. But don't worry about pressurization and temperature—the airlines won't accept your dog for carrying unless the compartment is pressurized and temperature-controlled, which almost all are. You can, and should, put familiar bedding in the kennel to help make your dog comfortable and at home. And don't feed him or give him water just before you put him in the shipping kennel, for obvious reasons.

Show dogs are shipped around the country all the time by air, and losses or problems are rare, but they *can* occur. If a naturally nervous dog is suddenly put into a crate, shoved in with other baggage, and then carried for several hours in total darkness in a lurching, jet-screaming airline baggage compartment, it could have serious consequences. The airlines handle these shipments well, but they take no responsibility beyond that of reasonable care.

The airlines also advise that you check beforehand on whether there are any special regulations in the state you're taking your dog to by air. Despite the fact that anyone can drive into the state with a car full of dogs and nobody will say nay, there are often special regulations (usually relating to health certificates and inoculations) about dogs arriving commercially.

FOREIGN TRAVEL

If you plan to take your dog with you into Canada or Mexico, those countries have certain health regulations that will have to be observed. Canada requires a health certificate signed by a veterinarian, plus a certificate that your dog has been vaccinated against rabies within the last thirty days.

Mexico requires the health and rabies vaccination certificates also, and a Mexican consul must visa the papers before you present them at the border. If there is no consul in your city, you will probably be able to find one in any of the larger cities of Texas along the way. Reentry into the United States from Mexico requires no further papers if you have stayed less than thirty days; if longer your certificate of vaccination must indicate that the rabies shot was given within six months of the date of reentry. Check the regulations, though. They change from time to time.

For further travel regulations, check with the nearest consul of the country or countries you plan to visit. Some few countries, England especially, will admit no dogs whatever except after a six-month quarantine. There is no rabies in England, for example, and they are scared silly that an infected dog might get in and start it up there. You could have a vaccination a day for six months, plus a certificate signed by the President stating that the dog was pure and healthy and it wouldn't make the slightest difference to the British authorities. They're very stuffy about that sort of thing, and make no exceptions, not even for Seeing Eye dogs, among whom the incidence of rabies is somewhat small.

KENNELS AND BOARDING

When the trip requires, or your personal preferences dictate, that you leave your dog behind for days or weeks, the problem of what to do with him can be bothersome. Friends or relatives are of course one solution. But willing friends or relatives are a breed apart. Even if willing at the outset, you may find relations somewhat strained when you return after a week or more. People who do not have dogs often have no real conception of how much attention a dog requires, in feeding and exercising and such. Beyond that, a lonely dog can often make a wreck of the lives of his temporary keepers, so think long and choose well, remembering too that some people, no matter how pleasant personally, have no concept of how to care for a dog properly.

The other alternative is a boarding kennel that will keep him at a flat per diem charge for room and board. There are kennels and kennels, some with no more than a fairly roomy cage for your dog, some with an elaborate hut plus fenced run for him. Just which kennel you pick is a matter only you can decide, for there are no rules we can give you. If it's clean, and the owner or owners seem to know and love dogs, your chances of having

BOARDING CONTRACT

RECEIVED on this date, _____ 19 ___, from:

Name _____ 'phone _____

Address _____

ONE DOG: Breed _____, Sex _____, Age _____

Color _____ ☐ for BOARDING. ☐ for TRAINING and BOARDING.

For other purposes _____

State yes or no, Has had distemper: ___ Inoculated against distemper___ Against rabies ___

Veterinarian to be called in case of illness _____ 'phone _____

CHARGES are to be _____

payable IN ADVANCE on the first day of each ___ week ___ each month ___ until owner calls
for dog or gives other instructions for disposal.

I have received this date $_____as advance payment to and including_____19 ___

The next payment of $_____ will be due on _____ 19 ___, and a

similar amount _____ weekly _____ monthly_____ _____thereafter.

The dog is to be fed properly and regularly, and to be housed in clean, safe quarters. Dogs are
boarded or trained, or otherwise handled or cared for by me without liability on my part for loss or damage from disease, death, running away, theft, fire, injury to persons, other dogs, or other unavoidable
causes. At least once weekly the dog is to be brushed, cleaned and groomed. The dog is not to be taken
off the premises except by consent of the owner. If dog becomes seriously ill, the owner shall be notified
at once in case no particular veterinarian has been designated. If the owner does not inform immediately
regarding measures to be taken, or if the state of the dogs health reasonably demands quick action, I
reserve the right to call a veterinarian or administer or give other advisable attention, within my discretion and judgment, and such expenses, being reasonable in amount, shall be paid promptly by the
owner of the dog.

If any charges for boarding, training, medicines, or veterinary services are not paid within thirty
days after they are due or if dog is not called for within thirty days after time for return of dog, the
dog will be sold by me publicly, privately or otherwise for the best price available. Notice in writing
of such intended sale shall be mailed by registered mail to the owner of the dog at the address given
hereon, not less than ten days before such date of intended sale, and no further notice shall be deemed
necessary. Any excess amount over charges will be given to the owner; any deficiency is to paid by the
owner.

The owner represents that he is the legal owner of said dog, that title to said dog is not mort-
gaged in any way, and that said dog has not been exposed to distemper or rabies within the last thirty
days, and that the required annual license has been obtained.

This agreement is signed in duplicate by both parties, each party having a copy.

Signed _____ Signed _____

Owner of dog   Owner of Kennel

Kennel address _____

Received back in good condition the foregoing dog on _____ 19 ___

Signed_____

found a good one are high. Try to investigate any local kennels long before your trip by getting opinions of other dog owners or from the local humane society.

We have reproduced here a sample boarding contract form. The one you will sign for your dog will probably not be too unlike it. You will notice that the small print legally releases the kennel owner from any responsibility for a great number of things. This is only right; don't think you have walked into something unsuitable if the kennel owner points this out to you when you appear with your dog. You cannot expect to find a kennel owner who will accept total responsibility for sickness, accidents, damage, or death. Although he knows dogs, he cannot know whether your dog is harboring some germ, or whether he will pine away from loneliness, or what. The great majority of kennel owners take every possible precaution, for although they may not be legally responsible for mishaps, their reputations and business are at stake. A few vocally unhappy former customers can bankrupt a boarding kennel, and the owners well know it.

Feeding is up to the kennel owner unless you specify otherwise. He will feed your dog the kennel's standard food in sufficient quantities, and that is included in the basic charge. If your dog cannot or will not eat anything but his special diet, be sure to give the kennel people full instructions and if possible supply a quantity of the food. You will otherwise have to pay for special diets supplied by the kennel.

Some people are able to put a dog in a kennel and walk away without so much as a backward look; some have a hard time even thinking of the poor dog closed away in a cage or a run with no one to pet or play with him. If you have to travel, though, and can't find an accommodating friend, it's got to be the kennel. The loneliness and confinement probably won't hurt him, and he will be in good hands. Kennel owners are "dog people" or they wouldn't be in the business. They know dogs and how to care for them, and will take every reasonable precaution to see that yours is well and happy when you return.

THE DOG'S SENSES

Throughout this book we have spoken, in one light or another, of the dog's senses and capacities—his sight, hearing, smell, and memory as they are different from those of the human. To expand a bit on these mentions, and in a way to justify ourselves in case you have been thinking, "Oh, come now, how do *you* know how a dog sees?," we will try to explain what is known about dogs and the way they receive their impressions of the world around them.

The fact that dogs are nearsighted, at least by human standards, is not only a matter of continued observation but of laboratory experiment. Any number of studies of dog eyesight have been run in various laboratories interested in such things. Generally the procedure is to train a dog to respond differently to certain shapes. He is taught, say, to sit up when he sees one figure and to lie down when he sees another. Then the figures are shown to him at increasing distances. The dog begins to encounter confusion at distances far short of those at which humans can still easily differentiate. Thus the dog's nearsightedness is established. You may say, of course, that this simply means that after a while the dog just didn't care, but this is only a minor example of the type of experiment used to establish the fact. Others, for example, use recognition or nonrecognition of objects at a distance as a food signal.

"Nearsighted" is not really the proper term, but there isn't any better one to describe a dog's vision. In fact, a dog can't focus on fine detail. In the human eye, there is a tiny spot in the retina called the fovea, directly in the center of another area called the macula. It is here that light rays are brought into fine focus, and it is this area that is capable of perceiving tiny objects and focusing sharply on them, as would be required in reading small print. The fovea is missing in the dog's eye, and the macula is less well defined; thus the fine-focus capability is missing. You can get a general idea of what a dog sees by focusing or fixing your eyes on something a few feet away, then trying to make out fine detail in the area a few feet away from where you are looking directly. This may also explain why a dog is so sensitive to movement in his field of vision. *You* will often catch movement "out of the corner of your eye" that you might not notice otherwise. A dog's entire eye, for all practical purposes, is like the "corner" of yours, the non-focusing area.

The color blindness of dogs and most other animals has also been established in experiments similar to those mentioned above. The actual effects of color blindness are almost as difficult to describe and imagine as is describing color to a totally color-blind person. It is a little easier, because you have seen black-and-white pictures of colored objects all your life. To a dog the world looks much like one long black-and-white movie. Just as in a picture you can tell the difference between light- and dark-colored objects, so can a dog. He can distinguish bright red from deep blue, for example.

But between two colors of the same shade and brightness, he simply cannot differentiate.

The dog's reaction to pictures is a curious aspect of things—whether of vision or of perception no one really quite knows. We do know that dogs do not recognize pictures of things as the things themselves. A picture, no matter how large, of another dog will not interest a dog in the slightest. Neither will he react to even a photo-mural of his beloved master. Perhaps the two-dimensional quality of pictures means nothing at all to a dog except as marks on a piece of paper. This seems to be borne out by the fact that a dog will react to things he sees in a mirror. There what he sees has a three-dimensional quality.

The subject of mirrors is another source of puzzlement as far as the dog is concerned. Young dogs and those who have never seen mirrors before will growl and challenge their reflections in a mirror, or even want to frisk and play with them. But with the passing of time and experience, a dog soon learns to ignore his reflection. It is hard to believe that he comes to realize that it is his reflection. It seems more likely that he eventually learns that that other dog is no menace and can't be reached and has no smell, and so he loses interest. Yet a dog who has learned to ignore his own image will often react throughout his life to seeing his master in a mirror. The exact nature of that particular perception is quite beyond us.

Along the line of pictures, there is the matter of dogs and television. Although an occasional dog is said by his owners to enjoy watching the television screen (and a few dogs are even reputed to have favorite programs, such as "Lassie"), the explanation is probably that the dog is fascinated by the light and movement on the screen. Just as with still pictures, the actual pictures on the screen mean nothing at all to a dog, other than as patterns and shapes of light and dark. There is another reason for a dog's seeming interest in the television set, but that is a matter of hearing.

It is a widely known fact that dogs can hear sounds far higher in the frequency range than humans can. It is generally accepted that dogs are able to hear sounds up to approximately 30,000 cycles per second, while the average human can hear only 15,000 cycles, with the exceptional individual just making out 20,000. (As a reference point, the highest note on a piano is 4,186 cycles.) Russian scientists, who seem to spend a good deal of their time trying things on dogs, claim to have established canine hearing as far as the 75,000–100,000 cycle range, but no evidence substantiates this.

The "silent" dog whistles you see in pet shops are one sure proof of the dog's higher hearing range. Although *you* will seem to be just blowing to no good effect, a dog can hear one of these whistles at distances up to half a mile. As with humans, a dog's hearing begins to fall off as the frequency gets higher, and so these whistles are designed to operate not far above the range of human perception. If you have exceptionally sensitive ears you may hear just a faint shrilling when you blow one. In any case, such a whistle is handy to have around if you want to call your dog without shouting up a storm and disturbing the neighbors. Train him to come when he hears the whistle and you can blast away at bedtime with no complaints from an aroused citizenry. The only drawback is that such whistles have no distinctive sound other than being in the high range—if several neighborhood dogs are trained to come at the blast of one, you may be inundated with dogs when you tootle away.

Hearing of this nature may explain the occasional case you hear of in which dogs seemingly respond to mental commands. We have never seen these exhibitions (for some reason, Indians seem to have a corner on this sort of thing), but there are fairly well authenticated stories of such. It may be just that the handler in question has trickily mastered the art of ultrasonic whistling and has trained his dog to respond to whistled signals. We don't really know, but it's a thought.

Back on the subject of television, this higher hearing will cause some dogs to exhibit an unseemly interest in the set when it is turned on. In many sets, perhaps in all, there is an inaudible (to humans) frequency generated that performs certain vital functions. This tone, somewhere in the neighborhood of 25,000 cycles, is perfectly audible to dogs. Whether it is an attractive sound to them or an irritating one, it's true that many dogs perk up their ears when the set goes on, and perhaps even sit and listen attentively for some time with every appearance of enjoying the program.

About music we can say little, for lack of effective communication limits our knowledge rather sharply in this sphere. Animals do respond to certain types of music—dairymen have found that soothing classics or other smooth background music will tranquilize cows, while jazz has the opposite effect. The dog howling while you play the piano may or may not be a critic, but dogs do seem to recognize music or musical attempts as being somehow different from other sounds. Dogs can be trained to respond differently to different tones in a laboratory, but it has been found that they generally cannot distinguish intervals of less than a whole tone (or at least they can't be persuaded to react to less), whereas the average untrained human can hear quarter-tone intervals or less.

As with sensitivity to movement, dogs seem to have very selective hearing—the ability to catch a familiar or expected sound through or above a veritable cataract of noise. A Doberman belonging to one of the authors demonstrates this constantly. Living in a New York City apartment, the dog is subjected to constant blasts of traffic and street noises and suffers the affliction of efficient stereo loudspeakers. Yet with a crashing symphonic number roaring from the machine and competing with heavy trucks outside, he can detect the faint noises of the elevator rising to the floor and will bristle protectively even before the car has arrived at the floor and the door opened. It may be that in this case the elevator gives off a loud (to him) noise in the ultrasonic range that rises above stereo and traffic. Other dogs, though, have demonstrated incredibly selective hearing under circumstances that do not seem to offer the ultrasonic explanation.

The extended range of hearing, or perhaps even of smell, may be an explanation for the often-heard stories of dogs being aware of ghosts and other psychic phenomena. We have had the experience of seeing a household dog suddenly stare fixedly at an ordinary corner of the room, and even bristle and snarl at it. In one case it was found that the dog was reacting to reflections in a window—to him it looked as though there were people moving about close outside the house. In other cases we have assumed that there was simply something earthly there that we couldn't detect, perhaps a peculiar reflection of sound waves beyond our hearing range. It may be that we are haunted, but the dogs' extended senses offer a more logical explanation. We must admit, however, that it is chilling to see a sudden bristling at empty air. It is easy to see how the thought of ghosts and other shiveries arose when dogs manifested this behavior.

Smell is the particular province of the dog. His sensitivity and analytical ability in the odor field are so widely known and appreciated as hardly to require comment. Partially it is the result of a considerably extended nasal range—the average large dog has four or five inches of nasal passages—and partially it is greater sensitivity. Even very short-nosed dogs such as Pugs and Bulldogs, who have hardly greater nasal length than humans, far exceed humans in smelling ability, even though they may rank in this talent far below their long-nosed colleagues.

A dog is able to break down a smell into its component parts, just as a music lover can distinguish all the simultaneous instrumental sounds in a symphony. A dog can detect minute quantities of a liked or disliked constituent in a hash of mixed foods, and he can detect and isolate a familiar smell from among a great range of other and stronger odors. It is in fact nearly impossible for us to imagine just how a dog smells and what the smells convey to him. Experiment is difficult because dogs detect odors of which we are not even aware, which we could not begin to reproduce.

Smell may be responsible for some otherwise unexplained reactions of dogs; for example, the curious business of dogs being somehow aware of fear in a human. It is our theory that dogs can smell fear. It is well enough known that fear causes an increase of adrenalin flow in the body, and that there are other minor physical changes involved in a fear reaction—cold sweat is only one of them. It follows that it is highly probable a dog can smell the results of these physical changes; for example, even a minute amount of "cold sweat" that the fearful person himself cannot detect on his skin.

The standard lie-detector test operates along much the same lines, detecting electrically the increased conductivity of the skin as a result of fear or anxiety sweating. And even as the polygraph also measures involuntary increases in muscular tensions when a subject is lying, the dog may also be able to detect physical signs that we ourselves are unaware of.

It is certain enough that dogs can and do recognize moods in humans, even above and beyond obvious anger, happiness, or depression. It is within the bounds of possibility that dogs actually "smell" moods. Or that they may be able to detect the tiny and unconscious movements and muscle tightenings that psychologists speak of as "subliminal cues," indications normally below the threshold of consciousness and average human perception. Whatever the mechanism of this in particular, it is certain that with their extended perceptions, dogs do react to many things we are not aware of—and this again is a point of importance to the trainer. When your dog reacts peculiarly in training, always examine the possibility that he sees, hears, smells, or otherwise detects something that is quite beyond your range of perception. When he balks or seems frightened or refuses to work in a certain place, give him the benefit of the doubt. You can't possibly know what he does, and attempts to "straighten him out" will be more useless than helpful.

TRICKS

Training of the "trick" variety is quite separate from obedience training for companionship, control, and convenience. Tricks are strictly for fun and display; obedience training is for practical purposes and sometimes for competition. Both, however, are taught by the same basic method of demonstration, correction, and praise. Tricks can be taught to a dog who has had no obedience training, although a trained dog who has acquired the habit of obedience and learning will pick up any trick you desire faster than his untrained colleague.

Thousands and perhaps millions of dogs in this country and around the world who can sit up, roll over, and shake hands wouldn't know a training collar if it bit them—far more, certainly, than there are obedience-trained dogs. Tricks are, in fact, the entire meaning of training to a very large segment of the population who have never seen or heard of an obedience-trained dog. This situation is at times trying in the extreme to the proud owner of an obedience dog. You modestly aver to an acquaintance that you have a well-trained dog, and he immediately reaches down to Rover and says, "Shake hands, boy." When you manage to stammer, "Oh, no, training doesn't mean just silly tricks," then your acquaintance says, "Well, what *does* he do?" You come back, if you have completed Novice training, with, "Uh, well, he heels real good. And he comes when I call him. And he stays there when I tell him to." From there the situation degenerates rapidly.

We suspect that even if you told an uninitiated friend that your dog could beat him two sets out of three at tennis, tell his fortune, and serve him coffee without slopping it into the saucer, you would get a reply something on the order of, "Yeah, yeah, but can he maybe sit up and beg?" Whatever your reason for training your dog to do the common tricks, be it in self-defense or just because you want to, here is the way to go about it.

Shake Hands: Probably the easiest of all tricks to teach, this can be given to even a very young dog, for it involves no more than the lifting of the right forepaw on command. With your dog or puppy sitting, reach down and take hold of his right paw with your right hand and lift it gently. Tell him, "Shake!" as you do it. Lift the paw until it is on the level of his chest, and then shake it gently just as though you were shaking hands with him. Praise him highly as you are shaking his paw, and give him an extra word of commendation when it is over. Do this half a dozen times a day for a few days, then try just reaching for his paw as you give the command. If he lifts it even a little, take it and shake it, praising him effusively. With application and a little practice he will soon be lifting it quite high for you.

Roll Over: Next in ease of teaching, the "roll over" can also be learned quite young, for it requires little muscular learning on the dog's part. Make it as much a game as possible when teaching. Whenever you normally play with him, get down on the floor with him and wait until he is lying down on his side. Then put one hand in the middle of his back and the other under his chest and shoulders. Give the command "Roll over!" and turn him gently over as you do so. When he is over, praise him highly, laugh with him at what he has done, and let him know what a colossal accomplishment he has managed. Do this three or four times in an evening. Once he seems to have the idea, cut down gradually on your assistance until he is doing it by himself at your command. Praise and an air of good-fellowship will make him happy and enthusiastic about rolling over, and you can, if you time your commands right, get him to go over twice, three times, or clear across the room. Be careful, though, about overdoing either in training or in demonstration. Even in the best of humor he may become bored with it as a repeated thing, and you will have a problem getting his interest up again.

Occasionally a dog objects quite violently to being manhandled to this extent, even in the spirit of play. If you have this problem, we can only suggest that you approach the subject more cautiously the next time you try it. Get him in a receptive mood by petting and praising him as he lies on his side (don't try to whisk him over from a sphinx-like down position with his rear legs braced—that can turn into a match for two falls out of three), get your hands sneakily into the proper position while petting him, then ease him over as you give the command in a friendly tone. If you do it right, he'll be over before he realizes he should be making an issue of it. This may work, but if not, give it up until he's older and perhaps more amenable to foolishness at your hands. Some few dogs for their own private reasons think that rolling over is a damn fool thing to do and will have no truck with it. It is not that important an accomplishment, and the same trouble will not occur with other tricks.

Sit Up: Because sitting up is an entirely unnatural position for a dog, he has to be helped at first. The best way is to sit him in a corner facing out. Give the command to sit up, and lift him gently by his front legs until he is in an erect sitting position. Keep him there a few moments, then release his feet and put one hand under his chin to help him keep his balance. Keep repeating to him as he sits, "Up, up," or whatever command you choose. Hold him there for only a few seconds, then let him down with much praise. Repeat this half a dozen times a day until he stays without your help once you have got him up, then keep working on it until he goes up by himself. A sufficient number of repetitions, along with praise to let him know he is doing something well when he raises himself up, will give him the idea.

Because sitting up requires the development of certain back muscles ordinarily not used in that way, be sure to go cautiously with this training. If you try to keep him in the sit-up position too long too early, he will slump over simply because he physically cannot hold it any longer. Once that has happened, he will become discouraged with trying, and your training will suffer a severe setback. If, on the first time you try it, he simply slumps down and your hand under his chin does not help, you will know that he is too young for this training. At too early an age a puppy can no more hold himself erect than can a human child. Let the sit-up training go for a month or two, until he is older and stronger.

When he finally does the sit up by himself, on command, try him in the center of the room. If at your command he runs over to the corner and sits up there, he is being only too logical and following out what he thinks you want, so praise him, do not reprimand him. Take hold of his legs the next time before you give the command, and assist him in sitting up *where he is.* A few repeats of this and he will come to understand that he is to sit up wherever he is at the time of your command.

Catch: A great many dogs do this quite naturally, catching any tidbit of food you throw them. To sharpen him up and make him realize that consistency and accuracy are important, give him a little practice just before his meal when he is hungry. Stand quite close in front of him and toss to him small bits of food, saying, "Catch!" as you throw them. What he catches he will of course eat—what he misses you must be quick to retrieve and not allow him to touch. Before long he will have the idea that the more catches he makes, the more he gets to eat, and there you have the training. Make it as easy as possible for him. Get in a little practice in pitching before you start with him; you don't want him to have to make shoestring catches, just plain easy ones. Later you can progress to systematic catching of a small, soft ball or any other soft toy from an appreciable distance. Praise him when he makes each catch and the training incentive will be doubled.

Bring the Slippers: Here tricks veer into the area of usefulness, for it is a handy thing indeed to have your dog bring your slippers, pipe, cigarettes, or whatever you happen to want and are too lazy or tired to get up and get yourself. Once your dog has learned the basics of getting and bringing to you any one thing, he can be taught to recognize the word for, and bring you, any number of items.

First, he must learn the simple retrieve. Without going into the regular

obedience retrieve, you can get the idea across to your dog by simply playing ball with him. Throw his ball and let him bring it back to you in play.
Go on from this to throwing a stick, a rolled-up newspaper, a glove, and
even your wallet. When you find that he chases and brings back almost any
object you throw for him, take the glove or paper or whatever and give it to
him as he sits near you, and coax him to follow you with it. If done in the
spirit of play, and gently, this will present no difficulties.

When he is carrying things happily for you, take him to the bedroom and
give him one of your slippers to carry. Give him the command "Bring the
slippers!" or "Fetch the slippers!" or whatever you like, and coax him to
follow you into the living room, carrying the slipper in his mouth. Sit down
and put it on, then give him the command again. He won't understand, of
course, but after you have given him the command, go with him again to
the bedroom and repeat the process with the second slipper. When you
have both on, praise him and let it go for that day.

The next night when you come home, tell him again to bring the slippers, pointing to the bedroom and going along with him to repeat the lesson of the night before. After a week or ten days, you will begin to see
progress. The first time he does go all by himself and bring one of your
slippers, heap the praise on him, for he has managed a very considerable
thing, and you should let him know it. Insist, then, that he go get the other
one, and keep this up every night until it takes only one command for him
to get both. Soon, in fact, you may find him going to get your slippers as
soon as you get inside the house, with no command. If he does this, stop
whatever you are doing and put them on so that he sees that all is as
before, and praise him as always.

From the slippers you can progress to having him bring you almost anything that is normally kept in the same place. Many a dog has learned to
fetch the leash on command when the owner is about to take him out for a
walk. It's easy enough for him to learn this; in fact, if you train your dog to
do this, you may well find him—when he wants to go out—bringing the
leash to you and standing there with leash in mouth and a longing in his
eye. Dogs are quite bright about such things.

Dogs can learn the names of dozens of items, and you can teach yours to
bring you just about anything he can carry. One dog we know of was
trained by his owner to bring a pack of cigarettes whenever the owner ran
out of them. The cigarettes were kept on a low table in another room, and
when his owner said, "Hey, I'm out of cigarettes," the dog would trot hap-

pily away and return in a moment with a fresh pack. In fact, having learned it so well, the dog came to overdo it. Whenever his owner said to a guest, "Would you like a cigarette?" the dog, hearing the key word, would trot away and return with yet another pack. The Surgeon General might not approve, but it is an impressive trick to show guests.

TRICKS FROM OBEDIENCE

For the fully trained obedience dog, and by this we mean one at the Utility level, there are many "tricks" that can be worked out, the number being limited only by your ingenuity. The three we suggest here actually require no new training. What they do require is a small amount of work with the new apparatus involved. But the Utility dog will find no difficulty in this.

Find the Dollar: Here you need a fairly good-sized grassy field, a dog trained in tracking, and a dollar bill. Get him used to the idea of carrying a crumpled dollar bill in his mouth, then practice a few short tracks with the dollar. With that you are ready to demonstrate to friends just how valuable your trained dog is. Leave him at the edge of the field, walk out into the middle with the crumpled bill, and drop it, returning over the same path. Send your dog out to find it, and hope for the best. If he is a good worker and you feel like living dangerously, try it with a ten or a twenty. It adds a certain something to the exercise, because a crumpled bill in a large grassy field is almost invisible and unfindable by you, even if you think you know where you dropped it.

Mind Reading: This is an exceptionally effective trick, but it consists of misdirection and can only be worked on friends who are not familiar with scent discrimination. In setting up the trick, you have half a dozen children's blocks with letters of the alphabet on one side. You ask one of your spectators to place them in a line on the floor or ground and to bring you the block he wants your dog to be mentally instructed to find. When you get the block, hold it against your forehead and do a bit of acting along the lines of "fierce concentration," then hand the block back to be placed in line with the others while you and your dog face away. Turn and send your dog with no other words to him but "Find it!" and, lo! he comes back with the proper block in his mouth!

The mechanism is simple enough—all you must do is train your dog to work scent discrimination with the blocks. In this practice, work with an assistant handling all the blocks, including the one that is handed to you and replaced in line. With a little work your dog will learn to ignore the assistant's smell on all the blocks and find the one that also has your smell on it. Your smell, of course, was fully transmitted to the block while you went through the business of holding it to your forehead and "concentrating" on your mental instructions. When the blocks are put in the line, have them placed with the letter face up, and when your dog sniffs along the line it will look to the uninitiated as though he were actually peering nearsightedly at the letters to find the right one. If you do it skillfully, it will puzzle your friends for months to come.

Find a Guest's Article: Perhaps the most effective trick of all is having a visiting friend go into another room and leave there something of his, then sending your dog to find it and bring it back. Here again, the basis is obvious: a combination of scent discrimination and retrieve. Work on it with one or two friends. Ask them first to take something of theirs (a wallet or a fresh handkerchief or a dollar bill they've rubbed), in a variation on "Find the Dollar," and put it on the floor across the room. Have the friend give your dog the scent by holding his cupped hand over the dog's nose for a moment, then send the dog to get and return with the article. Progress to leaving the article in the next room by being sure your dog watches as the guest goes into another room and leaves the article just a short distance inside the door.

You can work up from there to having a guest leave something in any room of the house—but always in easy reach, on a chair, on a bed, or on the floor—and your dog will take the scent and search, even sometimes using a bit of tracking, until he finds it and triumphantly brings it back. It never fails to astonish.

And there you have it. These later tricks that employ parts of regular obedience training can be great fun. And having fun is a good part of what obedience training is all about. As we've told you all along, training isn't a grim business of domination. It's fun—so have fun with it.

APPENDIX

AMERICAN KENNEL CLUB
OBEDIENCE REGULATIONS

AND

SOME AUTHORS' SUGGESTIONS
FOR
CONSTRUCTION OF OBEDIENCE EQUIPMENT

OBEDIENCE REGULATIONS

Purpose

Obedience trials are a sport and all participants should be guided by the principles of good sportsmanship both in and outside of the ring. The purpose of obedience trials is to demonstrate the usefulness of the pure-bred dog as a companion of man, not merely the dog's ability to follow specified routines in the obedience ring. While all contestants in a class are required to perform the same exercises in substantially the same way so that the relative quality of the various performances may be compared and scored, the basic objective of obedience trials is to produce dogs that have been trained and conditioned always to behave in the home, in public places, and in the presence of other dogs, in a manner that will reflect credit on the sport of obedience. The performances of dog and handler in the ring must be accurate and correct and must conform to the requirements of these Regulations. However, it is also essential that the dog demonstrate willingness and enjoyment of its work, and that smoothness and naturalness on the part of the handler be given precedence over a performance based on military precision and peremptory commands.

CHAPTER 1

General Regulations

Section 1. **Obedience Clubs.** An obedience club that meets all the requirements of The American Kennel Club and wishes to hold an Obedience Trial at which qualifying scores toward an obedience title may be awarded, must make application to The American Kennel Club on the form provided for permission to hold such trial. Such a trial, if approved, may be held either in conjunction with a dog show or as a separate event. If the club is not a member of The American Kennel Club it shall pay a license fee for the privilege of holding such trial, the amount of which shall be determined by the Board of Directors of The American Kennel Club. If the club fails to hold its trial at the time and place which have been approved, the amount of the license fee paid will be returned.

Section 2. **Dog Show and Specialty Clubs.** A dog show club may be granted permission to hold a licensed or member obedience trial at its dog show, and a specialty club may also be granted permission to hold a licensed or member obedience trial if, in the opinion of the Board of Directors of The American Kennel Club, such clubs are qualified to do so.

Section 3. **Obedience Classes.** A licensed or member obedience trial need not include all of the regular obedience classes defined in these Regulations, but a club will be approved to hold Open classes only if it also holds Novice classes, and a club will be approved to hold a Utility class only if it also holds Novice and Open classes. A specialty club which has been approved to hold a licensed or member obedience trial, if qualified in the opinion of the Board of Directors of The American Kennel Club, or an obedience club which has been approved to hold a licensed or member obedience trial may, subject to the approval of The American Kennel Club, offer additional nonregular classes for dogs not less than six months of age, provided a clear and complete description of the eligibility requirements and performance requirements for each such class appears in the premium list. However, the nonregular classes defined in these Regulations need not be described in the premium list. Pre-Novice classes will not be approved at licensed or member obedience trials.

Section 4. **Tracking Tests.** A club that has been approved to hold licensed or member obedience trials and that meets the requirements of The American Kennel Club, may also make application to hold a tracking test. A club may not hold a tracking test on the same day as its show or obedience trial, but the tracking test may be announced in the premium list for the show or trial, and the tracking test entries may be included in the show or obedience trial catalog. If the entries are not listed in the catalog for the show or obedience trial, the club must provide, at the tracking test, several copies of a sheet, which may be typewritten, giving all the information that would be contained in the catalog for each entered dog. If the tracking test is to be held within 7 days of the obedience trial the entries must be sent to the same person designated to receive the obedience trial entries, and the same closing date should apply. If the tracking test is not to be held within 7 days of the obedience trial the club may name someone else in the premium list to receive the tracking test entries, and may specify a different closing date for entries at least 7 days before the tracking test.

The presence of a veterinarian shall not be required at a tracking test.

Section 5. Obedience Trial Committee.
If an obedience trial is held by an obedience club, an Obedience Trial Committee must be appointed by the club, and this committee shall exercise all the authority vested in a dog show's Bench Show Committee. If an obedience club holds its obedience trial in conjunction with a dog show, then the Obedience Trial Committee shall have sole jurisdiction only over those dogs entered in the obedience trial and their handlers and owners; provided, however, that if any dog is entered in both obedience and breed classes, then the Obedience Trial Committee shall have jurisdiction over such dog, its owner, and its handler, only in matters pertaining to the Obedience Regulations, and the Bench Show Committee shall have jurisdiction over such dog, its owner and handler, in all other matters.

When an obedience trial is to be held in conjunction with a dog show by the club which has been granted permission to hold the show, the club's Bench Show Committee shall include one person designated as "Obedience Chairman." At such event the Bench Show Committee of the show-giving club

shall have sole jurisdiction over all matters which may properly come before it, regardless of whether the matter has to do with the dog show or with the obedience trial.

Section 6. Sanctioned Matches.
A club may hold an obedience match by obtaining the sanction of The American Kennel Club. Sanctioned obedience matches shall be governed by such regulations as may be adopted by the Board of Directors of The American Kennel Club. Scores awarded at such matches will not be entered in the records of The American Kennel Club nor count towards an obedience title.

All of these Obedience Regulations shall also apply to sanctioned matches except for those sections in which it is specified that the provisions apply to licensed or member trials, and except where specifically stated otherwise in the Regulations for Sanctioned Matches.

Section 7. American Kennel Club Sanction.
American Kennel Club sanction must be obtained by any club that holds American Kennel Club obedience trials, for any type of match for which it solicits or accepts entries from non-members.

Section 8. Dog Show Rules.
All the Dog Show Rules, where applicable, shall govern the conduct of obedience trials and tracking tests, and shall apply to all persons and dogs participating in them except as these Obedience Regulations may provide otherwise.

Section 9. Identification.
No badges, club jackets, coats with kennel names thereon or ribbon prizes shall be worn or displayed, nor other visible means of identification used, by an individual when exhibiting a dog in the ring.

Section 10. Immediate Family.
As used in this Chapter, "immediate family" means husband, wife, father, mother, son, daughter, brother, or sister.

Section 11. Pure-Bred Dogs Only.
As used in these Regulations the word "dog" refers to either sex but only to dogs that are pure-bred of a breed eligible for registration in The American Kennel Club stud book or for entry in the Miscellaneous Class at American Ken-

nel Club dog shows, as only such dogs may compete in obedience trials, tracking tests, or sanctioned matches. A judge must report to The American Kennel Club after the trial or tracking test any dog shown under him which in his opinion appears not to be purebred.

Section 12. **Unregistered Dogs.** Chapter 15, Section 1 of the Dog Show Rules shall apply to entries in licensed or member obedience trials and tracking tests, except that an eligible unregistered dog for which an ILP number has been issued by The American Kennel Club may be entered indefinitely in such events provided the ILP number is shown on each entry form.

Section 13. **Dogs That May Not Compete.** No dog belonging wholly or in part to a judge or to a Show or Obedience Trial Secretary, Superintendent, or official Veterinarian, or to any member of such person's immediate family or household, shall be entered in any dog show, obedience trial, or tracking test at which such person officiates or is scheduled to officiate. This applies to both obedience and dog show judges when an obedience trial is held in conjunction with a dog show. However, a tracking test shall be considered a separate event for the purpose of this section.

No dogs shall be entered or shown under a judge at an obedience trial or tracking test if the dog has been owned, sold, held under lease, handled in the ring, boarded, or has been regularly trained or instructed, within one year prior to the date of the obedience trial or tracking test, by the judge or by any member of his immediate family or household, and no such dog shall be eligible to compete. "Trained or instructed" applies equally to judges who train professionally or as amateurs, and to judges who train individual dogs or who train or instruct dogs in classes with or through their handlers.

Section 14. **Qualifying Score.** A qualifying score shall be comprised of scores of more than 50% of the available points in each exercise and a final score of 170 or more points, earned in a single regular or nonregular class at a licensed or member obedience trial or sanctioned match.

Section 15. **When Titles Are Won.** Where any of the following sections of the Regula-

tion exclude from a particular obedience class, dogs that have won a particular obedience title, eligibility to enter that class shall be determined as follows: a dog may continue to be shown in such a class after its handler has been notified by three different judges of regular classes in licensed or member trials, that it has received three qualifying scores for such title, but may not be entered or shown in such a class in any obedience trial of which the closing date for entries occurs after the owner has received official notification from The American Kennel Club that the dog has won the particular obedience title.

Where any of the following sections of the Regulations require that a dog shall have won a particular obedience title before competing in a particular obedience class, a dog may not be shown in such class at any obedience trial before the owner has received official notification from The American Kennel Club that the dog has won the required title.

Section 16. **Disqualification and Ineligibility.** A dog that is blind or deaf or that has been changed in appearance by artificial means (except for such changes as are customarily approved for its breed) may not compete in any obedience trial or tracking test and must be disqualified. Blind means having useful vision in neither eye. Deaf means without useful hearing.

When a judge finds any of these conditions in any dog he is judging, he shall disqualify the dog marking his book "Disqualified" and stating the reason. He shall not obtain the opinion of a veterinarian.

The judge must disqualify any dog that attempts to attack any person in the ring. He may excuse a dog that attacks another dog or that appears dangerous to other dogs in the ring. He shall mark the dog disqualified or excused and state the reason in his, judge's book, and shall give the Superintendent or Show or Trial Secretary a brief report of the dog's actions which shall be submitted to AKC with the report of the show or trial.

When a dog has been disqualified under this section as being blind or deaf or having been changed in appearance by artificial means or for having attempted to attack a person in the ring, all awards made to the dog at the trial shall be cancelled by The American Kennel Club and the dog may not again compete unless and until, following application by the owner to The American Kennel Club, the owner has received official notification from The American Kennel Club that the dog's eligibility has been reinstated.

Spayed bitches, castrated dogs, monorchid or cryptorchid males, and dogs that have faults which would disqualify them under the standards for their breeds, may compete in obedience trials if otherwise eligible under these Regulations.

A dog that is lame in the ring at any obedience trial or at a tracking test may not compete and shall not receive any score at the trial. It shall be the judge's responsibility to determine whether a dog is lame. He shall not obtain the opinion of a veterinarian. If in the judge's opinion a dog in the ring is lame, he shall not score such dog, and shall promptly excuse it from the ring and mark his book "Excused—lame."

No dog shall be eligible to compete if it is taped or bandaged in any way or if it has anything attached to it for medical or corrective purposes. Such a dog must be immediately excused from the ring, and under no circumstances may it be returned later for judging after the tape, bandage or attachment has been removed.

With the exception of Maltese, Poodles, Shih Tzu and Yorkshire Terriers, which may be shown with the hair over the eyes tied back as they are normally shown in the breed ring, no dog shall be eligible to compete if it appears to have been dyed or colored in any way or if the coat shows evidence of chalk or powder, or if the dog has anything attached to it for protection or adornment. Such a dog may, at the judge's sole discretion, be judged at a later time if the offending condition has been corrected.

An obedience judge is not required to be familiar with the breed standards nor to scrutinize each dog as in dog show judging, but shall be alert for conditions which may require disqualification or exclusion under this section.

Section 17. **Disturbances.** Bitches in season are not permitted to compete. The judge of an obedience trial or tracking test must remove from competition any bitch in season, any dog which its handler cannot control, any handler who interferes willfully with another competitor or his dog, and any handler who abuses his dog in the ring, and may excuse from competition any dog which he considers unfit to compete, or any bitch which appears so attractive to males as to be a disturbing element. If a dog or handler is expelled or excused by a judge, the reason shall be stated in the judge's book or in a separate report.

Section 18. **Obedience Ribbons.** At licensed or member obedience trials the following colors shall be used for prize ribbons or rosettes in all regular classes and for the ribbon or rosette for Highest Scoring Dog in the Regular Classes:

First Prize .... Blue
Second Prize .... Red
Third Prize .... Yellow
Fourth Prize .... White
Qualifying Prize .... Dark Green
Highest Scoring Dog in the
  Regular Classes ...... Blue and Gold

and the following colors shall be used for Nonregular Classes:

First Prize .... Rose
. Second Prize .... Brown
Third Prize .... Light Green
Fourth Prize .... Gray

Each ribbon or rosette shall be at least two inches wide and approximately eight inches long, and shall bear on its face a facsimile of the seal of The American Kennel Club, the words "Obedience Trial," the name of the prize, the name of the trial-giving club, the date of the trial, and the name of the city or town where the trial is given.

Section 19. **Match Ribbons.** If ribbons are given at sanctioned obedience matches they shall be of the following colors and shall have the words "Obedience Match" printed on them, but may be of any design or size:

First Prize .... Rose
Second Prize .... Brown
Third Prize .... Light Green
Fourth Prize .... Gray
Qualifying Prize ..... Green with Pink
  edges

Section 20. **Ribbons and Prizes.** Ribbons for the four official placings and all prizes offered for competition within a single regular or nonregular class at licensed or member trials or at sanctioned matches shall be awarded only to dogs that earn qualifying scores.

Prizes for which dogs in one class compete against dogs in one or more other classes at licensed or member trials or at sanctioned matches shall be awarded only to dogs that earn qualifying scores.

Prizes at a licensed or member obedience trial must be offered to be won outright, with the exception that a prize which requires three wins by the same owner, not necessarily with the same dog, for permanent possession, may be offered for the dog with the highest qualifying score in one of the regular classes, or the dog with the highest qualifying score in the regular classes, or the dog with the highest combined qualifying scores in the Open B and Utility classes.

Subject to the provisions of paragraphs 1 and 2 of this section, prizes may be offered for the highest scoring dogs of the Groups as defined in Chapter 2 of the Dog Show Rules, or for the highest scoring dogs of any breeds, but not for a breed variety. Show varieties are not recognized for obedience. In accordance with Chapter 2, all Poodles are in the Non-Sporting Group and all Manchester Terriers in the Terrier Group.

Prizes offered only to members of certain clubs or organizations will not be approved for publication in premium lists.

Section 21. **Highest Scoring Dog in the Regular Classes.** The dog receiving the highest qualifying score in the regular classes shall be awarded the ribbon and any prizes offered for this placement, after the announcement of final scores of the last regular class to be judged. The Superintendent or Show Trial Secretary shall mark the catalog to identify the dog receiving this award.

In case of a tie between dogs receiving the highest qualifying score in two or more regular classes, the dogs shall be tested again by having them perform at the same time some part or parts of the Heel Free exercise. The judge for the run-off shall be designated by the Bench Show or Obedience Trial Committee from among the judges of the obedience trial. When the run-off has been completed, the judge shall record the results on a special sheet which shall identify the dogs taking part in the run-off by catalog number, class and breed. When the judge has marked and signed the sheet, it shall be turned over to the Superintendent or Show or Trial Secretary who shall mark the catalog accordingly and forward the sheet to The American Kennel Club as part of the records of the trial.

Section 22. **Risk.** The owner or agent entering a dog in an obedience trial does so at his own risk and agrees to abide by the rules of The American Kennel Club and the Obedience Regulations.

Section 23. **Decisions.** At the trial the decisions of the judge shall be final in all matters affecting the scoring and the working of the dogs and their handlers. The Obedience Trial Committee, or the Bench Show Committee, if the trial is held by a show-giving club, shall decide all other matters arising at the trial, including protests against dogs made under Chapter 19 of the Dog Show Rules, subject, however, to the rules and regulations of The American Kennel Club.

Section 24. **Dogs Must Compete.** Any dog entered and received at a licensed or member obedience trial must compete in all exercises of all classes in which it is entered unless disqualified, expelled, or excused by the judge or by the Bench Show or Obedience Trial Committee, or unless excused by the official veterinarian to protect the health of the dog or of other dogs at the trial. The excuse of the official veterinarian must be in writing and must be approved by the Superintendent or Show or Trial Secretary, and must be submitted to The American Kennel Club with the report of the trial. The judge must report to The American Kennel Club any dog that is not brought back for the Group exercises.

Section 25. **Judging Program.** Any club holding a licensed or member obedience trial must prepare, after the entries have closed, a program showing the time scheduled for the judging of each of the classes. A copy of this program shall be mailed to the owner of each entered dog and to each judge, and the program shall be printed in the catalog. This program shall be based on the judging of no more than 8 Novice entries, 7 Open entries, or 6 Utility entries, per hour during the time the show or trial will be open as published in the premium list, taking into consideration the starting hour for judging if published in the premium list, and the availability of rings. No judge shall be scheduled to exceed this rate of judging. In addition, one hour for rest or meals must be allowed if, under this formula, it will take more than five hours of actual judging to judge the dogs entered under him. No judge shall be assigned to judge for more than eight hours in one day under this formula, including any breed judging assignment if the obedience trial is held in conjunction with a dog show.

If any nonregular class is to be judged in the same ring as any regular class, or by the judge of any regular class, the nonregular class must be judged after the regular class.

Section 26. **Limitation of Entries.** If a club anticipates an entry in excess of its facilities for a licensed or member trial, it may limit entries in any or all regular classes, but nonregular classes will not be approved if the regular classes are limited. A club may limit entries in any or all regular classes to 64 in a Novice class, 56 in an Open class, or 48 in a Utility class.

Prominent announcement of such limits must appear on the title or cover page of the premium list for an obedience trial or immediately under the obedience heading in the premium list for a dog show, with a statement that entries in one or more specified classes or in the obedience trial will automatically close when a certain limit or limits have been reached, even though the official closing date for entries has not arrived.

Section 27. **Additional Judges, Reassignment, Split Classes.** If when the entries have closed, it is found that the entry under one or more judges exceeds the limit established in Section 25, the club shall immediately secure the approval of The American Kennel Club for the appointment of one or more additional judges, or for reassignment of its advertised judges, so that no judge will be required to exceed the limit.

If a judge with an excessive entry was advertised to judge more than one class, one or more of his classes shall be assigned to another judge. The class or classes selected for reassignment shall first be any nonregular classes for which he was advertised, and shall then be either the regular class or classes with the minimum number of entries, or those with the minimum scheduled time, which will bring the advertised judge's schedule within, and as close as possible to, the maximum limit. If a judge with an excessive entry was advertised to judge only one class, the Superintendent, Show Secretary,

or Obedience Trial Secretary, shall divide the entry as evenly as possible between the advertised judge and the other judge by drawing lots.

The club shall promptly mail to the owner of each entry affected, a notification of any change of judge. The owner shall be permitted to withdraw such entry at any time prior to the day of the show, and the entry fee shall then be refunded. If the entry in any one class is split in this manner, the advertised judge shall judge the run-off of any tie scores that may develop between the two divisions of the class, after each judge has first run off any ties resulting from his own judging.

Section 28. **Split Classes in Premium List.** A club may choose to announce two or more judges for any class in its premium list. In such case the entries shall be divided by lots as provided above. The identification slips and judging program shall be made up so that the owner of each dog will know the division, and the judge of the division, in which his dog is entered, but no owner shall be entitled to a refund of entry fee. In such case the premium list shall also specify the judge for the run-off of any tie scores which may develop between the dogs in the different divisions, after each judge has first run off any ties resulting from his own judging.

Section 29. **Split Classes, Official Ribbons, Prizes.** A club which holds a split class, whether the split is announced in the premium list or made after entries close, shall not award American Kennel Club official ribbons in either division. The four dogs with the highest qualifying scores in the class, regardless of the division or divisions in which such scores were made, shall be called back into the ring and awarded the four American Kennel Club official ribbons by one of the judges of the class. This judge shall be responsible for recording the entry numbers of the four placed dogs in one of the judge's books.

If a split class is announced in the premium list, duplicate placement prizes may be offered in each division. If prizes have been offered for placements in a class that must be split after entries close, duplicate prizes or prizes of equal value may be offered in the additional division of the class.

Section 30. **Stewards.** The judge is in sole charge of his ring until his assignment is completed. Stewards are provided to assist him, but they may act only on the judge's instructions. Stewards shall not give information or instructions to owners and handlers except as specifically instructed by the judge, and then only in such a manner that it is clear that the instructions are those of the judge.

Section 31. **Ring Conditions.** If the judging takes place indoors the ring should be rectangular and should be about 35' wide and 50' long for all obedience classes. In no case shall the ring for a Utility class be less than 35' by 50', and in no case shall the ring for a Novice or Open class be less than 30' by 40'. The floor shall have a surface or covering that provides firm footing for the largest dogs, and rubber or similar non-slip material must be laid for the take off and landing at all jumps unless the surface, in the judge's opinion, is such as not to require it. At an outdoor show or trial the rings shall be about 40' wide and 50' long. The ground shall be clean and level, and the grass, if any, shall be cut short. The Club and Superintendent are responsible for providing, for the Open classes, an appropriate place approved by the judge, for the handlers to go completely out of sight of their dogs. If inclement weather at an outdoor trial necessitates the judging of obedience under shelter, the requirements as to ring size may be waived.

Section 32. **Obedience Rings at Dog Shows.** At an outdoor dog show a separate ring or rings shall be provided for obedience, and a sign forbidding anyone to permit any dog to use the ring, except when being judged, shall be set up in each such ring by the Superintendent or Show Secretary. It shall be his duty as well as that of the Show Committee to enforce this regulation. At an indoor show where limited space does not permit the exclusive use of any ring for obedience, the same regulation will apply after the obedience rings have been set up. At a dog show the material used for enclosing the obedience rings shall be at least equal to the material used for enclosing the breed rings. The ring must be thoroughly cleaned before the obedience judging starts if it has previously been used for breed judging.

Section 33. **Judge's Report on Ring and Equipment.** The Superintendent and the officials of the club holding the obedience trial are responsible for providing rings and equipment which meet the requirements of these Regulations. However, the judge must check the ring and equipment provided for his use before starting to judge, and must report to The American Kennel Club after the trial any undesirable ring conditions or deficiencies that have not been promptly corrected at his request.

CHAPTER 2

Regulations for Performance and Judging

Section 1. **Standardized Judging.** Standardized judging is of paramount importance. Judges are not permitted to inject their own variations into the exercises, but must see that each handler and dog executes the various exercises exactly as described in these Regulations. A handler who is familiar with these Regulations should be able to enter the ring under any judge without having to inquire how the particular judge wishes to have any exercise performed, and without being confronted with some unexpected requirement.

Section 2. **Standard of Perfection.** The judge must carry a mental picture of the theoretically perfect performance in each exercise and score each dog and handler against this visualized standard which shall combine the utmost in willingness, enjoyment and precision on the part of the dog, and naturalness, gentleness, and smoothness in handling. Lack of willingness or enjoyment on the part of the dog must be penalized, as must lack of precision in the dog's performance, roughness in handling, military precision or peremptory commands by the handler. There shall be no penalty of less than ½ point or multiple of ½ point.

Section 3. **Qualifying Performance.** A judge's certification in his judge's book of a qualifying score for any particular dog constitutes his certification to The American Kennel Club that the dog on this particular occasion has performed all of the required exercises at least in accordance with the minimum standards and that its performance on this occasion would justify the awarding of the obedience title associated with the particular class. A qualifying score must never be awarded to a dog whose performance has not met the minimum requirements, nor to a dog that shows fear or resentment, or that relieves itself at any time while in an indoor ring for judging, or that relieves itself while performing any exercise in an outdoor ring, nor to a dog whose handler disciplines or abuses it in the ring, or carries or offers food in the ring.

In deciding whether a faulty performance of a particular exercise by a particular dog warrants a qualifying score, the judge shall consider whether the awarding of an obedience title would be justified if all dogs in the class performed the exercise in a similar manner. The judge must not give a qualifying score for the exercise if he decides that it would be contrary to the best interests of the sport if all dogs in the class were to perform in the same way.

Section 4. **Judge's Directions.** The judge's orders and signals should be given to the handlers in a clear and understandable manner, but in such a way that the work of the dog is not disturbed. Before starting each exercise, the judge shall ask "Are you ready?" At the end of each exercise the judge shall say "Exercise finished." Each contestant must be worked and judged separately except for the Group exercises, and in running off a tie.

Section 5. **No Added Requirements.** No judge shall require any dog or handler to do anything, nor penalize a dog or handler for failing to do anything, that is not required by these Regulations.

Section 6. **A and B Classes and Different Breeds.** The same methods and standards must be used for judging and scoring the A and B Classes, and in judging and scoring the work of dogs of different breeds.

Section 7. **Interference and Double Handling.** A judge who is aware of any assistance, interference, or attempts to control a dog from outside the ring, must act promptly to stop such double handling or interference, and shall penalize the dog substantially or, if in the judge's opinion the circumstances warrant, shall give the dog a score of zero for the exercise during which the aid was received.

Section 8. **Rejudging.** If a dog has failed in a particular part of an exercise, it shall not ordinarily be rejudged nor given a second chance; but if in the judge's opinion the dog's performance was prejudiced by peculiar and unusual conditions, the judge may at his own discretion rejudge the dog on the entire exercise.

Section 9. **Ties.** In case of a tie for any prize in a Novice or Open class, the dogs shall be tested again by having them perform at the same time all or some part of the Heel Free exercise. In the Utility class the dogs shall perform at the same time all or some part of the Signal exercise. The original scores shall not be changed.

Section 10. **Judge's Book and Score Sheets.** The judge must enter the scores and sub-total score of each dog in the judge's book immediately after each dog has been judged on the individual exercises and before judging the next dog. Scores for the group exercises and total scores must be entered in the official judge's book immediately after each group of dogs has been judged. No score may be changed except to correct an arithmetical error or if a score has been entered in the wrong column. All final scores must be entered in the judge's book before prizes are awarded. No person other than the judge may make any entry in the judge's book. Judges may use separate score sheets for their own purposes, but shall not give out nor allow exhibitors to see such sheets, nor give out any other written scores, nor permit anyone else to distribute score sheets or cards prepared by the judge. Carbon copies of the sheets in the official judge's book shall be made available through the Superintendent or Show or Trial Secretary for examination by owners and handlers immediately after the prizes have been awarded in each class. If score cards are distributed by a club after the prizes are awarded they must contain no more information than is shown in the judge's book and must be marked "Unofficial score."

Section 11. **Announcement of Scores.** The judge shall not disclose any score or partial score to contestants or spectators until he has completed the judging of the entire class or, in case of a split class, until he has completed the judging of his division; nor shall he permit anyone else to do so. After all the scores are recorded for the class, or for the division in case of a split class, the judge shall call for all available dogs that have won qualifying scores to be brought into the ring. Before awarding the prizes, the judge shall inform the spectators as to the maximum number of points for a perfect score, and shall then announce the score of each prize winner, and announce to the handler the score of each dog that has won a qualifying score.

Section 12. **Explanations and Errors.** The judge is not required to explain his scoring, and need not enter into any discussion with any contestant who appears to be dissatisfied. Any interested person who thinks that there may have been an arithmetical error or an error in identifying a dog may report the facts to one of the stewards or to the Superintendent or Show or Trial Secretary so that the matter may be checked.

Section 13. **Compliance with Regulations and Standards.** In accordance with the certification on the entry form, the handler of each dog and the person signing each entry form must be familiar with the Obedience Regulations applicable to the class in which the dog is entered.

Section 14. **Handicapped Handlers.** Judges may modify the specific requirements

of these Regulations for handlers to the extent necessary to permit physically handicapped handlers to compete, provided such handlers can move about the ring without physical assistance or guidance from another person, except for guidance from the judge or from the handler of a competing dog in the ring for the Group exercises.

Dogs handled by such handlers shall be required to perform all parts of all exercises as described in these Regulations, and shall be penalized for failure to perform any part of an exercise.

Section 15. **Catalog Order.** Dogs should be judged in catalog order to the extent that it is practicable to do so without holding up the judging in any ring.

Judges are not required to wait for dogs for either the individual exercises or the group exercises. It is the responsibility of each handler to be ready with his dog at ringside when required, without being called. The judge's first consideration should be the convenience of those exhibitors who are at ringside with their dogs when scheduled, and who ask no favors.

A judge may agree, on request in advance of the scheduled starting time of the class, to judge a dog earlier or later than the time scheduled by catalog order. However, a judge should not hesitate to mark absent and to refuse to judge any dog and handler that are not at ringside ready to be judged in catalog order if no arrangement has been made in advance.

Section 16. **Use of Leash.** All dogs shall be kept on leash except when in the obedience ring or exercise ring. Dogs should be brought into the ring and taken out of the ring on leash. Dogs may be kept on leash in the ring when brought in to receive awards, and when waiting in the ring before and after the Group exercises. The leash shall be left on the judge's table or other designated place, between the individual exercises, and during all exercises except the Heel on Leash and Group exercises. The leash may be of fabric or leather and, in the Novice classes, need be only of sufficient length to provide adequate slack in the Heel on Leash exercise.

Section 17. **Collars.** Dogs in the obedience ring must wear well-fitting plain buckle or slip collars. Slip collars of an appropriate single length of leather, fabric or chain with two rings, one on each end are acceptable. Fancy collars, or special training collars, or collars that are either too tight or so large that they hang down unreasonably in front of the dogs, are not permitted. There shall not be anything hanging from the collars.

Section 18. **Heel Position.** The heel position as used in these Regulations, whether the dog is sitting, standing, or moving at heel, means that the dog shall be straight in line with the direction in which the handler is facing, at the handler's left side, and as close as practicable to the handler's left leg without crowding, permitting the handler freedom of motion at all times. The area from the dog's head to shoulder shall be in line with the handler's left hip.

Section 19. **Hands.** In all exercises in which the dog is required to come to or return to the handler and sit in front, the handler's arms and hands shall hang naturally at his sides while the dog is coming in and until the dog has sat in front. A substantial deduction shall be made if a handler's arms and hands are not hanging naturally at his sides.

Section 20. **Commands and Signals.** Whenever a command or signal is mentioned in these Regulations, a single command or signal only may be given by the handler, and any extra commands or signals must be penalized; except that whenever the Regulations specify "command and/or signal" the handler may give either one or the other or both command and signal simultaneously. When a signal is permitted and given, it must be a single gesture with one arm and hand only, and the arm must immediately be returned to a natural position. Delay in following a judge's order to give a command or signal must be penalized, unless the delay is directed by the judge because of some distraction or interference.

The signal for downing a dog may be given either with the arm raised or with a down swing of the arm, but any pause in holding the arm upright followed by a down swing of the arm will be considered an additional signal.

Signaling correction to a dog is forbidden and must be penalized. Signals must be inaudible and the handler must not touch the dog. Any unusual noise or motion may be considered to be a signal. Movements of the body that aid the dog shall be considered additional signals except that a handler may bend as far as necessary to bring his hand on a level with the dog's eyes in giving a signal to a dog in the heel position, and that in the Directed Retrieve exercise the body and knees may be bent to the extent necessary to give the direction to the dog. Whistling or the use of a whistle is prohibited.

The dog's name may be used once immediately before any verbal command or before a verbal command and signal when these Regulations permit command and/or signal. The name shall not be used with any signal not given simultaneously with a verbal command. The dog's name, when given immediately before a verbal command, shall not be considered as an additional command, but a dog that responds to its name without waiting for the verbal command shall be scored as having anticipated the command. The dog should never anticipate the handler's directions, but must wait for the appropriate commands and/or signals. Moving forward at the heel without any command or signal other than the natural movement of the handler's left leg, shall not be considered as anticipation.

Loud commands by handlers to their dogs create a poor impression of obedience and should be avoided. Shouting is not necessary even in a noisy place if the dog is properly trained to respond to a normal tone of voice. Commands which in the judge's opinion are excessively loud will be penalized.

Section 21. **Additional Commands or Signals.** If a handler gives an additional command or signal not permitted by these Regulations, either when no command or signal is permitted, or simultaneously with or following a permitted command or signal, or if he uses the dog's name with a permitted signal but without a permitted command, the dog shall be scored as though it had failed completely to perform that particular part of the exercise.

Section 22. **Praise.** Praise and petting are allowed between and after exercises, but points must be deducted from the total score for a dog that is not under reasonable control while being praised. A handler shall not carry or offer food in the ring. There shall be a substantial penalty for any dog that is picked up or carried at any time in the obedience ring.

Section 23. **Handling Between Exercises.** In the Novice classes the dog may be guided gently by the collar between exercises and to get it into proper position for an exercise. No other physical guidance, such as placing the dog in position with the hands or straightening the dog with the knees or feet, is permitted and shall be substantially penalized even if occurring before or between the exercises.

In the Open and Utility classes there shall be a substantial penalty for any dog that is physically guided at any time or that is not readily controllable.

Posing for examination and holding for measurement are permitted. Imperfections in heeling between exercises will not be judged. Minor penalties shall be imposed for a dog that does not respond promptly to its handler's commands or signals before or between exercises in the Open and Utility classes.

Section 24. **Orders and Minimum Penalties.** The orders for the exercises and the standards for judging are set forth in the following chapters. The lists of faults are not intended to be complete but minimum penalties are specified for most of the more common and serious faults. There is no maximum limit on penalties. A dog which makes none of the errors listed may still fail to qualify or may be scored zero for other reasons.

Section 25. **Misbehavior.** Any disciplining by the handler in the ring, any display of fear or nervousness by the dog, or any uncontrolled behavior of the dog such as snapping, barking, relieving itself while in the ring for judging, or running away from its handler, whether it occurs during an exercise, between exercises, or before or after judging, must be penalized according to the seriousness of the misbehavior, and the judge may expel or excuse the dog from further competition in the class. If such behavior occurs during an exercise, the penalty must first be applied to the score for that exercise. Should the penalty be greater than the value of the exercise during which it is incurred, the additional points shall be deducted from the total score under Misbehavior. If such behavior occurs before or after the judging or between exercises, the entire

penalty shall be deducted from the total score.

The judge must disqualify any dog that attempts to attack any person in the ring. He may excuse a dog that attacks another dog or that appears dangerous to other dogs in the ring.

Section 26. **Training on the Grounds.** There shall be no drilling nor intensive or abusive training of dogs on the grounds or premises at a licensed or member obedience trial or at a sanctioned match. No practice rings or areas shall be permitted at such events. All dogs shall be kept on leash except when in the obedience ring or exercise ring. Special training collars shall not be used on the grounds or premises at an obedience trial or match. These requirements shall not be interpreted as preventing a handler from moving normally about the grounds or premises with his dog at heel on leash, nor from giving such signals or such commands in a normal tone, as are necessary and usual in everyday life in heeling a dog or making it stay, but physical or verbal disciplining of dogs shall not be permitted except to a reasonable extent in the case of an attack on a person or another dog. The Superintendent, or Show or Trial Secretary, and the members of the Bench Show or Obedience Trial Committee, shall be responsible for compliance with this section, and shall investigate any report of infractions.

Section 27. **Training and Disciplining in the Ring.** The judge shall not permit any handler to train his dog nor to practice any exercise in the ring either before or after he is judged, and shall deduct points from the total score of any dog whose handler does this. A dog whose handler disciplines it in the ring must not receive a qualifying score. The penalty shall be deducted from the points available for the exercise during which the disciplining may occur, and additional points may be deducted from the total score if necessary. If the disciplining does not occur during an exercise the penalty shall be deducted from the total score. Any abuse of a dog in the ring must be immediately reported by the judge to the Bench Show or Obedience Trial Committee for action under Chapter 2, Section 29.

Section 28. **Abuse of Dogs.** The Bench Show or Obedience Trial Committee shall investigate any reports of abuse of dogs or severe disciplining of dogs on the grounds or premises of a show, trial or match. Any person who, at a licensed or member obedience trial, conducts himself in such manner or in any other manner prejudicial to the best interests of the sport, or who fails to comply with the requirements of Chapter 2, Section 26, shall be dealt with promptly, during the trial if possible, after the offender has been notified of the specific charges against him, and has been given an opportunity to be heard in his own defense in accordance with Chapter 2, Section 29.

Any abuse of a dog in the ring must be immediately reported by the judge to the Bench Show or Obedience Trial Committee for action under Chapter 2, Section 29.

Article XII Section 2 of the Constitution and By-Laws of The American Kennel Club Provides:

Section 29. **Discipline.** The Bench Show, Obedience Trial or Field Trial Committee of a club or association shall have the right to suspend any person from the privileges of The American Kennel Club for conduct prejudicial to the best interests of pure-bred dogs, dog shows, obedience trials, field trials or The American Kennel Club, alleged to have occurred in connection with or during the progress of its show, obedience trial or field trial, after the alleged offender has been given an opportunity to be heard.

Notice in writing must be sent promptly by registered mail by the Bench Show, Obedience Trial or Field Trial Committee to the person suspended and a duplicate notice giving the name and address of the person suspended and full details as to the reasons for the suspension must be forwarded to The American Kennel Club within seven days.

An appeal may be taken from a decision of a Bench Show, Obedience Trial or Field Trial Committee. Notice in writing claiming such appeal together with a deposit of five ($5.00) dollars must be sent to The American Kennel Club within thirty days after the date of suspension. The Board of Directors may itself hear said appeal or may refer it to a committee of the Board, or to a Trial Board to be heard. The deposit shall become the property of The American Kennel Club if the decision is confirmed, or shall be returned to the appellant if the decision is not confirmed.

(See Guide for Bench Show and Obedience Trial Committees in Dealing with Misconduct at Dog Shows and Obedience Trials for proper procedure at licensed or member obedience trials.)

(The Committee at a Sanctioned event does not have this power of suspension, but must investigate any allegation of such conduct and forward a complete and detailed report of any such incident to The American Kennel Club.)

CHAPTER 3

Novice

Section 1. **Novice A Class.** The Novice A class shall be for dogs not less than six months of age that have not won the title C.D. A dog that is owned or co-owned by a person who has previously handled or regularly trained a dog that has won a C.D. title may not be entered in the Novice A class, nor may a dog be handled in this class by such person.

Each dog in this class must have a different handler who shall be its owner or co-owner or a member of the immediate family of the owner or co-owner, provided that such member has not previously handled or regularly trained a C.D. dog. The same person must handle the same dog in all exercises. No person may handle more than one dog in the Novice A class.

Section 2. **Novice B Class.** The Novice B class shall be for dogs not less than six months of age that have not won the title C.D. Dogs in this class may be handled by the owner or any other person. A person may handle more than one dog in this class, but each dog must have a separate handler for the Long Sit and Long Down exercises when judged in the same group. No dog may be entered in both Novice A and Novice B classes at any one trial.

Section 3. **Novice Exercises and Scores.** The exercises and maximum scores in the Novice classes are:

1. Heel on Leash . . . . 40 points
2. Stand for Examination . . . . 30 points
3. Heel Free . . . . 40 points
4. Recall . . . . 30 points
5. Long Sit . . . . 30 points
6. Long Down . . . . 30 points

    Maximum Total Score . . . 200 points

Section 4. **C.D. Title.** The American Kennel Club will issue a Companion Dog certificate for each registered dog, and will permit the use of the letters "C.D." after the name of each dog that has been certified by three different judges to have received qualifying scores in Novice classes at three licensed or member obedience trials, provided the sum total of dogs that actually competed in the regular Novice classes at each trial is not less than six.

Section 5. **Heel on Leash & Figure Eight.** The principal feature of this exercise is the ability of the dog and handler to work as a team.

Orders for the exercise are "Forward," "Halt," "Right turn," "Left turn," "About turn," "Slow," "Normal" and "Fast." "Fast" signifies that the handler must run, handler and dog moving forward at noticeably accelerated speed. In executing the About turn, the handler will always do a Right About turn.

The orders may be given in any sequence and may be repeated as necessary, but the judge shall attempt to standardize the heeling pattern for all dogs in any class.

The leash may be held in either hand or in both hands, providing the hands are in a natural position. However, any tightening or jerking of the leash or any act, signal or command which in the judge's opinion gives the dog assistance shall be penalized.

The handler shall enter the ring with his dog on a loose leash and stand with the dog sitting in the Heel Position. The judge shall ask if the handler is ready before giving the order, "Forward." The handler may give a command or signal to Heel, and shall walk briskly and in a natural manner with his dog on a loose leash. The dog shall walk close to the left side of the handler without swinging wide, lagging, forging or crowding. Whether heeling or sitting, the dog must not interfere with the handler's freedom of motion at any time. At each order to Halt, the handler will stop and his dog shall sit straight and promptly in the Heel Position without command or signal, and shall not move until the handler again moves forward on order from the judge. It is permissible after each Halt, before moving again, for the handler to give a command or signal to Heel. The judge shall say "Exercise finished" after this portion of the exercise.

Before starting the Figure Eight the judge shall ask if the handler is ready. Figure Eight signifies that on specific orders from the judge to Forward and Halt, the handler and dog, from a starting position midway between two stewards and facing the judge, shall walk briskly twice completely around and between the two stewards, who shall stand 8 feet apart. The Figure Eight in the Novice classes shall be done on leash. The handler may choose to go in either direction. There shall be no About turn or Fast or Slow in the Figure Eight, but the judge must order at least one Halt during and another Halt at the end of this portion of the exercise.

Section 6. **Heel on Leash & Figure Eight Scoring.** If a dog is unmanageable, or if its handler constantly controls its performance by tugging on the leash or adapts pace to that of the dog, the dog must be scored zero.

Substantial deductions shall be made for additional commands or signals to Heel and for failure of dog or handler to change pace noticeably for Slow and Fast.

Substantial or minor deductions shall be made for such things as lagging, heeling wide, poor sits, handler failing to walk at a brisk pace, occasional guidance with leash and other imperfections in heeling.

In scoring this exercise the judge shall accompany the handler at a discreet distance so that he can observe any signals or commands given by the handler to the dog. The judge must do so without interfering with either dog or handler.

Section 7. **Stand for Examination.** The principal features of this exercise are that the dog stand in position before and during the examination, and that the dog display neither shyness nor resentment.

Orders are "Stand your dog and leave when you are ready," "Back to your dog" and "Exercise finished." There will be no further command from the judge to the handler to leave the dog.

The handler shall take his dog on leash to a place indicated by the judge, where the handler shall remove the leash and give it to a steward who shall place it on the judge's table or other designated place.

On judge's order the handler will stand and/or pose his dog off leash by the method of his choice, taking any reasonable time if he chooses to pose the dog as in the show ring. When he is ready, the handler will give his command and/or signal to the dog to Stay, walk forward about six feet in front of the dog, turn around and stand facing the dog.

The judge shall approach the dog from the front, and shall touch only the dog's head, body and hindquarters, using the fingers and palm of one hand only. He shall then order, "Back to your dog," whereupon the handler shall walk around behind his dog and return to the Heel Position. The dog must remain standing until after the judge has said "Exercise finished."

Section 8. **Stand for Examination, Scoring.** The scoring of this exercise will not start until the handler has given the command and/or signal to Stay, except for such things as rough treatment of the dog by its handler or active resistance by the dog to its handler's attempts to make it stand. Either of these shall be penalized substantially.

A dog that displays any shyness or resentment or growls or snaps at any time shall be scored zero, as shall a dog that sits before or during the examination or a dog that moves away before or during the examination from the place where it was left.

Minor or substantial deductions, depending on the circumstance, shall be made for a dog that moves its feet at any time or sits or moves away after the examination has been completed.

Section 9. **Heel Free, Performance and Scoring.** This exercise shall be executed in the same manner as Heel on Leash and Figure Eight except that the dog shall be off leash and that there shall be no Figure Eight. Orders and scoring shall also be the same.

Section 10. **Recall.** The principal features of this exercise are that the dog stay where left until called by its handler, and that the dog respond promptly to the handler's command or signal to "Come."

Orders are "Leave your dog," "Call your dog" and "Finish."

On order from the judge, the handler may give command and/or signal to the dog to Stay in the sit position while the handler walks forward about 35 feet to the other end of the ring, where he shall turn and stand in a natural manner facing his dog. On judge's order or signal, the handler will give command or signal for the dog to Come. The dog must come straight in at a brisk pace and sit straight, centered immediately in front of the handler's feet, close enough that the handler could readily touch its head without moving either foot or having to stretch forward. The dog must not touch the handler or sit between his feet.

On judge's order the handler will give command or signal to Finish and the dog must go smartly to the Heel Position and Sit. The manner in which the dog finishes shall be optional with the handler provided that it is prompt and that the dog sit straight at heel.

Section 11. **Recall, Scoring.** A dog must receive a score of zero for the following: not staying without additional command or signal, failure to come on the first command or signal, moving from the place where left before being called or signalled, not sitting close enough in front that the handler could readily touch its head without moving either foot or stretching forward.

Substantial deductions shall be made for a slow response to the Come, varying with the extent of the slowness; for extra command or signal to Stay if given before the handler leaves the dog; for the dog's standing or lying down instead of waiting in the sit position; for extra command or signal to Finish and for failure to Sit or Finish.

Minor deductions shall be made for slow or poor Sits or Finishes, for touching the handler on coming in or while finishing, and for sitting between the handler's feet.

Section 12. **Group Exercises.** The principal feature of these exercises is that the dog remain in the sitting or down position, whichever is required by the particular exercise.

Orders are "Sit your dogs" or "Down your dogs," "Leave your dogs" and "Back to your dogs."

All the competing dogs in the class take these exercises together, except that if there are 12 or more dogs they shall, at the judge's option, be judged in groups of not less than 6 nor more than 15 dogs. When the same judge does both Novice A and Novice B, the two classes may be combined provided that there are not more than 15 dogs competing in the combined classes. The dogs that are in the ring shall be lined up in catalog order along one of the four sides of the ring. Handlers' armbands, weighted with leashes or other articles if necessary, shall be placed behind the dogs.

For the Long Sit the handlers shall, on order from the judge, command and/or signal their dogs to Sit if they are not already sitting. On further order from the judge to leave their dogs, the handlers shall give a command and/or signal to Stay and immediately leave their dogs. The handlers will go to the opposite side of the ring, turn and stand facing their respective dogs.

If a dog gets up and starts to roam or follows its handler, or if a dog moves so as to interfere with another dog, the judge shall promptly instruct the handler or one of the stewards to take the dog out of the ring or to keep it away from the other dogs.

After one minute from the time he has ordered the handlers to leave their dogs, the judge will give the order to return, whereupon the handlers must promptly go back to their dogs, each walking around and in back of his own dog to the Heel Position. The dogs must not move from the Sitting Position until after the judge has said, "Exercise finished." The judge shall not give the order "Exercise finished" until the handlers have returned to the Heel Position.

Before starting the Long Down the judge shall ask if the handlers are ready. The Long Down is done in the same manner as the Long Sit except that instead of sitting their dogs the handlers shall, on order from the judge, down their dogs without touching either the dogs or their collars, and except further that the judge will order the handlers to return after three minutes. The dogs must not move from the down position until after the judge has said, "Exercise finished."

The dogs shall not be required to sit at the end of the Down exercise.

Section 13. **Group Exercises, Scoring.** During these exercises the judge shall stand in such position that all of the dogs are in his line of vision, and where he can see all the handlers in the ring without having to turn around.

Scoring of the exercises will not start until after the judge has ordered the handlers to leave their dogs, except for such things as rough treatment of a dog by its handler or active resistance by a dog to its handler's attempts to make it Sit or lie Down. These shall be penalized substantially; in extreme cases the dog may be excused.

A score of zero is required for the following: the dog's moving at any time during either exercise a substantial distance away from the place where it was left, or going over to any other dog, or staying on the spot where it was left but not remaining in whichever position is required by the particular exercise until the handler has returned to the Heel Position, or repeatedly barking or whining.

A substantial deduction shall be made for a dog that moves even a minor distance away from the place where it was left or that barks or whines only once or twice. Depending on the circumstance, a substantial or minor deduction shall be made for touching the dog or its collar in getting the dog into the Down position.

There shall be a minor deduction if a dog changes position after the handler has returned to the Heel Position but before the judge has said, "Exercise finished." The judge shall not give the order "Exercise finished" until the handlers have returned to the Heel Position.

CHAPTER 4

Open

Section 1. **Open A Class.** The Open A class shall be for dogs that have won the C.D. title but have not won the title C.D.X. Obedience judges may not enter or handle dogs in this class. Each dog must be handled by its owner or by a member of his immediate family. Owners may enter more than one dog in this class but the same person who handled each dog in the first five exercises must handle the same dog in the Long Sit and Long Down exercises, except that if a person has handled more than one dog in the first five exercises he must have an additional handler, who must be the owner or a member of his immediate family, for each additional dog, when more than one dog that he has handled in the first five exercises is judged in the same group for the Long Sit and Long Down.

Section 2. **Open B Class.** The Open B class will be for dogs that have won the title C.D. or C.D.X. A dog may continue to compete in this class after it has won the title U.D. Dogs in this class may be handled by the owner or any other person. Owners may enter more than one dog in this class but the same person who handled each dog in the first five exercises must handle each dog in the Long Sit and Long Down exercises, except that if a person has handled more than one dog in the first five exercises he must have an additional handler for each additional dog, when more than one dog that he has handled in the first five exercises is judged in the same group for the Long Sit and Long Down. No dog may be entered in both Open A and Open B classes at any one trial.

Section 3. **Open Exercises and Scores.** The exercises and maximum scores in the Open classes are:

1.	Heel Free	40 points
2.	Drop on Recall..........	30 points
3.	Retrieve on Flat.........	20 points
4.	Retrieve over High Jump .	30 points
5.	Broad Jump	20 points
6.	Long Sit	30 points
7.	Long Down.............	30 points

Maximum Total Score ... 200 points

Section 4. **C.D.X. Title.** The American Kennel Club will issue a Companion Dog Excellent certificate for each registered dog, and will permit the use of the letters "C.D.X." after the name of each dog that has been certified by three different judges of obedience trials to have received qualifying scores in Open classes at three licensed or member obedience trials, provided the sum total of dogs that actually competed in the regular Open classes at each trial is not less than six.

Section 5. **Heel Free, Performance and Scoring.** This exercise shall be executed in the same manner as the Novice Heel on Leash and Figure Eight exercise, except that the dog is off leash. Orders and scoring are the same as in Heel on Leash and Figure Eight.

Section 6. **Drop on Recall.** The principal features of this exercise, in addition to those listed under the Novice Recall, are the dog's prompt response to the handler's command or signal to Drop, and the dog's remaining in the Down position until again called or signalled to Come. The dog will be judged on the promptness of its response to command or signal and not on its proximity to a designated point.

Orders for the exercise are "Leave your dog," "Call your dog," an order or signal to Drop the dog, another "Call your dog" and "Finish." The judge may designate in advance a point at which, as the dog is coming in, the handler shall give his command or signal to the dog to Drop. The judge's signal or designated point must be clear to the handler but not obvious or distracting to the dog.

On order from the judge, the handler may give command and/or signal for the dog to Stay in the sit position while the handler walks forward about 35 feet to the other end of the ring, where he shall turn and stand in a natural manner facing his dog. On judge's order or signal, the handler shall give command or signal to Come and the dog must start straight in at a brisk pace. On judge's order or signal, or at a point designated in advance by the judge, the handler shall give command or signal to Drop, and the dog must immediately drop completely to the down position, where he must remain until, on judge's order or signal, the handler again gives command or signal to Come. The dog must come straight in at a brisk pace and sit straight, centered immediately in front of the handler's feet, close enough that the handler could readily touch the dog's head without moving either foot or having to stretch forward. The dog must not touch the handler nor sit between his feet.

The Finish shall be executed as in the Novice Recall.

Section 7. **Drop on Recall, Scoring.** All applicable penalties listed under the Novice Recall as requiring a score of zero shall apply. In addition, a zero score is required for a dog that does not drop completely to the down position on a single command or signal, and for a dog that drops but does not remain down until called or signalled.

Substantial deductions, varying with the extent, shall be made for delayed or slow response to the handler's command or signal to Drop, for slow response to either of the Comes, for extra command or signal to Stay if given before the handler leaves the dog, for the dog's standing or lying down instead of waiting where left in a sit position, for extra command or signal to Finish and for failure to finish.

Minor deductions shall be made for slow or poor sits or finishes, for touching the handler on coming in or while finishing, or for sitting between the handler's feet.

Section 8. **Retrieve on the Flat.** The principal feature of this exercise is that the dog retrieve promptly.

Orders are "Throw it," "Send your dog," "Take it" and "Finish."

The handler shall stand with his dog sitting in the Heel Position in a place designated by the judge. On order, "Throw it," the handler shall give command and/or signal to Stay, which signal may not be given with the hand that is holding the dumbbell, and throw the dumbbell. On order to send his dog, the handler shall give command or signal to retrieve. The retrieve shall be executed at a fast trot or gallop, the dog going directly to the dumbbell and retrieving it without un-

necessary mouthing or playing with the dumbbell. The dog must sit straight to deliver, centered immediately in front of the handler's feet, close enough that the handler can readily take the dumbbell without moving either foot or having to stretch forward. The dog must not touch the handler nor sit between his feet. On order from the judge to take it, the handler shall give command or signal and take the dumbbell.

The Finish shall be executed as in the Novice Recall.

The dumbbell, which must be approved by the judge, shall be made of one or more solid pieces of one of the heavy hardwoods, which shall not be hollowed out. It may be unfinished, or coated with a clear finish, or painted white. It shall have no decorations or attachments but may bear an inconspicuous mark for identification. The size of the dumbbell shall be proportionate to the size of the dog. The judge shall require the dumbbell to be thrown again before the dog is sent if, in his opinion, it is thrown too short a distance, or too far to one side, or too close to the ringside.

Section 9. **Retrieve on the Flat, Scoring.** A dog that fails to go out on the first command or signal, or goes to retrieve before the command or signal is given, or fails to retrieve, or does not return with the dumbbell sufficiently close that the handler can easily take the dumbbell as described above, must be scored zero.

Substantial deductions, depending on the extent, shall be made for slowness in going out or returning or in picking up the dumbbell, for not going directly to the dumbbell, for mouthing or playing with or dropping the dumbbell, for reluctance or refusal to release the dumbbell to the handler, for extra command or signal to finish and for failure to sit or finish.

Substantial or minor deductions shall be made for slow or poor sits or finishes, for touching the handler on coming in or while finishing, or for sitting between the handler's feet.

Section 10. **Retrieve over High Jump.** The principal features of this exercise are that the dog go out over the jump, pick up the dumbbell and promptly return with it over the jump.

Orders are "Throw it," "Send your dog," "Take it" and "Finish."

This exercise shall be executed in the same manner as the Retrieve on the Flat, except that the dog must clear the High Jump both going and coming. The handler must stand at least 8 feet, or any reasonable distance beyond 8 feet, from the jump but must remain in the same spot throughout the exercise.

The jump shall be as nearly as possible one and one-half times the height of the dog at the withers, as determined by the judge, with a minimum height of 8 inches and a maximum height of 36 inches. This applies to all breeds with the following exceptions:

The jump shall be once the height of the dog at the withers or 36 inches, whichever is less, for the following breeds—

Bloodhounds
Bullmastiffs
Great Danes
Great Pyrenees
Mastiffs
Newfoundlands
St. Bernards

The jump shall be once the height of the dog at the withers or 8 inches, whichever is greater, for the following breeds—

Spaniels (Clumber)
Spaniels (Sussex)
Basset Hounds
Dachshunds
Welsh Corgis (Cardigan)
Welsh Corgis (Pembroke)
Australian Terriers
Cairn Terriers
Dandie Dinmont Terriers
Norwich Terriers
Scottish Terriers
Sealyham Terriers
Skye Terriers
West Highland White Terriers
Maltese
Pekingese
Bulldogs
French Bulldogs

The jumps may be preset by the stewards based on the handler's advice as to the dog's height. The judge must make certain that the jump is set at the required height for each dog. He shall verify in the ring with an ordinary folding rule or steel tape to the nearest one-half inch, the height at the withers of each dog that jumps less than 36 inches. He shall not base his decision as to the height of the jump on the handler's advice.

The side posts of the High Jump shall be 4 feet high and the jump shall be 5 feet wide and shall be so constructed as to provide adjustment for each 2 inches from 8 inches to 36 inches. It is suggested that the jump have a bottom board 8 inches wide including the space from the bottom of the board to the ground or floor, together with three other 8 inch boards, one 4 inch board, and one 2 inch board. A 6 inch board may also be provided. The jump shall be painted a flat white. The width in inches, and nothing else, shall be painted on each side of each board in black 2 inch figures, the figure on the bottom board representing the distance from the ground or floor to the top of the board.

Section 11. **Retrieve over High Jump, Scoring.** Scoring of this exercise shall be as in Retrieve on the Flat. In addition, a dog that fails, either going or returning, to go over the jump, or that climbs or uses the jump for aid in going over, must be scored zero. Touching the jump in going over is added to the substantial and minor penalties listed under Retrieve on the Flat.

Section 12. **Broad Jump.** The principal features of this exercise are that the dog stay sitting until directed to jump and that the dog clear the jump on a single command or signal.

Orders are "Leave your dog," "Send your dog" and "Finish."

The handler will stand with his dog sitting in the Heel Position in front of and at least 8 feet from the jump. On order from the judge to "Leave your dog," the handler will give his dog the command and/or signal to Stay and go to a position facing the right side of the jump, with his toes about 2 feet from the jump, and anywhere between the lowest edge of the first hurdle and the highest edge of the last hurdle.

On order from the judge the handler shall give the command or signal to jump and the dog shall clear the entire distance of the Broad Jump without touching and, without further command or signal, return to a sitting position immediately in front of the handler as in the Recall. The handler shall change his position by executing a right angle turn while the dog is in mid-air, but shall remain in the same spot. The dog must sit and finish as in the Novice Recall.

The Broad Jump shall consist of four hurdles, built to telescope for convenience, made of boards about 8 inches wide, the largest measuring about 5 feet in length and 6 inches high at the highest point, all painted a flat white. When set up they shall be arranged in order of size and shall be evenly spaced so as to cover a distance equal to twice the height of the High Jump as set for the particular dog, with the low side of each hurdle and the lowest hurdle nearest the dog. The four hurdles shall be used for a jump of 52″ to 72″, three for a jump of 32″ to 48″, and two for a jump of 16″ to 28″. The highest hurdles shall be removed first. It is the judge's responsibility to see that the distance jumped is that required by these Regulations for the particular dog.

Section 13. **Broad Jump, Scoring.** A dog that fails to stay until directed to jump, or refuses the jump on the first command or signal, or walks over any part of the jump, or fails to clear the full distance, with its forelegs, must be scored zero. Minor or substantial deductions, depending on the specific circumstances in each case, shall be made for a dog that touches the jump in going over or

that does not return directly to the handler. All other applicable penalties listed under the Recall shall apply.

Section 14. **Open Group Exercises, Performance and Scoring.** During the Long Sit and the Long Down exercises the judge shall stand in such a position that all of the dogs are in his line of vision, and where he can see all the handlers in the ring, or leaving and returning to the ring, without having to turn around.

These exercises in the Open classes are performed in the same manner as in the Novice classes except that after leaving their dogs the handlers must cross to the opposite side of the ring, and then leave the ring in single file as directed by the judge and go to a place designated by the judge, completely out of sight of their dogs, where they must remain until called by the judge after the expiration of the time limit of three minutes in the Long Sit and five minutes in the Long Down, from the time the judge gave the order to "Leave your dogs." On order from the judge the handlers shall return to the ring in single file in reverse order, lining up facing their dogs at the opposite side of the ring, and returning to their dogs on order from the judge.

Orders and scoring are the same as in the Novice Group exercises.

CHAPTER 5

Utility

Section 1. **Utility Class.** The Utility class shall be for dogs that have won the title C.D.X. Dogs that have won the title U.D. may continue to compete in this class. Dogs in this class may be handled by the owner or any other person. Owners may enter more than one dog in this class, but each dog must have a separate handler for the Group Examination when judged in the same group.

Section 2. **Division of Utility Class.** A club may choose to divide the Utility class into Utility A and Utility B classes, provided such

division is approved by The American Kennel Club and is announced in the premium list. When this is done the Utility A class shall be for dogs which have won the title C.D.X. and have not won the title U.D. Obedience judges may not enter or handle dogs in this class. Owners may enter more than one dog in this class but the same person who handled each dog in the first five exercises must handle the same dog in the Group Examination, except that if a person has handled more than one dog in the first five exercises he must have an additional handler, who must be the owner or a member of his immediate family, for each additional dog, when more than one dog he has handled in the first five exercises is judged in the same group for the Group Examination. All other dogs that are eligible for the Utility class but not eligible for the Utility A class may be entered only in the Utility B class to which the conditions listed in Chapter 5, Section 1 shall apply. No dog may be entered in both Utility A and Utility B classes at any one trial.

Section 3. **Utility Exercises and Scores.** The exercises, maximum scores and order of judging in the Utility classes are:

1. Signal Exercise . . . . 40 points
2. Scent Discrimination
   Article No. 1 . . . . 30 points
3. Scent Discrimination
   Article No. 2 . . . . 30 points
4. Directed Retrieve . . . . 30 points
5. Directed Jumping . . . . 40 points
6. Group Examination . . . . . . 30 points

   Maximum Total Score . . . 200 points

Section 4. **U.D. Title.** The American Kennel Club will issue a Utility Dog certificate for each registered dog, and will permit the use of the letters "U.D." after the name of each dog that has been certified by three different judges of obedience trials to have received qualifying scores in Utility classes at three licensed or member obedience trials in each of which three or more dogs actually competed in the Utility class or classes.

Section 5. **Signal Exercise.** The principal features of this exercise are the ability of dog and handler to work as a team while heeling, and the dog's correct responses to the signals to Stand, Stay, Drop, Sit and Come.

Orders are the same as in Heel on Leash and Figure Eight, with the additions of "Stand your dog," which shall be given only when dog and handler are walking at normal pace, and "Leave your dog." The judge must use signals for directing the handler to signal the dog to Drop, to Sit and to Come, in that sequence, and to finish.

Heeling in the Signal Exercise shall be done in the same manner as in Heel Free, except that throughout the entire exercise the handler shall use signals only and must

not speak to his dog at any time. On order from the judge, "Forward," the handler may signal his dog to walk at heel, and on specific order from the judge in each case, shall execute a "Left turn," "Right turn," "About turn," "Halt," "Slow," "Normal" and "Fast." These orders may be given in any sequence and may be repeated as necessary, but the judge shall attempt to standardize the heeling pattern for all dogs in the class.

On order from the judge, and while the dog is walking at heel, the handler shall signal his dog to Stand in the heel position near one end of the ring. On further order, "Leave your dog," the handler shall signal his dog to Stay, go to the other end of the ring and turn to face his dog. On separate and specific signals from the judge, the handler shall give his signals to Drop, to Sit, to Come and to Finish as in the Recall. During the heeling part of this exercise the handler may not give any signal except when a command or signal is permitted in the Heeling exercises.

Section 6. **Signal Exercise, Scoring.** A dog that fails, on a single signal from the handler, to stand or remain standing where left, or to drop, or to sit and stay, or to come, or that receives a command or audible signal from the handler to do any of these parts of the exercise, shall be scored zero.

Minor or substantial deductions depending on the specific circumstances in each case, shall be made for a dog that walks forward on the Stand, Drop or Sit portions of the exercise.

A substantial deduction shall be made for any audible command during the Heeling or Finish portions of the exercise.

All the penalties listed under the Heel on Leash and Figure Eight and the Recall exercises shall also apply.

Section 7. **Scent Discrimination.** The principal features of these exercises are the selection of the handler's article from among the other articles by scent alone, and the prompt delivery of the right article to the handler.

Orders are "Send your dog," "Take it" and "Finish."

In each of these two exercises the dog must select by scent alone and retrieve an article which has been handled by its handler. The articles shall be provided by the handler and shall consist of two sets, each comprised of five identical objects not more than six inches in length, which may be items of everyday use. One set shall be made entirely of rigid metal, and one of leather of such design that nothing but leather is visible except for the minimum amount of thread or metal necessary to hold the object together. The articles in each set must be legibly numbered, each with a different number and must be approved by the judge.

The handler shall present all 10 articles to the judge, who shall designate one from each set and make written note of the numbers of the two articles he has selected. These two handler's articles shall be placed on a table or chair within the ring until picked up by the handler, who shall hold in his hand only one article at a time. The judge or steward will handle each of the remaining 8 articles as he places them on the floor or ground about 15 feet in front of the handler and dog, at random about 6 inches apart. The judge must make sure that the articles are properly separated before the dog is sent, so that there may be no confusion of scent between the articles.

Handler and dog shall turn around after watching the judge or steward spread the articles, and shall remain facing away from those articles until the judge has taken the handler's scented article and give the order, "Send your dog."

The handler may use either article first, but must relinquish each one immediately when ordered by the judge. The judge shall make certain that the handler imparts his scent to each article only with his hands and that, between the time the handler picks up each article and the time he gives it to the judge, the article is held continuously in the handler's hands which must remain in plain sight.

On order from the judge, the handler will immediately place his article on the judge's book or work sheet. The judge, without touching the article with his hands, will place it among those on the ground or floor.

On order from the judge to "Send your dog," the handler may give the command to Heel before turning, and will execute a Right about Turn, stopping to face the articles, the dog in Heel Position. The handler shall then give the command or signal to retrieve. Han-

dlers may at their discretion on order from the judge to "Send your dog," execute with their dog a Right about Turn to face the articles, simultaneously giving the command or signal to retrieve. In this instance the dog shall not assume a sitting position, but shall go directly to the articles. The handler may give his scent to the dog by gently touching the dog's nose with the palm of one open hand, but this may only be done while the dog and handler have their backs to the articles and the arm and hand must be returned to a natural position before handler and dog turn to face the articles.

The dog shall go at a brisk pace to the articles. It may take any reasonable time to select the right article, but only provided it works continuously. After picking up the right article the dog shall return at a brisk pace and complete the exercise as in the Retrieve on the Flat.

These procedures shall be followed for both articles. Should a dog retrieve a wrong article in the first exercise, that article shall be placed on the table or chair. The correct article must be removed, and the second exercise shall be conducted with one less article on the ground or floor.

Section 8. **Scent Discrimination, Scoring.** Deductions shall be the same as in the Retrieve on the Flat. In addition, a dog that fails to go out to the group of articles, or retrieves a wrong article, or fails to bring the right article to the handler, must be scored zero for the particular exercise.

Substantial deductions shall be made for a dog that picks up a wrong article, even though he puts it down again immediately, for any roughness by the handler in imparting his scent to the dog, and for any excessive motions by the handler in turning to face the articles.

Minor or substantial deductions, depending on the circumstance in each case, shall be made for a dog that is slow or inattentive, or that does not work continuously. There shall be no penalty for a dog that takes a reasonably long time examining the articles provided the dogs works smartly and continuously.

Section 9. **Directed Retrieve.** The principal features of the exercise are that the dog stay until directed to retrieve, that it go directly to the designated glove, and that it retrieve promptly. The orders for the exercise are "One," "Two" or "Three," "Take it" and "Finish." In this exercise the handler will provide three predominantly white, cotton work gloves, which must be open and must be approved by the judge. The handler will stand with his back to the unobstructed end of the ring with his dog sitting in the Heel Position mid-way between and in line with the two jumps. The judge or steward will then drop the three gloves across the end of the ring, while the handler and dog are facing the opposite direction, one glove in each corner and one in the center, about 3 feet from the end of the ring and for the corner gloves, about 3 feet from the side of the ring. All three gloves will be clearly visible to the dog and handler, when the handler turns to face the glove designated by the judge. There shall be no table or chair at this end of the ring.

The gloves shall be designated "One," "Two" or "Three" reading from left to right when the handler turns and faces the gloves. The judge will give the order "One," or "Two," or "Three." The handler then must give the command to Heel and turn in place, right or left to face the designated glove. The handler will come to a halt with the dog sitting in the Heel Position. The handler shall not touch the dog to get it in position. The handler will then give his dog the direction to the designated glove with a single motion of his left hand and arm along the right side of the dog, and will give the command to retrieve either simultaneously with or immediately following the giving of the direction. The dog shall then go directly to the glove at a brisk pace and retrieve it without unnecessary mouthing or playing with it, completing the exercise as in the Retrieve on the Flat.

The handler may bend his knees and body in giving the direction to the dog, after which the handler will stand erect in a natural position with his arms at his sides.

The exercise shall consist of a single retrieve, but the judge shall designate different glove numbers for successive dogs.

Section 10. **Directed Retrieve, Scoring.** A dog must receive a score of zero for the following: not going out on a single command, not going directly to the designated glove,

not retrieving the glove, anticipating the handler's command to retrieve, not returning promptly and sufficiently close so that the handler can readily take the glove without moving either foot or stretching forward.

Depending on the extent, substantial or minor deductions shall be made for a handler who over-turns, or touches the dog or uses excessive motions to get the dog in position.

All other deductions listed under Retrieve on the Flat shall also apply.

Section 11. **Directed Jumping.** The principal features of this exercise are that the dog go away from the handler in the direction indicated, stop when commanded, jump as directed and return as in the Recall.

The orders are "Send your dog," the designation of which jump is to be taken, and "Finish."

The jumps shall be placed midway in the ring at right angles to the sides of the ring and 18 to 20 feet apart, the Bar Jump on one side, the High Jump on the other. The judge must make certain that the jumps are set at the required height for each dog by following the procedure described in Retrieve over the High Jump.

The handler, from a position on the center line of the ring and about 20 feet from the line of the jumps, shall stand with his dog sitting in the Heel Position and on order from the judge shall command and/or signal his dog to go forward at a brisk pace to a point about 20 feet beyond the jumps and in the approximate center. When the dog has reached this point the handler shall give a command to Sit; the dog must stop and sit with his attention on the handler but need not sit squarely.

The judge will designate which jump is to be taken first by the dog, and the handler shall command and/or signal the dog to return to him over the designated jump. While the dog is in mid-air the handler may turn so as to be facing the dog as it returns. The dog shall sit in front of the handler and, on order from the judge, finish as in the Recall. The judge will say "Exercise finished" after the dog has returned to the Heel Position.

When the dog is again sitting in the Heel Position the judge shall ask, "Are you ready?" before giving the order to send the dog for the second part of the exercise. The same procedure shall be followed for the second jump.

It is optional with the judge which jump is taken first, but both jumps must be taken to complete the exercise and the judge must not designate the jump until the dog is at the far end of the ring. The dog shall clear the jumps without touching them.

The height of the jumps shall be the same as required in the Open classes. The High Jump shall be the same as that used in the Open classes, and the Bar Jump shall consist of a bar between 2 and 2½ inches square with the four edges rounded sufficiently to remove any sharpness. The bar shall be painted a flat black and white in alternate sections of about 3 inches each. The bar shall be supported by two unconnected 4 foot upright posts about 5 feet apart. The bar shall be adjustable for each 2 inches of height from 8 inches to 36 inches, and the jump shall be so constructed and positioned that the bar can be knocked off without disturbing the uprights.

Section 12. **Directed Jumping, Scoring.** A dog must receive a score of zero for the following: anticipating the handler's command and/or signal to go out, not leaving the handler, not going out between the jumps, not going at least 10 feet beyond the jumps, not stopping on command, anticipating the handler's command and/or signal to jump, not jumping as directed, knocking the bar off the uprights, climbing or using the top of the High Jump for aid in going over.

Substantial deductions shall be made for a dog that does not stop in the approximate center of the ring; for a dog that turns, stops or sits before the handler's command to Sit, and for a dog that fails to sit.

Substantial or minor deductions, depending on the extent, shall be made for slowness in going out or for touching the jumps. All of the penalties listed under Recall shall also apply.

Section 13. **Group Examination.** The principal features of this exercise are that the dog stand and stay, and show no shyness or resentment.

All the competing dogs take this exercise together, except that if there are 12 or more dogs, they shall be judged in groups of not less than 6 nor more than 15 dogs, at the judge's option. The handlers and dogs that are in the ring shall line up in catalog order, side by side down the center of the ring, with the dogs sitting in the Heel Position. Each handler shall place his armband, weighted with leash or other article if necessary, behind his dog. The judge must instruct one or more stewards to watch the other dogs while he conducts the individual examination, and to call any faults to his attention.

On order from the judge, "Stand your dogs," all the handlers will stand or pose their dogs and on further order, "Leave your dogs," will give command and/or signal to Stay and walk forward to the side of the ring where they shall turn and stand facing their respective dogs. The judge will approach each dog in turn from the front and examine it, going over the dog with his hands as in dog show judging except that under no circumstance shall the examination include the dog's mouth or testicles.

When all dogs have been examined and after the handlers have been away from their dogs for at least three minutes, the judge will promptly order the handlers, "Back to your dogs," and the handlers will return, each walking around and in back of his own dog to the Heel Position, after which the judge will say, "Exercise Finished." Each dog must remain standing at its position in the line from the time its handler leaves it until the end of the exercise, and must show no shyness or resentment. The dogs are not required to sit at the end of this exercise.

Section 14. **Group Examination, Scoring.** There should be no attempt to judge the dogs or handlers on the manner in which the dogs are made to stand. The scoring will not start until after the judge has given the order to leave the dogs, except for such general things as rough treatment of a dog by its handler, or active resistance by a dog to its handler's attempts to make it stand. Immediately after examining each dog the judge must make a written record of any necessary deductions, subject to further deductions for subsequent faults.

A dog must be scored zero for the following: displaying shyness or resentment, moving a minor distance from the place where it was left, going over to any other dog, sitting or lying down before the handler has returned to the Heel Position, growling or snapping at any time during the exercise, repeatedly barking or whining.

Substantial or minor deductions, depending on the circumstance, must be made for a dog that moves its feet at any time during the exercise, or sits or lies down after the handler has returned to the Heel Position.

CHAPTER 6

Obedience Trial Championship

Section 1. **Dogs That May Compete.** Championship points will be recorded only for those dogs which have earned the Utility Dog Title. Any dog that has been awarded the Title of Obedience Trial Champion may continue to compete, and if such dog earns a First or Second place ribbon, that dog shall also earn the points.

Section 2. **Championship Points.** Championship points will be recorded for those dogs which have earned a First or Second place ribbon competing in the Open B or Utility Class (or Utility B, if divided), according to the schedule of points established by the Board of Directors of The American Kennel Club. In counting the number of eligible dogs in competition, a dog that is disqualified, or is dismissed, excused or expelled from the ring by the judge shall not be included.

Requirements for the Obedience Trial Champion are as follows:

1. Shall have won 100 points; and
2. shall have won a First place in Utility (or Utility B, if divided) provided there are at least three dogs in competition; and
3. shall have won a First place in Open B, provided there are at least six dogs in competition; and
4. shall have won a third First place under the conditions of 2 or 3 above; and
5. shall have won these three First places under three different judges.

Section 3. **O.T.Ch. Title Certificate.** The American Kennel Club will issue an Obe-

dience Trial Championship Certificate for each registered dog and will permit the use of the letters O.T.Ch. preceding the name of each dog, that meets these requirements.

Section 4. **Ineligibility and Cancellation.** If an ineligible dog has been entered in any licensed or member obedience trial or dog show, or if the name of the owner given on the entry form is not that of the person or persons who actually owned the dog at the time entries closed, or if shown in a class for which it has not been entered, or if its entry form is deemed invalid or unacceptable by The American Kennel Club, all resulting awards shall be cancelled. In computing the championship points, such ineligible dogs, whether or not they have received awards, shall be counted as having competed.

Section 5. **Move Ups.** If an award in any of the regular classes is cancelled, the next highest scoring dog shall be moved up and the award to the dog moved up shall be counted the same as if it had been the original award. If there is no dog of record to move up, the award shall be void.

Section 6. **Return of Awards.** If the win of a dog shall be cancelled by The American Kennel Club, the owner of the dog shall return all ribbons and prizes to the show-giving club within ten days of receipt of the notice of cancellation from The American Kennel Club.

Section 7. **Point Schedule.**

<table>
<tr><th colspan="3" align="center">OPEN B CLASS</th><th colspan="3" align="center">UTILITY CLASS</th></tr>
<tr>
<th>NUMBER
COMPETING</th><th>POINTS
FOR FIRST
PLACE</th><th>POINTS
FOR SECOND
PLACE</th>
<th>NUMBER
COMPETING</th><th>POINTS
FOR FIRST
PLACE</th><th>POINTS
FOR SECOND
PLACE</th>
</tr>
<tr><td>6–10</td><td>2</td><td>0</td><td>3–5</td><td>2</td><td>0</td></tr>
<tr><td>11–15</td><td>4</td><td>1</td><td>6–9</td><td>4</td><td>1</td></tr>
<tr><td>16–20</td><td>6</td><td>2</td><td>10–14</td><td>6</td><td>2</td></tr>
<tr><td>21–25</td><td>10</td><td>3</td><td>15–19</td><td>10</td><td>3</td></tr>
<tr><td>26–30</td><td>14</td><td>4</td><td>20–24</td><td>14</td><td>4</td></tr>
<tr><td>31–35</td><td>18</td><td>5</td><td>25–29</td><td>18</td><td>5</td></tr>
<tr><td>36–40</td><td>22</td><td>7</td><td>30–34</td><td>22</td><td>7</td></tr>
<tr><td>41–45</td><td>26</td><td>9</td><td>35–39</td><td>26</td><td>9</td></tr>
<tr><td>46–50</td><td>30</td><td>11</td><td>40–44</td><td>30</td><td>11</td></tr>
<tr><td>51–56</td><td>34</td><td>13</td><td>45–48</td><td>34</td><td>13</td></tr>
</table>

CHAPTER 7

Tracking

Section 1. **Tracking Test.** This test shall be for dogs not less than six months of age, and must be judged by two judges. With each entry form for a licensed or member tracking test for a dog that has not passed an AKC tracking test there must be filed an original written statement, dated within six months of the date the test is to be held, signed by a person who has been approved by The American Kennel Club to judge tracking tests, certifying that the dog is considered by him to be ready for such a test. These original statements cannot be used again and must be submitted to The American Kennel Club with the entry forms. Written permission to waive or modify this requirement may be granted by The American Kennel Club in unusual circumstances. Tracking tests are open to all dogs that are otherwise eligible under these Regulations.

This test cannot be given at a dog show or obedience trial. The duration of this test may be one day or more within a 15 day period after the original date in the event of an unusually large entry or other unforeseen emergency, provided that the change of date is satisfactory to the exhibitors affected.

Section 2. **T.D. Title.** The American Kennel Club will issue a Tracking Dog certificate to a registered dog, and will permit the use of the letters "T.D." after the name of each dog which has been certified by the two judges to have passed a licensed or member tracking test in which at least three dogs actually participated.

The owner of a dog holding both the U.D. and T.D. titles may use the letters "U.D.T." after the name of the dog, signifying "Utility Dog Tracker."

Section 3. **Tracking.** The tracking test must be performed with the dog on leash, the length of the track to be not less than 440 yards nor more than 500 yards, the scent to be not less than one half hour nor more than two hours old and that of a stranger who will leave an inconspicuous glove or wallet, dark in color, at the end of the track where it must be found by the dog and picked up by the dog or handler. The article must be approved in advance by the judges. The tracklayer will follow the track which has been staked out with flags a day or more earlier, collecting all the flags on the way with the exception of one flag at the start of the track and one flag about 30 yards from the start of the track to indicate the direction of the track; then deposit the article at the end of the track and leave the course, proceeding straight ahead at least 50 feet. The tracklayer must wear his own shoes which, if not having leather soles, must have uppers of fabric or leather. The dog shall wear a harness to which is attached a leash between 20 and 40 feet in length. The handler shall follow the dog at a distance of not less than 20 feet, and the dog shall not be guided by the handler. The dog may be restrained by the handler, but any leading or guiding of the dog constitutes grounds for calling the handler off and marking the dog "Failed." A dog may, at the handler's option, be given one, and only one, second chance to take the scent between the two flags, provided it has not passed the second flag.

Section 4. **Tracking Tests.** A person who is qualified to judge Obedience Trials is not necessarily capable of judging a tracking test. Tracking judges must be familiar with the various conditions that may exist when a dog is required to work a scent trail. Scent conditions, weather, lay of the land, ground cover, and wind, must be taken into consideration, and a thorough knowledge of this work is necessary.

One or both of the judges must personally lay out each track, a day or so before the test, so as to be completely familiar with the location of the track, landmarks and ground conditions. At least two of the right angle turns shall be well out in the open where there are no fences or other boundaries to guide the dog. No part of any track shall follow along any fence or boundary within 15 yards of such boundary. The track shall include at least two right angle turns and should include more than two such turns so that the dog may be observed working in different wind directions. Acute angle turns should be avoided whenever possible. No conflicting tracks shall be laid. No track shall cross any body of water. No part of any track shall be laid within 75 yards of any other track. In the case of two tracks going in opposite directions, however, the first flags of these tracks may be as close as 50 yards from each other. The judges shall make sure that the track is no less than 440 yards nor more than 500

yards and that the tracklayer is a stranger to the dog in each case. It is the judges' responsibility to instruct the tracklayer to insure that each track is properly laid and that each tracklayer carries a copy of the chart with him in laying the track. The judges must approve the article to be left at the end of each track, must make sure that it is thoroughly impregnated with the tracklayer's scent, and must see that the tracklayer's shoes meet the requirements of these regulations.

There is no time limit provided the dog is working, but a dog that is off the track and is clearly not working should not be given any minimum time, but should be marked Failed. The handler may not be given any assistance by the judges or anyone else. If a dog is not tracking it shall not be marked Passed even though it may have found the article. In case of unforeseen circumstances, the judges may in rare cases, at their own discretion, give a handler and his dog a second chance on a new track. A track for each dog entered shall be plotted on the ground by one or both judges not less than one day before the test, the track being marked by flags which the tracklayer can follow readily on the day of the test. A chart of each track shall be made up in duplicate, showing the approximate length in yards of each leg, and major landmarks and boundaries, if any. Both of these charts shall be marked at the time the dog is tracking, one by each of the judges, so as to show the approximate course followed by the dog. The judges shall sign their charts and show on each whether the dog "Passed" or "Failed," the time the tracklayer started, the time the dog started and finished tracking, a brief description of ground, wind and weather conditions, the wind direction, and a note of any steep hills or valleys.

The Club or Tracking Test Secretary, after a licensed or member tracking test, shall forward the two copies of the judges' marked charts, the entry forms with certifications attached, and a marked and certified copy of the catalog pages or sheets listing the dogs entered in the tracking test, to The American Kennel Club so as to reach its office within seven days after the close of the test.

CHAPTER 8

Nonregular Classes

Section 1. **Graduate Novice Class.** The Graduate Novice class shall be for C.D. dogs that have not been certified by a judge to have received a qualifying score toward a C.D.X. title prior to the closing of entries. Dogs in this class may be handled by the owner or any other person. A person may handle more than one dog in this class, but each dog must have a separate handler for the Long Sit and Long Down exercises when judged in the same group. Dogs entered in Graduate Novice may also be entered in one of the Open classes.

Performances and judging shall be as in the Regular classes, except that the Figure 8 is omitted from the Heel on Leash exercise. The exercises, maximum scores and order of judging in the Graduate Novice class are:

1. Heel on Leash (no Figure 8) 30
2. Stand for Examination.......... 30
3. Open Heel Free 40
4. Open Drop on Recall 40
5. Open Long Sit 30
6. Open Long Down 30

    Maximum Total Score 200

Section 2. **Brace Class.** The Brace class shall be for braces of dogs of the same breed that are eligible under these Regulations and capable of performing the Novice exercises. The dogs need not be owned by the same person, but must be handled by one handler. Dogs may be shown unattached or coupled, the coupling device to be not less than six inches over-all length; whichever method is used must be continued throughout all exercises. A separate Official Entry Form must be completed in full for each dog entered.

Exercises, performances and judging shall be as in the Novice class. The brace should work in unison at all times. Either or both dogs in a brace may be entered in another class or classes at the same trial.

Section 3. **Veterans Class.** The Veterans class shall be for dogs that have an obedience title and are eight or more years old prior to the closing of entries. The exercises shall be performed and judged as in the Novice class. Dogs entered in the Veterans class may not be entered in any Regular class.

Section 4. **Versatility Class.** The Versatility class shall be for dogs that are eligible under these Regulations and capable of performing the Utility exercises. Owners may enter more than one dog. Dogs in this class may be handled by the owner or any other person, and may be entered in another class or classes at the same trial.

Six exercises will be performed, two each from the Novice, Open and Utility classes, except that there will be no Group exercises. The exercises will be performed and judged as in the Regular classes. For the purpose of this class, Scent Discrimination articles number 1 and number 2 shall be considered as a single Utility exercise. The exercises to be performed by each dog will be determined by the handlers drawing one of a set of cards listing combinations of the six exercises totaling 200 points. These cards will be furnished by the trial-giving clubs. Each handler shall provide a dumbbell, Scent Discrimination articles and Directed Retrieve gloves.

Novice exercise No. 1 25
Novice exercise No. 2 25
Open exercise No. 1 35
Open exercise No. 2 35
Utility exercise No. 1 40
Utility exercise No. 2 40

    Maximum Total Score 200

Section 5. **Team Class.** The Team class shall be for teams of any four dogs that are eligible under these Regulations. Five dogs may be entered, one to be considered an alternate for which no entry fee shall be required. However, the same four dogs must perform all exercises. Dogs need not be owner-handled, need not be entered in another class at the same trial, and need not have obedience titles. A separate Official Entry Form must be completed in full for each dog entered.

There shall be two judges, one of whom will call commands while the other scores the teams' performances. The teams will be judged one at a time, except for the Long Sit and Long Down exercises which shall be done with no more than four teams (16 dogs) in the ring.

The dogs on a team will perform the exercises simultaneously and will be judged as specified for the Novice class, except that a Drop on Recall will be used in place of the Recall exercise. In all exercises except the Drop on Recall, the teams have the option of executing the judge's commands on the team captain's repeat of the command.

In the Figure Eight portion of the Heel on Leash exercise, five stewards will be used. The stewards shall stand 8 feet apart in a straight line. One dog and his handler shall stand between two stewards, all members of the team facing in the same direction. On orders from the judge, the team shall perform the Figure Eight, each handler starting around the steward on his left and circling only the two stewards between whom he had been standing.

In the Drop on Recall exercise, the handlers will leave their dogs simultaneously on command of the judge. The dogs shall be called or signalled in, one at a time, on a separate command from the judge to each handler. The handler shall, without any additional command from the judge, command or signal his dog to drop at a spot midway between the line of dogs and the handlers. Each dog shall remain in the Down position until all four have been called and dropped, whereupon the judge shall give the command to call the dogs, which shall be called or signalled simultaneously. The finish shall be done in unison on command from the judge.

Section 6. **Team Class, Scoring.** Scoring of the Team class shall be based on the performance of the dogs and handlers individually plus team precision and coordination. Each dog and handler will be scored against the customary maximum, for a team total of 800 maximum available points. Individual dog's scores need not be recorded. The exercises and maximum scores are:

1. Heel on Leash 160
2. Stand for Examination 120
3. Heel Free 160
4. Drop on Recall 120
5. Long Sit 120
6. Long Down 120

   Maximum Total Score 800

SOME AUTHORS' SUGGESTIONS FOR
CONSTRUCTION OF OBEDIENCE EQUIPMENT

The authors recommend the construction of the following obedience equipment:

THE BROAD JUMP

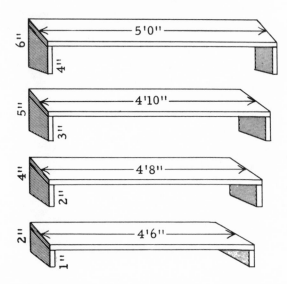

These jumps are made of 1″ x 8″ board, any wood. The decreasing dimensions enable you to "nest" them for storage or carrying. Angle brackets underneath add strength, but are not necessary. Paint the jumps flat white, and in use arrange them in order of increasing height, with the lowest nearest to your dog.

THE "CRIB"

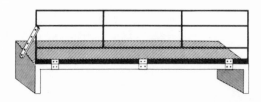

We recommend you make this of metal (iron, aluminum) in roughly the design pictured here. It can be made of dowels, 1″ x 1″ sticks or lath, but a wooden version will not be too strong. Dimensions are 8″ x 4′8″, with the holed bar at left for changing the angle of the crib. Mount it at the front of the second jump, as pictured here.

THE HIGH JUMP

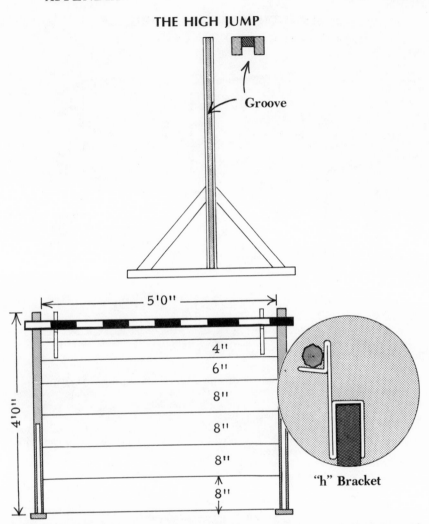

Groove

5'0"

4'0"

4"
6"
8"
8"
8"
8"

"h" Bracket

The high-jump uprights consist of two 1″ x 3″ and one 1″ x 2″ pieces nailed together, with the 1″ x 2″ forming the groove for the jump boards to slide into. The boards are 5′ long, of 1″ x 8″ stock. The bottom 8″ board is slightly less than 8″—just wide enough to measure 8″ from the ground to the top of the board. Paint the entire jump flat white.

The bar-jump standards are two 3″ x 3″ pieces, 4′ long, braced at the bottom as illustrated for the high-jump standards. Drill slightly slanting holes at one- or two-inch intervals down the "far" side of each standard, and have two nails or pegs to slip into the holes to support the bar at varying heights. The bar is 6′ long, 2″ to 2½″ in diameter, painted black and white in alternate sections of about 3″. The standards are flat white.

The "h" Brackets are made as shown in the inset, of iron or wood, to hold the bar on top of the high-jump boards in early jump training (see illustration here, and "Open" text). You will not need these if you drill the high-jump standards to carry the bar as well as the boards.

SCENT-DISCRIMINATION ARTICLES

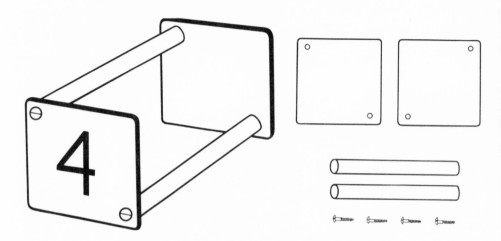

The size of these depends on your dog. Make the bars about 1″ longer than the width of your dog's muzzle, just behind the long canine teeth, and the reminder of the article in proportion as drawn here. Make six of each kind, and number them from 1 to 6 on the ends, using number 6 as your practice article.

Wood: (These are for transition training only.) Cut plywood squares to size, round the corners slightly, drill screw holes in opposite corners. Sand end-pieces and dowels well before assembling, to avoid splinters in your hands when scenting, and in the dog's mouth. Then screw the end-pieces on to the dowels to make an article as pictured here. *Do not paint!*

Metal: Cut thin aluminum sheet to size for ends, cut proper size of aluminum tubing to size for bars, drill holes in opposite corners of end pieces. Then cut dowels (slightly smaller than inside diameter of tubing) ¼″ shorter than tubing bars. With the dowels inside the bars, screw the end pieces on, with the screw through the end-piece hole and into the end of the dowel. You may not be able to do the metalwork, but a local shop will do it quite cheaply.

Leather: Get heavy sole leather from a shoemaker and cut it into proper squares for end pieces, with rounded corners and screw holes. Glue strips of thin leather around dowels, butting the ends for a smooth single layer of leather. Screw the end pieces to the dowels.

INDEX